“She ‘Shot’ Her Way to Success”

How China’s Empress Dowager Ci Xi Launched a Photographer’s Trailblazing Career

By Wilbur D. Jones Jr. and Carroll Robbins Jones

"She 'Shot' Her Way to Success":
How China's Empress Dowager Ci Xi Launched a Photographer's Trailblazing Photographer's Career

First paperback edition

Published by
Wilbur Jones Compositions LLC
3002 Joy Place
Wilmington, NC 28409

www.WilburJonesCompositions.com

Unless otherwise noted, all photographs in which she is not shown are by Patricia O'Meara Robbins.

Cover design by Kathleen Beall Meyer; book design by Kathleen Beall Meyer and John Meyer of Cape Fear Images, Inc., doing business as Cape Fear Publishers (www.capefearpublishers.com)

Cover photographs, all by Patricia O'Meara Robbins:

Front cover:

Elderly Chinese deaf -mute—originally published as the 'Old Chinaman'—at the Inland Mission, Chefoo, North China, mid-1930s.

Christina "Tina" Crawford, daughter of actress Joan Crawford, age approximately nine, at her home in Los Angeles, late 1940s.

'Honolulu death car.' Honolulu, Territory of Hawaii, after Japanese attack on Pearl Harbor, December 8, 1941.

Actress Nancy Davis, future First Lady to President Ronald Reagan, for *Photoplay* magazine, outside the MGM Studio, Los Angeles, 1950.

Back cover:

Whore House No. 12, Chefoo, North China, mid-1930s.

Soviet Victory Memorial, Tiergarten Park, West Berlin, with ruins of Reichstag, May 1953.

Twenty-four-hour fast-food joint on infamous Hotel Street in downtown Honolulu, 1942.

ISBN 978-0-9980735-0-7

"She 'Shot' Her Way to Success"

DEDICATION AND ACKNOWLEDGMENTS

First and foremost, this book must be dedicated to my late wife, Carroll Robbins Jones, whose two families' history it portrays, in part, during major and turbulent eras in American history.

For many years we discussed, on and off, what we should do with the multitude of images and records that her mother, Pat Robbins, left her. Finally, several years ago, we decided to write a book centered on Carroll's remarkable photographer mother—her career, life, and times—sparked by a generational link to the Chinese Empress Dowager Ci Xi. A few months before she died in 2013, I promised Carroll I would finish it. Furthermore, I dedicate this book to my children, whose lives are enriched by the legacies of their mother and maternal grandparents. As well, this book also will substantially contribute to the study of photography.

For his work with me over the years, I sincerely thank John Meyer of Cape Fear Publishers in Wilmington, North Carolina, a world-class editor and layout designer who formatted these pages and acts as my agent. With his exceptionally talented wife Kate, who designed the book's cover and its typography, they are a formidable creative team.

I also thank the Randall Library of the University of North Carolina Wilmington, in particular University Librarian Sarah Watstein and Director of Special Collections Jerry Parnell, for their encouragement and assistance. Upon this book's publication, Randall Library will accession the entire Carroll Robbins Jones Collection from the Estate of Patricia O'Meara Robbins. Readers interested in pursuing the story in greater depth may view the collection there.

Wilbur D. Jones, Jr.
August 2016

TABLE OF CONTENTS

PREFACE

"My Mother Should Never have Had Children": Empress Dowager Ci Xi and Why We Wrote This Book

As a youngster and teenager, Carroll Eloise Robbins was "obliged" to pose for and assist her professional photojournalist mother in testing cameras, film, perspectives, settings, exposures, lighting, scenes, subjects, backgrounds, costumes, props, angles, darkroom developing, toting her equipment, and more—for time on end—regardless of the hour and mother's mood, or daughter's own preferences. This "subjugation" brewed discord between the two, resulting in a degree of alienation as Carroll grew older, ending only once we began writing this book.

"My mother should never have had children," . . .

. . . Carroll has since said, half seriously. "She was more like 'Auntie Mame' [see Rosalind Russell], and never changed a diaper, never warmed a milk bottle, never pushed a carriage. She was independent, lovely, genuinely personable, socially savvy; loved parties, loved attention, and loved being around successful and glamorous people, including herself.

"As my brother Berton and I grew up, mother was devoted to our father, whom she adored—a war hero, patient and loving husband, and wonderful, courageous but remote man—and her photography career. Photography was the burning, creative challenge for achieving professional heights and admiration. She didn't have to work. Our father was a career officer. Meanwhile, others looked after us: my Chinese amah in the 1930s, and later boarding schools and our vast Irish, very well-connected, early-Los Angeles family.

"Berton and I had first-class private school educations and social interactions, attended elite birthday parties, hob-nobbed with her client stars' kids, doted on our pushover grandfather, bolstered each other, and were mother's model showcase society children."

A few months before her own death in 2013, Carroll admitted: "After looking back at mother, who died in 1988, I appreciated her as an ambitious, talented, and accomplished woman, and came to favorable terms with her." Decades of their frosty relationship and Carroll's scorn ended. "She was indeed a pace-setter near the spear point of the women's movement. A role model in retrospect. A younger contemporary of Margaret Bourke-White, Toni Frissell, and Jean Howard, but with different motives on different professional courses.

"Fatefully placed to record history, her photojournalist legacy thus becomes an historical gold mine we now share with others."

So, this book about her career, life, and times, a tribute to her and a gift of history to our extended family, at last we write.

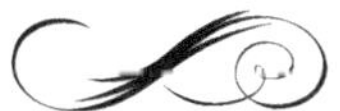

Mary Patricia O'Meara Robbins is buried in Arlington National Cemetery beside her husband, the highly decorated retired Navy Rear Admiral Berton A. Robbins, Jr., who died in 1983. Our family called her "Mutti," an affectionate German name she acquired while living in Occupied Germany in the early 1950s. For this book, I will call her Pat, as she was known professionally and to her countless friends. Also, using the pronoun "I" refers to myself as the eventual author, and "we" includes my late wife Carroll.

I met Carroll and her parents in Naples, Italy, in 1958 when then-Captain Robbins arrived to take command of the Service Force Sixth Fleet. As a young lieutenant junior grade, I served as his communications officer and flag aide, whose responsibilities included accompanying the commodore throughout the Mediterranean. Carroll and I began dating and developed a friendship that grew into love. On August 11, 1959, we were married in Christ Church in Naples, and with two weeks of leave, honeymooned in northern Italy, Switzerland, West Germany, and Austria. Our courtship was classical storybook. We were blessed with three children, Patricia, David, and Andrew, and raised our only grandchild at the time, Carrie.

Pat left us thousands of images she took beginning in the Pacific, China, and the Orient in the early 1930s, plus accompanying clippings and other family heirlooms and memorabilia. Her collection includes portraits, landscapes, formal and informal scenes both posed and un-posed, commercial advertisements, and random people and structures. Seemingly she shot anything except youth soccer games and lunar eclipses. It also includes images mounted for exhibits or contests, and examples of her client assignments and commissions.

Over the years she pasted or wedged many of the images into scrapbooks or albums so uncharacteristic of a true professional. Fortunately, they proved retrievable for cleanup. Unfortunately, we cannot locate any negatives covering the 1930s through 1950s. We do have hundreds of color slides and black and white negatives casually taken of family in the '60s and '70s as she shifted away from professional work, but using them would not improve this book.

For years, we occasionally discussed what should be done to preserve and exhibit her work, even writing a book, or just donating it to Randall Library at the University of North Carolina Wilmington. But we kept deferring. It would take lots of time to remember and write it down, to research, to cull the photographs, and to find other family items that would supplement them. And other important aspects of our lives, earning a living, heavy volunteer involvement, raising our granddaughter, our professional careers, and Carroll's rapidly deteriorating health—meant going from "maybe" to "let's hope, someday."

Finally, in 2011, we decided to write this book. We went through the photographs and documents and selected about three hundred images that we thought best represented Pat's work and recorded history. That year I completed most of the research. In 2012-13 Carroll's health dampened our motivation to finish the work, and again we put the project on hold.

Four months before she died, while still able, Carroll sat with me for several days to reminisce as we went through the stack. Although quite ill, her still-sharp long-term memory (I joked that she could remember the color socks she wore to the birthday party of her friend Christina Crawford—Joan Crawford's daughter—in Los Angeles in 1946) allowed a clear recall of details: what she experienced, and what her parents and family told her, which are this book's essential ingredients. To hers I added my own recollections of her parents, embellished by the respect I had for her father, my mentor, and for her mother's talent.

As we grappled with the book's purpose and direction, and coalesced facts and memories, soon we realized the story was much more than just about photographs. Rather, the story became Pat Robbins herself—the evolving woman, her professionalism, her interactions, influence and impact on family and friends, and her contributions to history. With that idea in mind, we proceeded to tell this story.

Near the end, I promised Carroll I would finish it. She is buried in Oakdale Cemetery in Wilmington, N.C., my native home town and her adopted one.

For many reasons, I dedicate this book to both Pat and my beloved wife of 54 years, Carroll.

Wilbur D. Jones, Jr.
Captain, U.S. Navy Reserve (Ret.)
Wilmington, N. C.
August 2016

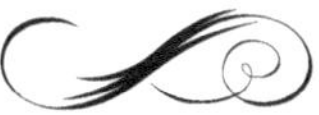

Now, back to Pat. She relished shooting other people, employing an impatient director's demands, but herself shied from the camera's other end. Thus, she appears in but a few photographs, and none, surprisingly, with camera in hand. This image of her seated in a ricksha at the entrance to the Temple of Ancestors in Peking in the mid-1930s must be the work of her husband, Bob.

It appears she shot virtually all her photographs of China and the Orient and most of Europe with only natural light, and nearly all were exterior scenes. If she kept a record of the particular cameras, film, and settings used for her individual or mass of photographs, we find only a couple of them that include the technical aspects for contests or exhibits.

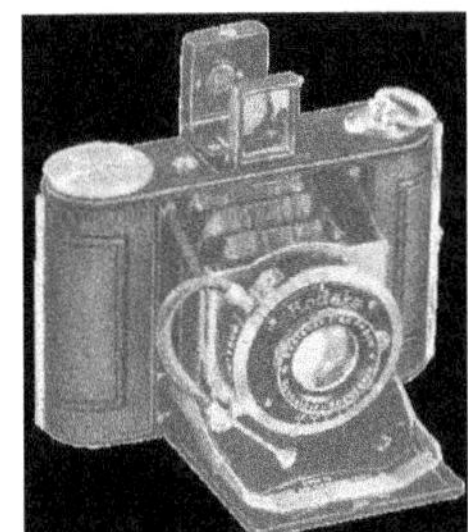

Kodak Vollenda

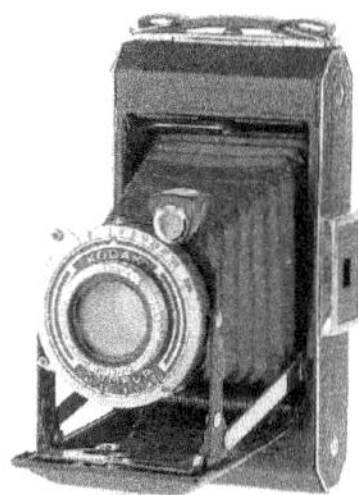

Kodak, ca. 1930s

We do know that as her career progressed she predominantly used German cameras such as Rolleiflexes and other twin lens reflex/viewfinder cameras, and much later 35mm Canons. Starting out she used an Eastman Kodak Vollenda, similar to these models of that era.

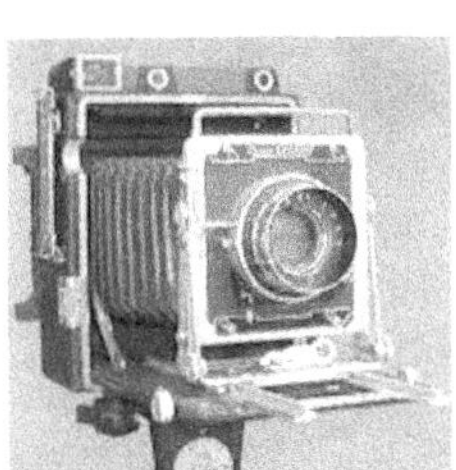

Graflex

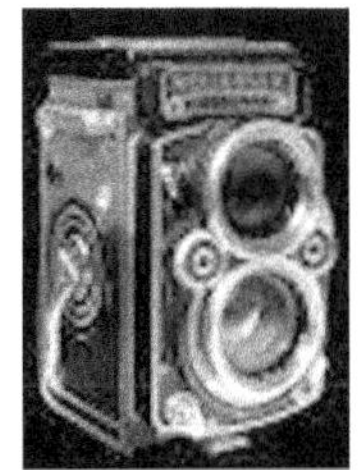

Rolleiflex

She used the customary assorted lenses, filters, flash attachments, and photo floodlights. Using primarily black and white film, later incorporating color, she processed and printed images by converting space in each home into a darkroom and laboratory, beginning apparently while in the Orient. As she progressed, her stock quality and quantity and treatment of artificial light increased, frequently in the "Golden Age of Hollywood" collection. She took early images with a Graflex view camera and evolved with a Rolleiflex twin-lens reflex.

Although she wrote that she took movies in the Orient, we found no reels, exposed film, or other evidence of motion pictures. She left us two cameras, an old viewfinder Rolleicord, and an 8mm Keystone Model K8 movie camera, about which we know nothing.

As a wife and mother, Pat combined family responsibilities and raised a daughter (born 1934 in China) and son Berton III (born 1936 in the US.) She always had hired household help, including amahs and houseboys in China and elsewhere in the Orient. Her husband, away at sea for three and a half years during the war and severely wounded at the battle of Iwo Jima, required a three-year recuperation. Later he commanded an amphibious attack transport ship during the Korean War. Although no "daredevil" seeking the unusual, Pat grew into a seasoned, resourceful, and undaunted international traveler.

Except for shooting the Pearl Harbor aftermath, she was a situational, portrait, society, and commissioned photographer rather than a straight news photographer, or one pursuing a social or political cause like her better-know woman contemporaries.

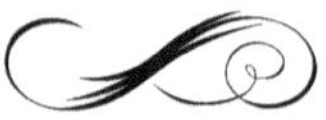

Because of one person, Pat instead might have chosen another profession, and this particular book might never have been written.

Soon after arriving in North China in 1933 as the new, twenty-one-year-old bride of a Navy ensign four years older, through high-level family intervention Pat befriended the Princess der Ling, who had been the last lady-in-waiting to the Qing Empress Dowager Ci Xi (Tzu Hsi) in the early 1900's. Ci Xi ruled China during the Boxer Rebellion of 1900.

Princess der Ling's nickname was "Venie." "She was very loving and smiling and outgoing, went to school in France, and was brought back to China to be a lady-in-waiting. She could handle herself in any occasion," Carroll said.

Der Ling arranged Pat's access to old imperial China, until then rarely granted and rather untouched by white Western women of the era. Such access facilitated her ability to roam through the Forbidden City, Summer Palace and Peking's other temples and imperial sites; The Great Wall, North China, Manchuria, and other places years before they became popular with sightseers.

Carroll's parents had no permanent China or Orient residence. At her birth on April 28 in Shanghai, they lived temporarily in the French Concession. "Mother chose to go to Shanghai to give birth in the British hospital," Carroll said. Pat and other Navy wives traveled to try to meet their husbands' ships. She had friends in Shanghai whom her father had alerted. "I don't think Mother needed to be taken care of. She was forceful, spoiled, and had a horrible temper at times." The family's 1935 itinerary included Manila, Hong Kong, Chefoo, Haiphong, Tokyo, and Shanghai among other places.

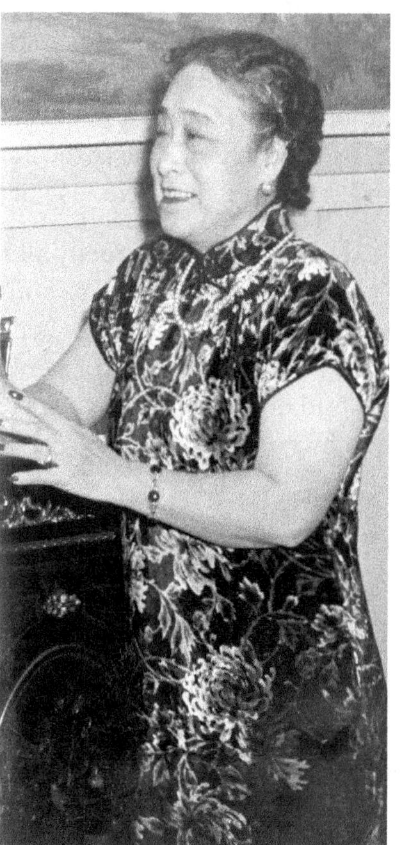

Princess der Ling (Deling), the last lady-in-waiting to the Qing Dynasty Empress Dowager Ci Xi (Tzu Hsi), taken by Pat Robbins in Los Angeles, mid-1940s.

Well, who was this woman? Born in Peking in 1885 to a Manchu nobleman and given the Christian name of Elisabeth Antoinette, der Ling served Ci Xi from March 1903 to October 1905. In 1907 she married Thaddeus C. White, an American. Ci Xi allowed her to use the title "princess." Although it might have undermined her credibility in China, it elevated her profile in America on the book lecture circuit. In 1911 she published the popular book, favorable to Ci Xi, titled *Two Years in the Forbidden City*. Later she wrote a biography aptly titled *Old Buddha*, and seven more books total about her life in China. She died in California in 1944.

Who was Ci Xi?

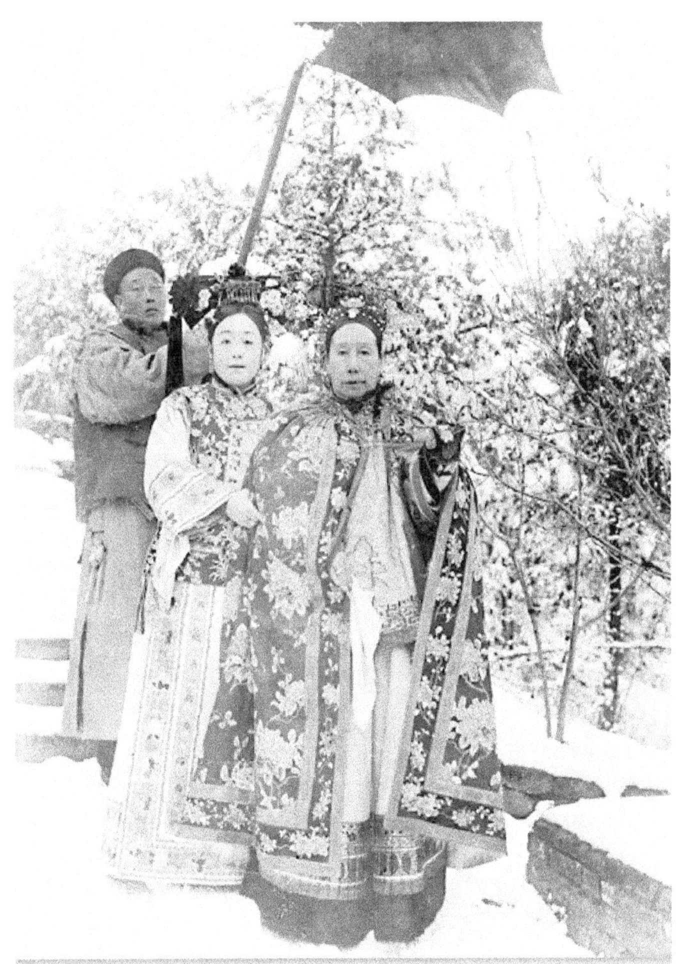

This photograph of der Ling with the Empress Dowager Ci Xi was taken by der Ling's brother Xunling, ca. 1905.[1]

Her name is spelled several ways: Ci Xi, Cixi, Tsu h' Si, and Tzu Hsi (pronounced Soo-She), and her nickname was the "Old Buddha" and sometimes, "Dragon Lady." We will use Ci Xi. The Empress Dowager in affect ruled China during the 1900 Boxer Rebellion, when Chinese insurgents known as the Righteous Fists of Harmony (the Boxers) rebelled against the Qing dynasty and Western influences. They slew Christians and foreign diplomats and their families. Ci Xi allied with the insurgents, but an eight-nation coalition, including the United States, doused the uprising in months.

While her nephew, the Guangxu Emperor (1875-1908), reigned, "Ci Xi was the defacto ruler of China and the Qing Empire. She was known for 'ruling from behind the curtain.'"[2]

"Ci Xi survived" the Boxers, Smithsonianmag.com reported, "but with a reputation for cruelty and treachery. She needed help dealing with the foreigners clamoring for greater access to her court, and was portrayed in the Western press as the "mother of all dragon ladies." So her advisers called in Lady Yugeng, the half-American wife of a Chinese diplomat, and her daughters, Deling [Princess der Ling] and Rongling, to familiarize Ci Xi with Western ways."

She eventually tried instituting western reforms, but largely was blamed for the dynasty's collapse in 1911 after her 1908 death. She appointed China's Last Emperor, Pu Yi. "The Dragon Lady may have been behind the curve when it comes to political reform, but she was ahead of it when it came to using the medium to control her image," *Smithsonian* magazine noted.[3]

Carroll recalled, "Der Ling took a liking to mother and easily introduced her to the arts and social communities, the upper crusts, the horse races, and the British community. The two were extremely fond of each other and enjoyed each other's company. Der Ling's husband had a big job in the States. I saw him occasionally. Never had children so she was always very fond of Berton and me. I was her Chinese girl. She gave me a Chinese girl's costume and loved telling me stories about little girls in China and how she grew up, like fairy tales about women and girls who might have lived in the palace. She developed a girl character.

"She insisted in speaking to me in Chinese but by that time [1940s] I had forgotten much of it. She told me to continue to try to speak Chinese so when I met Chinese people I could understand, but I didn't know too many

Chinese people in Los Angeles who couldn't speak English. She was around a lot and sent gifts to Mother. She told me that not having children was a lost joy."

God rest her soul.
Without der Ling, perhaps there might be no Patricia O'Meara Robbins
the photojournalist, and
thus no book about her life, career, and times.
Thank you, "Venie."

Pat's two most remarkable, memorable, and widely circulated images perhaps are these.

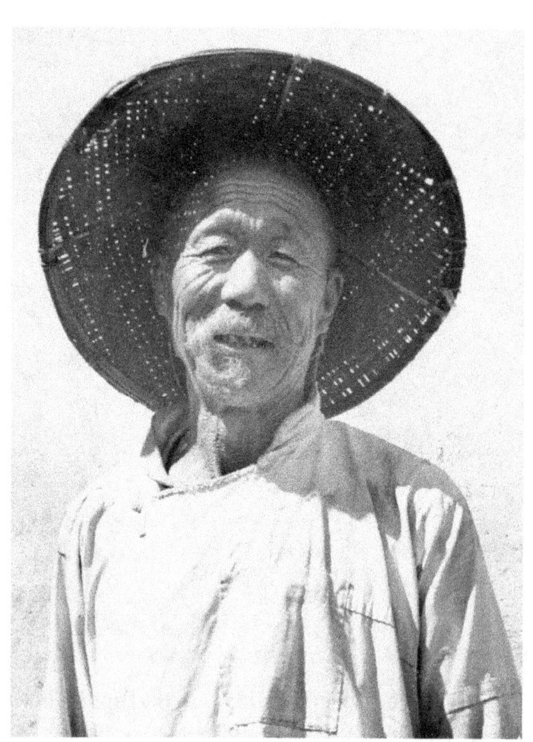

Elderly Chinese deaf -mute—the 'Old Chinaman'—at the Inland Mission, Chefoo, (now Yantai, Shandong Peninsula) North China, mid-1930s.

She won several awards for image, one of her personal all-time favorites, when her "Faces of China" collection was shown in New York and Los Angeles galleries. It played a large role in launching her career. To her family, this photograph embeds long-lasting value.

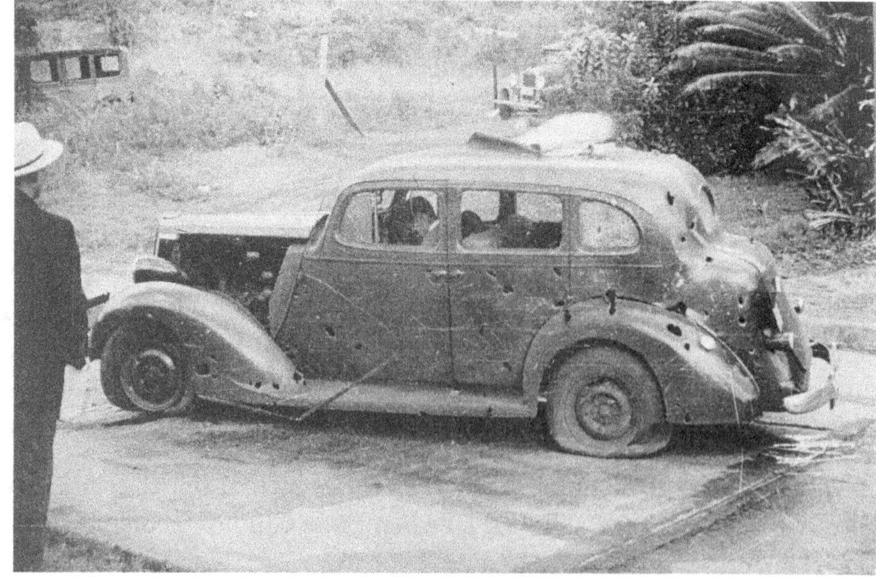

The 'Honolulu death car.' Pat took this enduring photograph of a four-door sedan, riddled with bullets or shrapnel, and the dead driver slumped over the wheel, on December 8, 1941, in Honolulu, Territory of Hawaii, following the Japanese attack.

She came upon this scene shortly after beginning her freelance assignment from the Associated Press, Army, and Navy to photograph the aftermath. The United States had entered World War II.

In Old Imperial China, a Career and Family Begin

Beginning in 1933, she gained access to old imperial China unheard of for a Western white woman. Following her husband's ships to Orient ports, speaking some Chinese, at five-feet-four and weighing 110 pounds, and often taking her infant daughter and amah, she shot indelible images of China and the Orient reflecting a fearlessness that begged, "It's there, why not?"

December 7, 1941

A witness to the Japanese attack on Pearl Harbor, Hawaii, and credentialed by the Associated Press, Army, and Navy, she took some of the historically most memorable photos of the aftermath and life on Oahu.

'Golden Age of Hollywood'

In her native Los Angeles amidst the "Golden Age of Hollywood" of the 1940's, she earned a "must-have" reputation among the movie and society sets by engaging fashionable family social connections and working tirelessly—while raising two children. Her portraits and informal shots included clients such as Joan Crawford and Christina Crawford, Jack Benny and Joan Benny, Maureen O'Sullivan and Mia Farrow, Eve Arden, Andrew Jergens, Loretta Young, Mrs. Lou Costello, and William Lear. She photographed Marine Corps Guadalcanal hero "Machine Gun Smitty," Jeanne Crain, Walter Chrysler, John Roosevelt, Alfred Hitchcock, Nancy Davis (Reagan), and Mrs. Walter Dillingham.

Occupied Germany and Post-War Europe

Living in Occupied Germany as her husband commanded the Rhine River Patrol in the early 1950's, her wide-ranging photos of post-war Europe included a clandestine interview with the White Russian underground leader and piece for *Colliers* magazine, parties with old nobility, behind the Iron Curtain for Hitler's bunker remains, palaces and castles, and Bavarian winter splendors.

Washington, DC, Scene

While engaging an active social schedule of giving and attending parties in Washington, D. C., her subjects included senior military and government officials and the breathtaking capture of an Arlington National Cemetery funeral procession for the *Saturday Evening Post*.

Credits and Tools

Look, *Photoplay*, *Mademoiselle*, *Popular Photography*, *Vogue*, *Town and Country*, and Honolulu, Los Angeles, and Washington newspapers were among the media publishing her images and pieces, including commissioned advertisements. Contests and exhibits gained her numerous awards and international respect.

Pat's Evolution

Through a chronological succession of art and vignettes, the reader tracks an experimental, evolutionary, and maturing professional. Through self-instruction and application, always with camera bag, Pat artfully employed subject, purpose, film, setting, lighting, angle, and perspective, and wrote with exceptional acquired skills. Topically in tune, she employed dashing positive personal traits of grace, small talk, and flattery in wooing and dealing with people she met. "Mother could, as the expression went, charm the hinges off of a door," Carroll remembered.

Profoundly Striking Images

Images of clients, scenes, and friends range from documentary and serious to informal and recreational. Contemporary observations and memories tempered with historical interpretations support this book's images, captions, and vignettes, embellishing the story beyond just identifying the images. The 1930s images of old imperial China and the Orient are profoundly striking, capturing people and vistas mainly unfamiliar to the outside world before becoming tourist destinations. The Pearl Harbor aftermath images, sometimes attributed as "Official Photograph," are valuable historical contributions, notably the dead Honolulu driver. A private intimacy with Hollywood stars and families and the Los Angeles "Old Guard" is revealed through images and personal associations and recollections.

As we shall see in Chapter One, Pat's well-entrenched Los Angeles family, particularly her father and family patriarch William Patrick O'Meara, used political persuasion to facilitate the new bride's 1933 passage to the Orient on the same ship as her naval ensign husband. A world completely alien to her upbringing enchanted and challenged her. Soon she adjusted and accepted the "obligated and indoctrinated" role of loyal, subservient Navy wife, quite normal and traditional for that age, successfully melding dedicated support for his career with her own ambition.

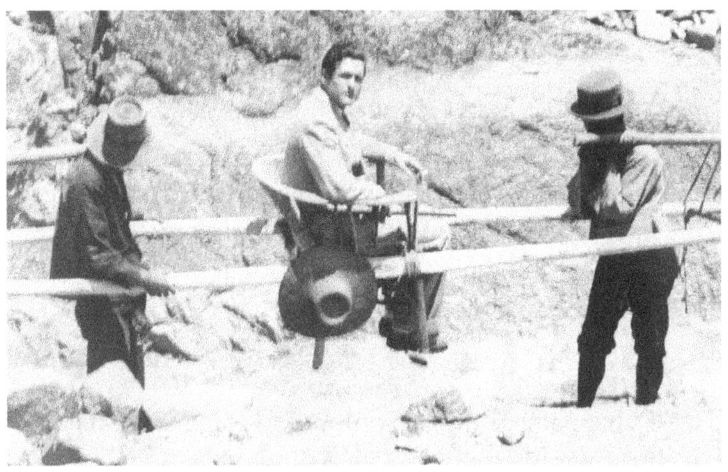

Lieutenant Berton A. Robbins, Jr., U.S. Navy, in low-budget sedan chair, somewhere in China, mid-1930s.

Lieutenant (Junior Grade) Bob Robbins quickly assimilated into the culture while practicing his junior officer duties in the glamorous 1930s Asiatic Fleet. Both before and after Carroll was born, a footloose and on-the-go Pat, traveling by steamships of questionable reliability or crowded local trains, frequently visited his ship's ports of call. Occasionally he accompanied her ashore wearing the prescribed civilian clothes for shore leave.

For then and forever, when available, the accommodating and supportive Bob became a favorite prop for photographs, beginning with his return from a serious 1945 war wound at Iwo Jima to a Long Beach, California, hospital.

In this image we find Bob looking uncomfortable but accommodating in a rather makeshift conveyance as they made their way from and to somewhere.

For reference, the reader will find Bob's service record of duty stations valuable in assessing the couple's travels. A highly decorated officer in World War II, and the esteemed mentor and role model for his son-in-law, co-author Wilbur, he retired in 1959 with a well-earned rear admiral's rank. Note the numerous assignments and changes of venue.

1931 - Graduated from the U.S. Naval Academy, Annapolis, Md., as an ensign
1931-33 - Communications and gunnery duties on battleship USS *Oklahoma* (BB-37), Long Beach, Calif.
1933 - Passenger to Orient on transport USS *Chaumont* (AP-5)
1933-34 - Engineering and gunnery officer on tender USS *Blackhawk* (AD-9), Chefoo, China
1934-36 - Gunnery officer on destroyer USS *Whipple* (DD-217), Chefoo/Shanghai (promoted to lieutenant junior grade)
1936-38 - Gunnery officer on cruiser USS *Portland* (CA-33), Long Beach
1938-39 - Instructor, U.S. Naval Academy (promoted to lieutenant)

1939-41 - Executive officer, destroyer USS *Kilty* (DD-137). Long Beach
1941 - Executive officer, destroyer USS *Tucker* (DD-374), Long Beach and Pearl Harbor, Territory of Hawaii
1941 - Executive officer, destroyer USS *Shaw* (DD-373), Pearl Harbor
1941-42 - Tactical instructor, tender USS *Tangier*, (AV-8) Pearl Harbor (promoted to lieutenant commander)
1942-43 - Cruiser Task Force/Group/Division staffs, on USS *Chicago* (CA-29), USS *Astoria* (CA-34), USS *Indianapolis*, (CA-35) USS *Detroit* (CL-8), USS *Richmond* (CL-9), Pearl Harbor
1943-45 - Commanding officer, destroyer USS *Leutze* (DD-481), Bremerton, Wash., and Pearl Harbor
1945 - Patient, Long Beach Naval Hospital
1946-47 - Staff, U.S. Naval Base, Long Beach
1947-51 - Staff, Armed Forces Radio Service, Los Angeles, Calif.
1951 - Promoted to captain
1951-53 - Commander, U.S. Navy Rhine River Patrol, Schierstein, West Germany
1953-55 - Commanding officer, amphibious attack transport USS *Pickaway* (APA-222), San Diego, Calif.
1955-58 - Staff, Office of the Secretary of Defense, Far East/International Security Affairs, The Pentagon, Washington, D.C.
1958-59 - Commander, Service Squadron Six/Service Force Sixth Fleet, and Task Force 63, on fleet oilers USS *Mississinewa* (AO-144) and USS *Truckee* (AO-147), Naples, Italy
Retired November 1, 1959, as rear admiral

Decorations:

Navy Cross - Battle of Surigao Strait, Battle of Leyte Gulf
Silver Star - Battle of Iwo Jima
Bronze Star w/Combat V - Battle of Lingayan Gulf
Purple Heart - Iwo Jima
World War II Campaigns:
Attack on Pearl Harbor, 1941; Battle of the Coral Sea, 1942; Battle of Midway, 1942; Aleutians and Battle of the Komandorskis, 1943; Invasions of Peleliu (Palaus), Battle of Surigao Strait (Battle of Leyte Gulf), Lingayan Gulf (Luzon, Philippines), and Iwo Jima, Bonins (seriously wounded)

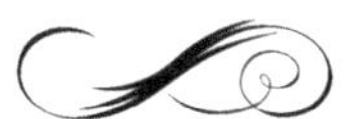

Principal research sources for Pat's "career and life" are Robbins family photographs, albums, periodical clippings, documents, and other items, and Carroll's memories and notes. Internet sources are used extensively for the "time" (historical) vignettes and to expand identification of the images.

CHAPTER 1

'She "Shot" Her Way to Success': The 'Washington Post' Captures Pat Robbins

She 'Shot' Her Way to Success

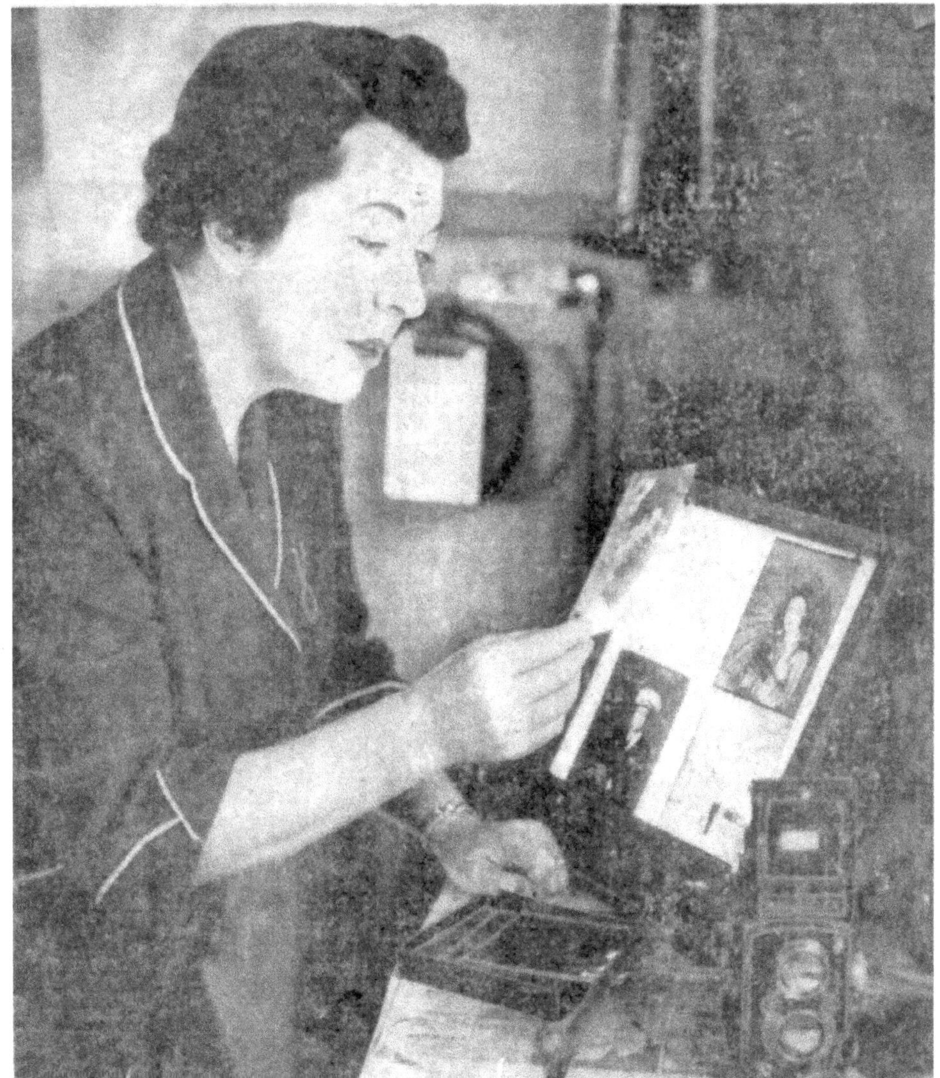

Caption with 1956 newspaper profile reads: 'Taking a close look at one of her color transparencies is photographer Patricia O'Meara Robbins, whose prize-winning photographs were taken while traveling with her husband, Navy Capt. Berton Aldrich Robbins, Jr. Mrs. Robbins' picture credit-line is well known in Vogue, Town and Country, Look, Mademoiselle and other national publications.'

Well-established and well-connected, and the wife of a highly decorated naval captain en route to choice Pentagon duty, by the time Pat Robbins hit Washington, D.C., in 1955, her reputation, charm, and doggedness landed her in the right circles, including with the print media.

She attracted Winzola "Winnie" McLendon, a popular women's/style section columnist for the *Washington Post* and *Times Herald* and an equally well-established, well-connected professional. Thus, mutual respect and social attraction. (The naval officer husband of the younger McLendon, later a best-selling author and newspaper icon whom *Time* Magazine in 1958 called a "newshen," would also make captain rank. More common ground.)

"Mrs. Robbins' picture credit-line is well known in Vogue, Town and Country, Look, Mademoiselle and many other national publications."

McLendon's 1956 feature on Pat smartly captured her career, life, and times to that point. She says it well, as if she were Pat's biographer. So, that's a good place to begin this book, and with it comes a quirky, teasing title.[1]

"That old adage about 'rolling stones gathering no moss' doesn't apply to photographers," McLendon wrote. "Pat's Robbins' roamings around the world with her husband . . . have gathered for her all sorts of top photographic awards. Her journeys from Shanghai to Wiesbaden have also put her 'in the right places at the right times' to get some mighty interesting news pictures. She was in Honolulu on December 7, 1941, and took some of the first pictures of the damage caused by the Japanese bombings and strafings.

"While in Germany in 1952, Pat scored another picture 'scoop' when she photographed the leader and staff of the National Alliance of Russian Solidarities (a movement which fights the Red regime). These color photos, along with a story on the underground movement, appeared in *Collier's* magazine."

Photography since childhood

McLendon continued. "All of this photographic 'know-how' has grown from a hobby started when Pat was a child in Los Angeles. Her parents . . . members of an old California family (her maternal grandfather was Patrick Joseph McCormick, who built the first railroad from San Diego to San Francisco)—had a German chauffeur who was also an amateur photographer. He not only took pictures but did his own developing as well.

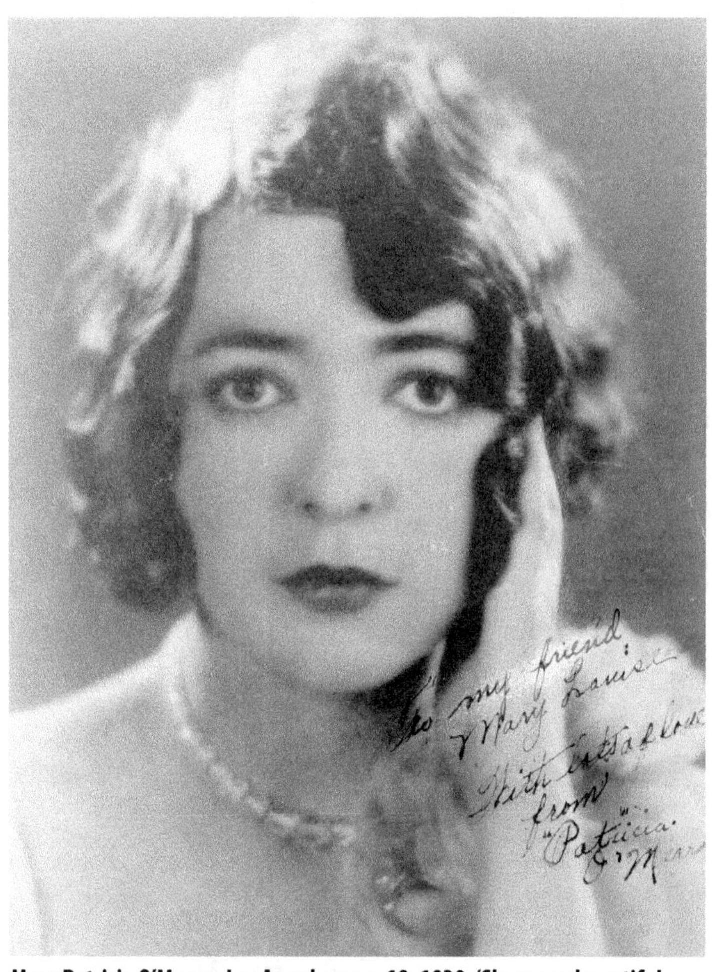

Mary Patricia O'Meara, Los Angeles, age 19, 1930. 'She was a beautiful young woman,' Carroll fondly recalled.

"Patricia was so fascinated with the chauffeur's photo hobby, relatives gave her a German folding camera and all the developing equipment for her seventeenth birthday. From the very beginning, she 'worked at it.' She shot all of her classmates at St. Mary's Academy; took pictures for the school yearbook; and kept a picture record of the debutante parties the year she made her debut at a gala party in the Los Angeles Biltmore Hotel.

"All of this time, photography was strictly a hobby. And, it might have stayed that way is she hadn't met and married Ens. Berton Aldrich Robbins, Jr. . . . They left immediately following the ceremony—via the Navy transport USS *Chaumont*—for Ens. Robbins' new duty in China."

A German folding camera

"With her one German folding camera (she now has seven cameras) Pat took shipboard pictures and when they arrived in China learned to speak Chinese so she could 'wander around' by herself to take more pictures.

"She 'took' the Forbidden City and the Imperial palace in Peking; Princess Der Ling—the last lady in waiting to the Empress Tsu Hsi (the 'Old Buddha') who became a close friend; the Great Wall of China; and studies of the

Chinese people and countryside.

"From China, the Robbineses (there were now three, daughter Carroll was born in Shanghai) went to the Philippines. There Pat traveled around the Islands adding photographs to her collection.

"Long Beach, Calif., was the next duty station for the Robbinses. (They were now four; son Berton . . . was born the week after returning from the Philippines). There Pat had another exhibit of her photographic studies of China; sold some more pictures; entered and won several national contests; and received letters from national advertising agencies which started her doing illustrative photography."

Pearl Harbor

"Two duty station changes and several hundred pictures later found Mrs. Robbins and her two children headed for Honolulu to join Capt. [sic, Lt.] Robbins who was then stationed on a destroyer. On Thanksgiving Day, 1941, Pat and the children arrived in Honolulu. They rented an apartment at Waikiki, just across the street from the Royal Hawaiian, and that is where they were on December 7 when the Japanese struck.

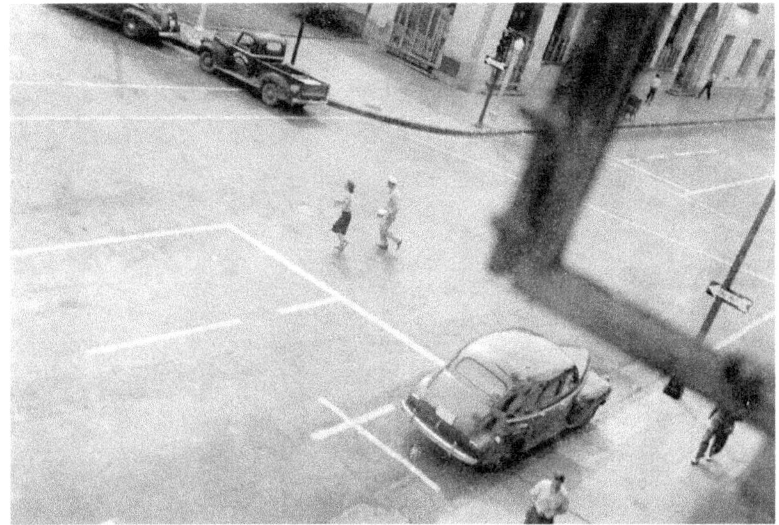

Pat's first photo during the Japanese air raid; a bomb fell in this area killing one and damaging buildings. Here two people scurry across an intersection. Waikiki, Honolulu, Territory of Hawaii, December 7, 1941.

"The noise and confusion was so terrifying to the children, Pat knew to calm them she must do 'something normal.' And, what would be more 'normal' than taking pictures? So, away they went—Pat with her camera and the children carrying flash bulbs and extra film.

"Her first 'December 7th' picture was taken one block from her apartment where a bomb had hit in the middle of the street, killing a man and ruining three buildings. She says, 'I was shaking so hard. I had to shoot at $^{1}/_{250\text{th}}$.'

"A strafed automobile was her next subject. There a reporter from one of the local papers asked if she would take some pictures for him. She and the children went along with the reporter in a press car, and the pictures she took that day were some of the first to go out from the Islands.

"The next day Associated Press hired her. . . . On the same day her husband, whose ship the USS *Shaw* was blown up in Pearl Harbor, was assigned to a new ship and sent to sea.

"With the children's help Pat worked for AP for several weeks. Then she did some illustrated stories for *Look* and *Mademoiselle*. (Yes, she can write, too. She doesn't like to write and will only do so when it is the only way to sell her pictures.) Some commercial illustrations, pictures for the photogravure section of a Los Angeles paper, and 'society' pictures for *Town and Country* were also part of her Honolulu work. In the fall of 1942 she went home to Los Angeles."

Hollywood small-fry

"Here she started another phase of her career. For some time she had been keeping a photographic history of her two children. The 'histories' were 11x14 pictures bound in volumes of 24 pictures. Friends who saw the books wanted sets of these 'story-telling' pictures.

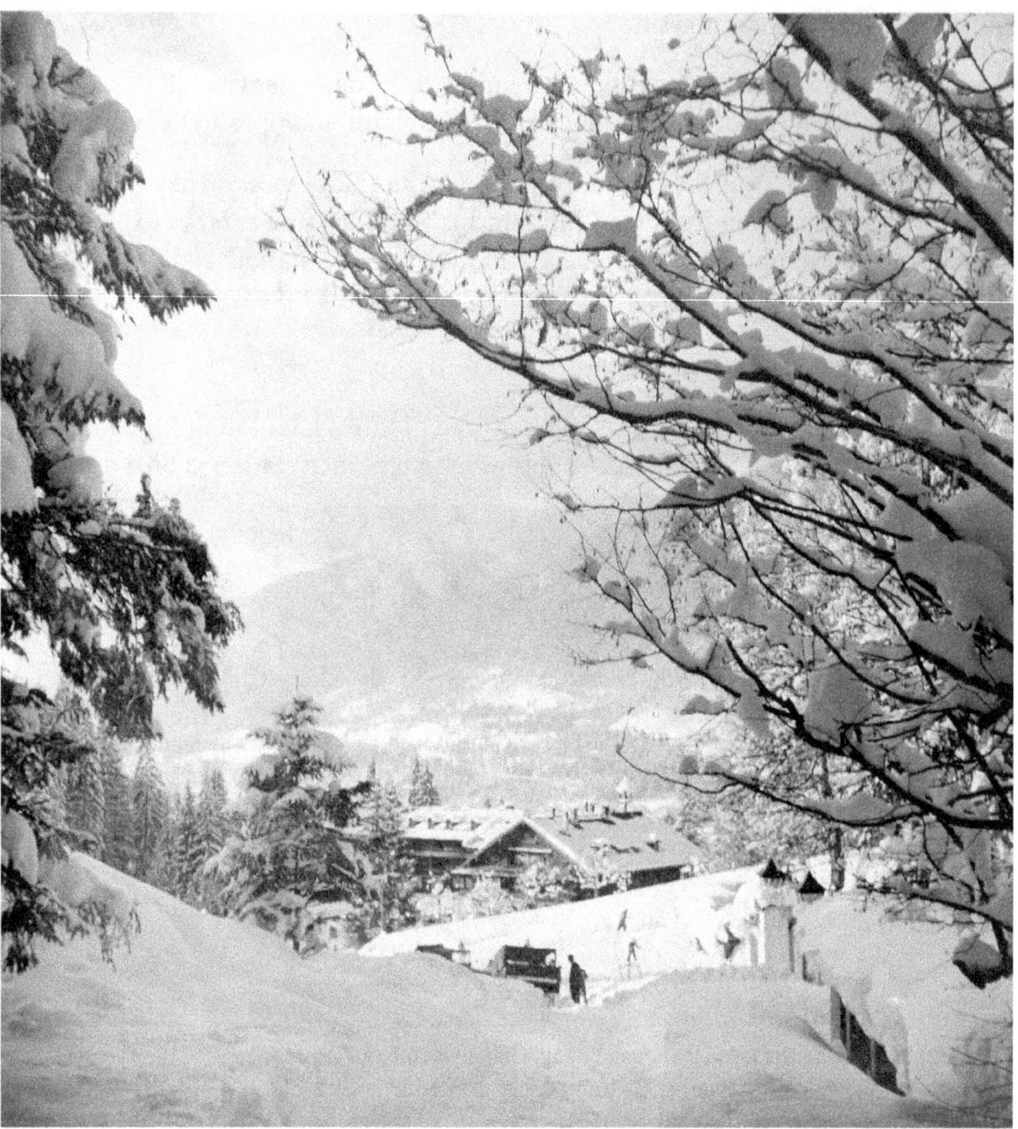

Garmisch, Bavarian Alps, West Germany, early 1950s. 'Mother carried her camera everywhere,' Carroll said. 'It bored me so much. She was always looking for an opportunity. She exhibited this one. A greeting card company asked her to buy the rights, and she said no.'

"In the next few years she made pictures by the hundreds of Hollywood and Los Angeles small-fry," McLendon's feature continued. "Included among them were the children of Jack Benny, Eve Arden, Joan Crawford and Loretta Young. She also got the the name of a Los Angeles service man each week from the Hollywood Canteen, made a 'picture' book of his children and sent it to him at sea.

"Color portraiture was next on the list for this adaptable and versatile photographer; subjects for her magnificent 16x20 color portraits which look like 'oils' include Andrew Jergens, Earl Anthony, and Maureen O'Sullivan.

"Early in 1951, the Robbins went to [West] Germany . . . . A villa on the Rhine at Eltville was 'home port' but Pat traveled over Europe with her many cameras. She took pictures of the Schonbrunn Palace in Vienna, Stalin's Memorial in Berlin (she still wonders why the Russians let her take pictures inside the memorial) and got her famous pictures of Dr. Victor Baydalakov the leader of the Limburg staff of NTS (National Trudovoi Soyuz) . . . which has been fighting 'Bolshevism' consistently for two decades."

'How's your courage?'

"That assignment came about when a representative of *Collier's* magazine called her and asked 'How's your courage?' Her courage was OK. She went to Limburg where part of the underground is located and took pictures of their headquarters. She went with them for a shortwave broadcast from a mobile sending and receiving station (complete with machine guns) which was an automobile disguised as a bakery truck. The men said it was a new truck. The old one 'was ambushed last week' and completely destroyed.

"Now the Robbins, who are 'five'—Princess Renata von Marchenschloss, an adorable black miniature poodle called 'Baby,' joined the family in Germany—live in Alexandria, Va . . . ."

They built a house "which would have the right size and shaped right for Pat's photographic equipment . . . . The laboratory is a photographer's dream. It houses her seven cameras, an enlarger, developing equipment and all those things photographers find necessary for taking and developing good pictures." She plays classical records "to give her 'quite a lift during the long hours spent developing her films.'"

Whew!

Whew, Winnie, thank you! Perhaps you should have written this book. You certainly had a huge head start.

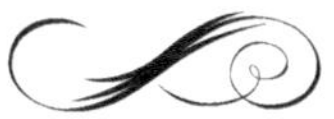

From socialite to junior officer's bride: the quick transition.

"Marked by charming simplicity was the marriage yesterday afternoon at 5:30 o'clock of Miss Patricia O'Meara . . . to Ensign Berton Aldrich Robbins, Jr., USN," per the *Los Angeles Times* piece on July 12, 1933. "The service was read in the O'Meara home in Van Ness Avenue by Rev. William Mullane of St. Brendan's Church, with only members of the immediate family and a few close friends in attendance . . . . [They] left last evening for Yosemite for a brief honeymoon. They will sail in a week for Honolulu, the South Seas and then to Shanghai, where Ensign Robbins is detailed to special duty." The piece identified Pat as "a popular member of the younger set of this city."[2]

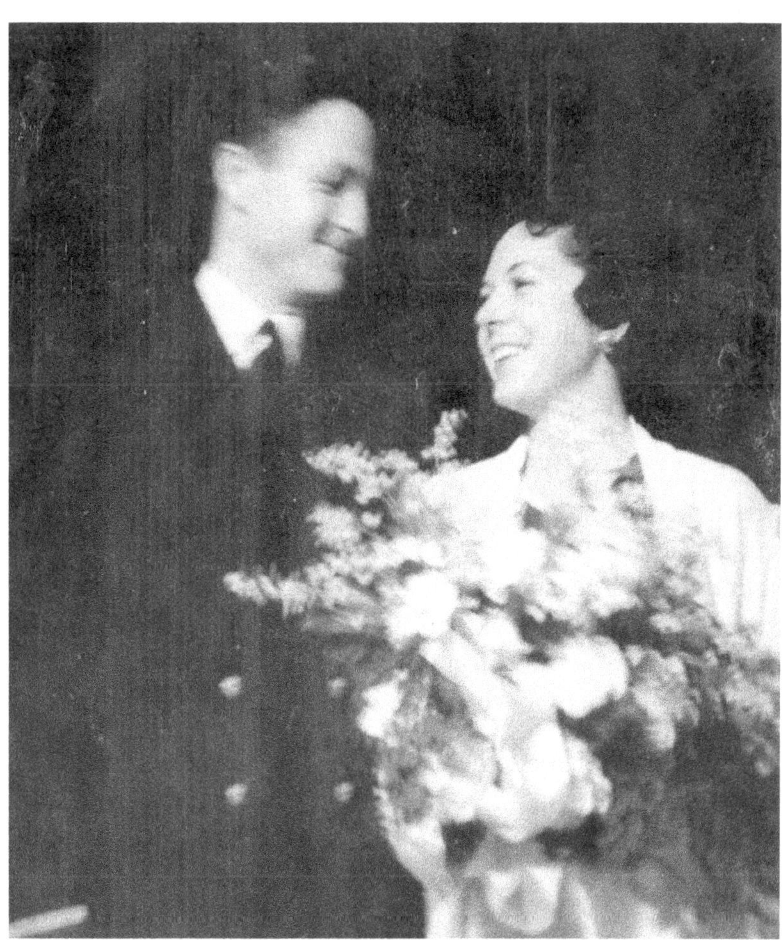

Ensign Berton Aldrich Robbins, Jr., US Navy, and his bride, Mary Patricia O'Meara Robbins, on their wedding day, July 12, 1933, Los Angeles.

Off they went to the Orient on July 17, sailing from San Francisco—but not before her father pulled enormous strings and cashed political chits.

Pat was the youngest of seven children of the esteemed, all-Irish William Patrick O'Meara, a gentleman and pillar of Los Angeles business and society. The domineering O'Meara controlled the family and used external persuasion for its benefit without hesitation. He overcame initial Navy and Army reluctance—

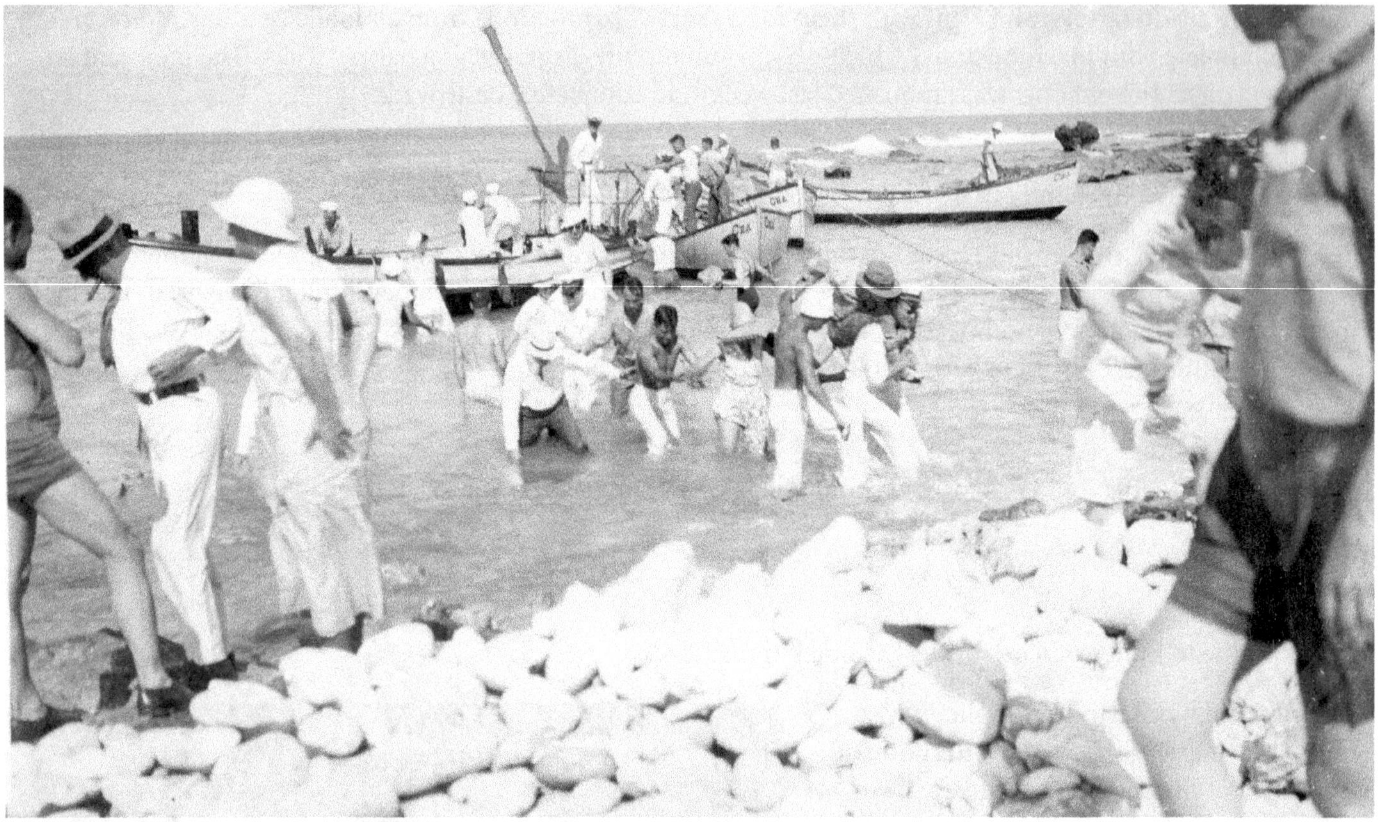

Landing party from the transport USS *Chaumont* (AP-5) going ashore at Wake Island, July 1933. Pat, marked by an arrow that she likely put on the print herself, is on the shoulders of a naval officer, probably her husband. She was aboard because her father had pulled strings in Washington.

lack of authority—to grant his daughter passage to the Orient on the same troop ship, in this case the Navy troop transport USS *Chaumont* (AP-5), with her husband by enlisting the intervention of his old friend, Nevada Democratic Senator Patrick McCarran, himself a huge presence on Capitol Hill.

McCarran's secretary wrote O'Meara on July 5 that McCarran had personally taken up the matter with the Navy, "and received full assurances that satisfactory arrangements would be made to carry out your desires." Also, the Administrator of Veterans Affairs contacted the Secretary of the Navy. During June and early July, Western Union made a mint from the telegrams between all parties involved. O'Meara prevailed, and perhaps the Navy was none the worse for it.

If Pat had been denied, there would have been no Carroll, no Princess der Ling, nor this book. For that blessing, we add the name of the late Senator McCarran to those we acknowledge.

On board the USS *Chaumont* en route to the Orient, one "Lieutenant Martin . . . happened to notice Ensign and Mrs. Robbins returning with the Wake Island expedition the other day and was heard to remark that 'They were probably the first 'Robbins' that have been on the

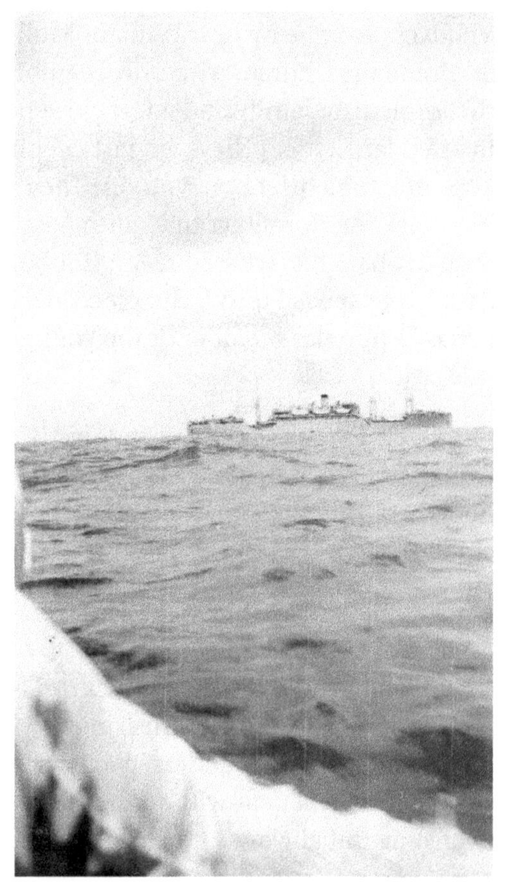

This photo of the troop transport USS *Chaumont* (AP-5) from a boat is noteworthy because it was one of Pat's first photos en route to China, July 1933.

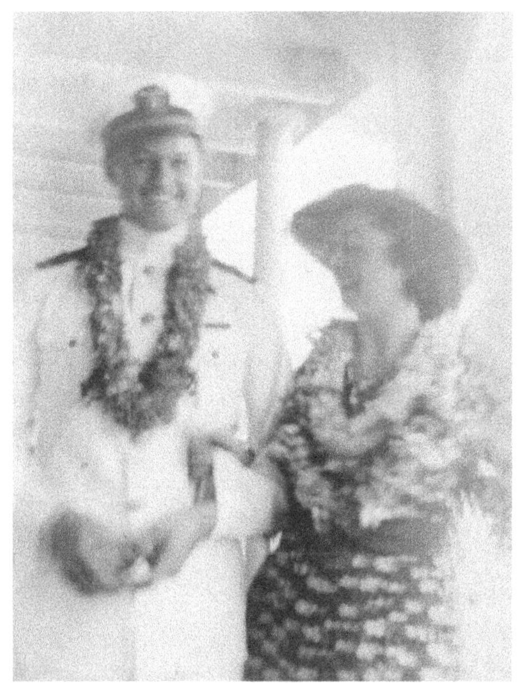

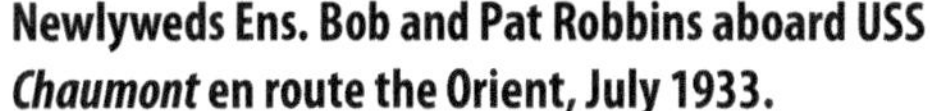

Newlyweds Ens. Bob and Pat Robbins aboard USS *Chaumont* en route the Orient, July 1933.

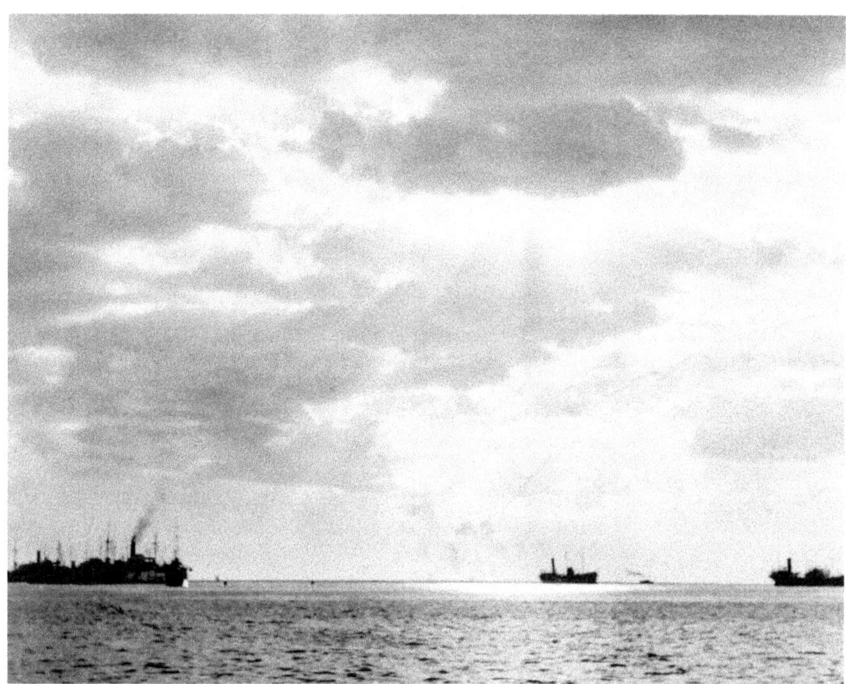

Ships in Manila Bay, Philippine Islands, on arrival of the USS *Chaumont* in 1933. Note the sun's rays spotlighting the middle ship. Pat was off and running.

island since the big tidal wave back in 1900,'" reported the *Morning Breeze* newsletter on August 5, 1933. That night's shipboard movie: *Possessed*, in nine reels, starring Joan Crawford and Clark Gable. The ship's itinerary included Honolulu, Guam, Manila on August 16, Shanghai on the 21st, and Chefoo on the 26th.[3]

Carroll always figured she had been conceived on that "Slow Boat to China." At least it always made for light conversation with guests.

On April 28, 1934, "Miss Robbins' Arrival Told," blurbed the *Los Angeles Examiner*'s society page. "News of the birth of baby Carol [sic] Eloise Robbins . . . was radioed by her parents, Mr. and Mrs. Bertram [sic—soon the O'Meara family would see that their local media got the names right] Robbins from Shanghai, China . . . . The couple were married in this city a year ago and left immediately for the Philippine Islands. Later Mr. Robbins was transferred to China, and recently to Vladivostok."[4] The father, somewhere else on his destroyer, sent a naval message from the USS *Sacramento* (PG-19) to a fellow officer in Shanghai: "Tell Pat all hats now too small. All my love, Bob."

And now, the Orient awaited a three-year visit. First stop, Manila.

CHAPTER 2

Whore House No. 12, a Marble Boat, and Vladivostok: Princess der Ling Opens Doors to 1930s Old Imperial China

Pat Robbins conquered old imperial China from 1933 to 1936 because Princess der Ling opened its doors to her, providing names, access, guidance, travel information, and sites to see. We can't say whether Pat prepped for this new world or for her role as a neophyte Navy junior officer's wife, what with her Los Angeles wedding and a hasty shuffle by politicians and ranking naval and government officials to authorize her transit to the Orient. But once she was there, the mysterious Middle Kingdom appeared naturally open to her inquisitiveness and initiative.

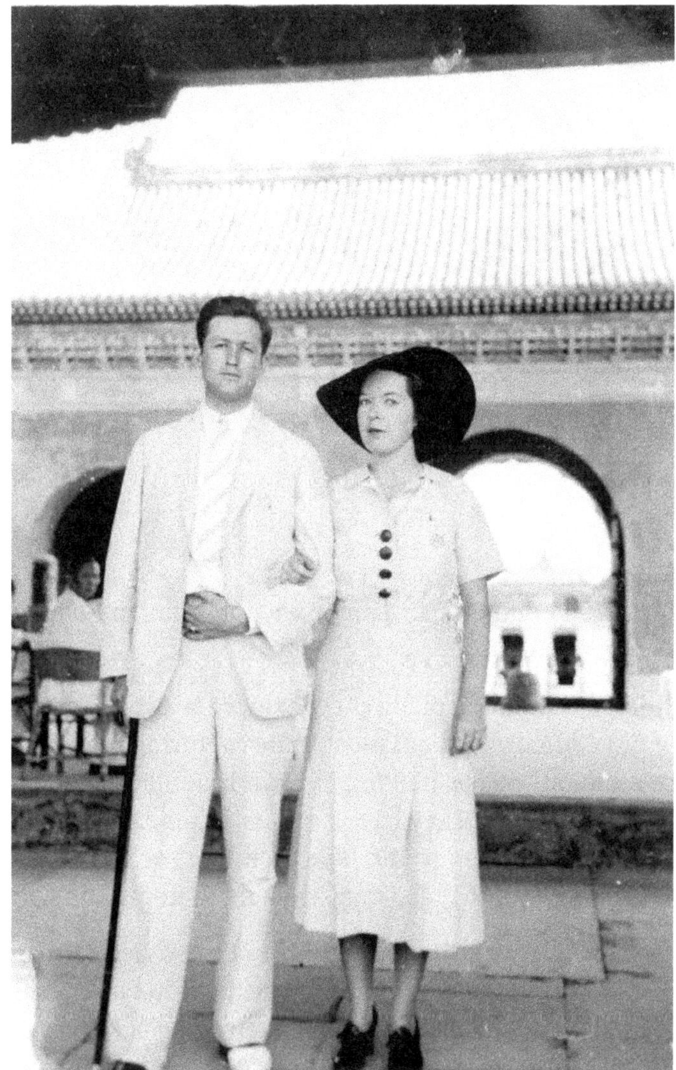
Bob and Pat Robbins in old imperial China, early 1930s.

Think of it. Can you imagine undertaking such a daring adventure in the unsettled mid-1930s when European influences, not American, permeated China? And, while China stumbled along under the Kuomintang Nationalist government before the all-out war with Japan in 1937, long before the Communist takeover in 1949, and before U.S. President Richard Nixon opened the country to the West in 1972? There she was, 22, a smart and privileged socialite from a well-to-do, long-time Los Angeles family, freshly married, ready to tread where other Caucasian women probably had not, a camera novice eagerly aiming to explore. The standard script more likely would have cast her as a missionary's wife on wheels.

Guts, ignorance, or egotistical fantasy? What possessed her besides "It was there, why not?" Then, had she any idea she was breaking ground, or of the contribution to history she had begun to make? Of course not. She was a driven, determined woman now detached from California roots with a husband often at sea. She either made it on her own, or not. And, from April 28, 1934 on, with her daughter Carroll and her Chinese amah, Ah Kwai. Carroll recalled, "It was so amazing for a very young white woman to be accepted into parts of China that no one from outside would go to. She always was a free spirit. Dad usually wasn't with her." By the time Carroll was two, reportedly she had been the youngest white child ever to take a sedan chair on the Great Wall

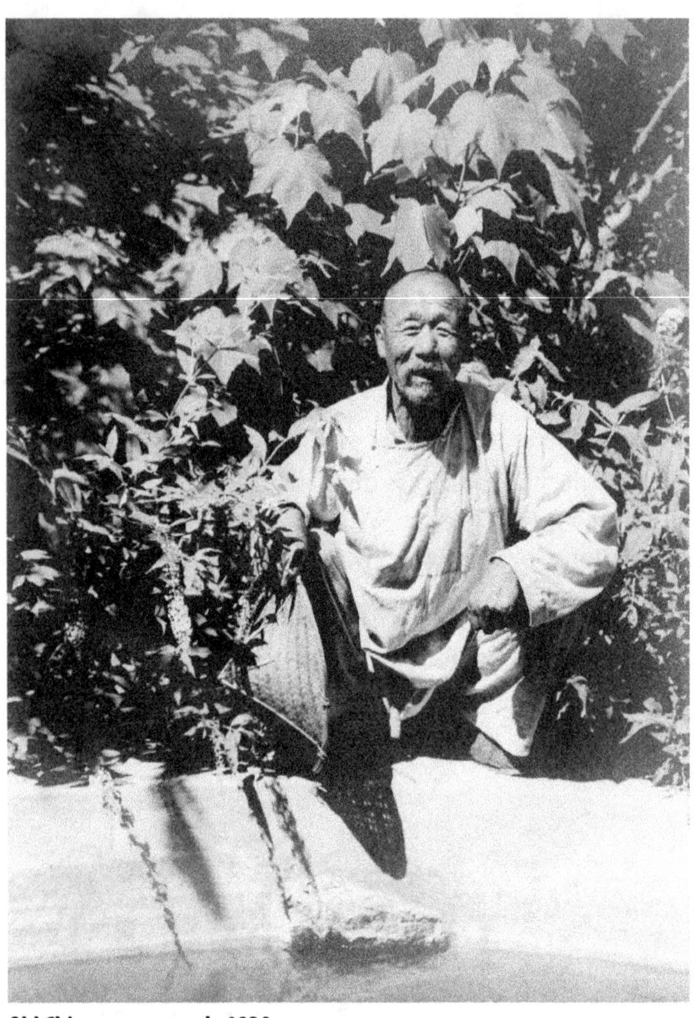

Old Chinese man, early 1930s.

of China.

From China, Pat visited French Indochina, the Philippines, Japan, and Hong Kong, then a British Crown Colony, following her man around the Western Pacific Ocean. Traveling to Manchuria, called Manchukuo after the Japanese seized control, to Vladivostok, Soviet Union, where she baptized her daughter, to Haiphong to be met on the docks by the city's Number One Madame, she obtained passage on passenger-cargo steamships and trains, and lodged in hotels of varying sophistication. Nothing deterred her, not the food, water, customs, traditions, poverty, or politics. Somehow she got film and somehow she developed it.

Pat also guest-rode her husband's two ships, the destroyer USS *Whipple* (DD-217) and tender USS *Black Hawk* (AD-9), which plowed the Asiatic Fleet's Yangtze River and China Sea patrols.

(This chapter presents only her China images. Remaining images of her Orient collection appear in Chapter Three.)

Almost alone, but not without domestic help, Pat launched a remarkable career without the slightest inclination of what would envelop her. A day, a week at a time. She saw opportunity ahead - first for a hobby, next for recognition, then for money, later for service.

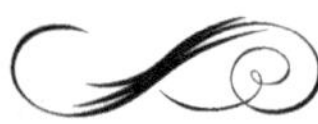

In a 1944 photojournalism piece published in *Popular Photography* magazine, Pat recalled her days in the Orient:[1]

"I had been taking pictures ever since I was seven years old and had studied art. I loved the drama and color of old China, and spent much time capturing, both with still and movie cameras, the quaintness, the Oriental color, and the slow-moving pageant I found there. However, it was very difficult to obtain pictures of the Chinese themselves. They have a superstition that your little black box will capture their souls along with their images. Most of them would hide their faces or turn their backs when I approached with one of my Graflexes ready for action. It didn't take long, though, to find some who would gladly let me 'capture their souls' for a small coin.

"I followed my husband over most of the Orient, usually finding that Uncle Sam wanted him somewhere else just as I caught up with him . . . clicking my camera shutters merrily all the way. "My daughter . . . was born in Shanghai . . . and almost immediately I began keeping a camera record of her week-to-week changes. Altogether we spent three years and hundreds of pieces of film and dozens of flashbulbs in the Orient. I had my own photographic exhibits in many of the countries I have visited."

We begin our journey through Pat's China photographs by reviewing that turbulent nation's political, military, and cultural conditions in the mid-1930s.

First, this map represents much of the geographic area of China that Pat visited. From her images it appears that she traveled, or at least took pictures, only in mild weather. North China has frigid winters and hot, humid summers. Judging from the landscape and what people are wearing, the images reflect neither extreme cold nor heat. What she did in extreme weather we do not know, except that she also traveled to warmer climes around the Western Pacific.

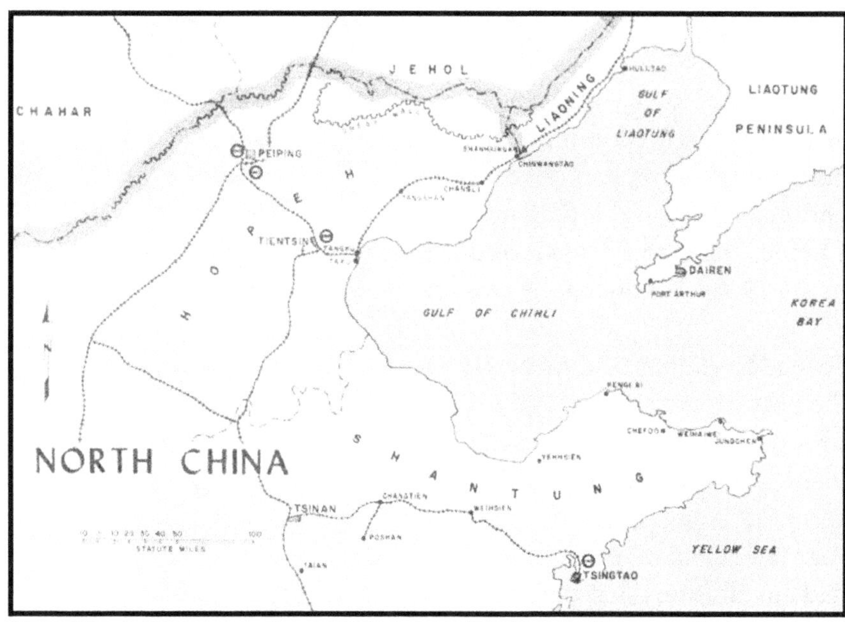

Map of North China centered around Tientsin and Chefoo (now known as Tianjin and Yantai), showing this area of operations of the U.S. Asiatic Fleet.

By this time, Japan had grabbed Manchuria from China, renamed it Manchukuo, and installed China's last emperor, Pu-Yi, as figurehead sovereign of this puppet state. The prelude to full war in Asia and the Western Pacific had begun, culminated by Japan's capture of Shanghai in a 1937 invasion, a year after the Robbinses departed. The Republic of China's Nationalist government, which emerged after Pu-Yi abdicated in 1912, was administered from the new capital of Nanking by General Chiang Kai-Shek's Kuomintang party. During the 1920s and 1930s, it nominally governed much of the rest of the country and continually attempted to consolidate power.

Until the late 1930s, Germany, needing raw materials, helped to modernize Chinese industry and China's military, as the threat was always Japan. In 1932, after subduing Manchuria, Japanese forces attacked the Chinese army from their Shanghai concession, "and settled into a de facto, but relatively quiescent, state of war with the divided Chinese nation. Increasingly, the U.S. Asiatic Fleet—and particularly the Yangtze Patrol—was called on to protect American citizens and national interest from Japanese incursions."[2]

Meanwhile, the Kuomintang faced an ongoing challenge from Communist revolutionaries headed by Mao Zedong. As the war against Japan expanded, Chiang's and Mao's forces began collaborating in 1936 to repel the invaders, but frequently fought each other as their civil war exploded. Meanwhile, large chunks of China remained controlled by local warlords and their coalitions and provincial military leaders, many with questionable allegiance to the Nationalists. Frequent foreign intervention also stirred turmoil.

In his official 1934 report, the commander of the U.S. Asiatic Fleet stated:

"China continues in a state of disruption with internecine strife and communist-bandit activities now engaging the wholesale attention of the Government forces," particularly "along the Yangtze Valley where our Yangtze Patrol and armed guards of Marines afford protection to American citizens and their interests. The spread of communism along the South China littoral has frequently necessitated, upon consular request, the presence of gunboats or destroyers at South China ports for varying periods. Their timely presence has had a steadying effect in these and other seaports. Piracy, with attacks on foreign coastwise vessels, remains widespread in the Canton area." The Fourth Marines regiment, with 94 officers and 1,669 enlisted men, was stationed in Shanghai. Another 29 Marine officers and 522 enlisted men guarded the Peking legation.[3]

Amid this instability and through pockets of chaos, Pat Robbins wandered.

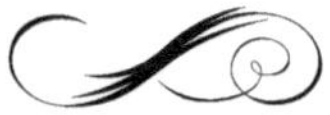

Chinese, Korean, and Japanese women served in intimate-contact professions as companions for international sailors and U.S. Marines in Chefoo, Tsingtao, Tientsin, and Peking in the 1930s. Following the reorder of Chinese society after 1911, women needed to support themselves or faced the necessity to sell sex. Printed business cards bore such names as Pleasure Pleasure Wong, Plain Lotus Chang, and Lilly Wong. In the pre-war years, very few Asian or Western prostitutes had any illusions that their hoped-for liaisons with Americans would lead to marriage, but some women still tried to arrange for monthly formal allotments from them.[4]

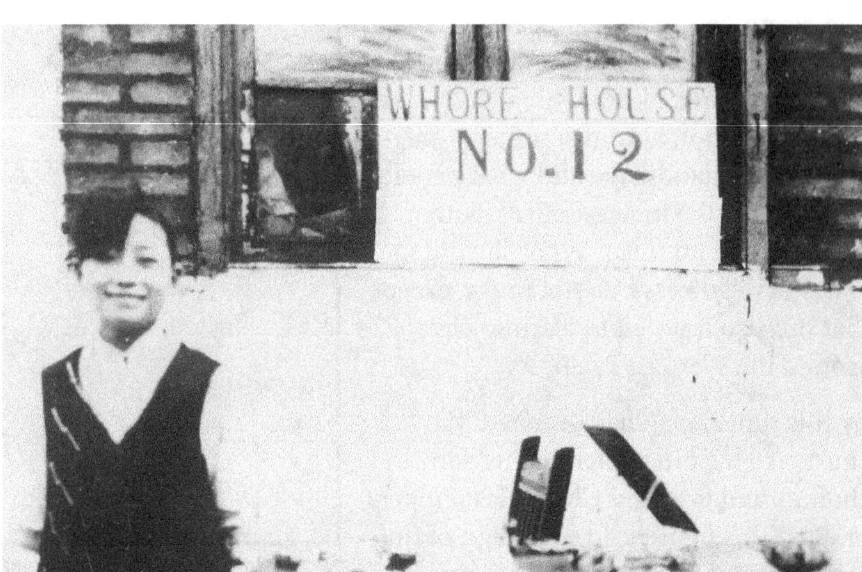

Whore House No. 12, Chefoo, North China, mid-1930s.

No potential subject escaped Pat's eye as she relentlessly crossed North China and the Orient, "good neighborhoods" and "otherwise." Always with camera and film, once she happened upon this establishment it was, naturally: point, focus, click.

The Chefoo (or China) Inland Mission School, or Protestant Collegiate School, was a Christian boarding school established in 1880 to educate children of foreign missionaries and the diplomatic communities in China. The China Inland Mission Headquarters was located in Shanghai. Based on the British education system, heavily emphasizing the classics to prepare students for Oxford and Cambridge, it became co-ed in 1934 and also taught Chinese studies. It had a reputation as the "best school east of Suez."

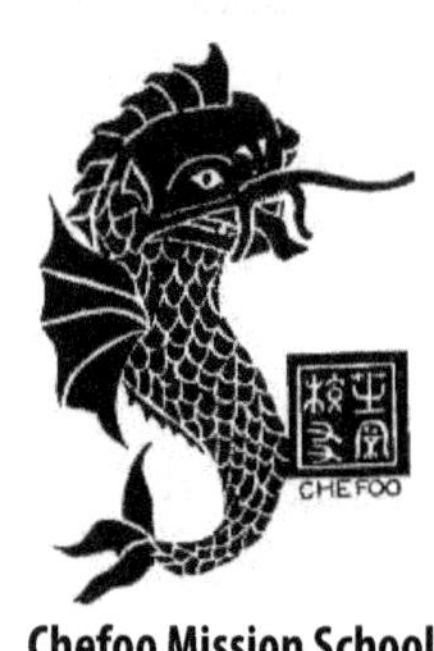

Chefoo Mission School's dragon-fish logo

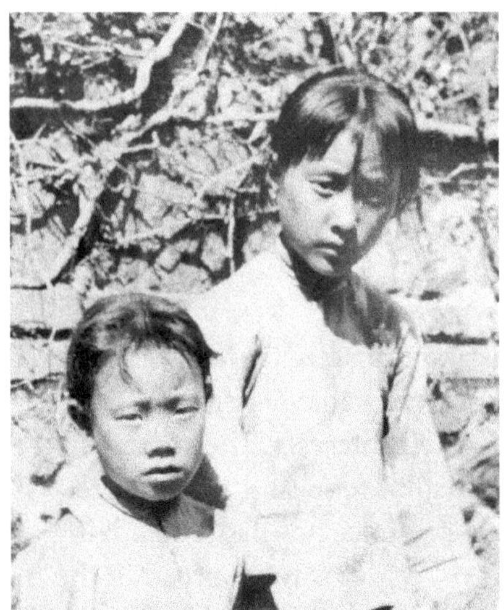

Portrait of Chinese peasant children at the Chefoo Inland Mission School, North China, mid-1930s.

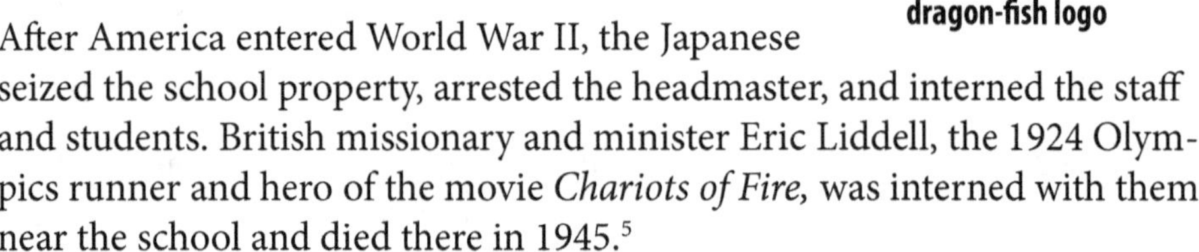

After America entered World War II, the Japanese seized the school property, arrested the headmaster, and interned the staff and students. British missionary and minister Eric Liddell, the 1924 Olympics runner and hero of the movie *Chariots of Fire,* was interned with them near the school and died there in 1945.[5]

From the *Los Angeles Times* in 1938, a piece that uses an old name for Beijing: "Arriving in China before the Japanese invasion, Patricia O'Meara Robbins brought back many fascinating photographic studies which have been arranged in an exhibit at the Villa Riviera in Long Beach . . . . Her ability to capture the real feeling of China is depicted in some of the studies which include wrinkled old men, boats on the Yangtze River and the Summer Palace in Peiping. While living in China Mrs. Robbins became adept at speaking the Chinese language. Her small daughter . . . was taught by her amah to speak the language.

"Mrs. Robbins, who is in her early twenties, found her greatest handicap in securing her pictures to be her youthfulness, since Chinese people revere old age and to the youth is given little consideration. Although Patricia Robbins with her charming personality and intelligent insight was able to see into the real China far more than any visitors, she feels that because of the vastness of the country penetrating into the real Chinese life is practically impossible . . . ."[6]

The O'Meara family knew the Los Angeles media, which accommodated Pat comfortably as she built her own web of those she wished to impress.

The Nankou Pass was a large gap in the mountains between China and Mongolia. Vast amounts of trade and travel between those lands passed through there. Hordes of barbaric Mongols for centuries used this pass to invade and devastate the plains and cities of China, necessitating construction of the Wall to stop them.

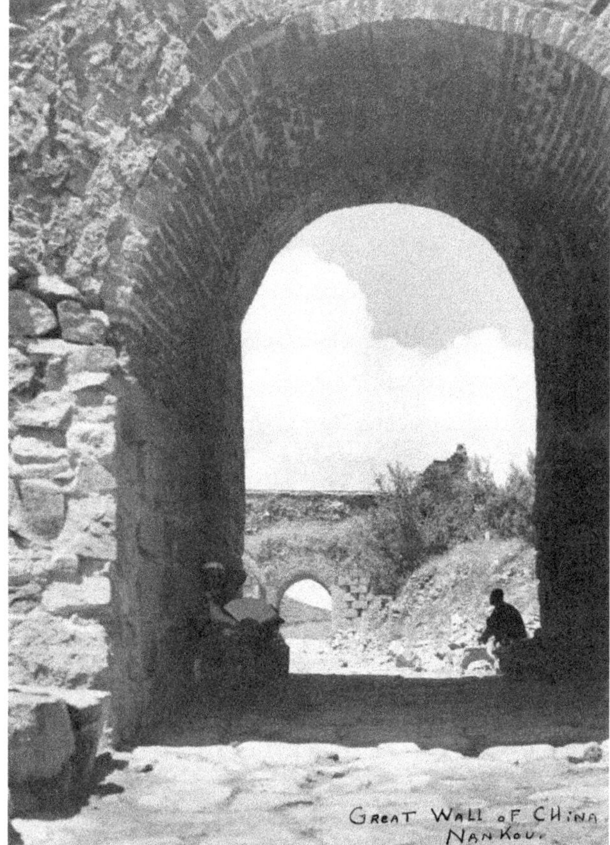

The Great Wall of China arch in Nankou, located northeast of Peking (as Beijing was then known to Westerners), mid-1930s.

"Mother took so many exquisite images of China," Carroll recalled, "concentrating on such as The Great Wall, that it is difficult to choose the finest among them. But this was one of her best. She exhibited it everywhere. She liked including archways, roofs, and pergolas. Her first exhibit in 1938-39 in Los Angeles highlighted The Great Wall, an endearing and popular subject yet to be retouched by tourism-minded preservationists. She shot it from multiple sections, angles, and panoramas. China was still a mystery to many and for a 'white woman' of 23-24 years to wander about without an older male was unheard of, especially with infant and amah. But she did it."

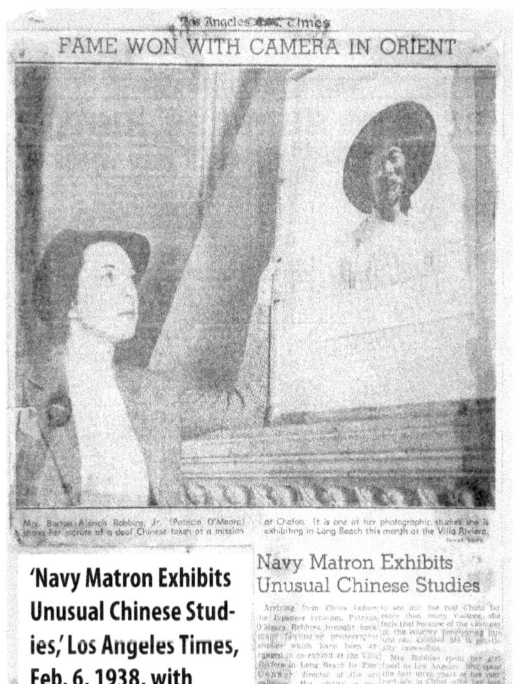
FAME WON WITH CAMERA IN ORIENT

Mrs. Burton Aldrich Robbins, Jr. (Patricia O'Meara) shows her picture of a deaf Chinese taken at a mission at Chefoo. It is one of her photographic studies she is exhibiting in Long Beach this month at the Villa Riviera.

Navy Matron Exhibits Unusual Chinese Studies

'Navy Matron Exhibits Unusual Chinese Studies,' Los Angeles Times, Feb. 6, 1938, with photo captioned at the time as 'Deaf and Dumb Chinaman.'

Titled "The Son of Heaven," the Chinese emperor was the country's supreme authority evolving from his ancestral lineage. He ruled and conducted affairs of state from this room. As magistrate, scholar, judge, supreme military commander, and family patriarch, he mediated between the earthly and heavenly realms.[7]

The photographs below were part of a series Pat shot of the school for the deaf in Chefoo, where she was welcomed and given unlimited access. Chinese with serious impairments to such faculties as hearing and speech were considered sub-standard and basically ignored. Visiting here bolstered her confidence and helped shape her view of how to photograph the Orient.

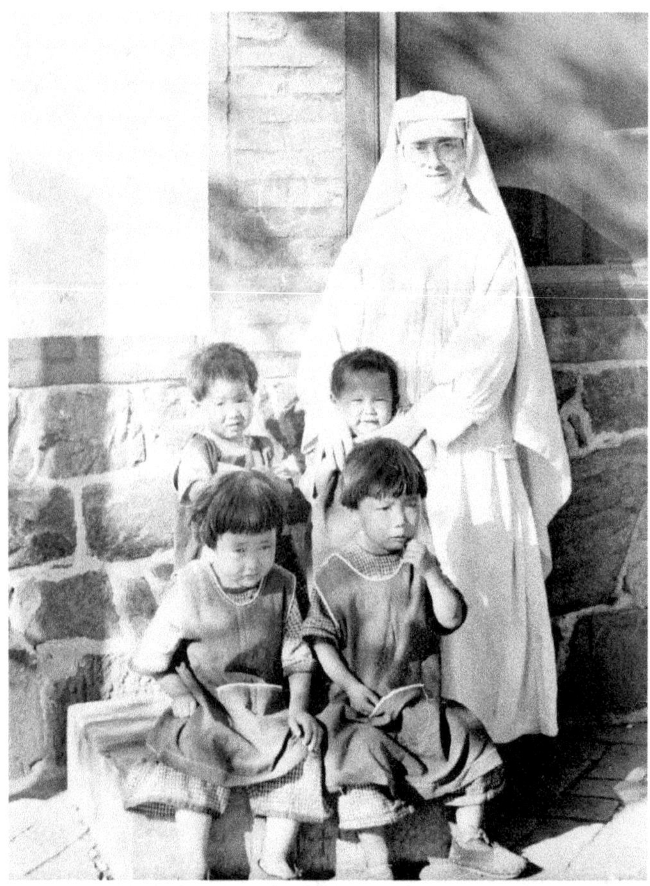

Catholic nun with school children. Chefoo, North China, mid-1930s.

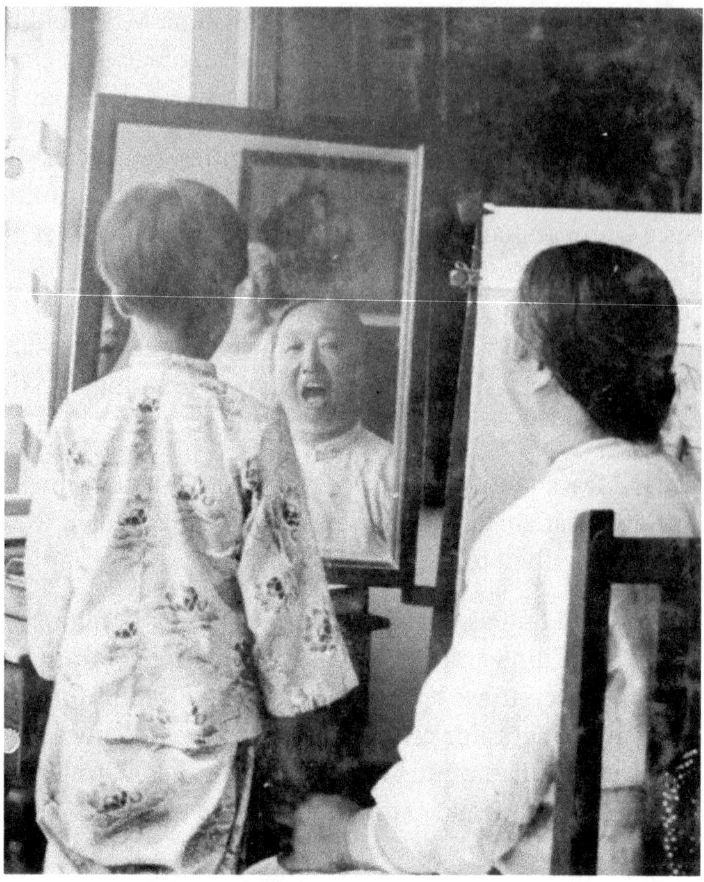

School teacher pronouncing words to deaf student, Chefoo, mid-1930s.

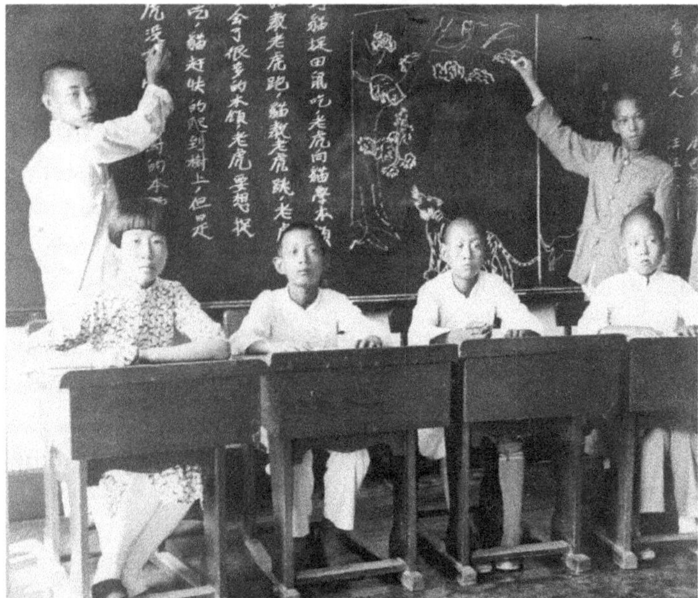

Teaching students at the school for the deaf, Chefoo, North China, mid-1930s. From the blackboard, the students are learning a fable. The wild cat catches the field mouse for food. The tiger learns a lot of skills from the cat, who teaches the tiger how to run and jump. Now the tiger wants to catch the cat for his food. But the cat runs up the tree. Alas, the tiger did not learn from the cat how to climb a tree.

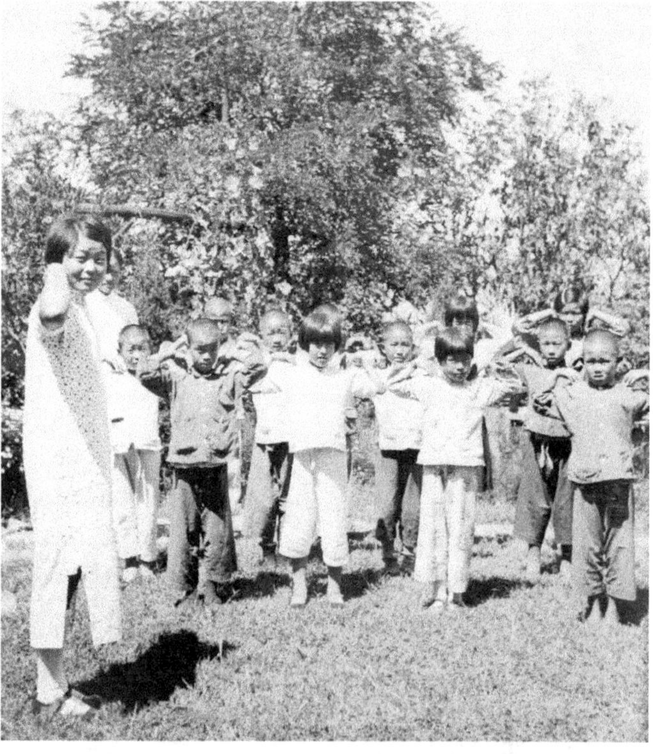

Caption: Children of what was then called the 'deaf-and-dumb school,' Chefoo, North China, mid-1930s.

Her diminutive presence, even at 5'4" and 110 pounds, and fair complexion, must have bewildered her subjects. What is this lily-white woman doing here? Eventually they posed anyway. (Unlike today, when photographers can immediately show a subject its digital or Polaroid image, while in the Orient she had to await later processing somewhere else – her own makeshift darkroom or in a studio - to judge her products, or share them with subjects.)

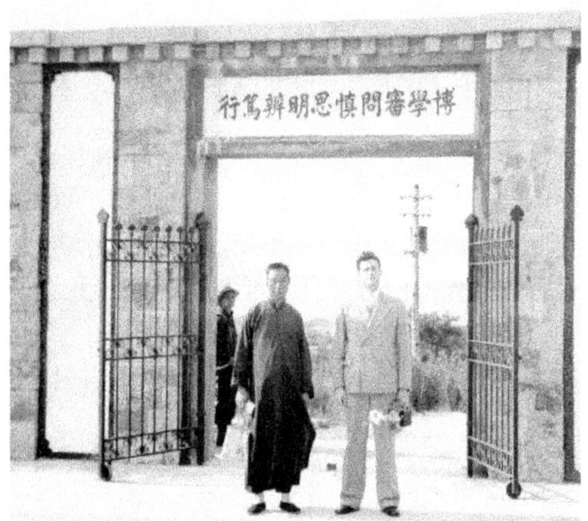

Bob Robbins at the Gate of Knowledge, Qinhuangdao, North China, mid-1930s. Its inscription implores the reader to learn broadly, ask questions, apply learned knowledge, make clear judgments, e.g., and think critically.

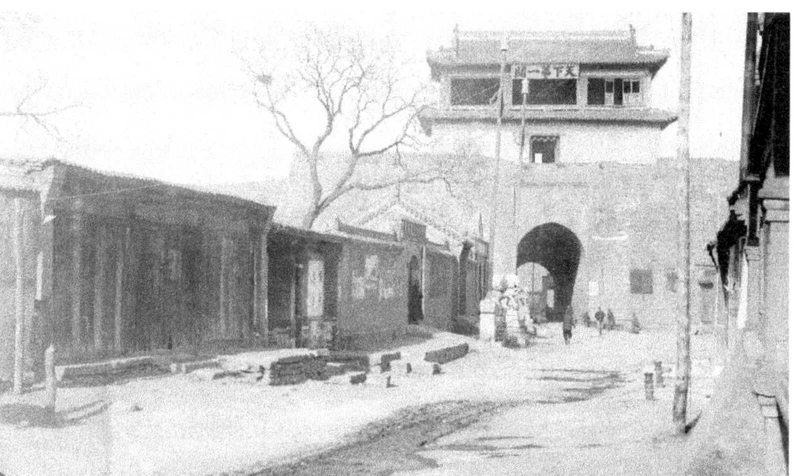

The Shanhai Pass (the Gateway) to Shanhaiguan, North China, of The Great Wall's northern defensive system mid-1930s. 'First Pass Under Here,' the entrance reads.

Qinhuangdao is China's only city named after the title of an emperor, referring to the Emperor Qin Shi Huang of the Qin Dynasty (221BC-206BC), the first Chinese emperor.

When my translator Lu Xue saw this image, she exclaimed: "That's my hometown, Qinhuangdao!" The Shanhaiguan District—in the image above—is an enclosed area encircled by walls linking the Great Wall. Laolongtou (Old Dragon's Head) is the east end of the Great Wall of the Ming Dynasty (1368-1644). In the center of the old town, the First Pass under Heaven (Shanhaiguan Pass) is the first pass of great military importance in the Great Wall.

The Ming Dynasty built the town, located in Hebei Province and bordering the Bohai Sea. During World War II, the Japanese mostly destroyed the pass, the town's main entrance, but now restored it survives as a tourist attraction. Lu Xue Googled its current image: the resemblance to Pat's photograph is remarkably clear.

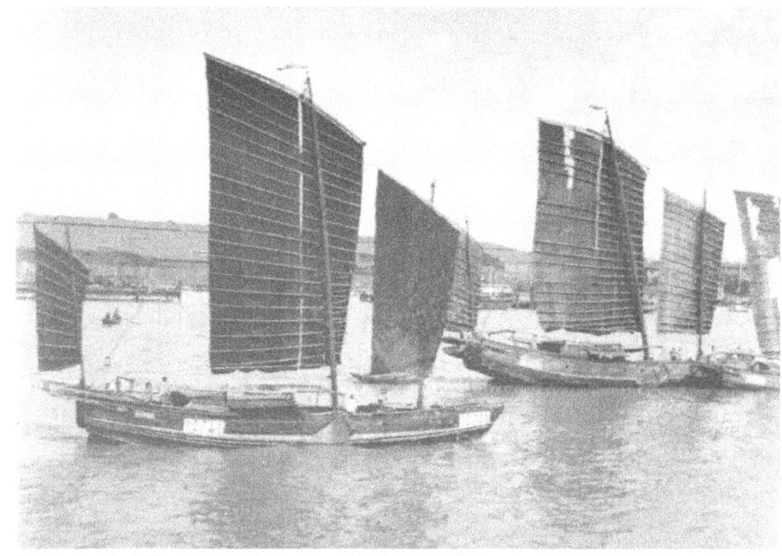

Junks on the Whangpoo River, Shanghai, mid-1930s.

Pat went to Shanghai, Asia's greatest city, to give birth to Carroll on April 28, 1934, in the British-run Country Hospital. She wandered around "Old Shanghai" unencumbered, and later in life reminisced about its vastness, culture, glamour, and mystique.

Historians, particularly in *Tales of Old Shanghai*, recall, "Old Shanghai was a very special time and place. The city was run by foreigners but was not a colony, most residents were Chinese but it was not ruled by China . . . . It was one of the most cosmopolitan places that ever existed, full of growth and speculation, of rogues and adventurers, of color and life, and of poverty and death. "Old Shanghai was the worst and the best of everything," the "Whore of Asia," the "Paris of the East," and a "paradise for adventurers" as a "haven to millions of people, both Chinese and non-Chinese, who sought refuge there from the wars and the poverty that surrounded it." Its bad reputation spawned the verb "to be Shanghai-ed," "which meant to be drugged and shipped off to sea as a sailor, a reflection of the problem ship's captains often had when they arrived in Shanghai in putting together enough of a crew to set sail again."

Modern Chinese television and films romanticized Shanghai of the 1920s and 30s as the city became the main center of Chinese entertainment, and the production source for many films and songs. The most well-known production was *The Bund*, produced in 1980 by Hong Kong's TVB, about the international section.

The largest and most industrialized Chinese city, Shanghai attracted adventuresome Westerners, intellectual activity, "bourgeois thinkers," and future revolutionaries, while developing a middle class influenced by Western fashion and habits yet living by themselves. Westerners lived in enclaves such as the International Settlement and French Concession and few ever spoke Chinese. "The world of the 'Shanghailanders' was based on the classic British colonial model—there was the racecourse and the Club, and a church. There were the trading houses and the banks. There was the arrogance of racial and cultural superiority." The city nevertheless "pointed the way to the future of China, but paid the price for being premature."[8]

Shanghai remains the historic foundation for past, present, and future China, and the place most associated globally with that nation. Carroll never returned to China, but always reveled in the fascination of her birthplace. Over the decades she and Wilbur called it to each other's attention when it hit the news. A favorite dinner-table story: As a teenager around 1950, she was held momentarily in a Mexican jail for truthfully answering a guard's question at the Tijuana-San Diego border regarding her birthplace. Mexican authorities at first did not believe her—something suspicious—until family intervened.

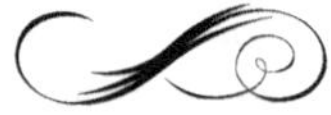

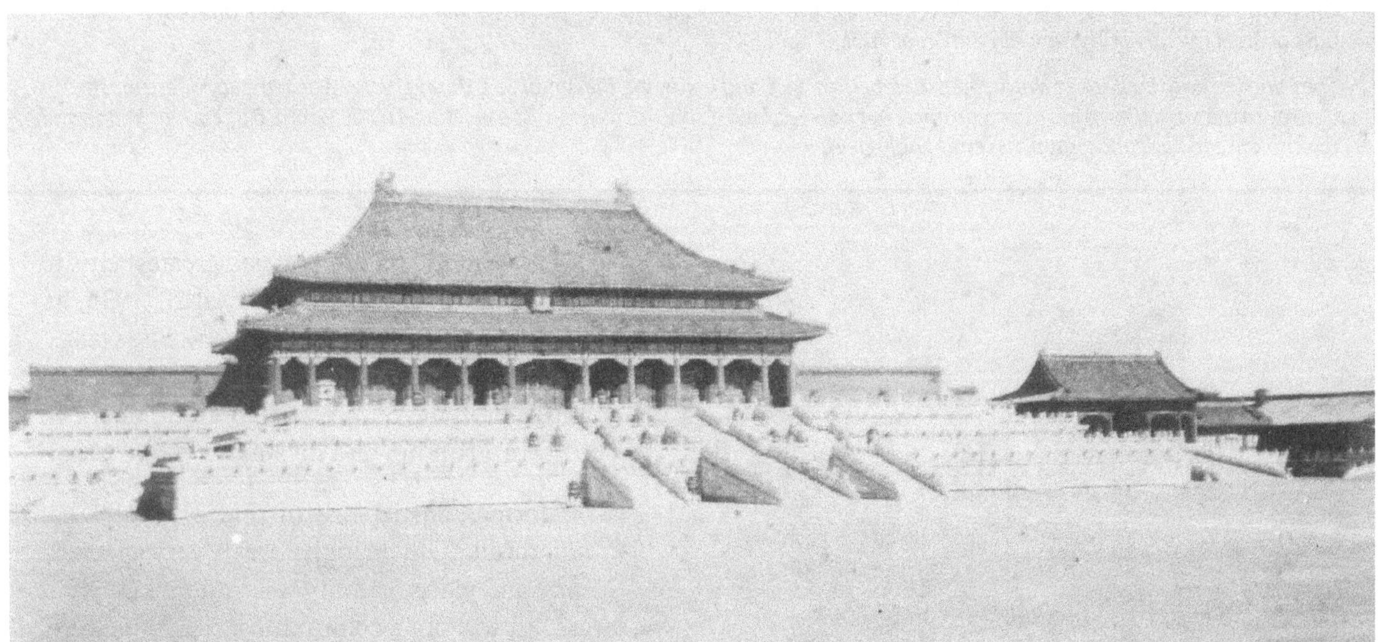

The Forbidden City, Peking, mid-1930s. Pat used her Eastman Kodak Vollenda camera, Panatomic film with K2 filter, settings of f-22 and 1/50.

Ahhh! Pat did leave a record of this shoot. We presume she used a Vollenda and processed her images while in the Orient.

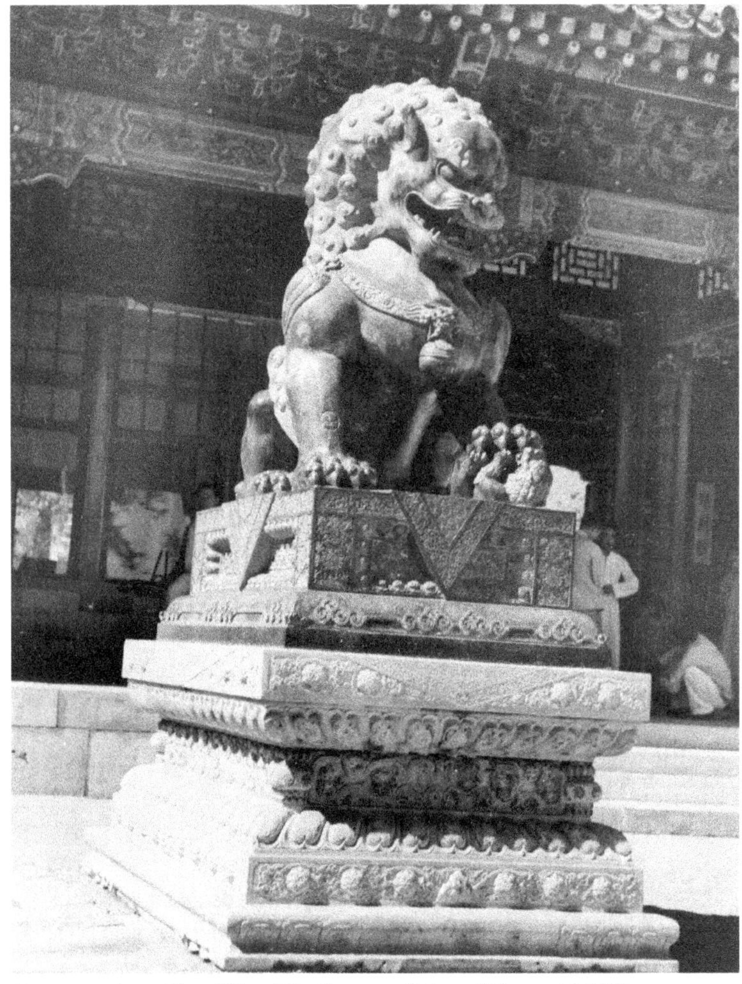

Bronze and marble griffin at the Summer Palace, China, mid-1930s.

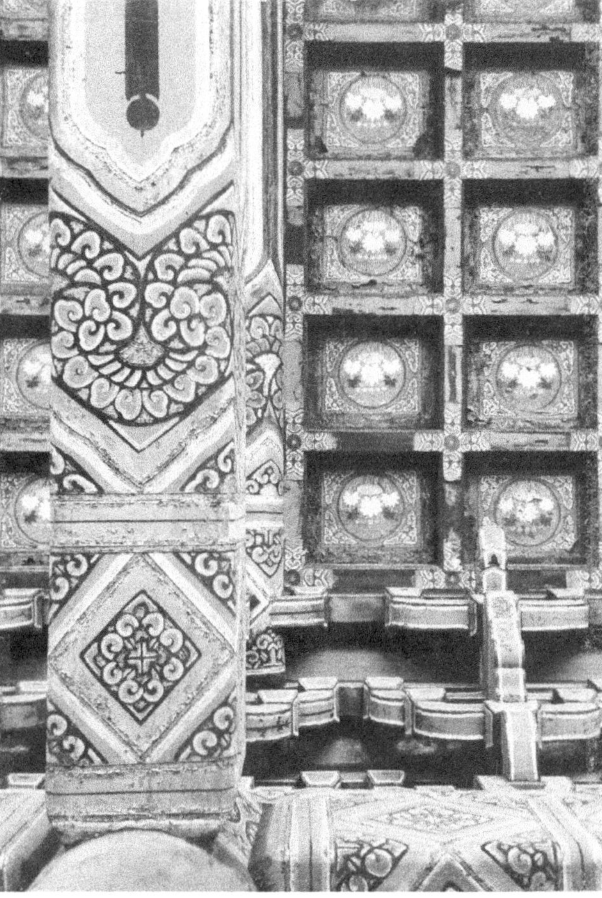

Ceiling in Throne Room in the Forbidden City, Peking, mid-1930s. The ceiling and beams are carved teakwood. The painted design is in shades of green, red, purple, and blue with inlaid gold.

Named Gu Gong in Chinese, for Former Palace, and lying in Peking's center, the Forbidden City served as the imperial palace for 24 emperors of the Ming (1368-1644) and Qing Dynasties. No one could enter the palace within, called "The Purple (Polaris) Forbidden City," without the emperor's permission. The Empress Dowager Ci Xi fled from the Forbidden City during the Boxer Rebellion, and the international treaty nations occupied it for a year. Before the last Chinese emperor, Pu Yi, abdicated in 1912, he sold many palace treasures "to finance his expensive lifestyle, while others were stolen by palace eunuchs." National treasures from the Palace Museum were evacuated in 1933 during the Japanese invasion.[9]

The Forbidden City then and now is a post-card representation of one's fantasies of old imperial China and its court intrigue, eunuchs, concubines, terra-cotta soldiers, coolie laborers, and imperial burial mounds.

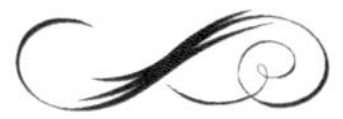

Pat began early keeping her Los Angeles family, friends, and media informed. She didn't hesitate to practice "outreach." From the society column in the Sunday *Los Angeles Times*, March 29, 1936, after Pat's return to give birth to a son, we have:

"Society as well as fashions this spring reveals a strong Chinese influence . . . . One of the most charming contributions from China in local social circles was the premiere appearance of tiny two-year old Carroll Robbins, blonde daughter of Lieut. and Mrs. Berton Aldrich Robbins, Jr., who are now living with Mrs. Robbins's (Patri-

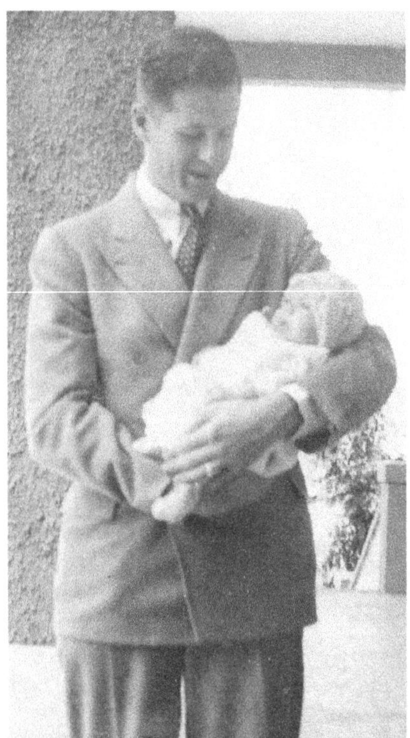

Bob cradles newborn daughter Carroll in Shanghai, 1934.

cia O'Meara) family on South Van Ness Avenue.

"Little Carroll . . . last Monday found she had a young brother who was born in St. Vincent's Hospital [Los Angeles] and named Berton Aldrich Robbins III. Carroll speaks and understands Chinese as well as or better than she does English, for she's had a Chinese amah ever since she was born in Shanghai where her father was stationed. She still has the Chinese nurse, a slim black-haired maiden named Ak-Wai [Ah Kwai] who takes Carroll for her walks up and down Van Ness Avenue and carries her little Chinese folding chair with her so she can sit down and knit while Carroll plays on all the neighbors' lawns. Ak-Wai coaxes and teases Carroll in Chinese while all the other neighborhood children stand around and wonder what's happening.

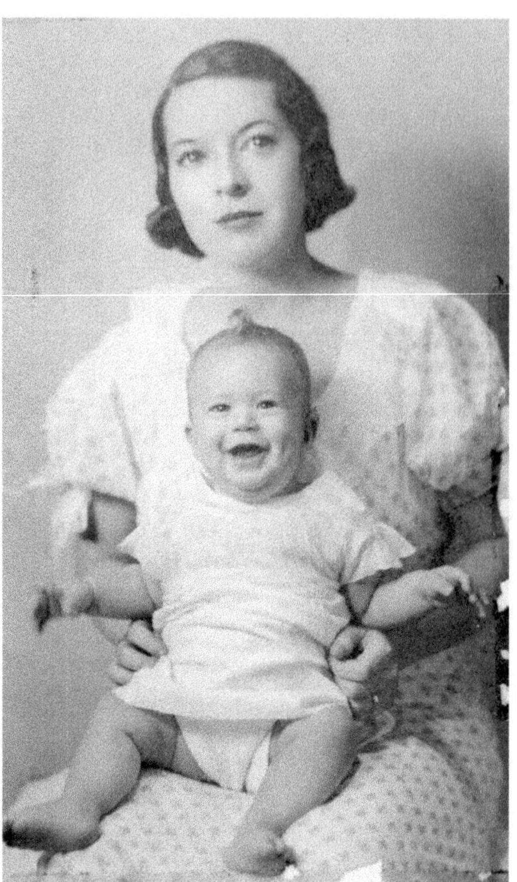

Pat Robbins with one-year old daughter Carroll, in Manila, the Philippines, 1935. While residing in China, Pat traveled to Manila more than once. This was a passport photo.

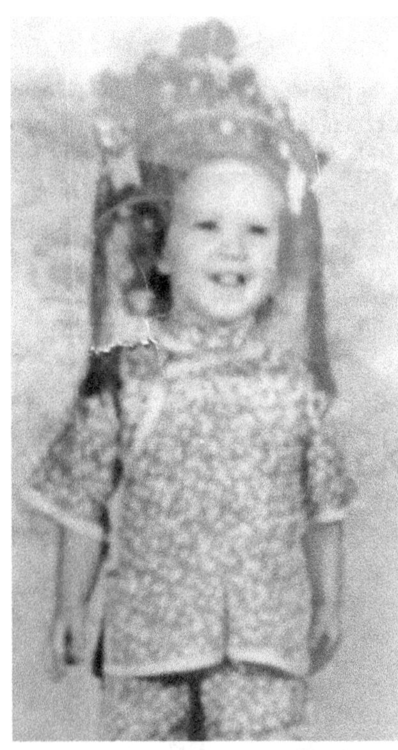

Carroll in Chinese outfit, mid-1930s.

"Carroll even has a Chinese dress made of red silk and embroidered by Ak-Wai's own hands. And her red Chinese hat has jewels on it and is quite the envy of the neighborhood. And all the little Carroll's aunts and uncles, to say nothing of her grandparents, the William P. O'Mearas, are quite enchanted with their almost-Chinese little relative whom they hadn't seen until a couple of weeks ago.

"We don't understand Chinese very well ourselves, so we're glad that Patricia and Bob, along with little Carroll, Ak-Wai, and tiny Bob, Jr., are going to be with us in San Pedro two and a half years. By that time, even Ak-Wai may be using Hollywood slang!"

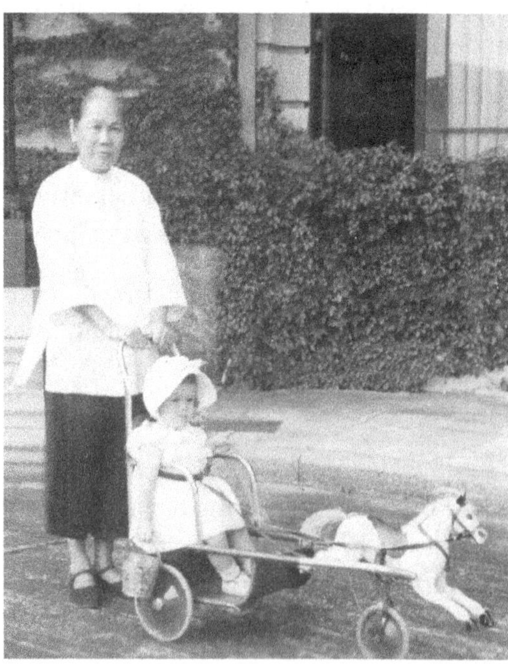

Carroll rides in toy pony cart. North China, ca. 1936.

Because of calendar adjustments, the Chinese new year occurs somewhere between the middle of January and end of February. "Chinese New Year celebrations were born out of fear and myth. Legend spoke of the wild beast Nien (which also is the word for 'year') that appeared at the end of each year, attacking and killing villagers. Loud noises and bright lights were used to scare the beast away . . . ." The event is the country's most important social and economic holiday, traditionally "a time to honor household and heavenly deities as well as ancestors . . . and a time to bring family together for feasting."[10] These characters appear more frightening than the wild beast.

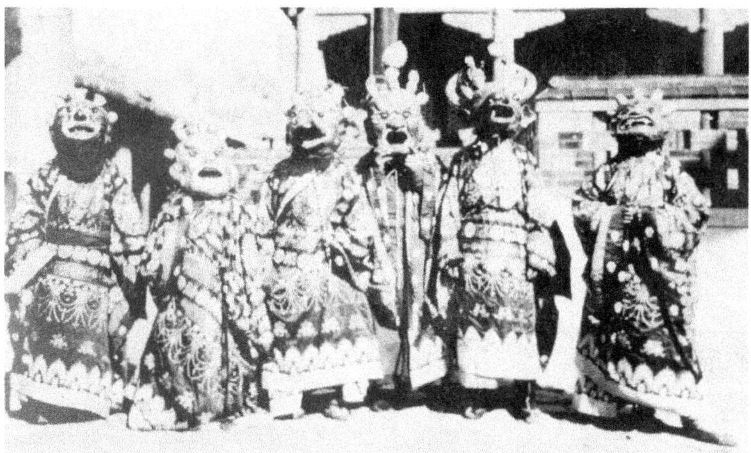

New Years game, streets of Chefoo, North China, mid-1930s.

The Great Wall is the imposing universal symbol of China. Chinese emperors began building it more than 2,000 years ago. Counter to traditional popular Western thought, the Wall was not primarily a defensive barrier to protect the interior from invading northern hordes. Often associated with war, the Wall also served during peacetime and always "was connected to the culture, foreign policies, and economy . . . . Philosophically, the Great Wall speaks well for a growth in the mixed soil of peace and war. It stands for some power, an unbeatable power despite all bitter conditions, known as the Great Wall Spirit among Chinese people." The Wall, therefore, is a powerful monument to Chinese history—the dynasties, the people, their myriad assemblage of states ultimately into one nation, and their enemies.[13]

A collection of short walls often following the crests of hills on the southern edge of the Mongolian plain, rather than one continuous structure, the Wall extends about 5,500 miles. And it cannot be seen from outer space, as fancied in a Twentieth-Century myth. Initially the Qin Dynasty (221-206 BCE) builders used earth and stones in wood frames. Modern construction, which one sees today, began during the Ming Dynasty (1388-1644 CE). The Ming dimensions ultimately uniformly reached about twenty-five feet high, fifteen to thirty feet wide at the base, and nine to twelve feet wide at the top to accom-

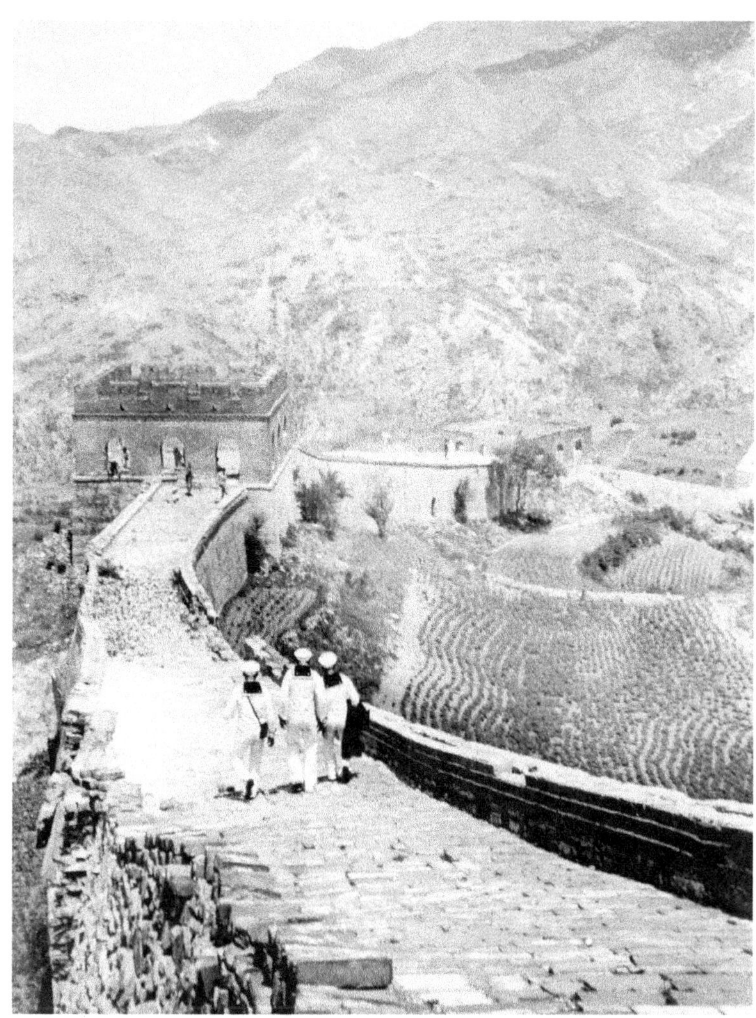

Western sailors, probably Americans, walk along the crumbling Great Wall, mid-1930s, giving it a feeling of vastness. This area was typical of many unrestored portions before the Wall became a tourist and promotional destination after World War II.

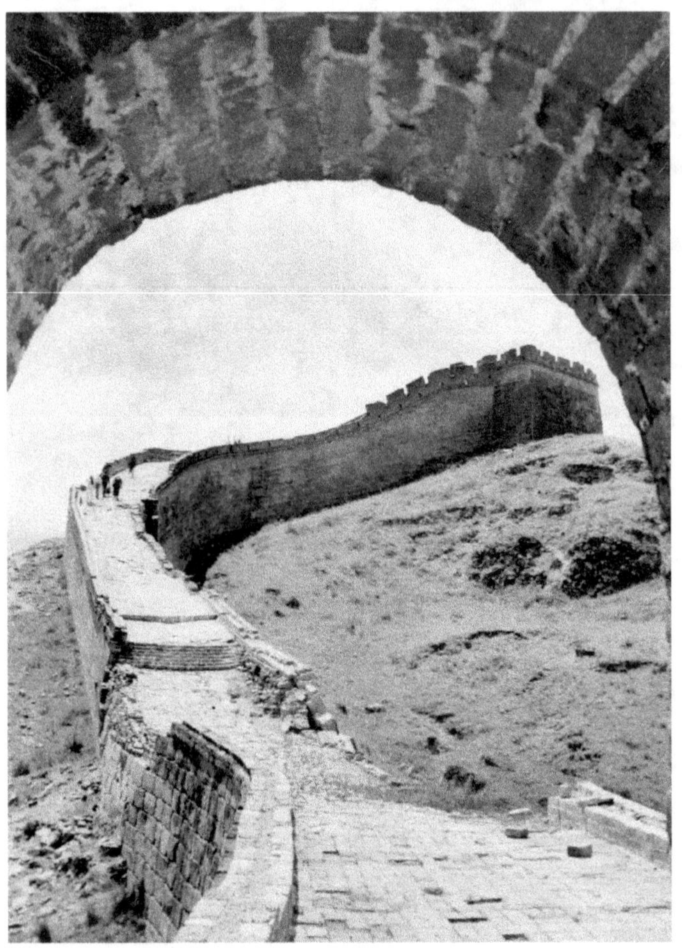

Great Wall of China near Peking, mid-1930s, many years before its restoration.

modate wagons and marchers, with guard towers and stations placed at regular intervals.

Because Mongol invaders breached the wall by flanking it, following subsequent pacification of Mongol chieftains the wall was eventually abandoned. In 1987 following rebuilding and restoration it was designated a World Heritage Site. Today thousands of tourists daily flock to that section about 50 miles from Beijing.[14]

Pat made multiple trips to various sections of the Wall and recorded some of her most memorable and favorite China images there.

For a Chinese Buddhist funeral, monks accompanied the bedecked bier with coffin through the deceased's neighborhood for one final association with its lifetime surroundings. A procession's trappings indicated the wealth or standing of the deceased, with the poor being borne on the shoulders of barefooted accomplices. The 1935 Shanghai procession of silent film icon Ruan Lingyu, who died at 24, reportedly stretched for three miles, and three women committed suicide during the event.[15] Family customarily placed money and belongings on the biers for use in the afterlife.

Pat brought back numerous Chinese artifacts and treasures including Ming Dynasty royal sleeves, which Carroll framed at our home, a meticulous silver junk model with oars, a majestic black mahogany floor chest, cloisonné vases, and a delicately and expertly hand-painted clay, wood, and fabric detailed funeral procession.

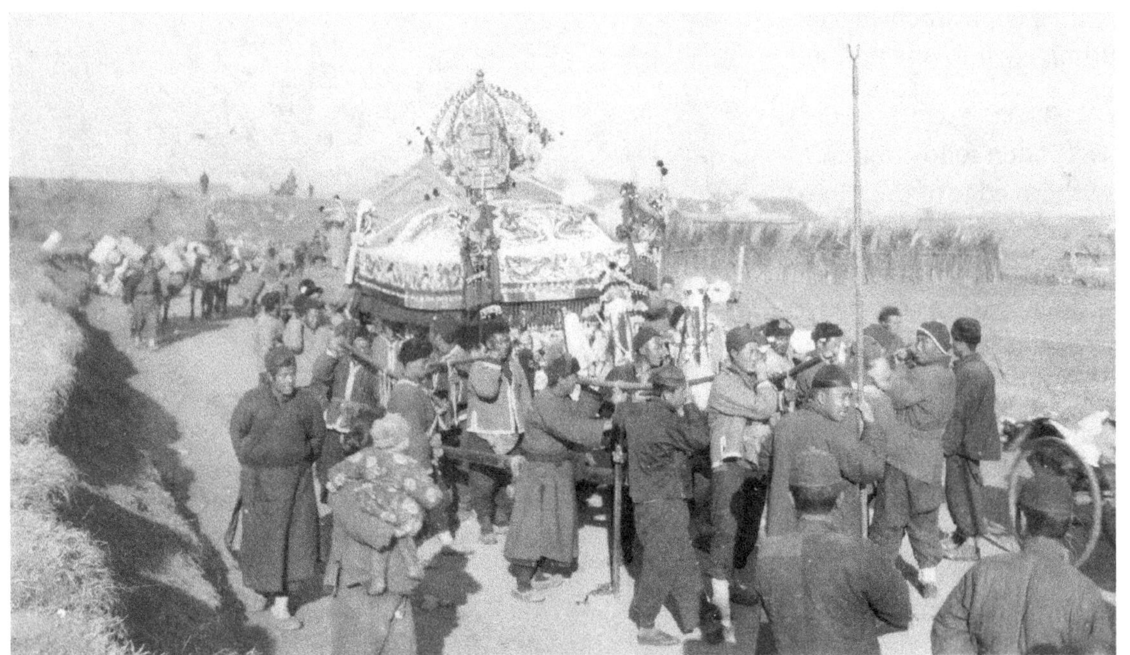

Traditional Chinese funeral procession, Chefoo, North China, mid-1930s.

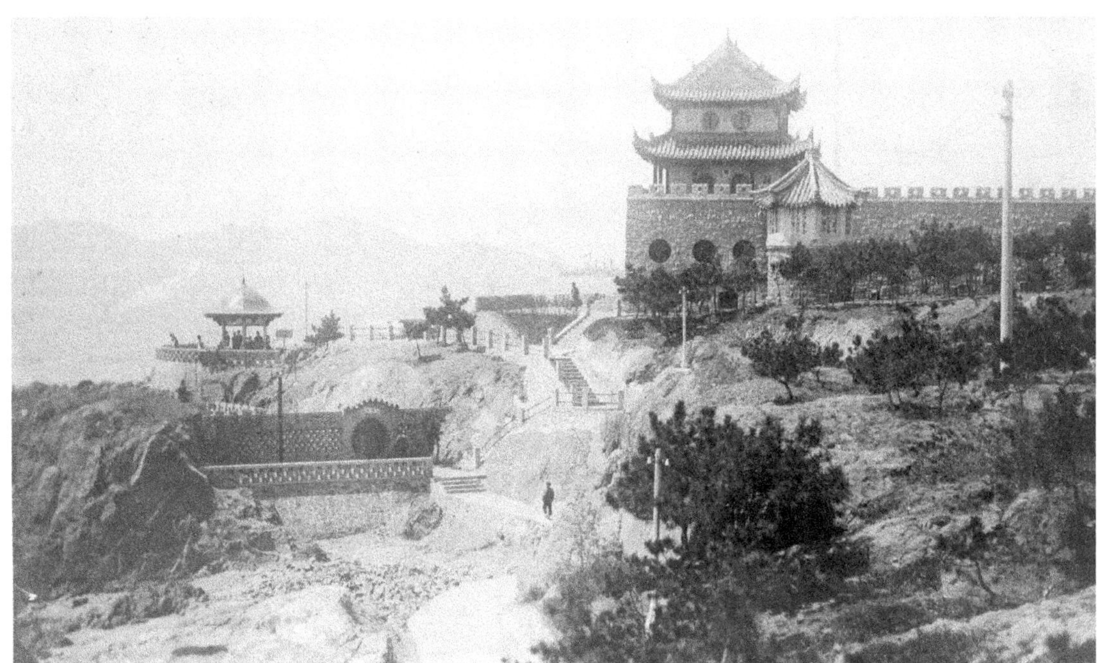

North China, with what appears to be a U.S. cruiser in the middle background.

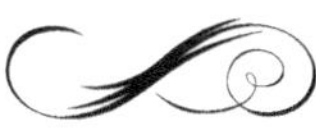

A scene awaited. Pat and camera arrived. Unabashed, done: More life and culture of pre-World War II China thus preserved. Such was her modus operandi.

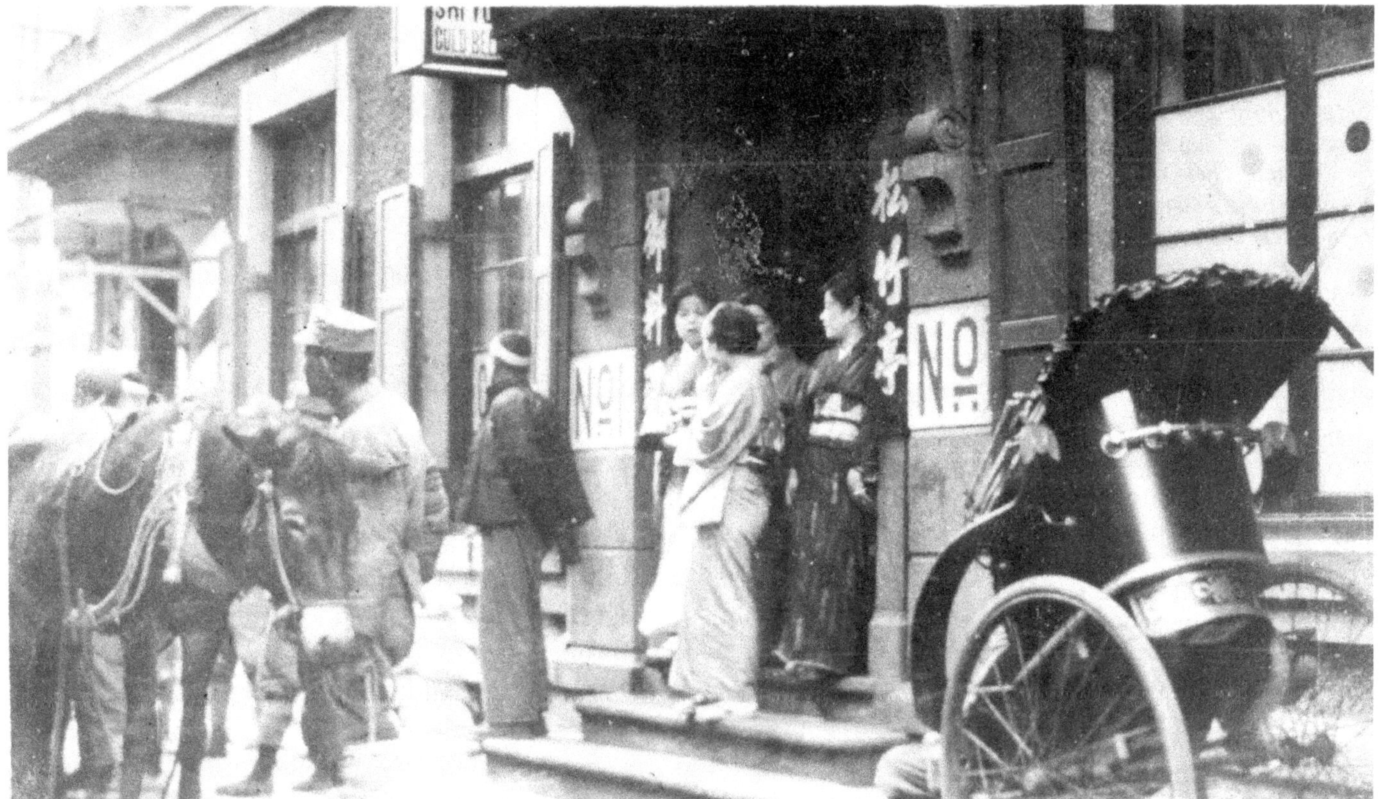

The infamous Tai Ping Street in Chefoo, North China, mid-1930s. Beneath a 'Cold Beer' sign, Chinese soldiers and street people seeking pleasure mixed with prostitutes at this gentlemen's pavilion, whose entrance forecast dignity and elegance once inside: ergo, the 'No. 1 whore house.'

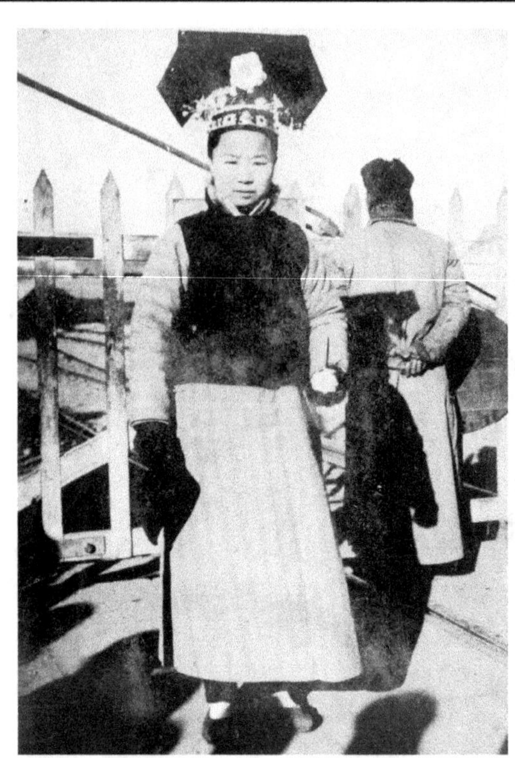

A Manchu lady, Peking, China, mid-1930s.

Northeast China is home to Manchu customs and traditions: their women coiled hair in high tufts on top of their heads and wore earrings, long gowns, and embroidered shoes. Women of lower social standing wore cotton clothing, while the upper crust wore silk and satin clothing. "Manchu girls were reported to be more independent and equal to male siblings, having more rights than Chinese girls. Manchu women were said to be more aggressive and irritable." Educating Manchu women was discouraged, whereas Chinese women nominally could read and write. Although Manchuria was intended for Manchus, after the Japanese conquered it in 1931 the predominant population was Han Chinese. After World War II the state reverted back to China.[11]

The Qing Dynasty, also known as the Manchu Dynasty, followed the Ming Dynasty and ruled China from 1644 to 1912, when the Republic of China replaced it. In 1917 it reemerged briefly. The Qing Dynasty was not majority Han Chinese, but rather Manchus, a hunting, fishing, and farming people who today are an ethnic minority. The 1912 collapse ended 2,000 years of imperial China "and began an extended period of instability or warlord factionalism" with "unorganized political and economic systems combined with widespread criticism of Chinese culture" and future doubts.[12] *These conditions existed when Pat and her husband lived in North China.*

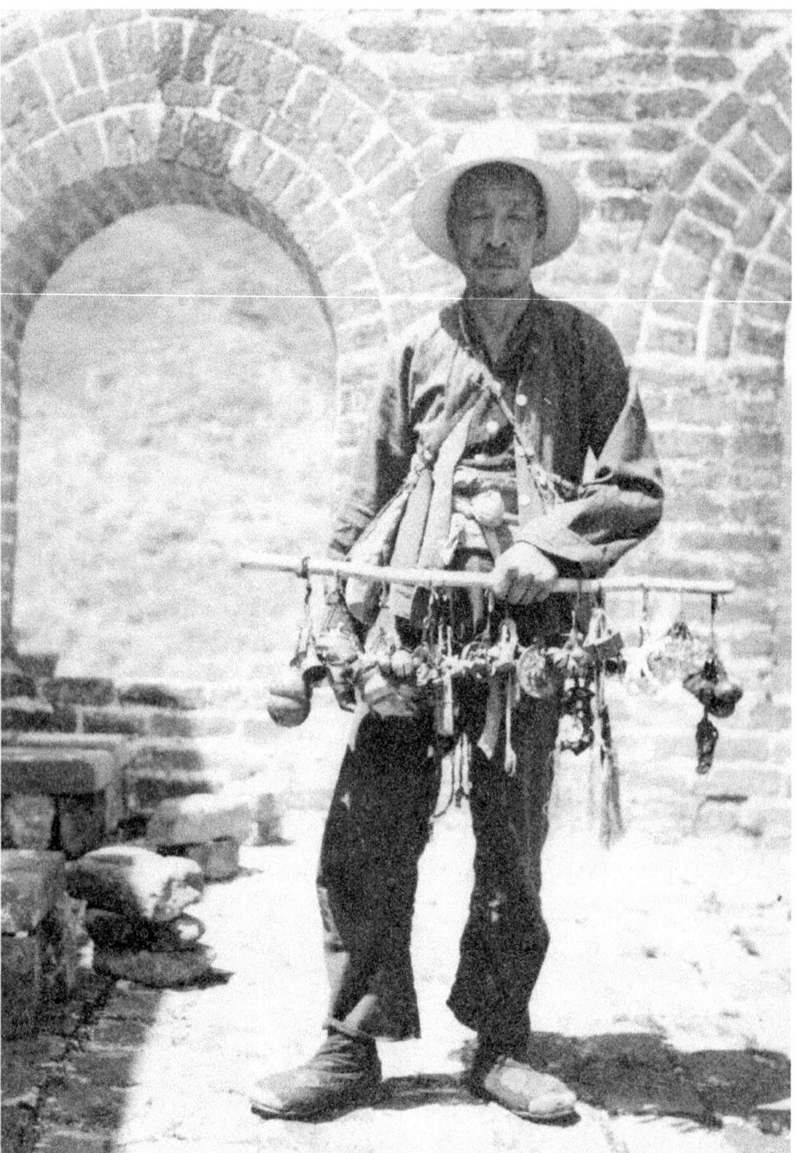

Mongolian peddler at the Great Wall of China near Shanhaikuan, Mid-1930s.

The daughter (born 1835) of an ordinary Manchu official, the future Empress Dowager Ci Xi's Manchu name was Yehenara, a combination of the names of the Yehe and Nara tribes. She felt mistreated and ignored as a child. The Emperor Xianfeng selected her as a royal concubine at age eighteen. She bore his only son, who later became Emperor Tongzhi, and began a career of politics, intrigue, power, and corruption, ruling behind the Qing Dynasty throne for nearly half a century. For background and context about her reign, and her influence on China's early twentieth-century revolution, see the movies *55 Days at Peking* (1963) and *The Last Emperor* (1987) and the Smithsonian Channel's *The Reign of the Concubine* (2007).

Titled "The Son of Heaven," the Chinese emperor was the country's supreme authority, evolving from indisputable family hierarchy. He ruled and conducted affairs of state from the Forbidden City's Throne Room. As magistrate, scholar, judge, supreme military commander, and family patriarch, he mediated between the earthly and heavenly realms.[15]

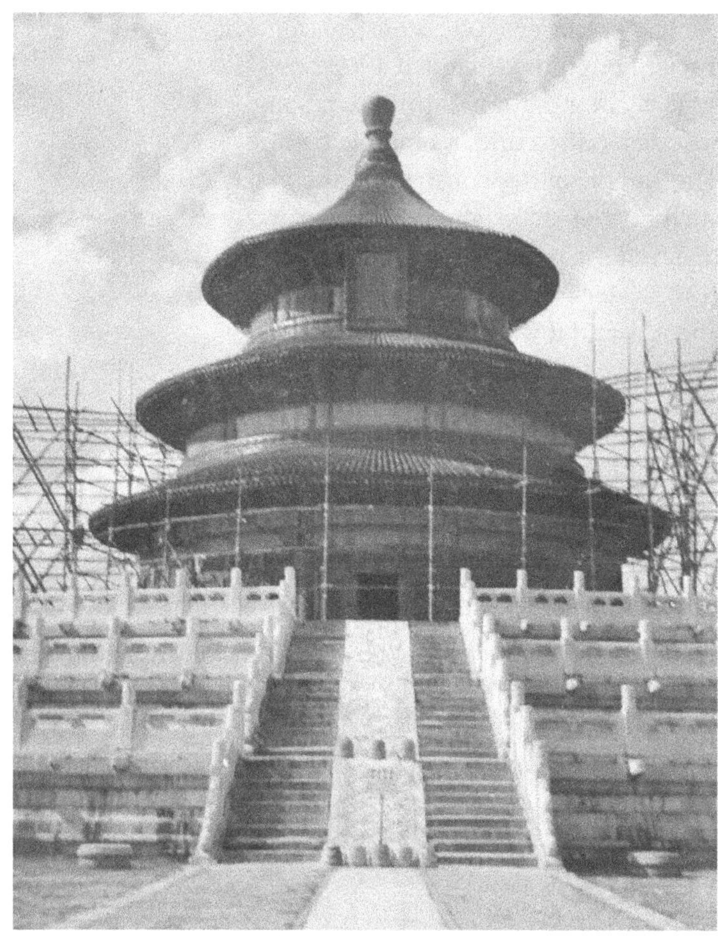

Temple of Heaven, Peking, China, mid-1930s.

Chinese emperors were considered the intermediary between Earth and Heaven. "To be seen to be showing respect to the source of his authority, in the form of sacrifices to heaven, was extremely important." The Temple of Heaven, completed in 1420 and used by all Ming and Qing emperors, housed these ceremonies. The most important was when the emperor prayed for good harvests at the winter solstice. Commoners were forbidden to see the annual imperial procession and were forced to bolt their windows and keep quiet indoors.

The emperor's animal sacrifice rituals were planned to the smallest details and had to be perfectly completed. Even minor mistakes "would constitute a bad omen for the whole nation in the coming year." In 1899 lightning destroyed the Hall of Prayer, deemed "divine punishment" because a caterpillar was about to crawl on the hall's roof. Thirty-two court dignitaries thus were executed.

Since 1914 the building has been a public museum, and is now on UNESCO's World Heritage List.[16]

One of the grandest structures of the imperial Summer Palace near Peking is the Marble Boat (Shifang). The existing boat, originally built in 1755 during Emperor Qianlong's reign (1711-99), suffered severe fire damage and was later saved by Empress Dowa-

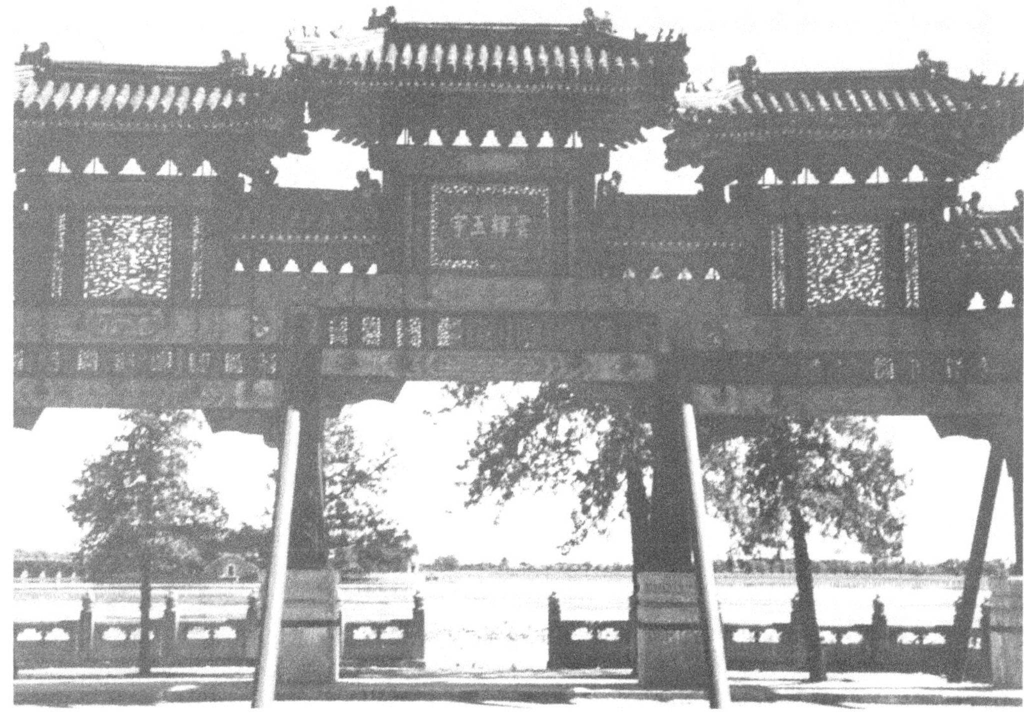

Imperial boat landing, Summer Palace, mid-1930s.

ger Ci Xi. Her general reconstruction of ancient buildings included a Western-style yacht imitation of this boat. Some wood is hidden under a marble texture. The Tang Dynasty constructed the first such boat of stone when the emperor believed the possibility that the people (the "waters") could overthrow him (the "boat"), and it was deemed a sturdy, protective talisman of sorts.[17]

"It is a great disappointment to all visitors," lamented Pat after a visit.

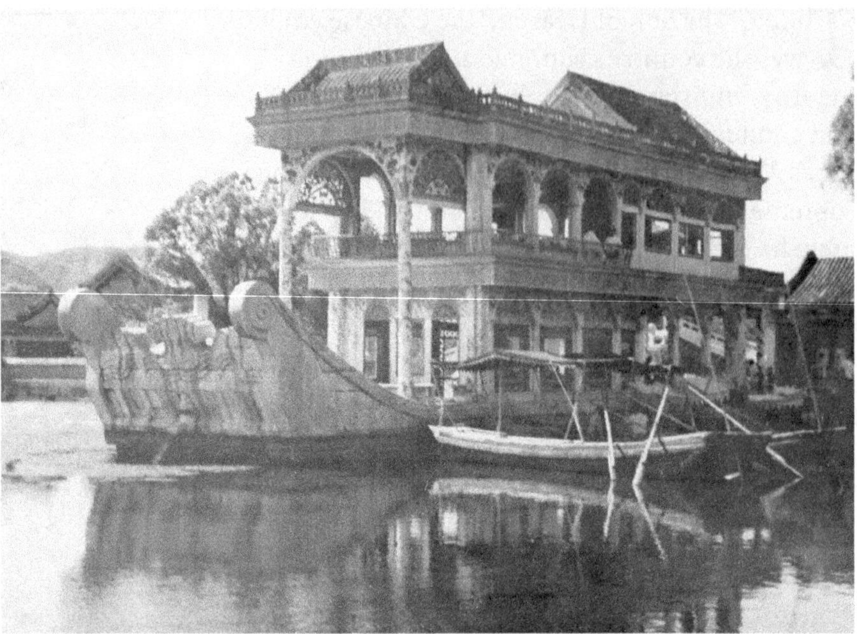

The Marble Boat, rebuilt by Empress Dowager Ci Xi with funds appropriated for her navy, photographed mid-1930s.

The Summer Palace lies northwest of central Peking and "is said to be the best preserved imperial garden in the world, and the largest of its kind still in existence in modern China." During summer, the Imperial Family preferred the gardens and airy pavilions to the walled-in Forbidden City of Peking.

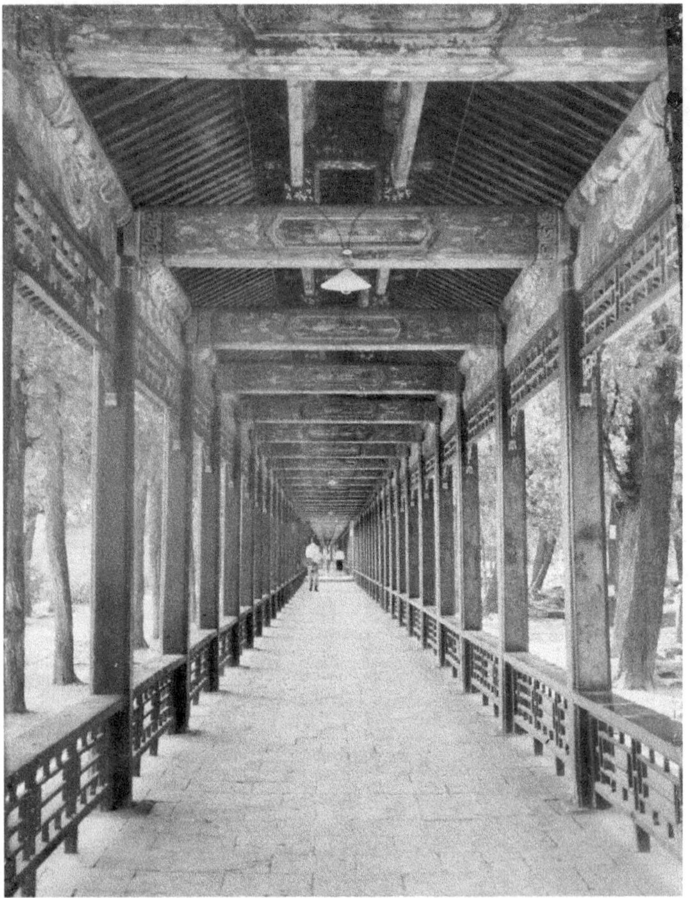

Colonnaded veranda of the Summer Palace, built to shelter the imperial court proceeding from the Summer Palace to the Marble Boat. Lotus blossoms and Chinese scrolls decorate the teakwood structure similar to the Throne Room ceiling. Peking, China, mid-1930s.

Empress Dowager Ci Xi occasionally resided here, creating "some wonderful tales of extravagance and excess."[18] In fact, in 1886 Ci Xi's brother-in-law embezzled funds earmarked for warships and built her a new Summer Palace. The restored grand garden received its current name, "Garden of Peace and Harmony," to which she relocated her administration. "Tales of Ci Xi's excesses (including the Marble Boat) are numerous and came to symbolize the decadence of the Imperial Family."

The Summer Palace Pat visited, now a popular tourist site, is essentially the same rebuilt palace of 1903.

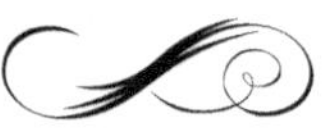

Vladivostok, the former Soviet Union's southeastern-most city, northeast of Korea and across from North China, in the 1930s served as a terminal for mass numbers of Soviet political prisoners and perceived enemies of the state, including Chinese, Koreans, Jews, Ukrainians, and Chechens, under terrible conditions. After taking Manchuria, Japan eyed Soviet territories, and in 1936 hostile relations commenced.

In the early 1930s, the Communist regime closed the city's Catholic church, and in 1934 selected Vladivostok as a model urban city on the Pacific in their plan to rid the nation of its czarist past and reconstruct it under Communism. The intent was to make it one of the USSR's great port cities and confirm its position as the "forepost" on the Pacific, the "Kronshtadt" of the Russian Far East.[19]

Hundreds of miles from Shanghai and Peking, how Pat traveled there (likely by train), and why she chose the city in the USSR for Carroll's baptism is unknown. If it was to follow her husband's ship there for a port call, we find no record of a U.S. warship visit there before 1937. A *Los Angeles Examiner* piece in May 1934 stated that Bob had been transferred to Vladivostok, but that's all we know.[20] One clue is the fact that the United States had resumed diplomatic relations with Russia in late 1933, and that a U.S. consulate was re-established in Vladivostok. Nevertheless, Pat must have arranged with the local priest regardless of the church's status, using her fearless ability to request, negotiate, and achieve. Navy people stood in for the godparents, Pat's Los Angeles friends Alfredo de la Vega and Eloise Jane Morgan. The Chefoo Catholic Mission priest signed the baptism certificate on July 15, 1934.

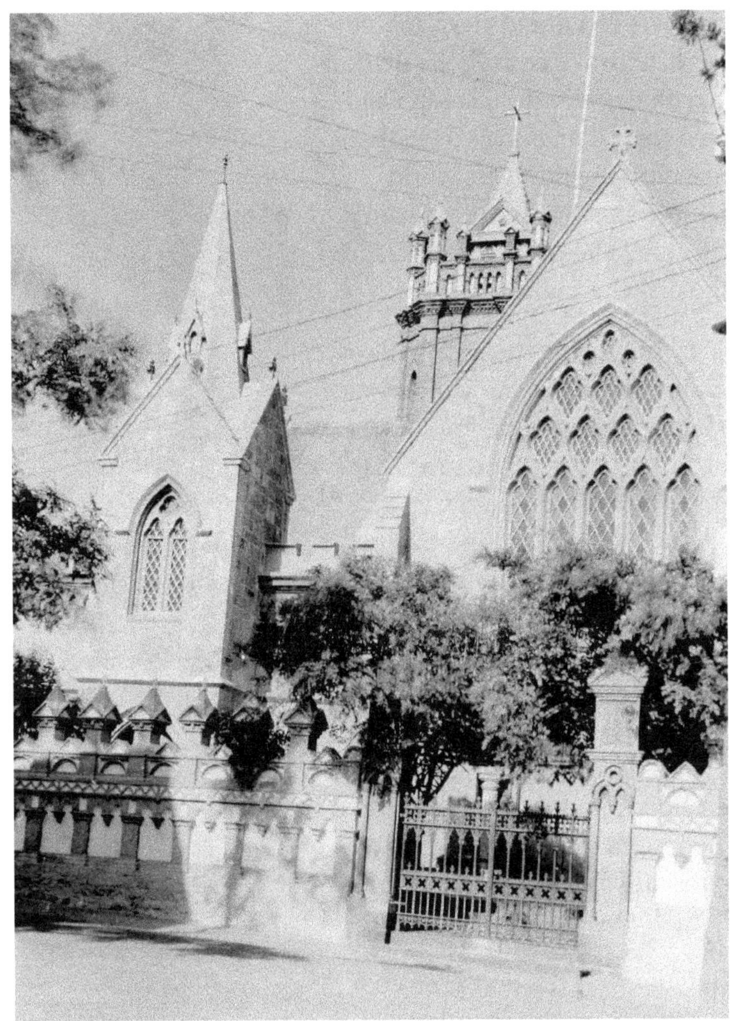

The Roman Catholic church in Vladivostok, USSR, where Carroll was baptized by a French priest in 1935.

As a port, no city in Shandong or Hebei provinces equaled the natural advantages of Tsingtao (now Qingdao). During the 1930s, the Asiatic Fleet, including its submarines, used facilities in Tsingtao as well as Chefoo. Japan's aggressive moves into Manchuria threatened China. "The American presence ... remained unhindered. It was an uneasy awareness of growing tensions, but the Navy did not interfere with the comfortable life" of its fleet.

"Wives moved back and forth on rickety old steamers, but lived lives of comfort with maids keeping furnished apartments. They spent their time shopping, sightseeing, and tea-drinking. The American community was isolated from the miserable living conditions of the Chinese. When the Japanese took over the administration of the area they were careful not to impose

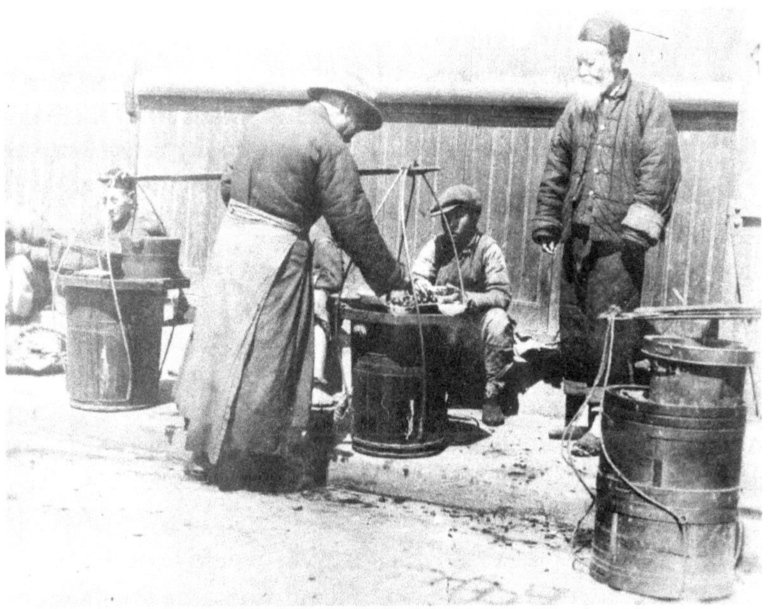

Street peddlers in Tsingtao (now Qingdao), North China, 1933.

problems for the Americans who were neutral 'guests.'" The neutral Germans, who decades ago had colonized Tsingtao as a German-like city (including its world famous brewery) before turning it over to the Chinese in 1922, ran the dispensary.[21]

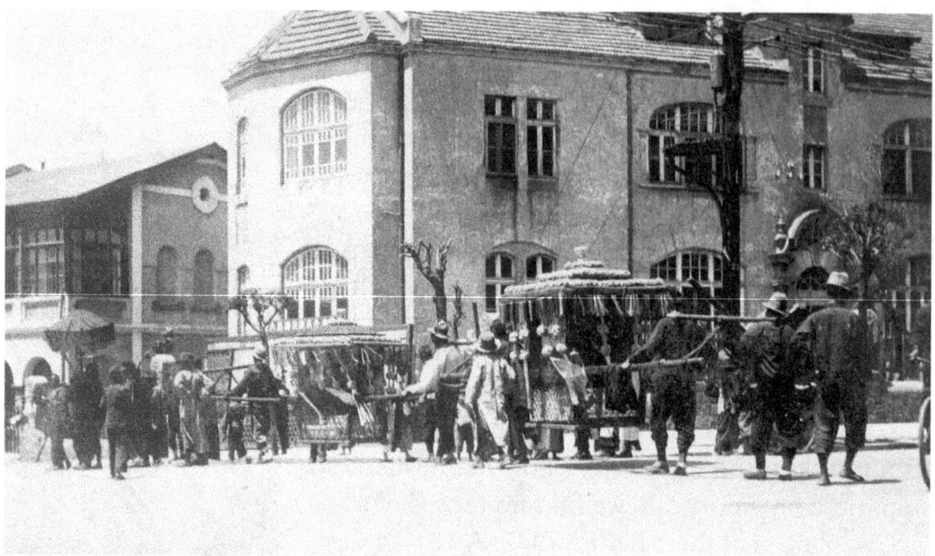

Wedding procession with sedan chairs, North China, mid-1930s.

By deploying the Asiatic Fleet in the 1930s, the United States maintained a strong presence in China, enforcing its Far East trade interests and coaxing an alliance with the Chinese Republic, loosely governed by Chiang Kai-shek's Kuomintang. Relations varied from cordial to severed, including violent anti-American protests. For young naval officers, such duty was a solid foundation for building a career. For enlisted men, such duty appealed as an interlude or a semi-permanent home.

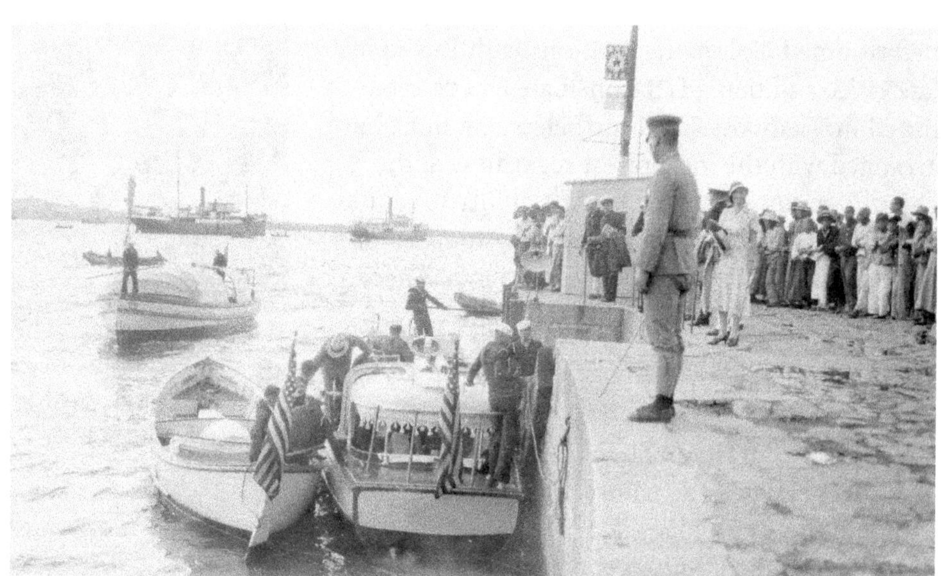

U.S. Navy boats at fleet landing, Chefoo, North China, mid-1930s. The ships appear to be the type of commercial steamer Pat would take around the western Pacific. The boat on the upper left showing 'BH' on the bow is probably from Ensign Robbins' ship, the tender USS *Black Hawk*—which might be why Pat is there.

Chefoo, with the best protected anchorage on the Shandong Peninsula's north shore on the Korea Bay, was a principal U.S. home port. "A classic image of the 'China Sailor' developed, as a large number of U.S. Navy members would remain at postings in China for 10 to 12 years, then retire and continue to live in the country. The classic film *The Sand Pebbles*," about a U.S. river gunboat attacked by the Japanese, "is a dramatization on the life of the China Sailors." As World War II approached, the U.S. military in China was slowly withdrawn to protect other Pacific interests.[22]

The Asiatic Fleet consisted of a few cruisers and mostly destroyers, augmented by support ships and submarines, which patrolled and trained in the South China Sea and Yangtze River areas. While maintaining alertness to potential Sino-Japanese demonstrations and hostilities, including firing on American naval and merchant vessels, the fleet also cruised to Japan, French Indochina, the Philippines, and other countries. In 1934 the cruiser USS *Augusta* (CA-31)—which in 1941 would host the President Franklin Roosevelt-Prime Minister Winston Churchill conference off Newfoundland—became the flagship.

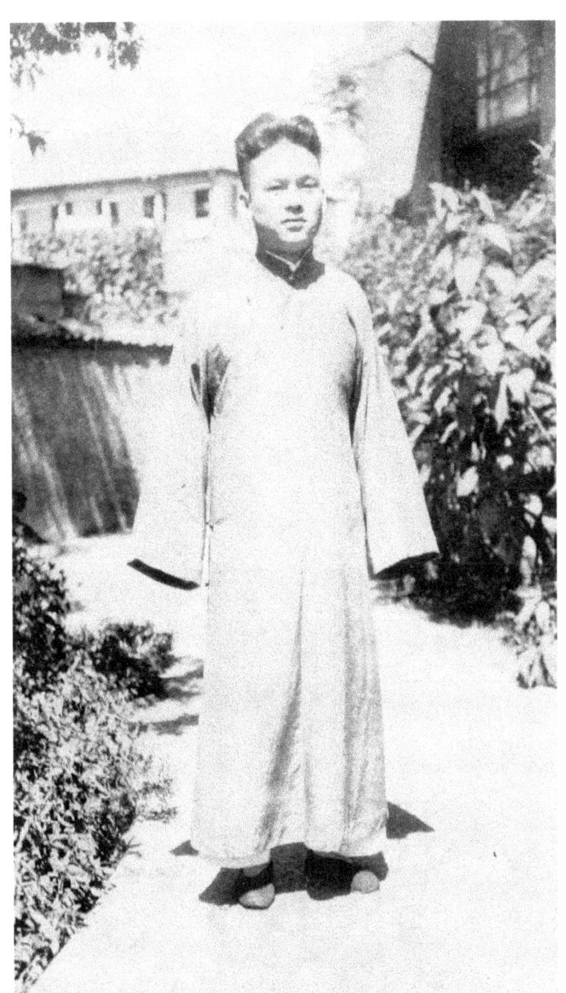

Chin, the Robbinses' house boy, North China, mid-1930s. Carroll recalled Pat asking him to wax the floors. 'He said yes, mum. Later she went into the kitchen and saw they hadn't been done. Asked him again. Later she saw him standing on two coconut halves skating across the floor trying to wax it.'

Chinese amahs were nannies or female domestic servants. The Robbinses employed at least two whose names are known. Ah Kwai stayed with them from shortly after Carroll's birth through their tour at the Naval Academy. Their first was Ah Fung. A *Los Angeles Examiner* column reported in 1934 that "Patricia O'Meara Robbins has a precious baby daughter over in China where her navy husband is stationed. They also have five Chinese servants who won't let them pick up a newspaper by themselves." Might have been, but likely pushing the facts.

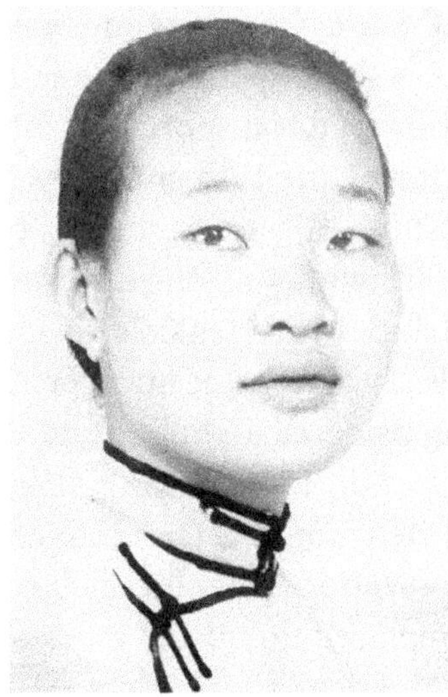

Ah Kwai, Carroll's principal Chinese amah, who accompanied Pat and her throughout China and the Orient and later to Annapolis, Md., from 1934 to 1938.

Many Chinese women who lost their jobs when the Guangdong silk industry collapsed in the early 1930s turned to this occupation, or as mail order brides, slaves, or prostitutes. Ah Kwai joined those who vowed to remain independent and became "devout, down-to-earth and utterly dependable servants with a style all their own." These women, also known as "black-and-whites," typically wore an outfit of white shirts and black pants.

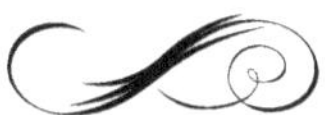

"Mesmerizing, viewers called it," Carroll recalled. "Mother took so many pictures all over China, concentrating on such as the Great Wall. This one meant a lot to her, and she showed it for her first exhibit in 1938 in Los Angeles."

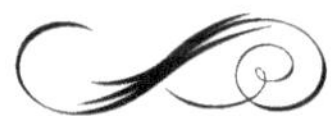

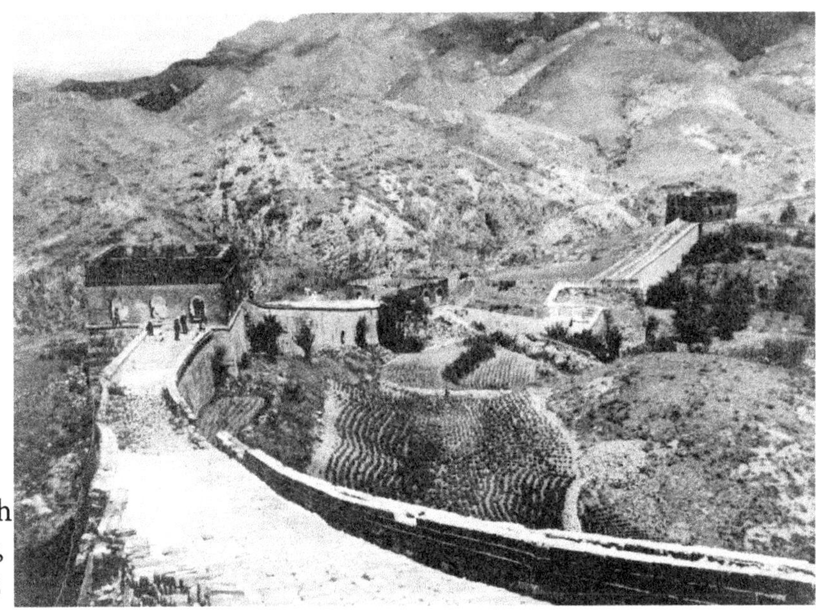

This shot of The Great Wall of China appeared in several professional photo magazines and a couple of exhibits to demonstrate how she was able to get such a panoramic view without a true professional camera. It shows the impact of the Wall's construction along ridges and hills. See similar image with walking sailors on page 29.

Rickshas, sometimes spelled rickshaws, a mode of one-man, human-powered transportation, became popular during the 19th and early 20th century China. A runner pulled a two-wheeled cart, with one long support bar in each hand, which seated one or two persons. Both covered or uncovered, they were considered among the cheapest transport. In 1930s Peking, rickshas constituted almost 20 per cent of local transportation. Later bicycle and auto rickshas replaced them.

Tsingtao boasts a museum named after the fictional 1930s Peking hero of the literary classic, *Rickshaw Boy* ("Luotuo Xiangzi" in pinyin), a novel by Chinese author Lao She and considered a classic of 20th-century Chinese literature.

The Camel Back Bridge, aka the Jade Belt Bridge and known for its distinctive arch, is perhaps the most famous of several bridges on the grounds of the Qing Summer Palace on Kunming Lake. "Its beauty remains timeless despite nearly two and a half centuries." Built in 1751-64 from marble and other white stone, "the ornate bridge railings are decorated with carvings of cranes and other animals. The clearance of the arch was chosen to accommodate the dragon boat of the Qianlong Emperor. As the Kunming Lake inlet to the neighboring Yu River, and during special occasions, the emperors and empress and their dragon boat would specifically pass under this bridge."[25]

The bridge shows Pat's strength of depth by framing it with close-by tree branches.

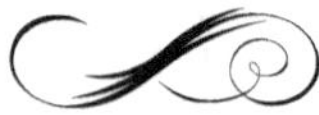

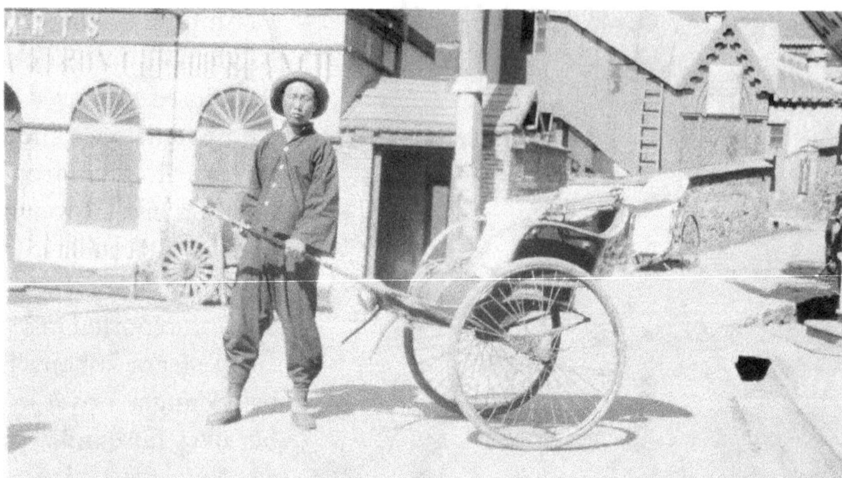

'Ricksha boy,' Chefoo, North China, mid-1930s.

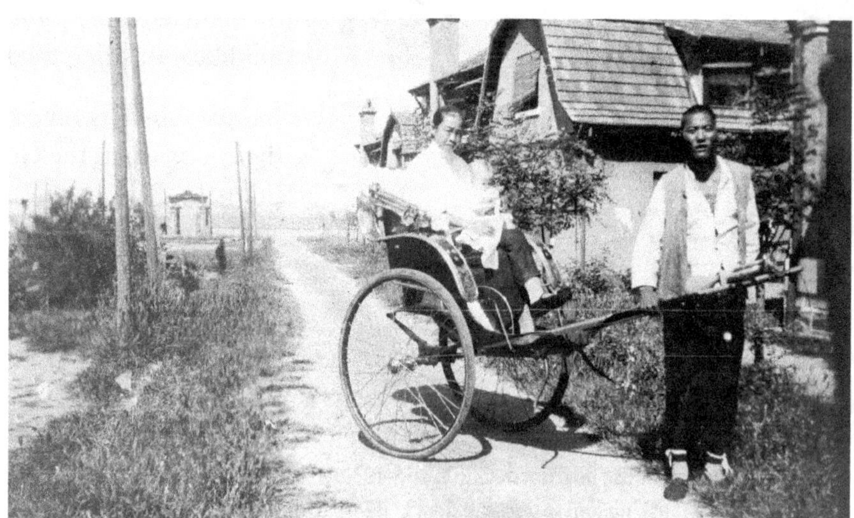

Carroll riding in a ricksha, 1934, with her amah.

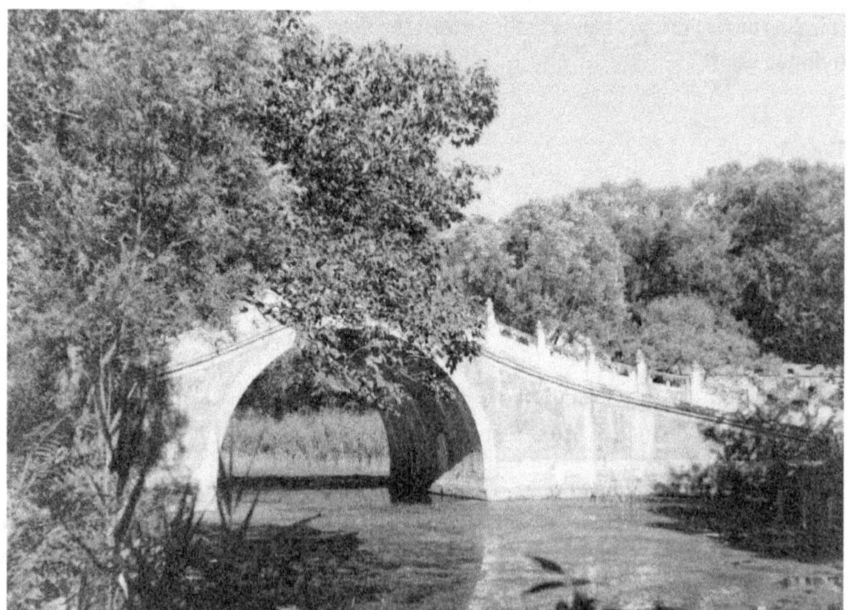

The Camel Back Bridge, Summer Palace, Peking, China, mid-1930s.

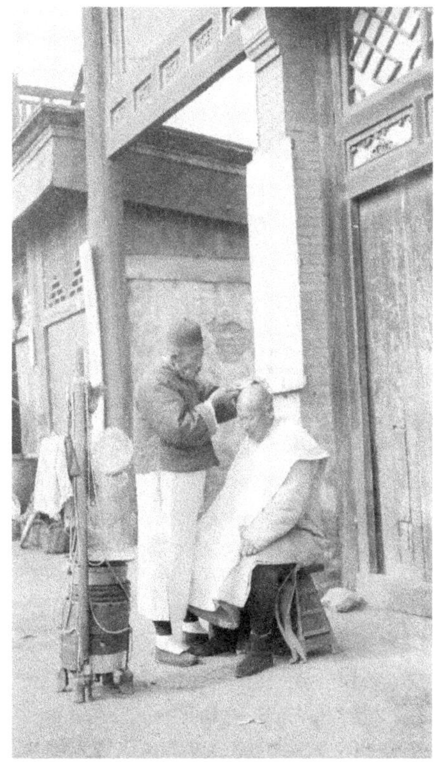
Street barber in Chefoo (now Yantai), North China, mid-1930s. Street barbers for men were popular then.

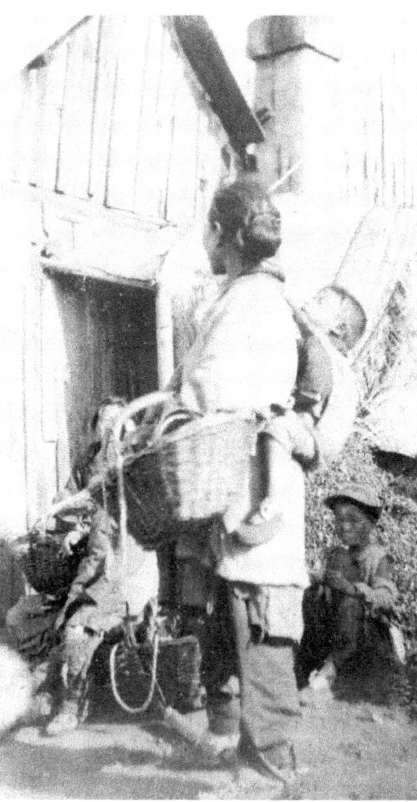
Coolie woman and child in back sling, Chefoo (now Yantai) North China, mid-1930s.

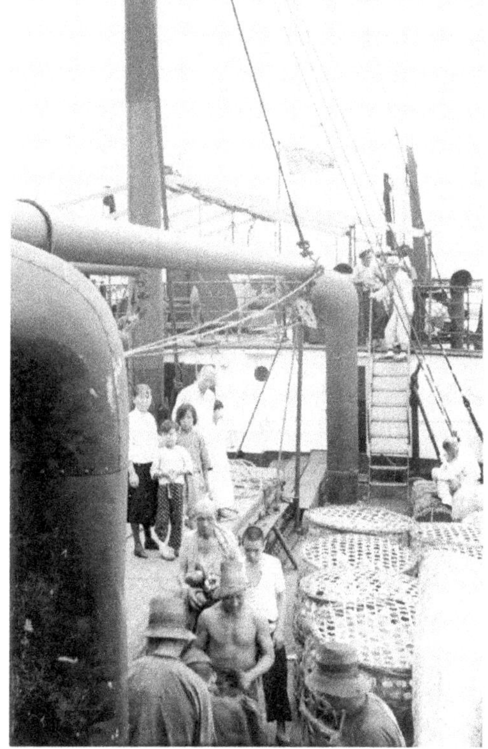
Steerage passengers on the SS *Tungchow* on the Hai-Ho River near Tientsin (now Tianjin), North China, mid-1930s.

The 1937 Chinese movie *Street Angel*, one of the early sound films made in China, is praised for its portrayal of the downtrodden in Shanghai in melodrama and comedy, including one sequence where the stars act as barbers. "Today, *Street Angel* is often considered one of the classics of the 'leftist' film-making period that reached its peak in the 1930s."[26]

Roaming the streets of North China safely invigorated Pat and proved her independence, agility, and plain good fortune and avoiding trouble.

Western superpowers by the 1900's set up concessions one after another in Tientsin, now Tianjin, and it became a spearhead for opening the Westernization movement in modern China. Until the 1930s it served as the largest industrial and commercial city and economic center of North China. The informal U.S. territory within was attached to the British concession, and garrisoned by U.S. Army troops until 1938.[27]

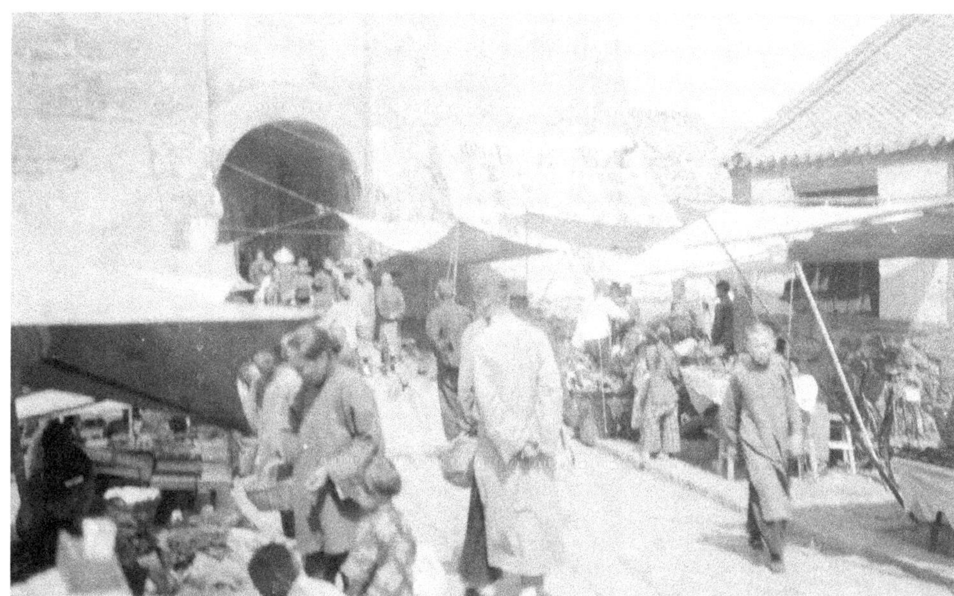
Street market in Chefoo, North China, mid-1930s.

In his memoirs, U.S. President

Herbert Hoover, a Tientsin resident during the Boxer Rebellion, wrote: "Tienstin is a universal city, like a world in miniature with all nationalities, all architectural styles, all kitchens." Another observer wrote: "The country is so flat and ordinary between Tienstin and Peking that one could almost imagine to be riding across our Midwest plains. The sudden appearance of the great walls of Peking comes as a startling experience, even when they are expected."[28] Tianjin remains a major seaport and the fourth largest Chinese city.

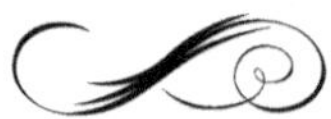

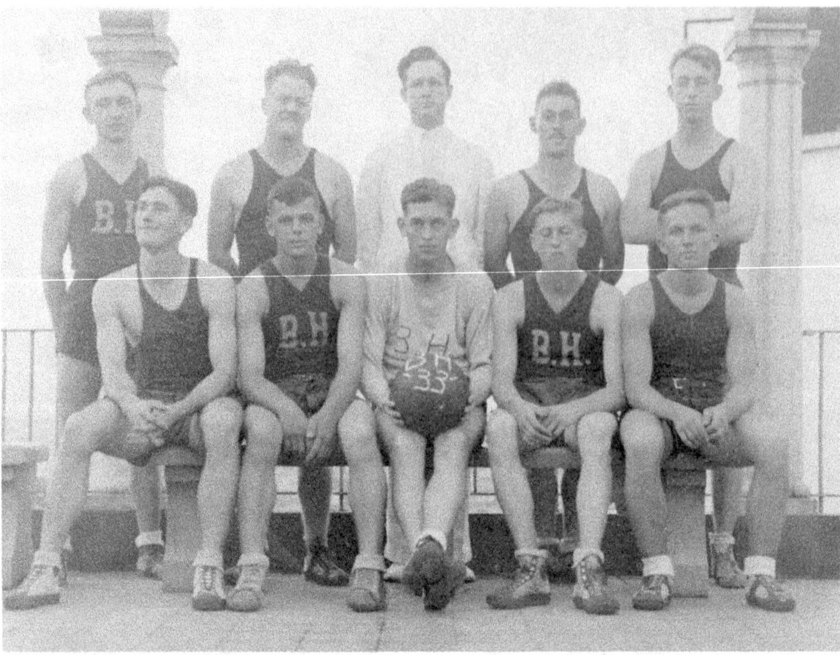

The basketball team of the destroyer tender USS *Black Hawk*, with its coach Ensign B. A. Robbins, Jr., in suit, Shanghai, China, 1933. The *Black Hawk*, Bob's first assignment in the Asiatic Fleet, served in the Far East for twenty years, at this time tending Destroyer Squadron 5.

Pat apparently took few nighttime photographs in China and the Orient, this one and several in Manila, the Philippines, and Hong Kong are identifiable. We do not know if she used a tripod, but seeing branches on the frame's left edge used for depth, she may have steadied her camera against that tree. The Chefoo waterfront, a liberty (shore leave) haven for U.S. sailors on the Shandong Peninsula facing the Korea Bay, was dubbed the "Brighton of China."

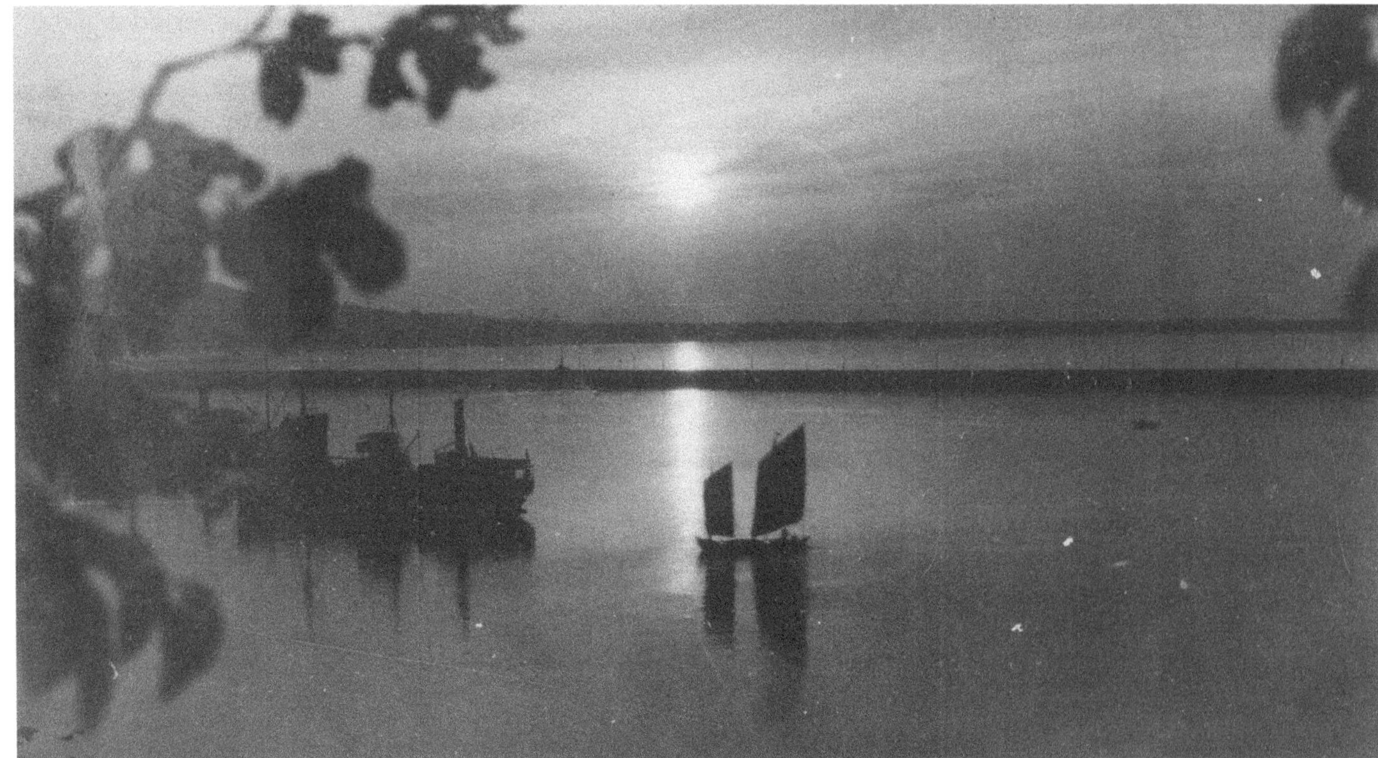

Nighttime over Chefoo harbor, North China, mid-1930s.

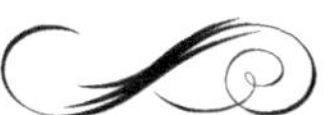

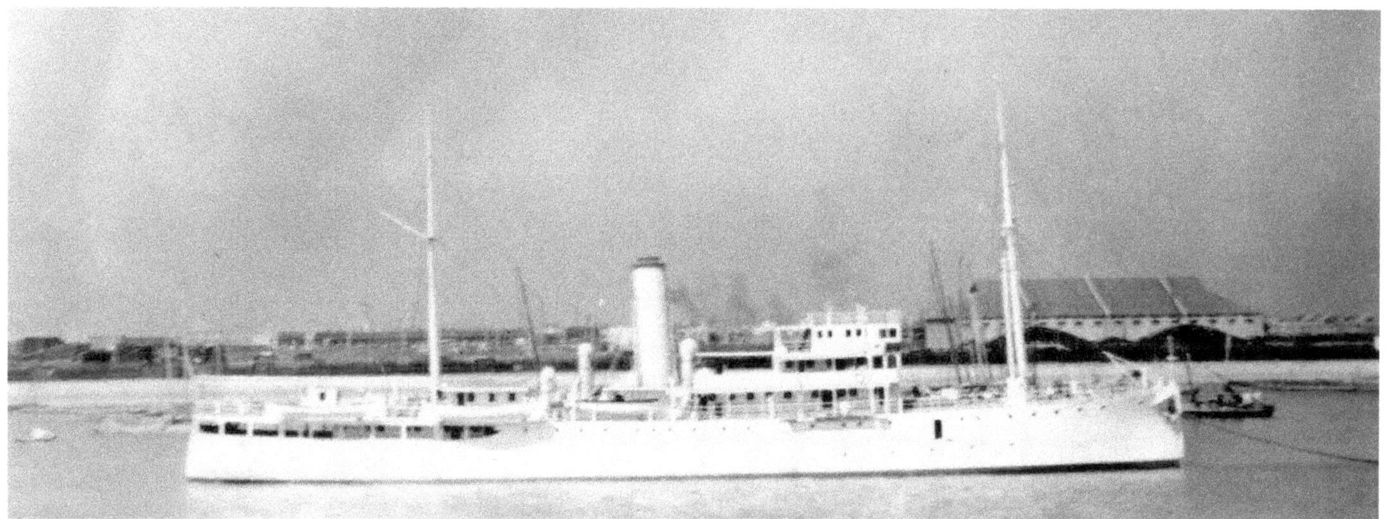

U.S. Navy gunboat on the Yangtze River, Shanghai, mid-1930s.

The U.S. Navy's Asiatic Fleet gunboats operated the Yangtze Patrol from 1854 to 1941 along China's longest river to protect American interests in its treaty ports, essential to commerce. Under treaties, the United States, Japan, and various European powers cruised the rivers and "patrolled coastal waters, protecting their citizens, their property, and their religious missions." The ships sailed the Yangtze as far inland as Chongqing, more than 1,300 miles from the sea, and occasionally beyond. The patrol triggered an unprovoked Japanese attack which sank the gunboat USS *Panay* (PR-5) on the Yangtze on December 12, 1937, a precursor to eventual war. "After the Japanese took control of much of the middle and lower Yangtze, American gunboats entered into a period of frustrating inactivity and impotence."[29]

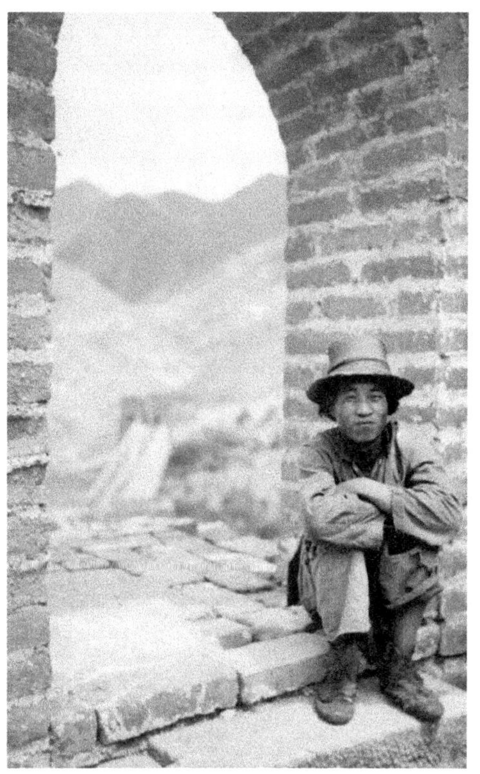

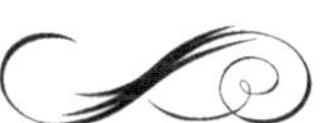

A sedan chair was a human or animal-powered transport vehicle for carrying a person, also called a "shoulder carriage," "sleeping sedan," and "warm sedan." The most familiar warm sedans saw service since the Ming and Qing Dynasties. The sedan body fitted into the bamboo or wood rectangular frames on the two thin log poles, borne by two to eight man-servants on their shoulders. Their design accommodated different social status and occasion, ranging from common people (plain) to high-ranking officials (decorated and ornamented). The higher an official's rank, "the more luxurious his sedan and the larger the number of men needed to carry it." Although popular for such as wedding processions, modern conveyances such as motor vehicles replaced them long since.[30]

Sedan chair bearer awaiting a customer on a parapet of the Great Wall of China, mid-1930s.

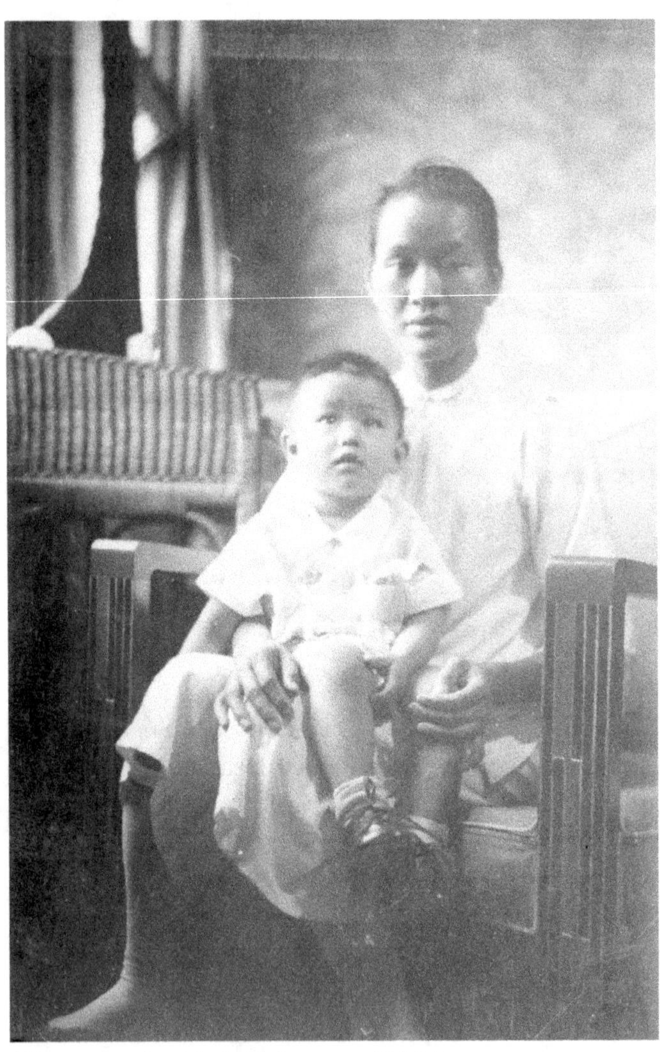

Chinese woman seated with her son, mid-1930s.

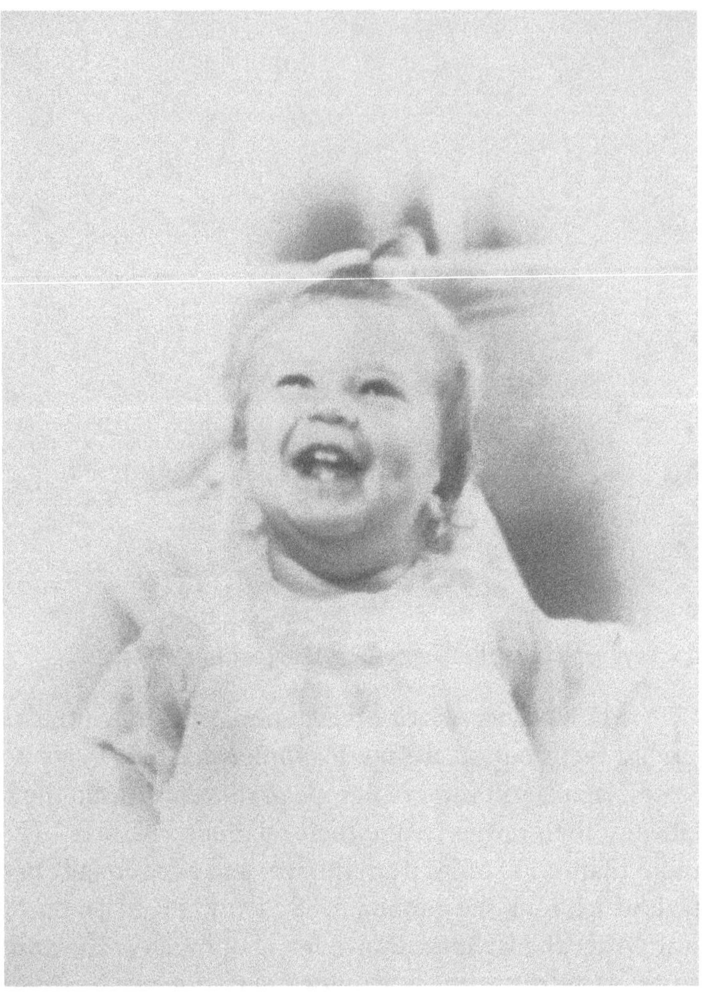

Carroll at one year-plus, one of Pat's early 'experiments' with lighting, setting, and developing the image, China, 1935.

CHAPTER 3

Intramuros, the Ginza, and Tonkinese People: Following the Asiatic Fleet Throughout the Pre-War Orient

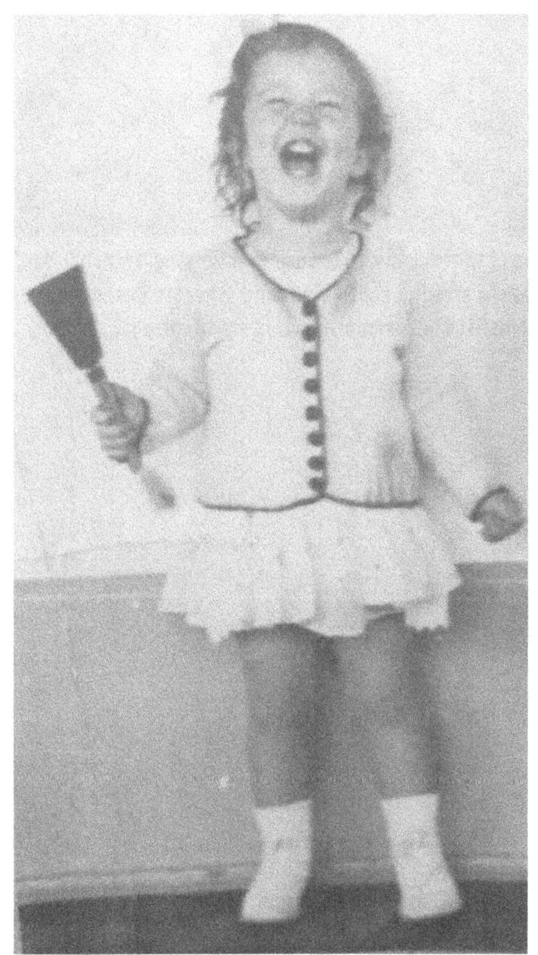

Carroll at age one on board USS *Henderson* (AP-1) sailing somewhere with her mother in the Western Pacific.

Odyssey aptly describes the travels of Pat Robbins in China and the Orient from 1933 to 1936. After she and husband Bob sailed from California on Navy transportation, goodness only knows the myriad and how many means she employed to cover thousands of miles on land and sea, besides known passages on Navy or commercial passenger and cargo steamships.

She and daughter Carroll sailed on the commercial SS *Jefferson* in 1934 to the Philippines. For one voyage, they boarded the Navy's first troop transport, the USS *Henderson* (AP-1), and in 1935 the commercial SS *President Van Buren* to Hong Kong. The family's ambitious 1935 schedule included Manila, Chefoo, Hong Kong, Indochina, Japan, and Shanghai.

The first time Pat traveled at sea with baby Carroll she developed mastitis, an inflammation of the breast. Her breast milk was no good and an arm was in sling. She took a nursemaid, likely Ah Kwai. "I didn't have Ah Kwai all the time," Carroll said. "Later on, Mother had her for years. She was about twenty-eight years old when she started. Mother almost had to ask permission to touch her baby—that's what they were trained to do."

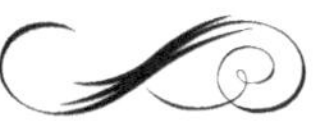

No shrinking society violet, Pat's determination and feet guided her to all corners of her new world. She saw first-hand vice, poverty, and the seedy side, as well as cavorting with the well-to-do. Here she learned how prostitution and female sex trade flourished in French Indochina (now Vietnam). "International commissions notwithstanding, the trade continued in Vietnam and in 1935 the newspaper *l'Annam Nouveau* reported that the kidnappings of Vietnamese girls were numerous . . . [and] that a human-trafficking network had been discovered in Tonkin . . . . Given the poverty levels of peasant society in Vietnam . . . women and children were all the more vulnerable to this sort of commerce. In addition, prostitution was a feature of traditional Confucian societies . . . [and] colonial Vietnam." *Maisons de tolerance* were legal in French Indochina, and brothels were legal in various forms also in China.[1]

We believe Pat limited her excursions in French Indochina to the Haiphong area. In 1887 the country formed from the provinces of Tonkin, Annam, Cochinchina (together, modern Vietnam), the Kingdom of Cambodia, and later, Laos. "The French formally left the local rulers in power . . . but in fact gathered all powers in their hands, the local rulers acting only as figureheads."[2] The country's history "is one of war, colonization and rebellion." Subsequently, Chinese occupation and French colonization seriously influenced Vietnamese culture, religion (Confucianism), social etiquette, and cuisine.[3]

The country experienced harsh French oversight and control into the mid-1930's, along with local corruption, although France ordered temporary liberalization in 1936. Rice consumption fell causing peasant hunger. Rural debt rose, but as the decade closed, rubber production (overwhelmingly owned by non-natives) and mining boosted the national economy. Vietnam, however, lacked industries and thus its foreign trade suffered.

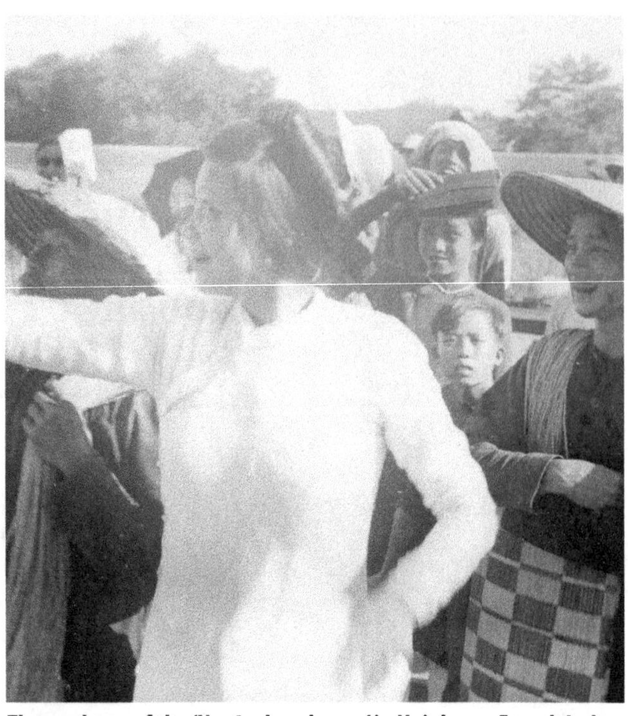

The madame of the 'No. 1 whorehouse' in Haiphong, French Indochina, welcomed arriving Pat Robbins and other steamship passengers and distributed promotional tickets on the dock, 1935.

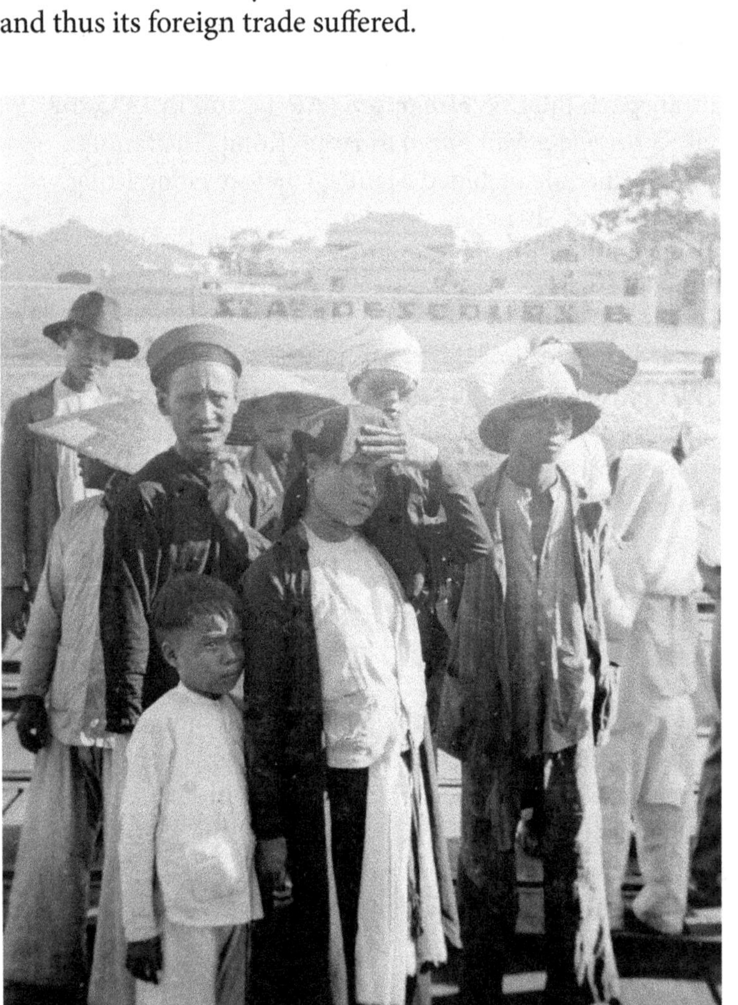

Tonkinese people at the dock at Haiphong, French Indochina, 1935.

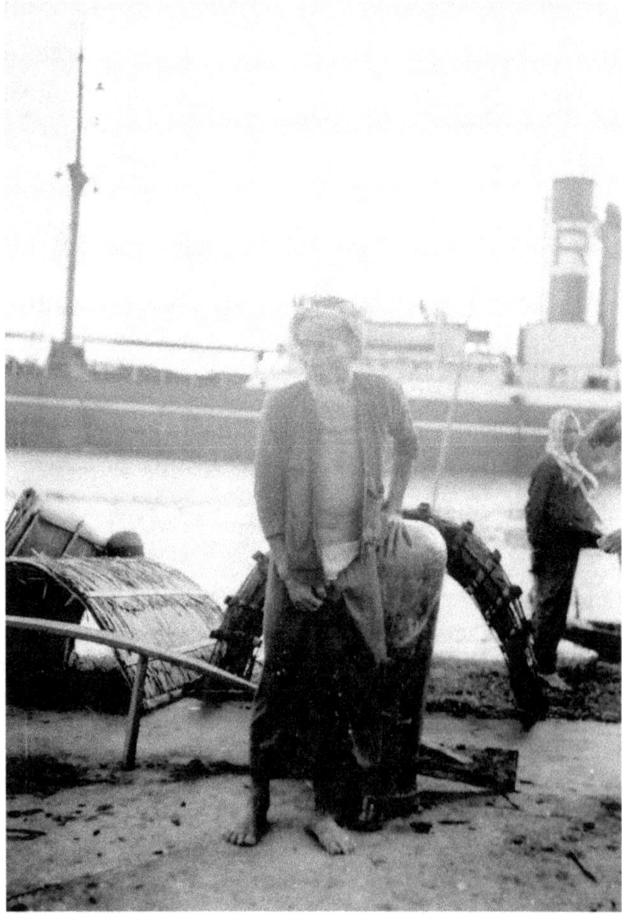

Old man on the docks at Saigon, French Indochina, 1935.

Pat's observant eye found numerous subjects on shipping docks everywhere. Naturally, ports gave her first impressions of a country. It appears she arrived ready to go to work.

The French seized Tonkin in 1883 as a protectorate and key region in forming French Indochina. Following its liberation from the Japanese after World War II it became a center of the Viet Minh Communists' anti-French fighting in the country that eventually became Vietnam. In 1964 President Lyndon Johnson used an alleged Communist attack on U.S. destroyers in the Tonkin Gulf as the pretext for inserting American ground forces into the ultimate Vietnam War.

The calm and unusually emerald waters of Halong Bay, now a popular Vietnam tourist attraction, contain nearly 2,000 islands. In 1994 UNESCO designated the bay as a World Heritage site. Here is another grand Halong Bay image.

The major port of Haiphong is ten miles from the Tonkin Gulf in northeast Vietnam, connected to the South China Sea by a narrow access channel. In the 1930's it served as the French Navy's principal Indochina base. That her husband's ship called there demonstrates the U.S. Asiatic Fleet's vast reach.

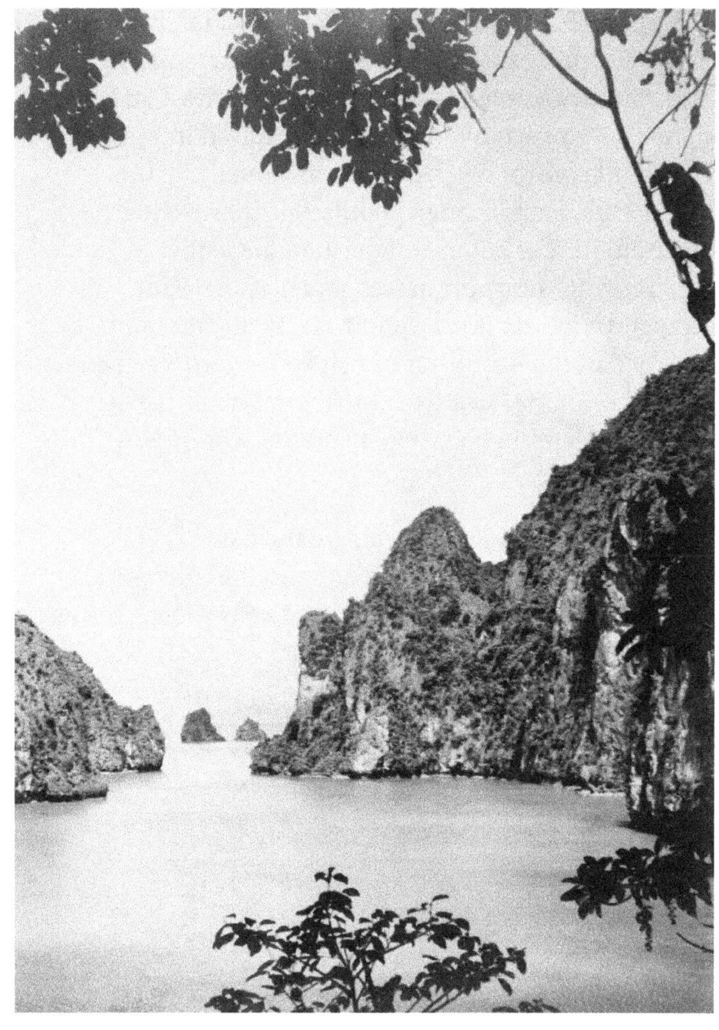

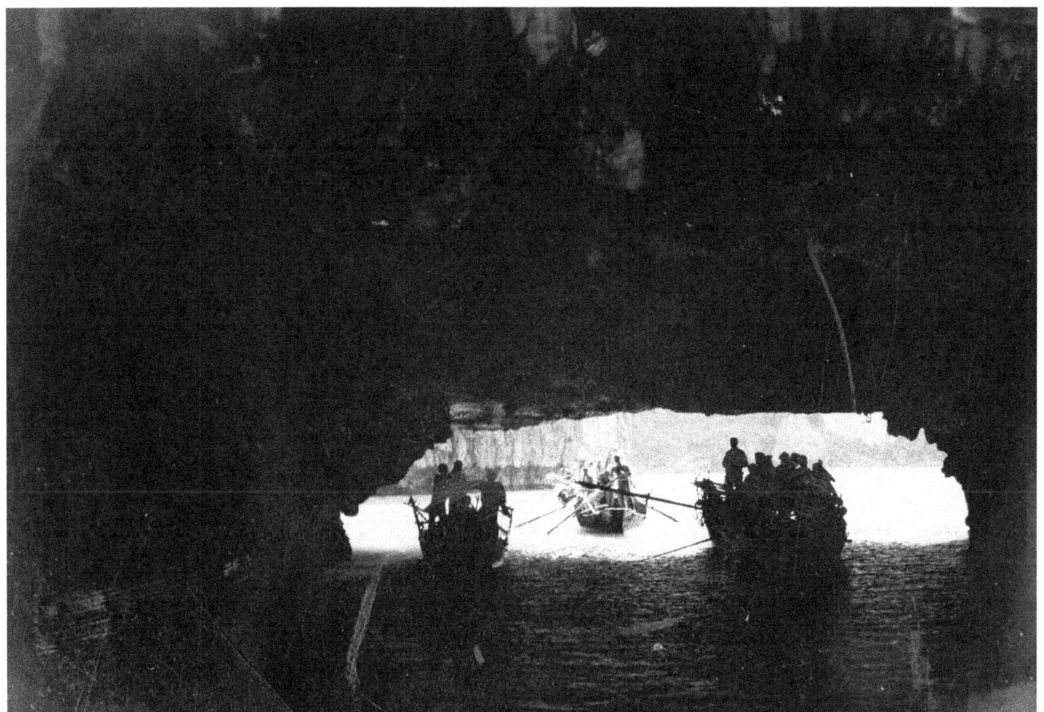

Above: the beautiful Halong Bay comprises 1,500 square kilometers on the Tonkin Gulf on the South China Sea. This image shows Pat's canny awareness of composition and depth. Near Haiphong, French Indochina, 1935.

Left: tour boats containing U.S. sailors (probably from Bob's destroyer, the USS *Whipple* (DD-217), pass through a rock opening in Halong Bay near Haiphong, French Indochina, 1935.

For the defense of Hong Kong, in 1898 the British Empire expanded its control of surrounding areas on the mainland—the New Territories—and signed a 99 year rent-free lease. (It expired in 1997, and control reverted back to China.) By the mid-1930's, Hong Kong's population approached one million. The colony established the iconic Star Ferry to transport passengers between Kowloon and Victoria Island, and Kai Tak airport, and emerged as the Royal Navy's prime Western Pacific base. The colony became Southeast Asia's prime economic giant in banking, insurance, commerce, and shipping.

In this street market scene, above the name "Chok Kee" is a grocery store where one can find oils, rice, and an assortment of goods. Chok Kee is probably a funeral home with its wreaths for sale. Signs in the middle denote a clinic, wine shop, and pawn shop.

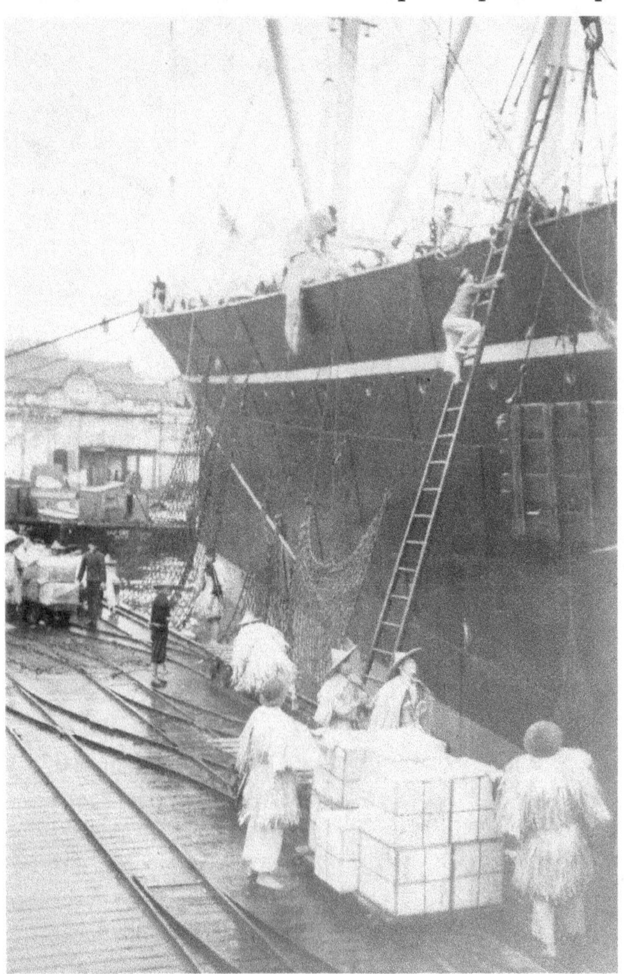

The docks on Victoria Island, Hong Kong, British Crown Colony, showing the workers in primitive straw rain gear and a dangerous method of boarding, 1935.

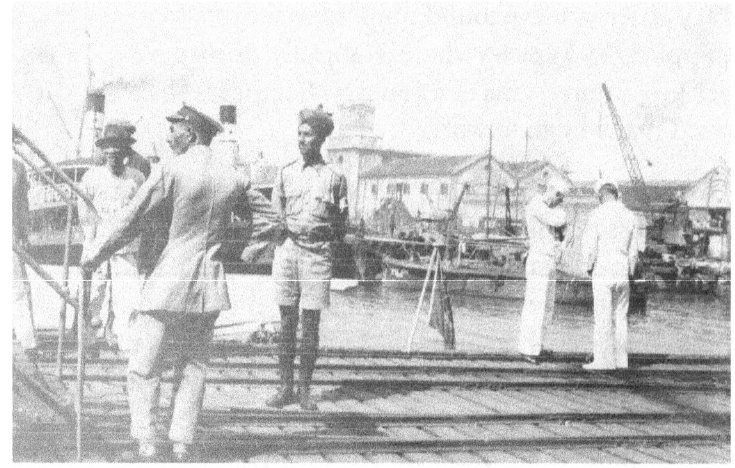

Hong Kong docks, its military personnel reflecting the British Empire's scope, and what also appear to be American sailors in teacup hats, 1935.

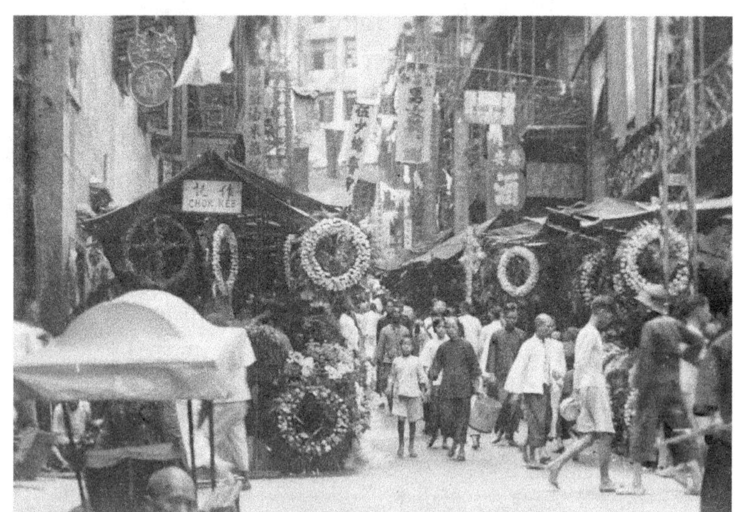

Flower market in Hong Kong, British Crown Colony, 1933.

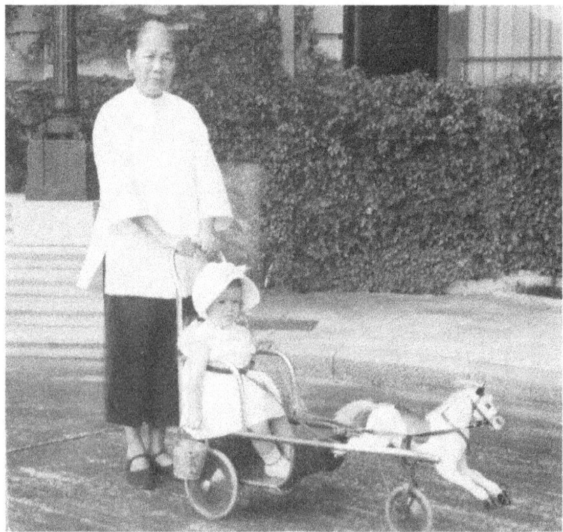

Carroll in her bonnet on a toy horse cart with temporary amah Ah Kuan at the Peninsula Hotel, Kowloon, Hong Kong, British Crown Colony, 1935.

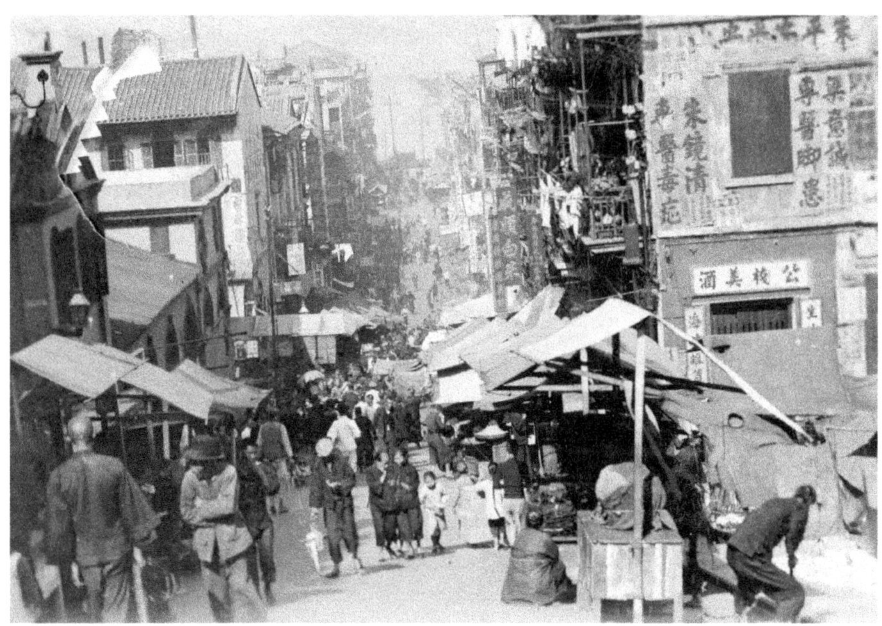

A street scene in Victoria, Hong Kong, 1933.

The Robbinses stayed at the world-famous Peninsula Hotel in Kowloon, the last stop on the trans-Siberian railroad, a refuge meeting their requirements for style and convenience. It opened in 1928 as "the finest hotel east of Suez," catering to the world's "rich, the famous, the titled and the titans of industry to a place of unsurpassed luxury and service."[4]

Pat apparently spent many days on both Victoria Island and in Kowloon, Hong Kong, a photographer's paradise, as we see in these diverse images.

The commercial street in the top image, rising from the Hong Kong harbor with its divergent enterprises, appears like a strip mall. Or, as my translator Lu Xue observed, like "Chinatown in New York City." The signs at top left sell white rice and list a doctor who specializes in "poisonous scars." The name of a doctor specializing in foot problems decorates the wall at top right. One also sees signs promoting a clinic, restaurant, pharmacy, wine shop, and barber shop.

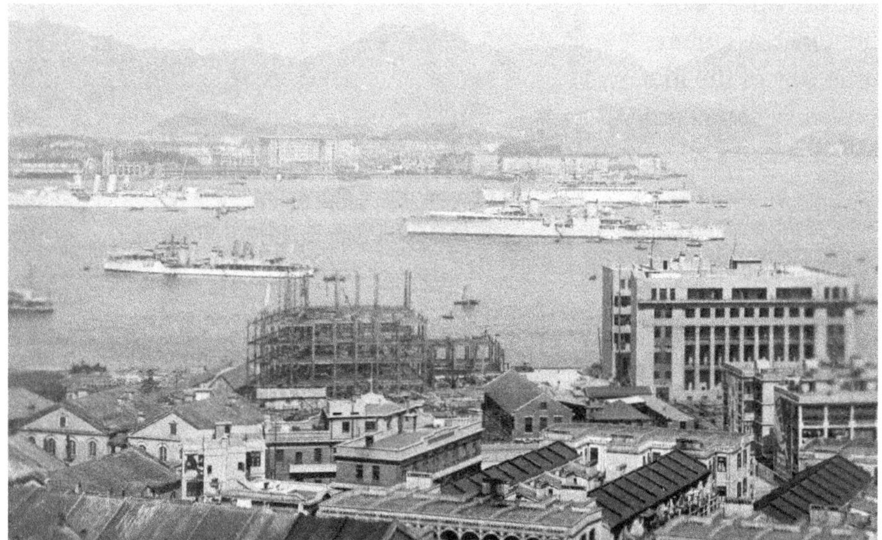

Harbor of Hong Kong from The Peak on Victoria Island looking toward Kowloon on the mainland, with a U.S. cruiser in the foreground and a British cruiser in the background, 1933.

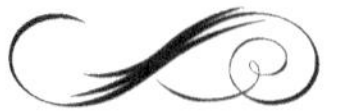

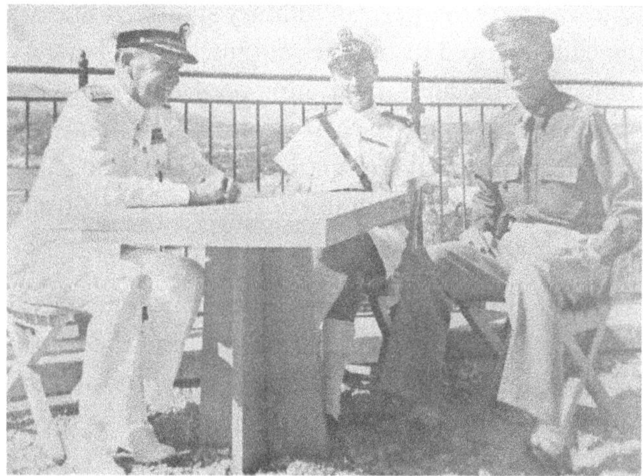

This trio of senior officers from two nations that had recently been allies and would be again soon, at rest in Hong Kong, British Crown Colony, mid-1930s: unidentified U.S. Navy admiral and Army general flank BrItIsh Royal Navy officer. Pat managed her way into diverse scenes.

Ceded to the United States by Spain as a trophy after the 1898 Spanish-American War, the Philippines remained totally under U.S. authority until 1935. American culture, customs, government, and language heavily influenced Filipino life and structure. American armed forces provided security.

In 1935 President Franklin Roosevelt signed a bill granting Filipinos a constitution and a limited autonomy. Their legislature and a plebiscite ratified the bill and constitution, thus establishing the Commonwealth of the Philippines. Manuel L. Quezon was inaugurated as its first president on November 15, 1935, while Pat, Bob, and Carroll were in Manila. The Philippines (aka Philippine Islands, now the Republic of the Philippines) received full independence in 1945.

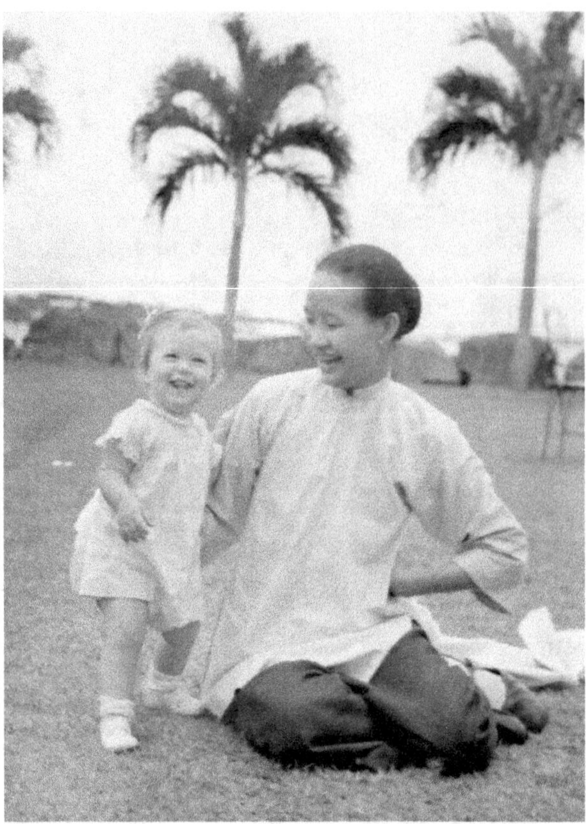

Carroll, nearly two, with her Chinese amah Ah Kwai at the Army and Navy Club on South Boulevard in Luneta on Manila Bay, Manila, Philippine Islands, 1935.

For the Robbinses, the Philippines became a base of operations for Bob's shipboard duties and Pat's ship-following photographic excursions. Other than North China, they spent more time on the ground in the islands than anywhere else in the Orient/Western Pacific from 1933-36. On November 29, 1935, they witnessed the arrival in Manila Bay of the first China Clipper, a four-engine Martin 130 passenger and cargo aircraft carrying 111,000 letters.

Pat and Bob Robbins joined the prestigious Army and Navy Club and used it when in Manila. Carroll remembered, "Dad joined to have drinks with the officers he would serve with and to take a furnished room that became his home away from home. Mother spent a lot of time over there. It was where most of the military wives would congregate with or without their babies. Dad played golf there when he was around. Ahmahs took care of the babies and the wives swam, played cards. Most of the wives were from upper-class families. It was expensive, hard to get passage over there—it was the Depression. I had teeth and dimples then."

Catering to the American military stationed there or visiting, the club featured its own restaurant, several bars, a reading room, bowling alley, swimming pool, and tennis courts, "a stark contrast to the bare frontier posts back home." Spanish-American War hero Admiral George Dewey had served as its first president. The building now houses the Museum of the City of Manila.

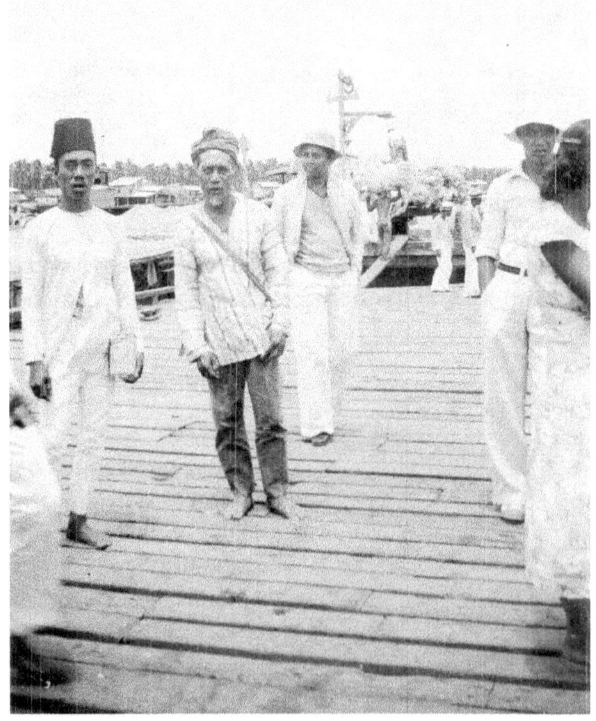

Pat encountered a 'rather ancient and dilapidated Moro on the dock at Davao, Mindanao, Philippine Islands. Teeth stained black with betel nut,' she noted. 1934

At the docks again. The ethnically indigenous Muslim Moros, located primarily in Mindanao, Sulu, and the southern islands, form the largest non-Catholic religious group in the country, today comprising about 10 percent of the total population. They fought the U.S. military from 1890-1913, and lost.

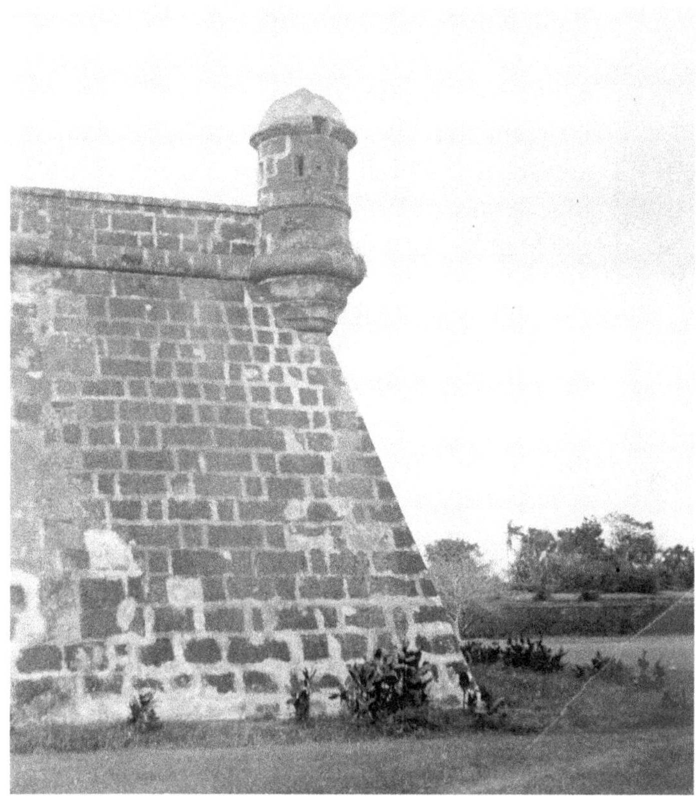

The Intramuros, Manila's ancient walled city, mid-1930s

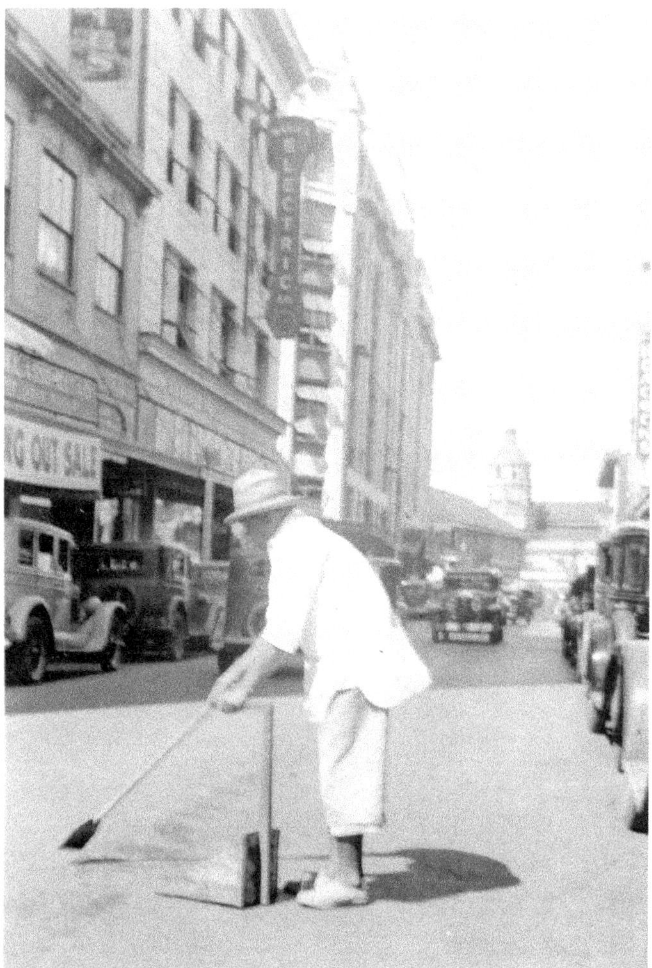

Street cleaner in Manila, Philippine Islands, mid-1930's.

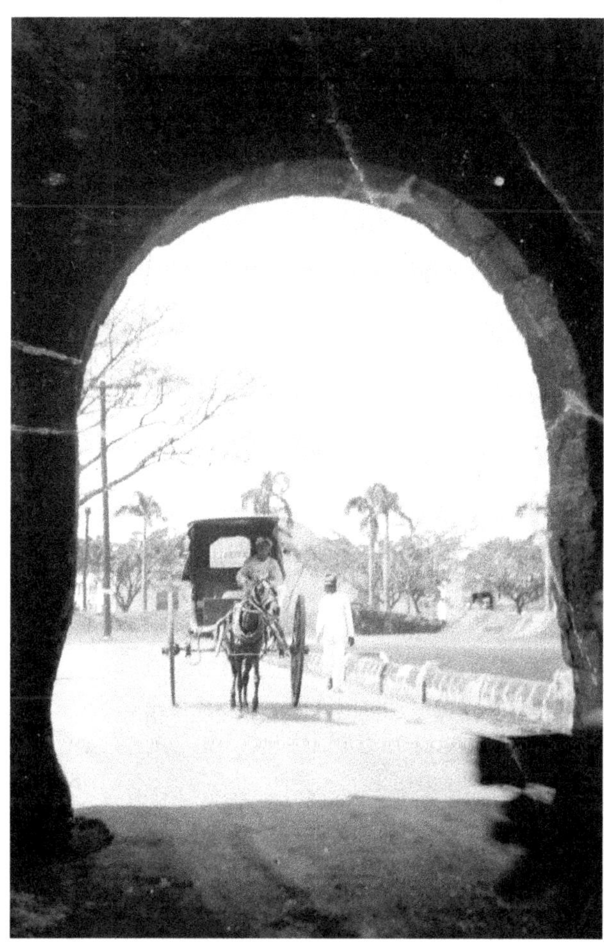

Fascinated by the history, design, and significance of Manila's Intramuros fascinated Pat, who photographed it from numerous directions.

The islands' original capital city served from Spain's colonial conquest in 1590 until their defeat in the Spanish-American War in 1898. The Intramuros, described as "tucked into a small corner of the city . . . is another world," a little more than a kilometer wide, and one-and-a-half kilometers long, fronted by Manila Bay, Luneta Park, and the Pasig River, into which was "literally crammed more than 350 years of Filipino history."[5]

In 1935 Commonwealth of the Philippines President Manuel L. Quezon invited General Douglas MacArthur, U.S. Army Chief of Staff, to build the

A horse-drawn carriage at an entrance gate into the Intramuros, the historic walled city in Manila, Philippine Islands, mid-1930s.

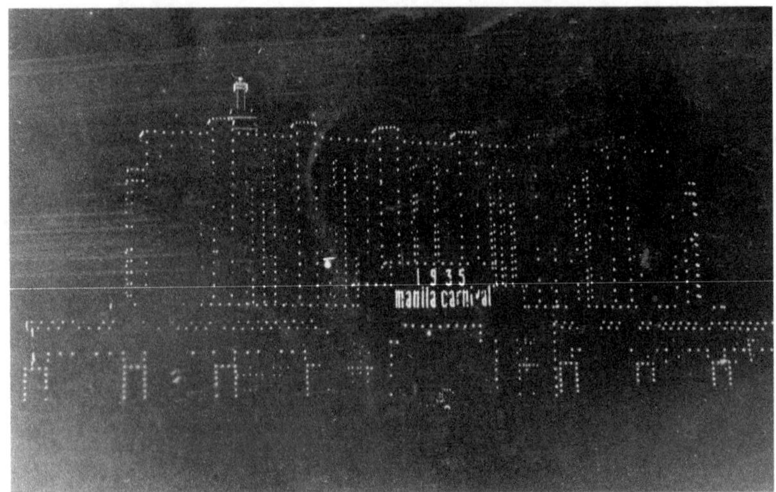

The Manila Hotel lighted for Carnival time, the Philippine Islands, 1935.

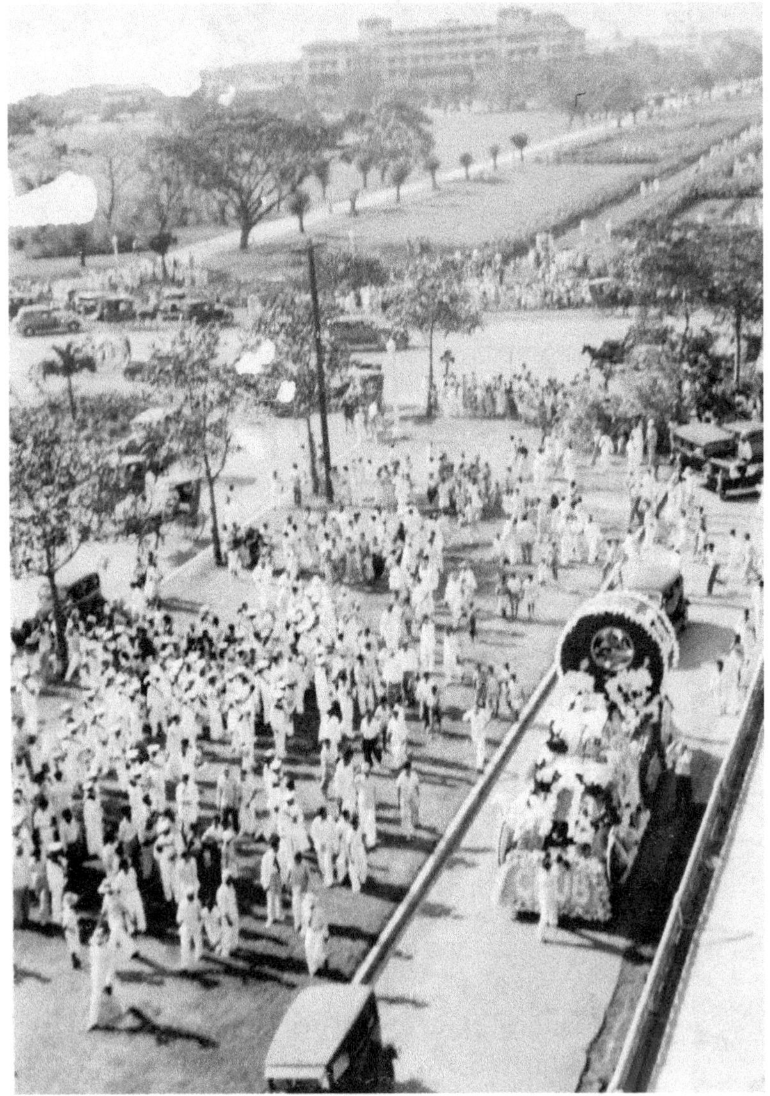

Carnival time along Dewey Boulevard looking across from the famed Luneta Park at the Manila Hotel where the Robbinses lived next door to General Douglas MacArthur and his family, Manila, Philippine Islands, November 1935.

Philippine army. MacArthur, who had served there earlier in his career, resigned and accepted the request from a man who had long been his confidant. During his tenure as the military advisor to the Philippine government, 1935-41, MacArthur, his wife Jean and son Arthur made the Manila Hotel their home.

"To handle the cost of MacArthur's suite, he was given the honorary title of 'General Manager'" and attended monthly meetings. MacArthur "ignored the figurehead status and instead took control of hotel management. MacArthur's favorite food at the hotel was lapu-lapu, a grouper fish native to the Philippines, wrapped in banana leaves."[6]

For a while, the Robbinses occupied a Manila Hotel room adjacent to the MacArthurs.

"Perhaps no other event has piqued the interest and stirred a nation's imagination more than the fabled Manila Carnivals," one source cited. Held from 1908-1939, the two-week fair was organized as a goodwill event to celebrate harmonious U.S.-Philippine relations and to showcase our commercial, industrial and agricultural progress. Spectacular parades, lavish shows, firework displays and the crowning of the Manila Carnival Queen highlighted the "greatest annual event in the Orient."[7]

The "rambunctious" Carnival featured five parades such as the one above, and crowning the Carnival Queen, that year Miss Conchita Chuidian Sunico. "The entrance fee range from 50 centavos and up and one can buy at the gate a mask, a horn and a bag of confetti. The children wore a harlequin, a clown's costume, or a dunce cap, while the elder ones wore dominoes or similar attractive attires. The scene was like New Year's Eve with all the gaiety, laughter and gossips in old Manila circling around. Everyone seemed to be tooting horns or throwing confetti."[8]

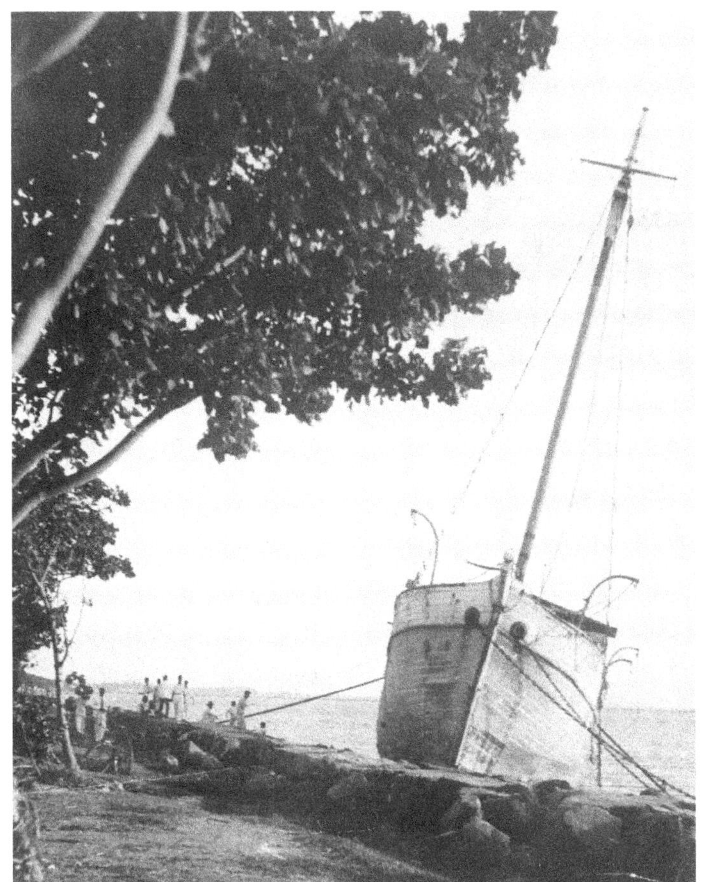

Shipwreck beached by typhoon, Manila Bay, mid-1930s.

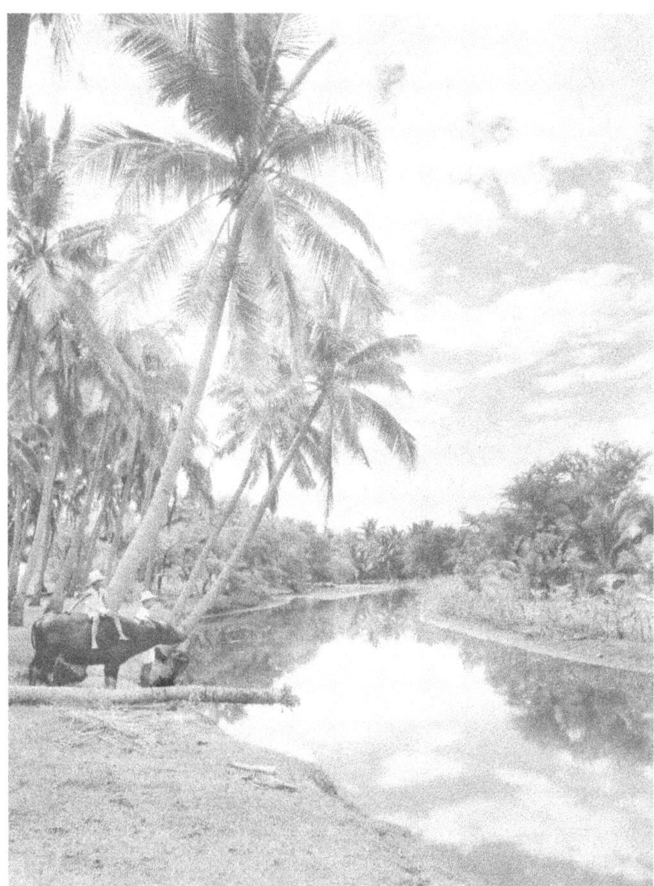

Water buffalo at the river, Philippine Islands, mid-1930s.

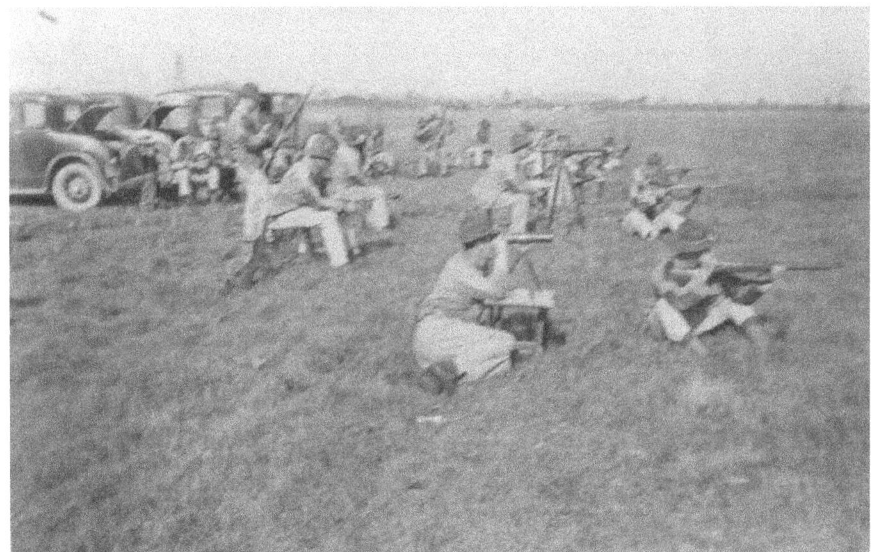

U.S. Army troops stationed in the Philippines on the firing range, mid-1930s.

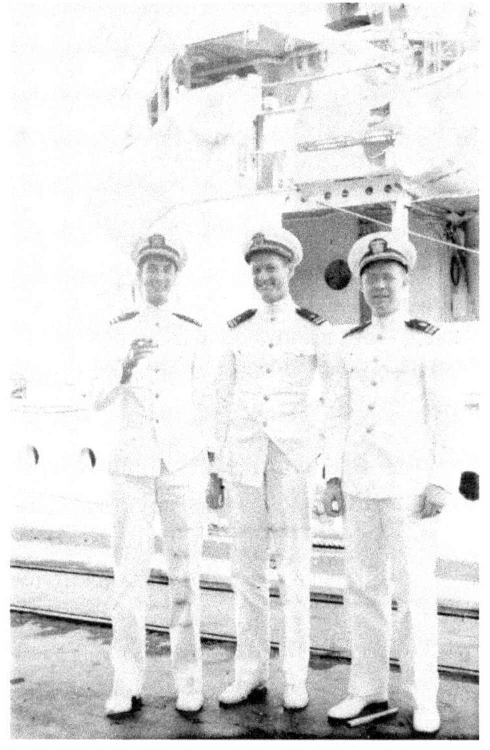

Lt.(jg) Bob Robbins (center) with fellow officers on the destroyer USS *Whipple* (DD-217), Far East, mid-1930s.

Bob served on the destroyer *Whipple* from 1934 to early 1936 before being transferred to California. Called a "four-piper" for its four smokestacks, the ship was commissioned in 1920, served for twelve years in the Asiatic Fleet, earned two World War II battle stars, and was decommissioned in 1945.

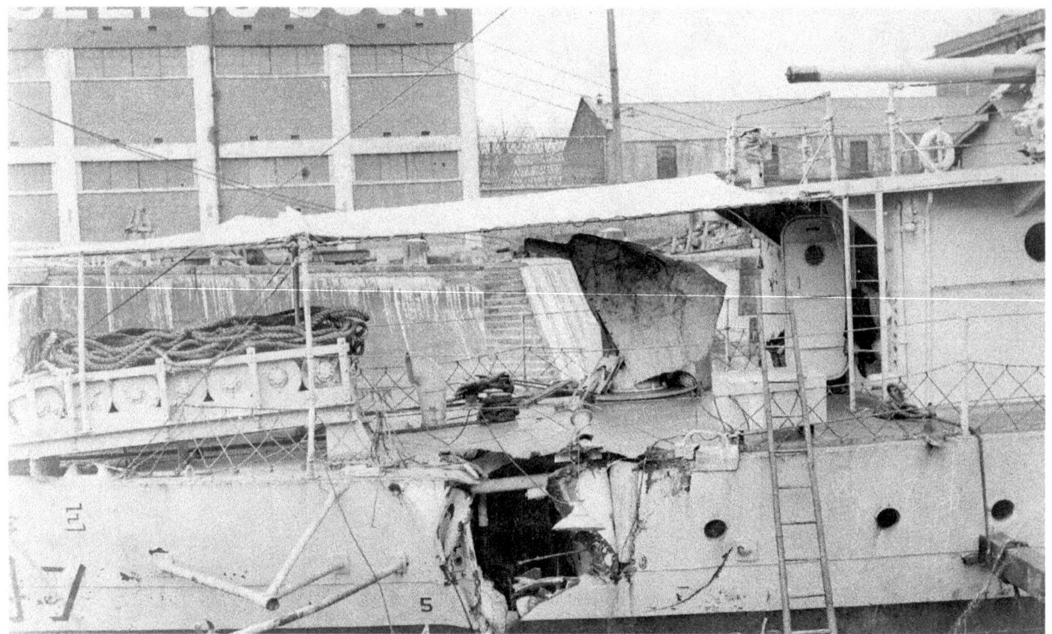

Collision damage to the after starboard side of the destroyer USS *Whipple*, spring 1936.

While maneuvering in Subic Bay on April 14, 1936, the *Whipple* collided with the destroyer USS *Smith Thompson* (DD-212). Serious damage caused the latter to be scrapped. *Whipple's* bow was twisted facing aft. She received *Smith Thompson*'s undamaged bow and returned to service.[9] Pat shot this photo of the *Whipple* while in for repairs at either Cavite or Subic Bay, Luzon, Philippine Islands.

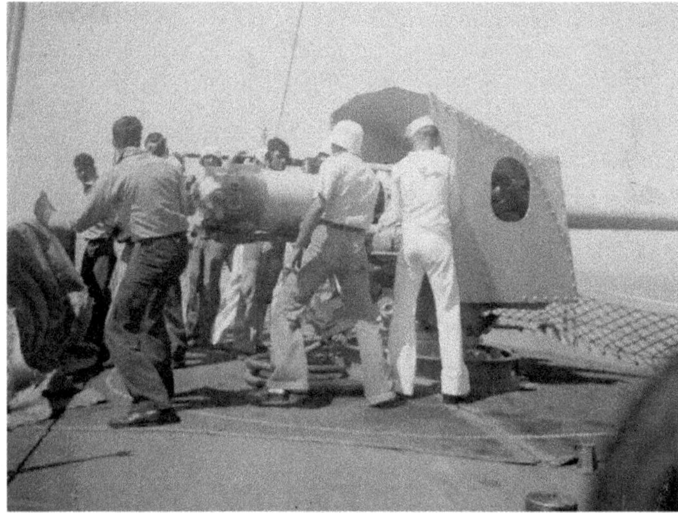

Crewmen during at-sea practice firing of 5-inch deck gun on what is believed to be the forward deck of the destroyer USS *Whipple*, of the U.S. Asiatic Fleet, mid-1930s.

The never-reluctant Pat somehow worked her way on board the ship to go to sea. Perhaps such was routine for family members, but doubtful, probably not for maneuvers. Needless to say, she always carried a camera.

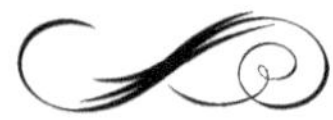

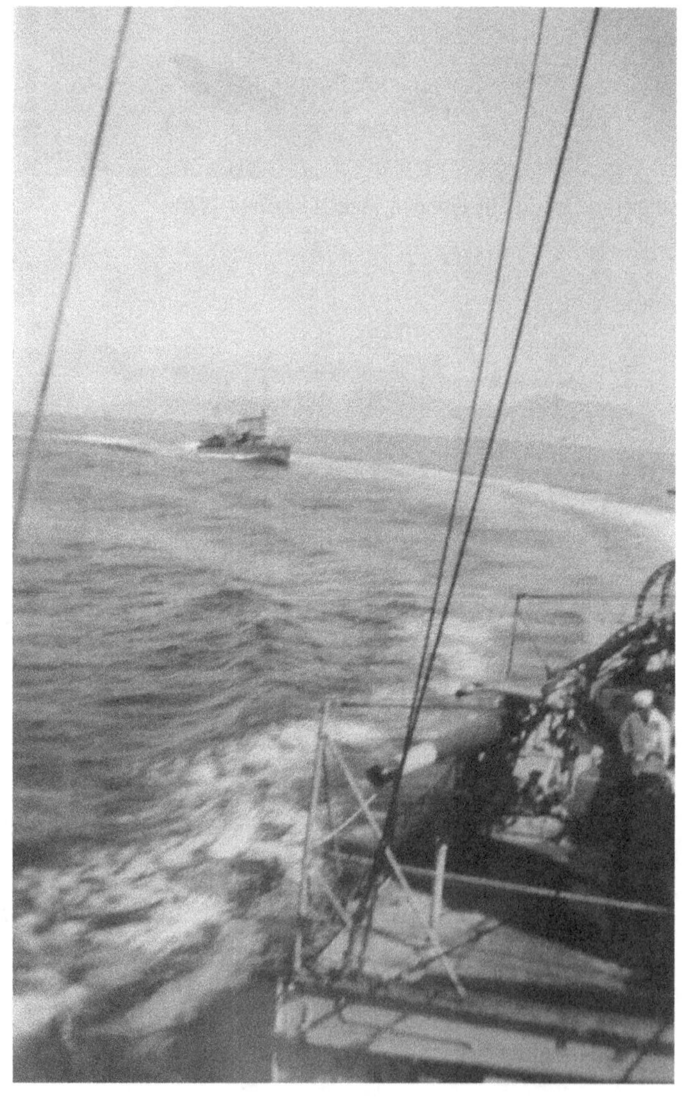

U.S. destroyers maneuver at 25 knots on the Western Pacific, mid-1930s. Pat rode Bob's ship to make these photographs.

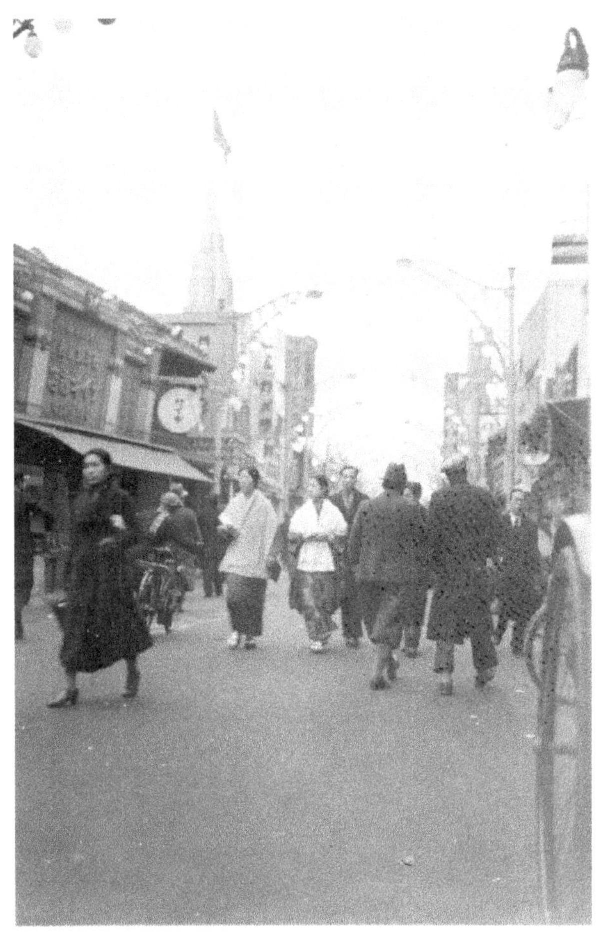
Street scene in Tokyo, Japan, 1936.

We assume Bob's ship called at Tokyo, or perhaps Yokohoma, or that he went there on an assignment. Following the 1923 Great Kanto Earthquake and the global Depression's start in 1929, Japan's economic situation had worsened by the early 1930's. The military seized totalitarian control of the national government, installing naval and army officers in major positions (including prime minister), assassinated or persecuted political enemies and Communists, and instituted indoctrination and censorship of the media and in education.

Within a few years, the economy recovered, thanks to rearmament, heavy industry, and "exploitation of captive East Asian markets . . . . Japan's quest for 'economic security'" drove its nationalists and militarists "forward into an expansionist foreign policy."[10] They anticipated and charted a potential Pacific conflict with the United States.

In 1931 Japanese forces occupied Chinese Manchuria, renaming it the "independent" puppet state of Manchukuo, and bombed Shanghai to protect its citizens living there from anti-Japanese movements. In 1936 Japan created a Mongolian state, another stab at China. Denounced for its actions against China, in 1933 Japan withdrew from the flaccid League of Nations. Tensions increased, leading to a full-fledged war in 1937, setting the stage for the vast Pacific War that would begin four years later. The Empire of Japan existed from 1868 until its defeat in 1945.

At the time of the Robbins visits, U.S-Japanese relations were gradually deteriorating, but we find no indication that Pat's movements were obstructed. However, we lack intimate or close-up photos or any notes she may have made on life and politics in Japan.

Since the early 1900's, the Ginza was Tokyo's principal business and shopping street, and entertainment and social hangout for the very wealthy, including tourists. Ginza means "place where silver is minted," which dates to the Seventeenth Century. After fire destroyed its wooden structures in 1872, the rebuilt "Bricktown" area "quickly gained a reputation as the height of fashion—that is, Western fashion—and the place has never looked back."[11]

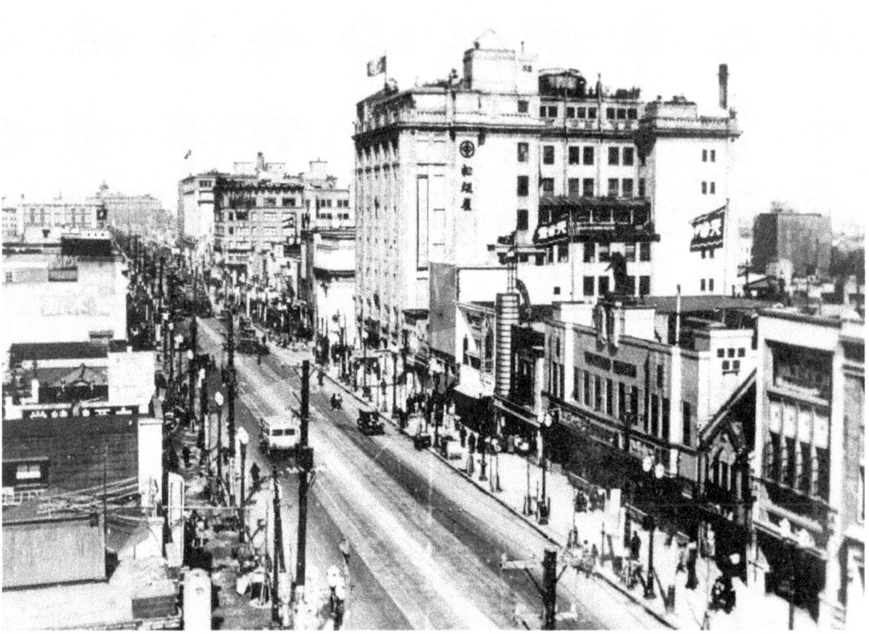
The Ginza, the iconic, world-famous commercial district of downtown Tokyo, Japan, 1934.

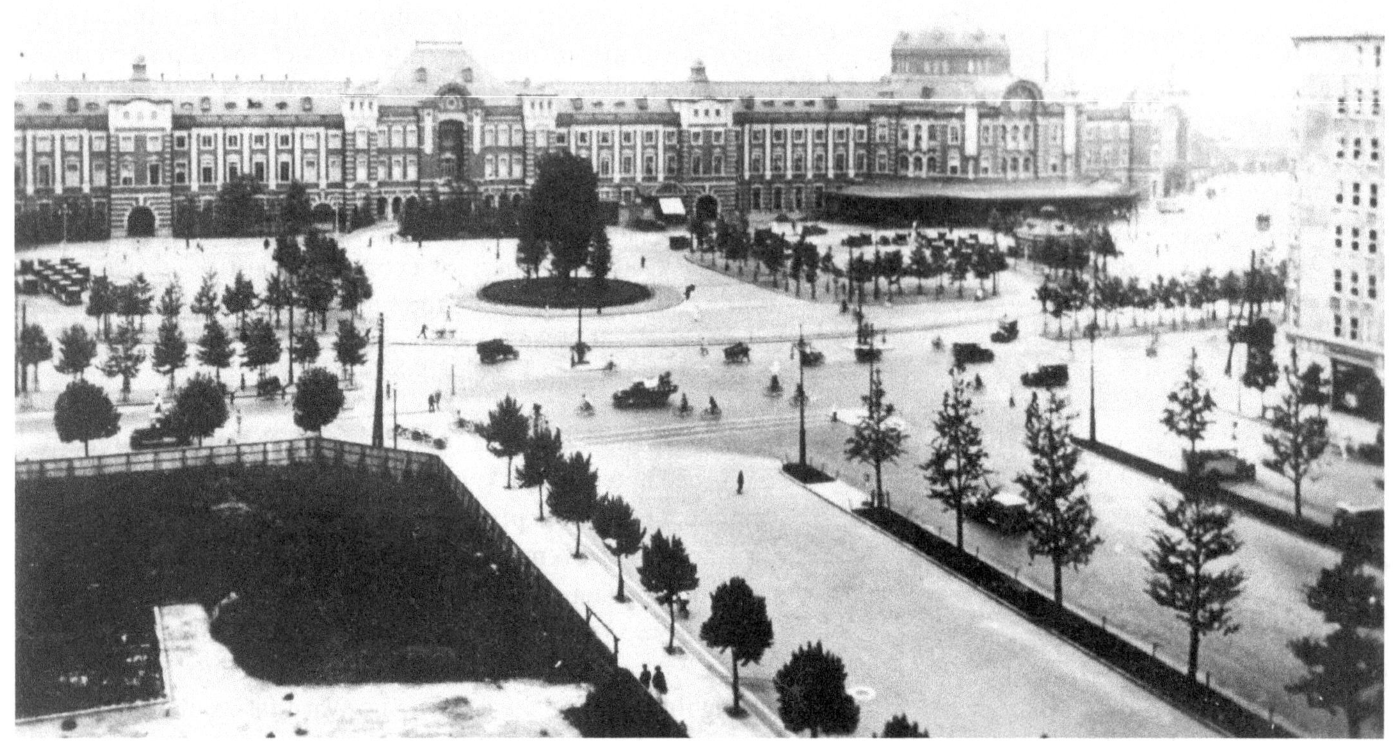

Main railroad station, Tokyo, Japan, 1934. Note the absence of vehicles and pedestrians.

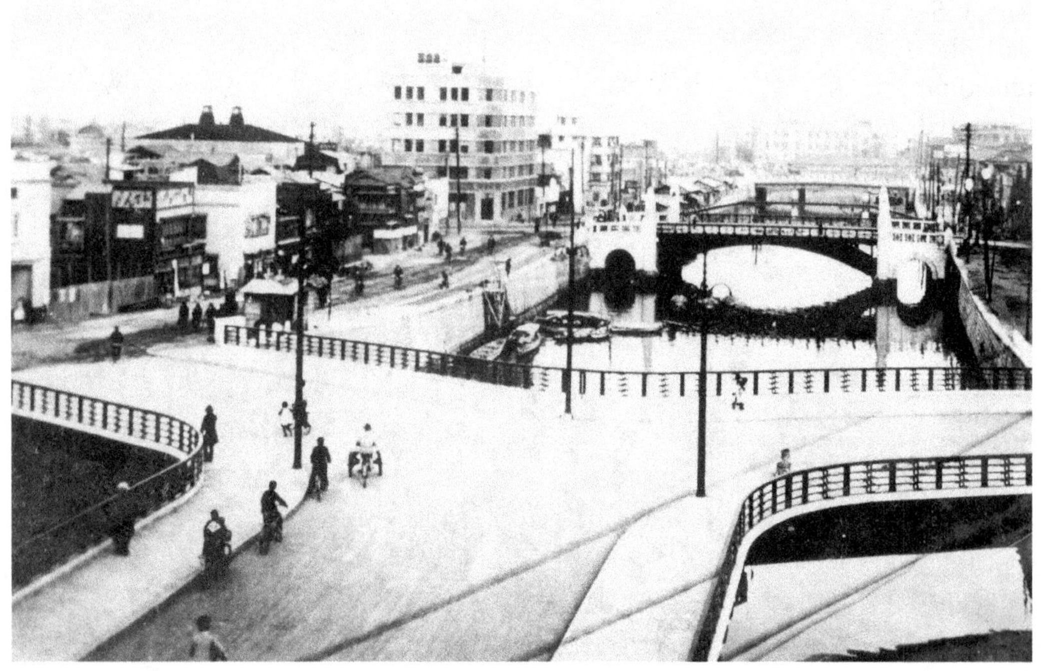

Bridges over the Sumida River which traverses the heart of central Tokyo, Japan, into Tokyo Bay, 1934.

The shot of Tokyo's train station required Pat to ascend to a high perch across the street. Tokyo Station opened in 1914 serving two electric trains and two steam. In the early years it had gates only on the Marunouchi side, the one seen here.

Hundreds of rivers flow throughout Tokyo. In the early Twentieth Century, one of the biggest, the Arakawa, was diverted in Kita Ward to reduce flooding, and was renamed Sumida. Twenty-six bridges spanned the Sumida.

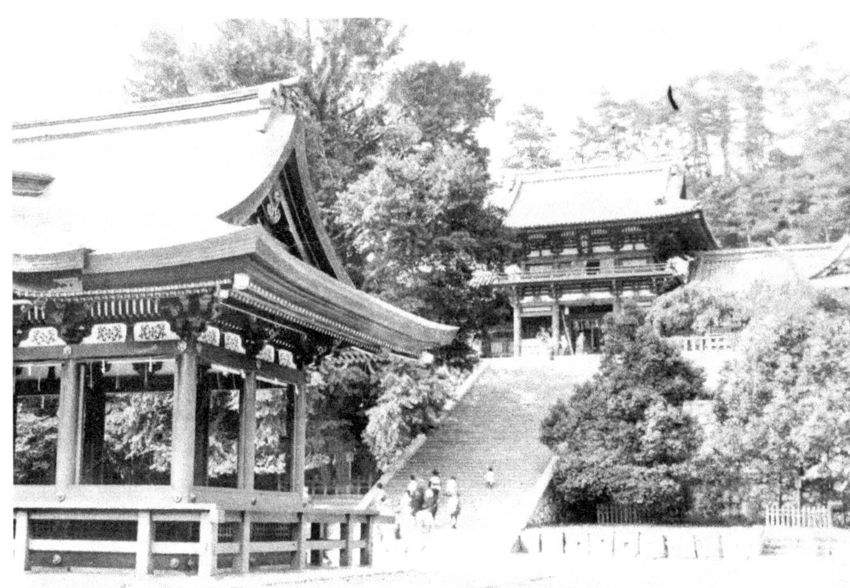
The Tsurugaoka Hachimabgu Shrine, founded in 1063, is the most important religious site of Kamakura, Japan. Photographed in 1934.

The Tsurugaoka Hachimabgu, dedicated to Hachiman, the patron god of the Minamoto family and the samurai, is Kamakura's most important shrine. in 1180 it was enlarged and relocated to its current site by the town's first shogun.

The tiny island of Enoshima connected to the mainland during low tide, and could be reached by boat during high tide. The Great Kanto Earthquake of 1923 caused land around Enoshima and its neighboring island of Shotenjima to rise, joining them. A place of worship and popular destination for pilgrims and foreigners since ancient times, Enoshima enshrined the Seven Lucky Gods and a protector of seafaring people.

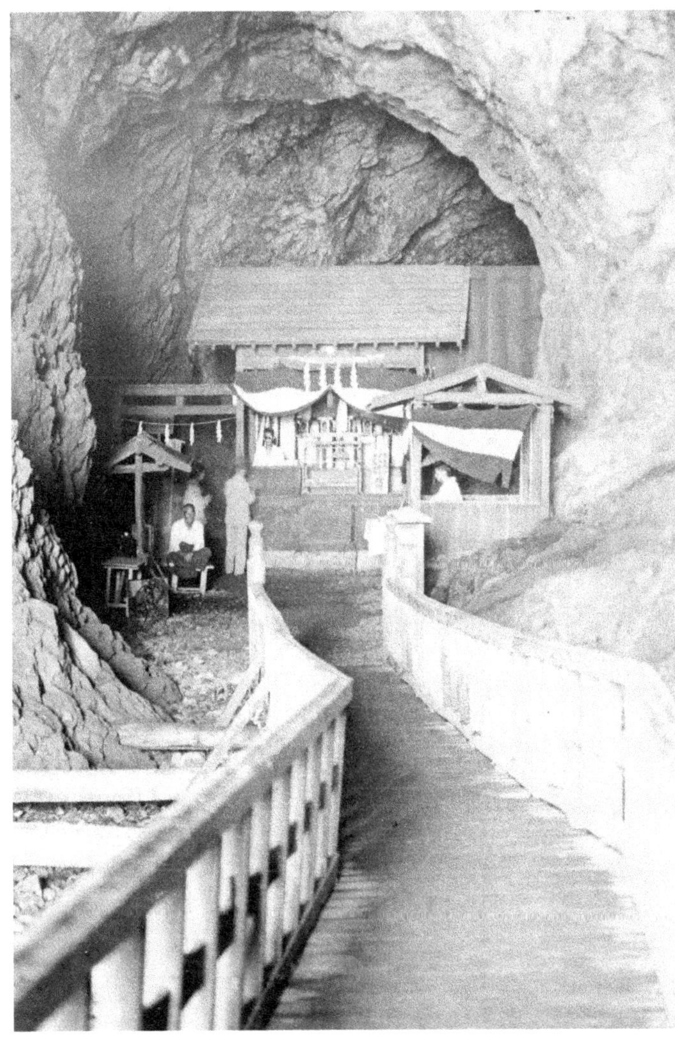
Enoshima island in Sagami Wan (Bay), Kanagawa Prefecture, Japan, a place of worship since ancient times, spring 1934.

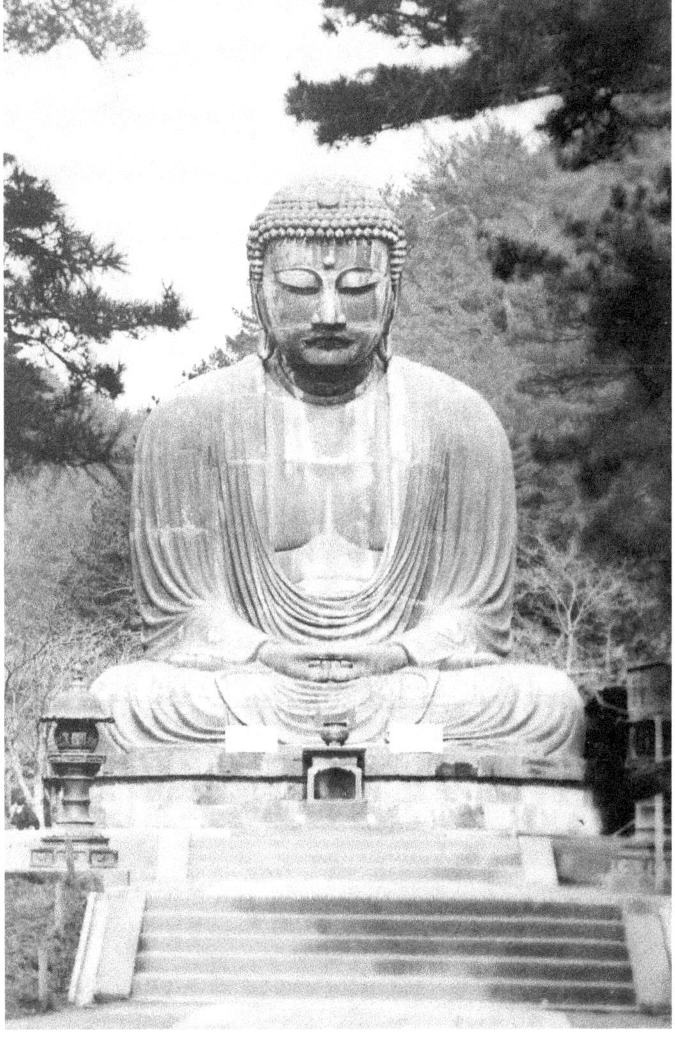
The Great Buddha of Kamakura, Kamakura, Japan, 1934.

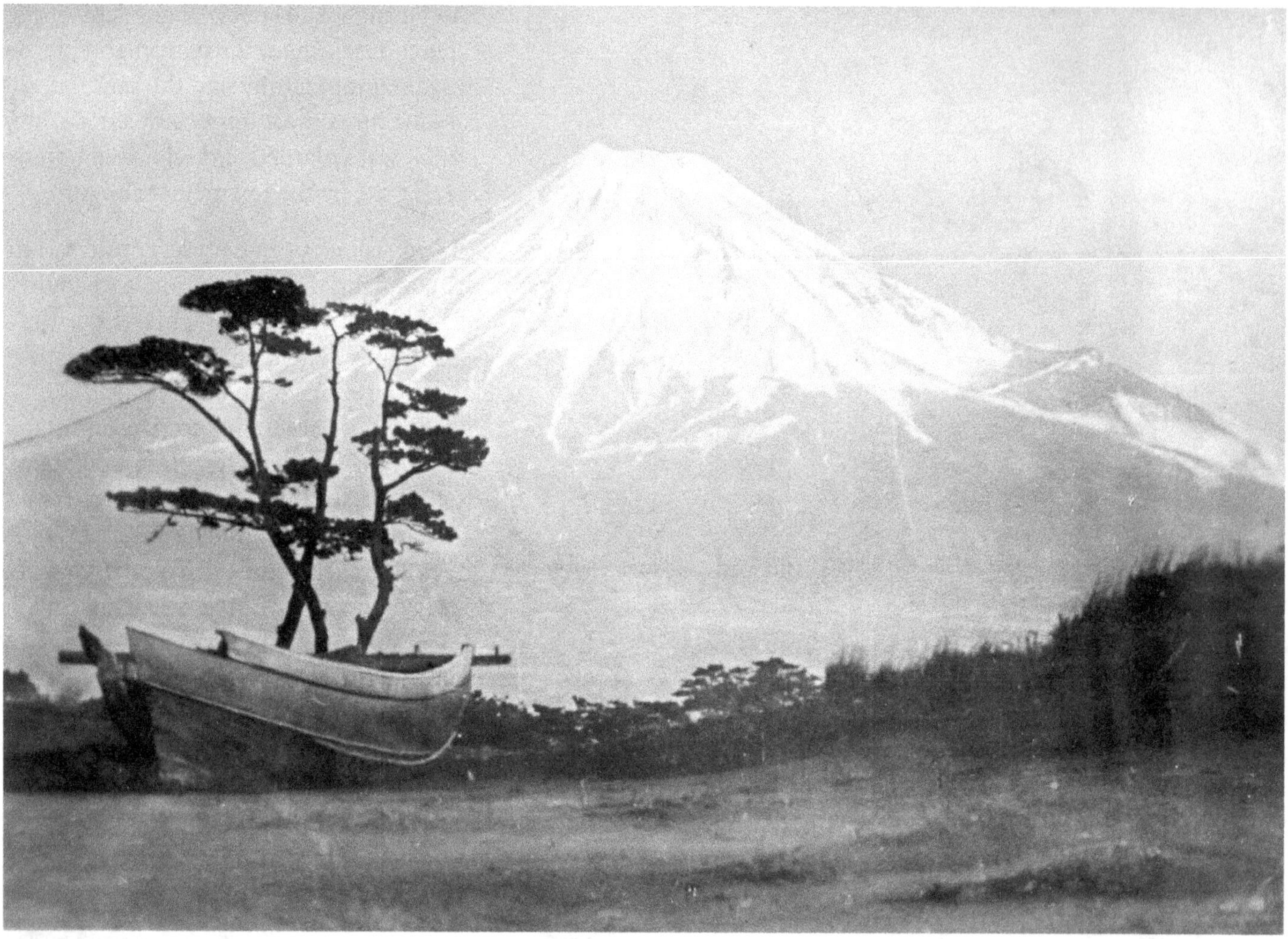

Mount Fujiyama looking from the north, Japan, 1934.

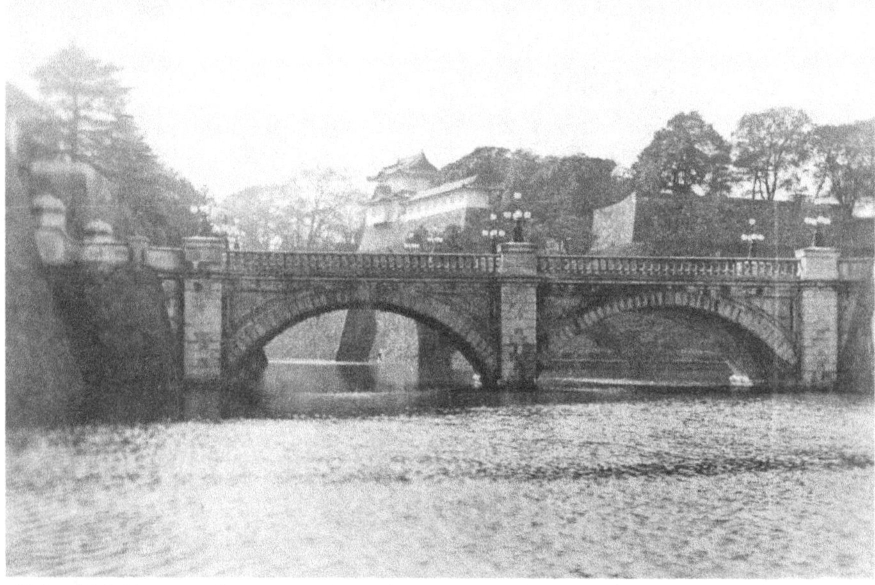

Nijubashi Bridge over the moat at the main entrance to the Imperial Palace, Tokyo, 1934.

The Great Buddha of Kamakura (Kamakura Daibutsu), cast in 1252, is a bronze statue of Amida Buddha, located at the Kotokuin Temple. Its height of 13.35 meters (nearly 44 feet) makes it the second tallest bronze Buddha statue in Japan.

How Pat got there is unknown, but this is as close to a "*National Geographic*" shot as any of her Orient images. Worshiped as a sacred mountain, Mount Fuji (Fujisan), Japan's highest peak and nearly perfectly shaped active volcano, has been a highly popular destination for tourists and artists for centuries. Standing on the border between Yamanashi and Shizuoka Prefectures, on clear days it can be seen from Tokyo and Yokohama.

Girl Travels 34,000 Miles In Four Years

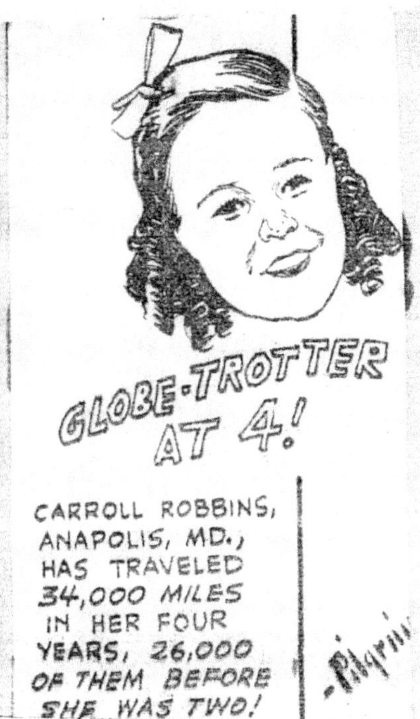

Globe Trotter at 4!

At 4, Carroll Robbins has traveled 34,000 miles—equal to one and one-third times around the world! Before she was 2, she had covered 26,000 of those miles, always on water.

Daughter of Navy people, she was born in Shanghai, China, and for the next 22 months practically lived aboard ships plowing between Japan, Hongkong, Manchuria, the Philippines and Hawaii.

A year ago she, her mother and father landed at Los Angeles. They drove across country—piling up mileage all the way—to Annapolis, Md., where Carroll now lives at 904 Dream's Landing.

So, though an American, she's learning about America for the first time. But that isn't all. "She learned to speak a little Chinese from her

'Girl Travels 34,000 Miles in Four Years.' Newspaper item believed to be from the *Washington Post and Times Herald*, ca. 1938.

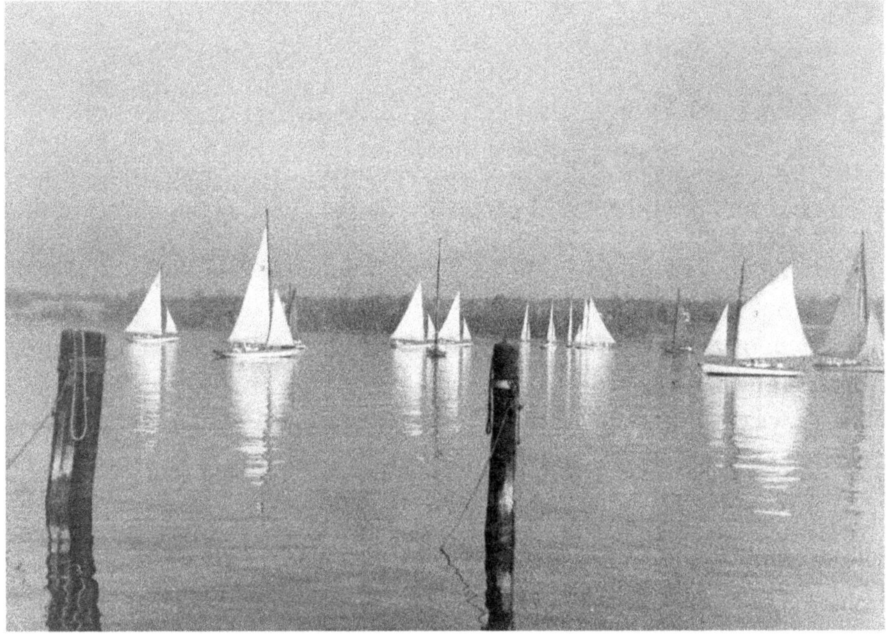

Sailboats at dusk on the Severn River at Annapolis, Md., late 1930s. Bob served on the Naval Academy faculty in 1938-39.

In early 1936 Lt.(jg) Robbins left his wife and daughter in the Orient and reported to Long Beach, Calif., as the gunnery officer for the cruiser USS *Portland* (CA-33). Pat and Carroll remained there until booking passage out of Yokohama, Japan, on the liner SS *President Taft* to California late that year, arriving in Los Angeles before Christmas. In 1938 Bob joined the faculty of the U.S. Naval Academy in Annapolis, Md., where he earned the rank of full lieutenant in 1939.

They traveled back to Long Beach that year for his two years of sea duty aboard the destroyer USS *Kilty* (DD-137) as executive officer, the ship's second in command. By that time, all three had recorded enormous mileage totals, but Carroll was spotlighted.

What a unique way to make news in that day and age: "Globe trotter at 4! Carroll Robbins, Annapolis, Md., has traveled 34,000 miles in her four years, 26,000 of them before she was two! . . . always on water. Daughter of Navy people, she was born in Shanghai, China, and for the next 22 months practically lived aboard ships plowing between Japan, Hong Kong, Manchuria, the Philippines, and Hawaii. A year ago, she, her mother and father landed at Los Angeles. They drove across country . . . to Annapolis, Md. . . . So, though an American, she's learning about America for the first time. She learned to speak a little Chinese from her amah."[12]

Coming into her own as a talented photographer, Pat always liked the restful image of sailboats because she chose the right time, place, and composition. Interestingly, for all the time she lived there while Bob taught midshipmen, she left us very few photographs of Annapolis.

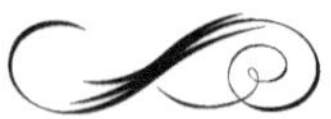

Pat spent much of these years in the Long Beach-Los Angeles area honing her professional skills, entering contests, earning awards, shooting the O'Meara family and friends, and taking advertising commissions.

So, let's look at a typical Los Angeles Sunday in 1938, as per the *Times:*[13]

"It's Sunday in Los Angeles, and the weekly real estate section features the floor plan of a modern home—cost $3,990 ($67,386 in 2016 dollars) . . . Japan builds a navy . . . As Hitler consolidates his power, Germany wants the return of colonies it lost after the World War . . . control of Danzig . . . and 'influence' in Austria . . . Dist. Atty. Buron Fitts expands his investigation of graft and corruption in Los Angeles . . . Former actress Hope Green says the bomb that injured Harry Raymond was made at her rooming house, 2032 W. 24th St. She implicates an unidentified 'high city official' in the bombing plot . . . The German ambassador says his country wants to be a 'good neighbor.'"

The headlines:

"Powers Warn Japan on Navy: America, Britain and France Threaten to Arm with Superdreadnaughts Unless Tokio Disclose Size of New Warships"

"Tokio Resists Naval Curb"

"Berlin Moves Worry Europe"

"World Fears Hitler's Plans May Bring on New War"

And the quote of the day: "The 'great goal' of the German government is peace—'real peace.'" – German Ambassador Hans Heinrich Dieckhoff, in an Associated Press story datelined Philadelphia.

An abnormally unsettled world awaited the Robbinses, yet three years away from their war.

Pat earned numerous awards early in her career. After these achievements, she concentrated on commissions and assignments rather than contests.

She received two 1939 awards—"Amateur, Special Merit"—for her "Old Chinaman" photo entered in the Sixth Annual and Third International Photographic Salon, sponsored by Marshall Field & Company, Chicago. And "Amateur, Special Prints" for "Haircut," showing son Berton in Annapolis looking into the mirror while Carroll holds scissors.

She earned a six-dollar check from *Picture: The Snapshot Magazine*, in 1940, for her China image "Temple Yard." The magazine printed her comment: "When you have an archway, you've the start of a good picture; add something picturesque beyond the arch, and you're all set. Note the nice interplay between the curves of the archway and that of the temple roof." For this shot she used Panatomic-X Film and a filter, with settings of f/22 at 1/25.[14]

In August 1940, for her Class C photograph of lilies, the *Los Angeles Times* wrote: "The *Times* takes pleasure in notifying you that your snapshot has been awarded first prize of $3.00 in our second weekly snapshot contest."[15]

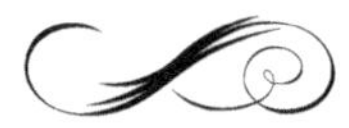

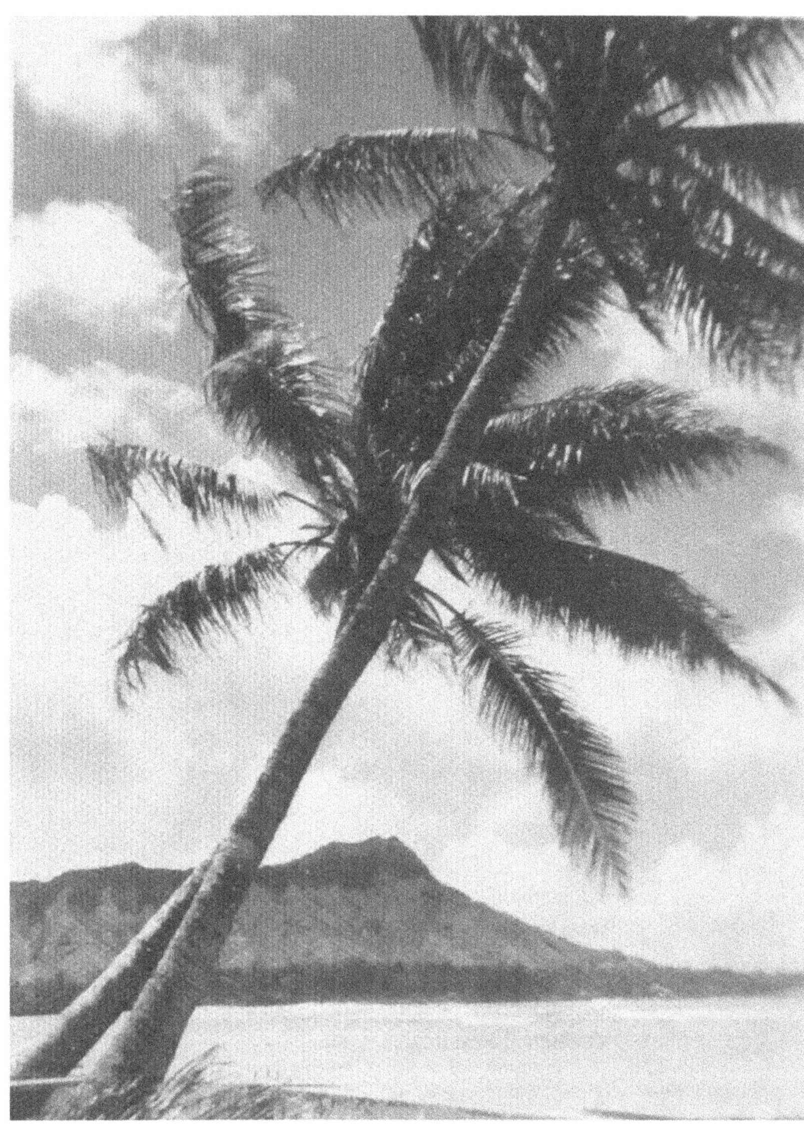

Pat's award-winning Diamond Head and palm trees along Waikiki Beach, 1940.

For her photograph of Diamond Head, Waikiki, Hawaii, she received the 1940 Kodak Award of Merit. This photo also appeared in a San Diego, Calif., newspaper, believed to be the *Tribune-Sun*, on November 14, 1940.

A January 25, 1938 letter from *Mademoiselle: The Magazine for Smart Young Women*, read: "Congratulations! Your shoe design, inspired by a childs barefoot sandal, has been judged one of the prize winners in *MADEMOISELLES*'s December 'Design for a Living' contest. Your prize will be a pair of these shoes made up in your size."[16]

Her photo "Dad's His Hero" in the December 1942 issue of *Popular Photography* garnered an award. "She has depicted a true case of hero worship of a son [Berton] whose father is on sea duty most of the time." She used a $2^1/_4$ x $2^1/_4$ National Graflex camera and 75mm Bausch & Lomb Tessar f3.5 lens; two photofloods in reflectors for illumination; and Eastman Plus-X film.

All told, in the 1930s and '40s she won six awards—nothing spectacular, not much cash—but ultimately she would exhibit her work in Los Angeles and New York, in Wiesbaden, West Germany, after the war, and with the Eastman [Kodak] Traveling Salon.

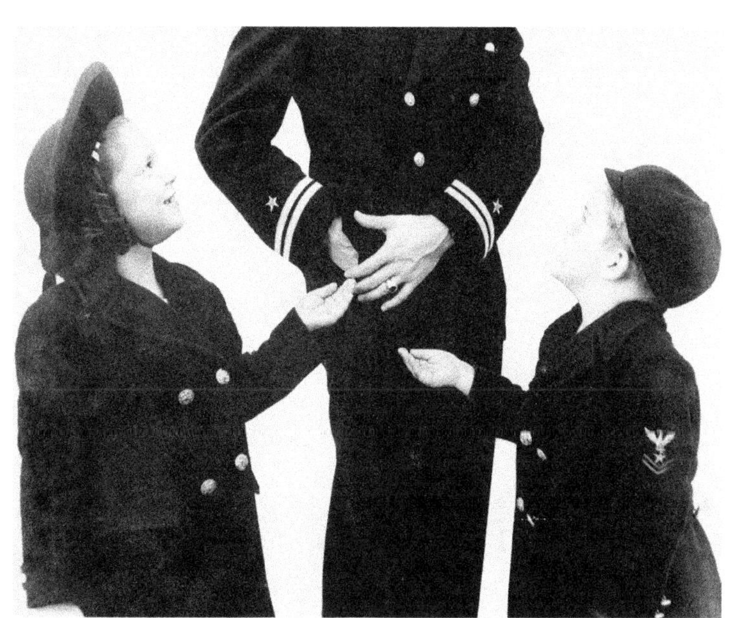

'Santa Claus lived at our house year-round,' remembered Carroll of the scenario for this scripted photo from 1940. 'Mother tried to dress us alike when we younger. She was always trying to pose us. The biggest problem with that was my eyes were very light sensitive [Carroll was mostly blind in one eye from birth]. She'd say, "Close your eyes real tight, and when I say open, I'll flash."'

Having not heard from a 1941 submission for potential publication, the persistent Pat sent Mademoiselle a self-designed jack-in-the-box cartoon card: "Here I am again," with both a "NO" and "YES" on each side. It must have worked. "We are delighted . . . to accept 'The Radio Actor' [photojournalism piece] which you submitted on December 11th! . . . If we had reported on this earlier we would have missed your very amusing follow-up which is now—sans comment—on our bulletin board and every *MLLE* editor knows just why you are here again!" Apologizing for the long delay, they asked her to shorten the article, for which they paid her $100.[17]

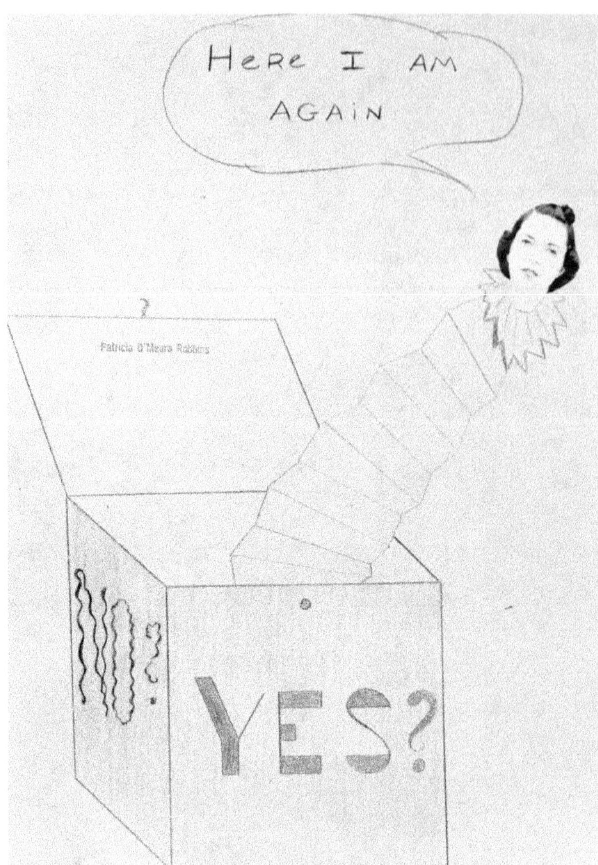

Pat Robbins' unique reminder that she'd received no feedback from a submission to *Mademoiselle*, 1941.

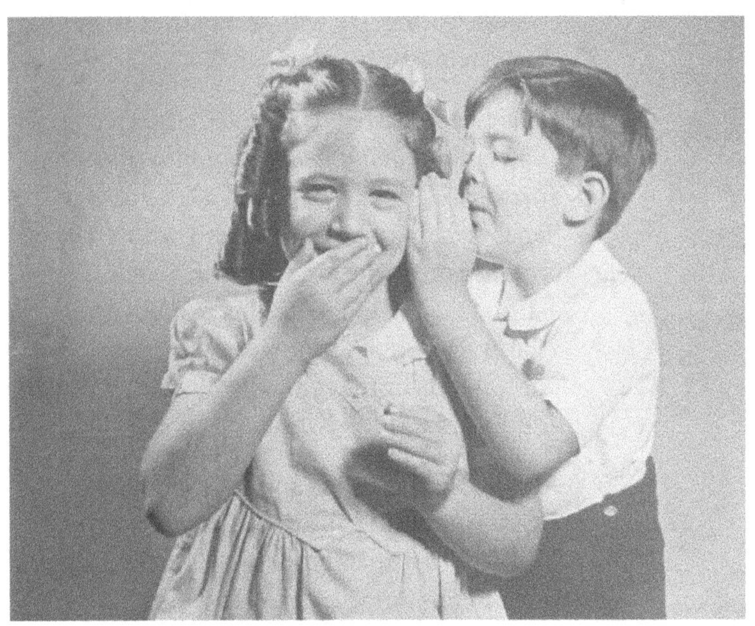

One of Pat's cutest among thousands of images taken of her children: 'The Secret,' ca. 1940.

After May 1940, in reaction to Japanese expansion in the Pacific expansion and the potential threats that posed to the United States, and over the objections of Pacific Fleet commander Admiral James O. Richardson, the Navy shifted the Fleet's warships and support ships from the Long Beach-San Diego bases to advanced positions in Pearl Harbor, on Oahu in the Territory of Hawaii. Richardson's personal protests led to his dismissal, and he was replaced by Admiral Husband E. Kimmel, who held command on December 7, 1941. The eventual result, for Bob, was reassignment to the destroyer USS *Shaw* (DD 373), which would put him in harm's way when war finally came.

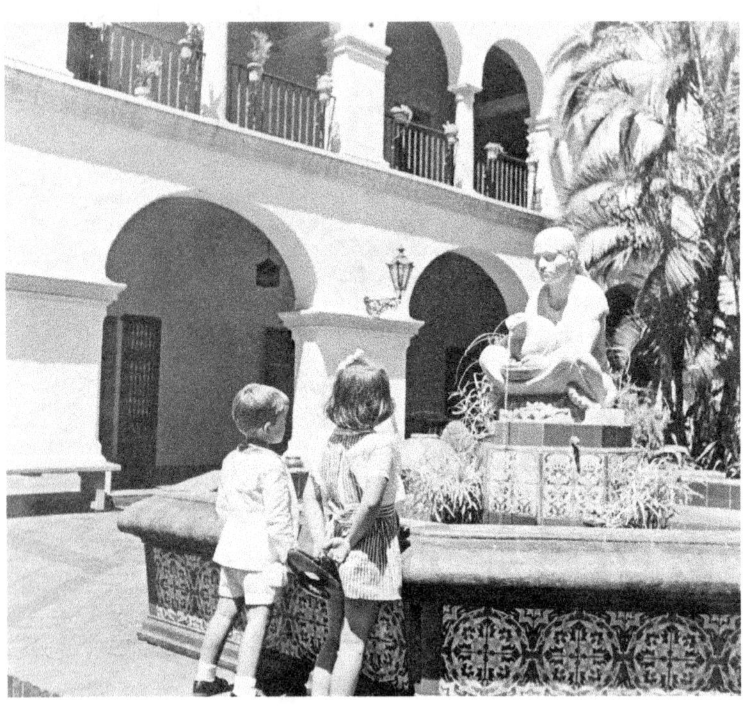

Berton and Carroll in Balboa Park, San Diego, Calif., July 1940. Then the family lived on Margarita Avenue in Coronado facing San Diego Bay.

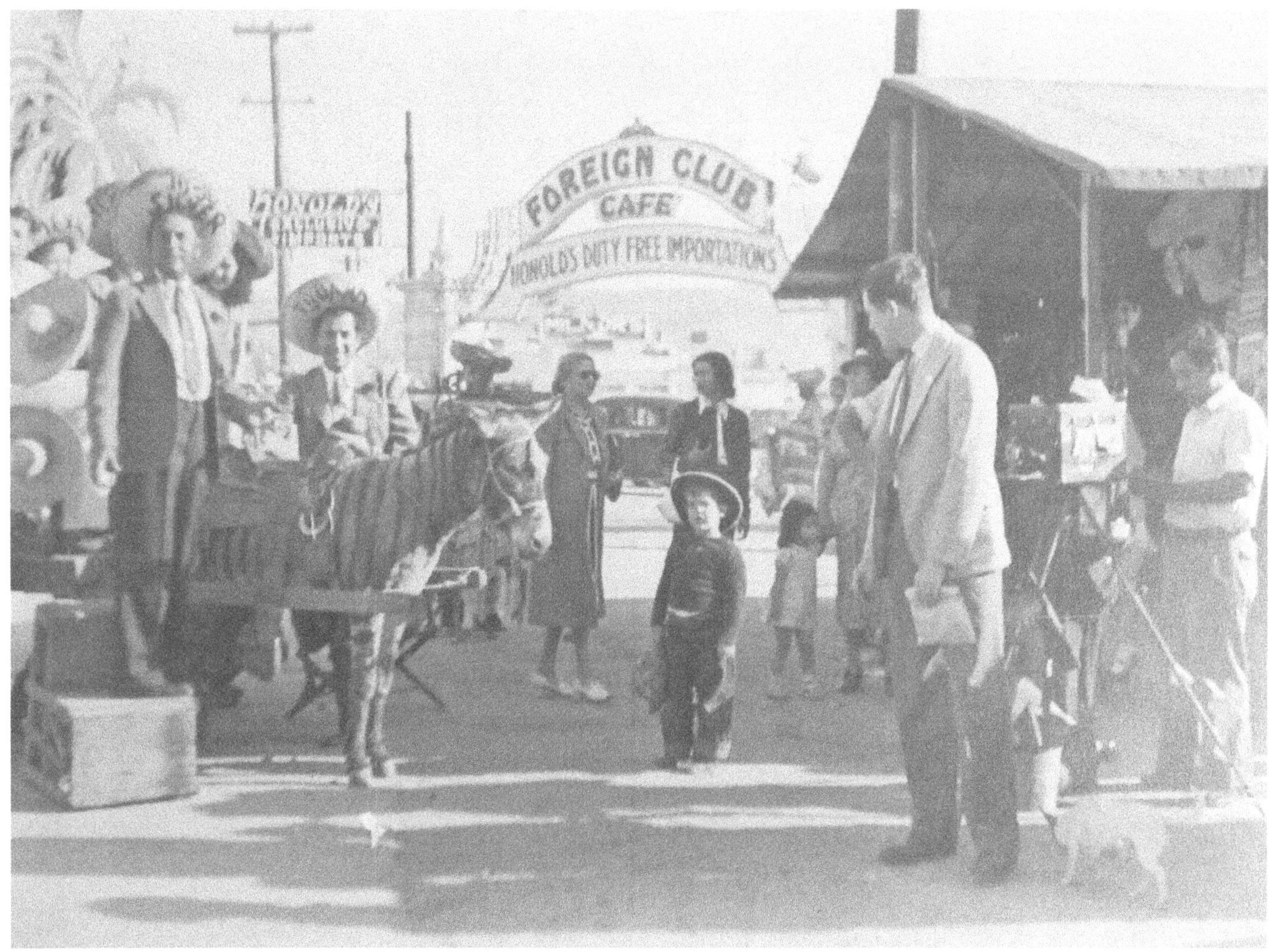

The Robbins clan and friends venture to Tijuana, Mexico, south of San Diego, ca. 1940. Berton III is in the middle.

Pat's outreach persona (one might say lifelong ego) included a close relationship with Princess Conchita Sepulveda Pignatelli, the local social arbiter and *Los Angeles Examiner* columnist, who wrote in August 1941: "Lovely Pat Robbins, in addition to being an ideal mother, is deeply interested in photography, and there is great demand for her work in smart set magazines. She is artistic and has traveled much, particularly in the Orient."[18]

Travels would continue, but never again to China and the Orient.

CHAPTER 4

'Mrs. Robbins Visiting Here': Pat and Children Record Hawaii in the Aftermath of Pearl Harbor

Pat Robbins' adventure in Hawaii, which expanded her career in new dimensions, began with a November 3, 1941, announcement (no less planted) in *The Honolulu Advertiser* newspaper: "Mrs. Robbins Visiting Here."

It read, in part: "Mrs. Berton Robbins, Jr., well known photographer, arrived recently to join her husband, Lt. Robbins, USN. Their two children accompanied Mrs. Robbins who has been residing in Los Angeles for the past six months . . . . Known professionally as Patricia O'Meara Robbins," she is working on an assignment for Look magazine titled "'Honolulu House Party' in which a dozen Southern California society girls, who came over earlier in the season for a prolonged visit, are to participate. She is . . . a member of an old and prominent Los Angeles family" who "left college in her first year to become a Navy bride. Her avocation of photography has developed to such an extent she is recognized as one of the foremost women photographers in the United States."

Earlier in 1941, sensing the Japanese threat, the Pacific Fleet had transferred husband Bob's ship, the destroyer USS *Kilty* (DD-137), and others from West Coast home ports to Pearl Harbor on Oahu, Territory of Hawaii. The day before the Japanese struck Hawaii on December 7, the Navy transferred Bob to the destroyer USS *Shaw* (DD-373) as executive officer.

Not long after the attack, the *Advertiser* introduced Pat's photography and verse to Hawaiians.

With her photo ran these words:

> "Dear God our Daddy's on the sea
> Please bring him safely home –
> Calm the winds and rolling waves
> And shield him from all harm
> When he walks the rain-swept deck
> The thought of home and us
> Kindles warmth within his heart –
> Oh, keep him ever thus.
> While Mother watches over us
> Our Daddy guards the sea,
> We all give thanks, dear God to You
> For Your care eternally."[1]

"The picture was taken in Coronado, Calif., before we left for Hawaii," Carroll said. The poem and photo also appeared in the *Los Angeles Times Home Magazine*, November 1, 1942.

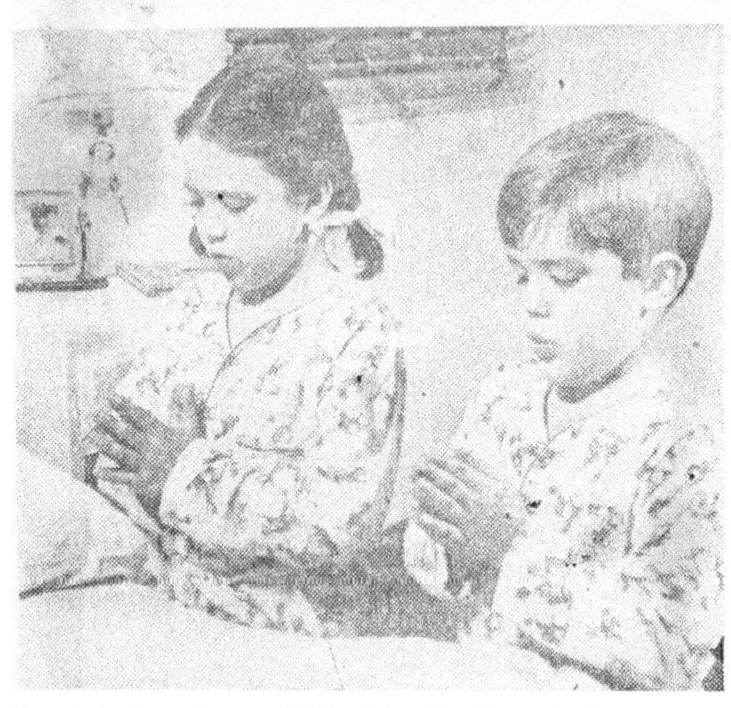

'Great is the force of prayer of children': Carroll and Berton in *The Honolulu Advertiser*, December 28, 1941.

"Mother thought the *Shaw* would return to California. The only way she could get to Honolulu was on an assignment. She got two of them, *Mademosielle* and *Look*. She paid her own way, was put on a waiting list, but Grandpa called his old friend Pat McCarran [Nevada U.S. senator, mentioned in Chapter 1] and made it happen. Originally she hadn't planned on taking us, wanted to leave us with our grandparents. Grandfather was old and wouldn't admit it and Grandmother was getting old, even though she continued her social work."

Carroll continued. "There was conflict in '*the Family*' about my mother dragging us kids off to that 'pagan place' with iffy schooling and her working with 'the Kodiak [Kodak] craze' (Grampa's terminology) and our not experiencing a normal childhood. I don't believe they quite trusted Mother's maternal instincts or her gypsy life and felt we kids would be better off left in Los Angeles, attending St. Brendan's School, eating regular meals at specific times, under the watchful eyes of Hancock Park and Windsor Park residents, ensuring that we would learn all the 'right' traditions of '*Family*.'"

But, oh never mind.

Over most of our marriage Carroll eschewed discussing the war or her parents' involvement in it. She never forgot, but considered it too painful, especially her father's three-year recuperation from wounds he sustained at Iwo Jima. Finally, in 1999, she began speaking around Wilmington about her remembrances of Pearl Harbor, and gave interviews to area media. No longer reluctant, she agreed to co-author with me the popular book *Hawaii Goes to War: The Aftermath of Pearl Harbor*, which my publisher requested for the sixtieth anniversary of the attack. Carroll divulged lucid wartime recollections including wartime life in Hawaii and Los Angeles. For inclusion in the book we broke out the multitude of photos Pat had left us, in myriad boxes and scrapbooks that largely had been stored out of mind.

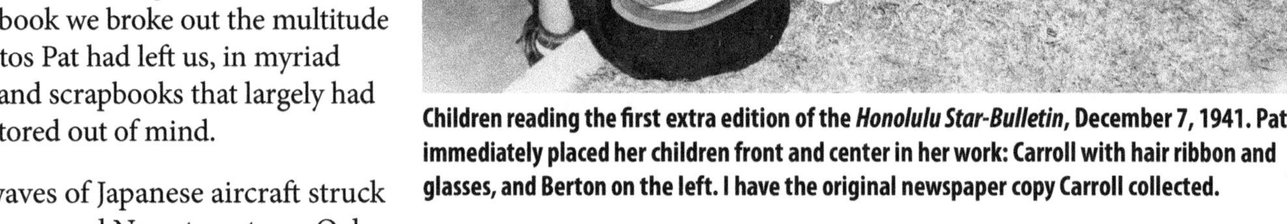

Children reading the first extra edition of the *Honolulu Star-Bulletin*, December 7, 1941. Pat immediately placed her children front and center in her work: Carroll with hair ribbon and glasses, and Berton on the left. I have the original newspaper copy Carroll collected.

Two waves of Japanese aircraft struck U.S. Army and Navy targets on Oahu the morning of December 7, paralyzing the naval forces at Pearl Harbor, and the Army Air Forces at Hickam and Wheeler Fields. Carroll and her mother witnessed the attack's second wave, which passed over their residence at the Comstock Apartments Hotel in the Waikiki Beach area, and saw, in open cockpits, the pilots' faces and flapping scarves.

One bomb from that wave obliterated the forward section of the *Shaw*, which was in drydock, causing an enormous white fireball explosion, made famous in the second-most-electrifying image from that day. Her father, in civilian clothes, arrived on the drydock at the moment of the impact, but went aboard uninjured. The very next day he departed for duty on another ship, leaving the family on its own.

Immediately Pat began shooting pictures, and soon the Associated Press, Army and Navy credentialed her to shoot for them. Thus began a nine-month saga during which she recorded for history Oahu's damage, defenses, life, and times, and proceeded with her professional career photographing various events and taking advertising assignments. Her work and deeds began appearing in Honolulu and mainland newspapers and magazines.

In August 1942, Pat, Carroll, then 8, and Berton, 6, returned to Los Angeles where she resumed her career amidst the large O'Meara family and began making inroads into the "Golden Age of Hollywood" crowds. The *Los Angeles Times* reported their sojourn on August 22: "Navy Wife Tells Life in Hawaii."

"There is no social life in Hawaii today . . . under martial law . . . . With the vanishment of the social scene in Honolulu went the once gay and carefree set of 'Navy wives': instead of cocktail parties . . . they attend first-aid and other emergency defense classes . . . . The paramount problem in the islands today is the entertainment of the armed forces and the vast number of civilian defense workers."

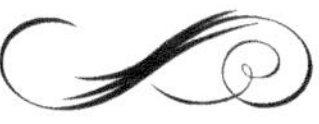

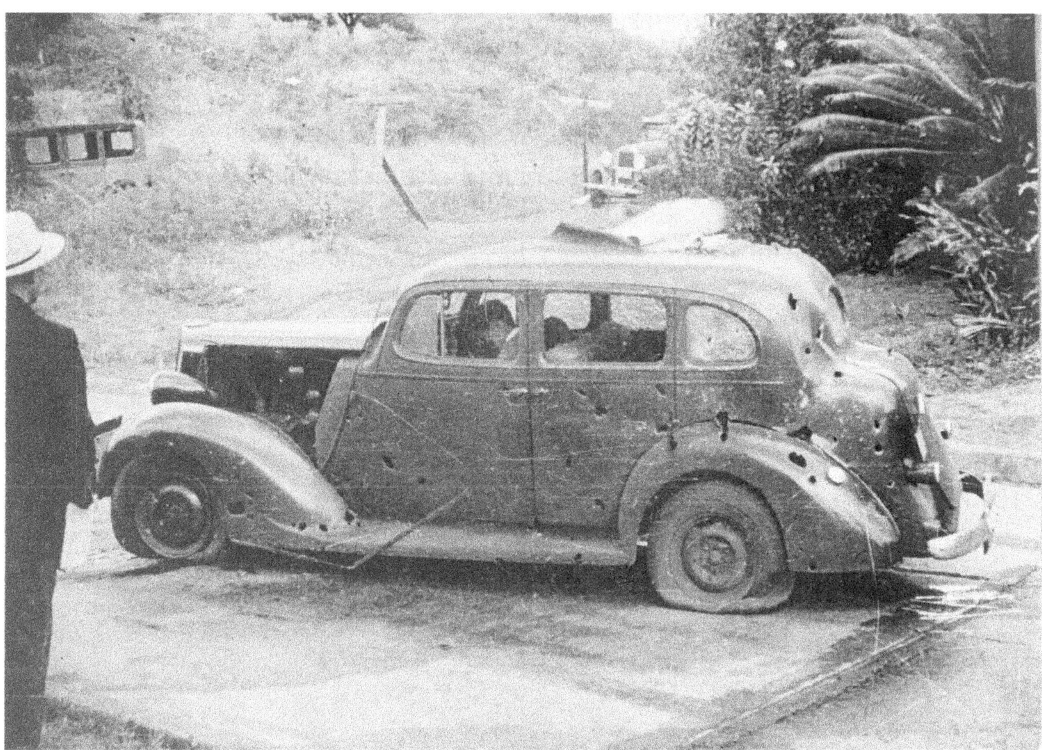

The 'Honolulu death car,' riddled by bullets or shrapnel, one of Pat's most notable photographs, December 8, 1941.

Her career-boosting photography of Oahu's aftermath is best known for this timeless image of some of the first Americans to die in World War II. "This is a widely published picture," Carroll said. "The car was dark green. I remember it well, seeing all that, and would throw up—that was my answer to everything bad. It was in a big field and a lot of bombed and strafed machinery. This was a day or so after the bombing. The Army and Navy had official rights to her pictures since she was credentialed by them. 'I would have taken them no matter what,' Mother said."

The *Honolulu Advertiser* website reported, "Initial reports said three civilians were killed when their car was hit by a Japanese bomb, but in fact the four were killed when the car was hit by errant US anti-aircraft fire. A photo of the shell-riddled car—victims still inside—was taken by *Look* magazine photographer Patricia Robbins and appeared in hundreds of publications. That photo has become one of the more recognizable shots from the Day of Infamy."[1]

This yellowed business card is a memento of how Pat learned what had happened to her husband. The card reads: "Your husband OK – Ship blown up." Carroll said Lt.Cdr. Glenn Jones, the *Shaw*'s commander, didn't go to the ship until that afternoon. "He wasn't very well liked." At least he courteously showed up with good news about Bob.

"Dad was in civilian clothes carrying a Harris tweed sports jacket and we didn't see him again until that night," Carroll remembered. "The ship's commanding officer never showed up that day. Dad rescued the flag, rolled it into his pocket, and gave it to Mother, who saved the jacket and the flag. We later discovered a 30 caliber bullet in a pocket, which I later placed on a bracelet. He came home for time enough to change clothes, collected some items, told Mother goodbye (Berton and I were asleep), and left. Mother sent the photo to the media who published it." The U.S. Naval Academy museum now exhibits the flag.

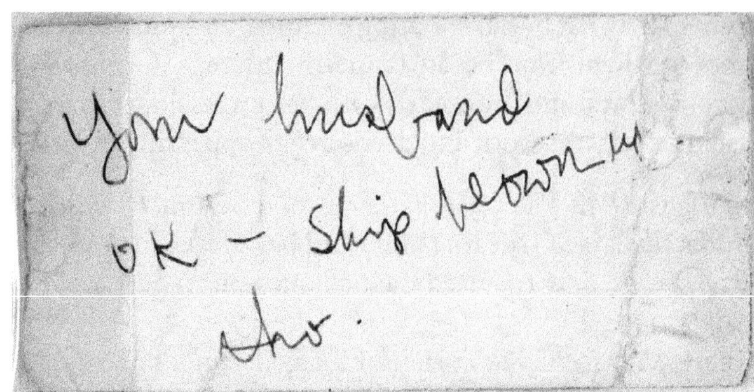

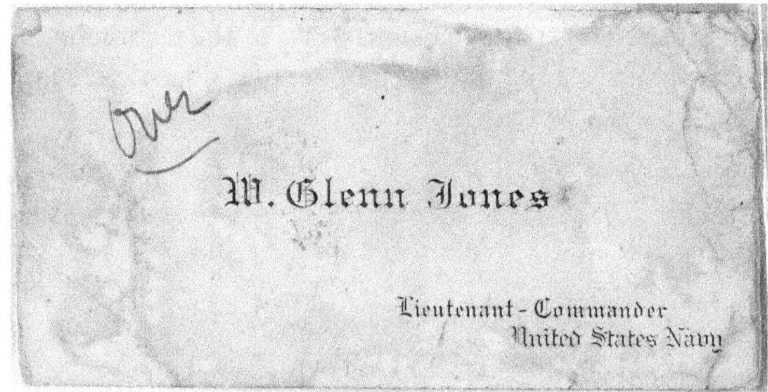

The business card of Lt.Cdr. W. Glenn Jones, commanding officer of the USS *Shaw* (DD-373), Bob Robbins' ship, which blew up in a Pearl Harbor dry dock on December 7, 1941. Lt.Cdr. Jones left it in Pat's apartment doorway that day.

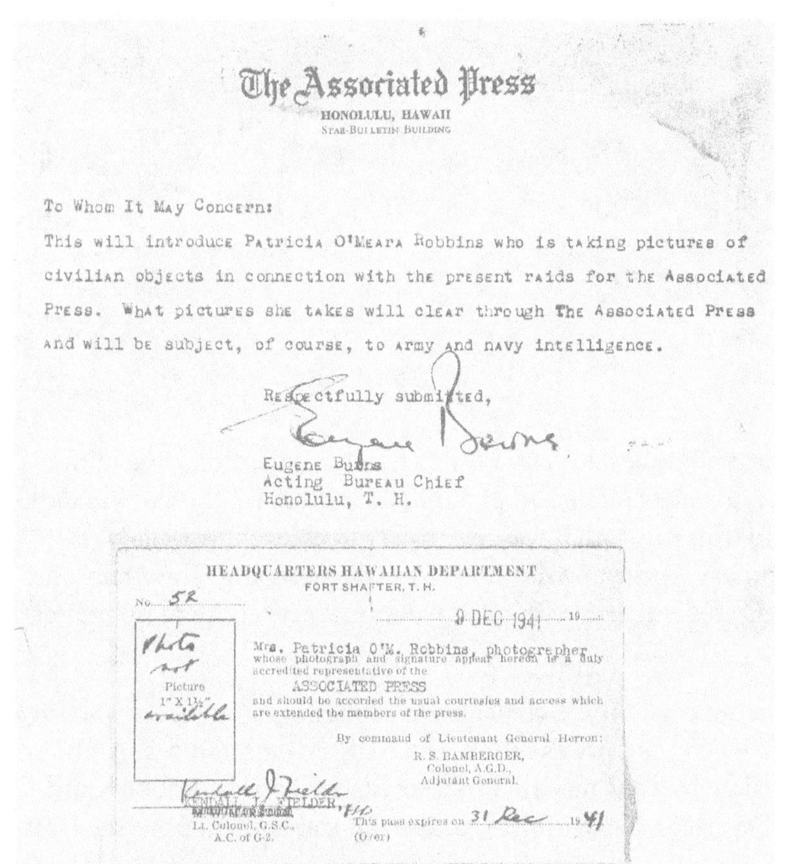

The Associated Press
HONOLULU, HAWAII
Star-Bulletin Building

To Whom It May Concern:

This will introduce Patricia O'Meara Robbins who is taking pictures of civilian objects in connection with the present raids for the Associated Press. What pictures she takes will clear through The Associated Press and will be subject, of course, to army and navy intelligence.

Respectfully submitted,

Eugene Burns
Acting Bureau Chief
Honolulu, T. H.

HEADQUARTERS HAWAIIAN DEPARTMENT
FORT SHAFTER, T. H.

No. 52

9 DEC 1941

Photo not available
Picture 1" X 1½"

Mrs. Patricia O'M. Robbins, photographer whose photograph and signature appear hereon is a duly accredited representative of the
ASSOCIATED PRESS
and should be accorded the usual courtesies and access which are extended the members of the press.

By command of Lieutenant General Herron:

R. S. BAMBERGER,
Colonel, A.G.D.,
Adjutant General.

KENDALL J. FIELDER,
Lt. Colonel, G.S.C.,
A.C. of G-2.

This pass expires on 31 Dec 1941
(Over)

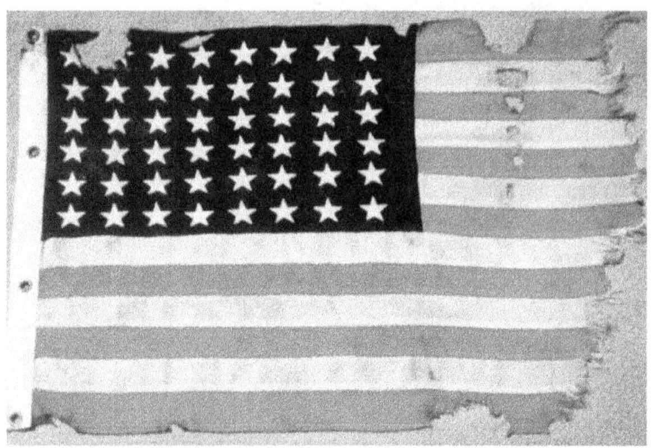

The ensign of the destroyer USS *Shaw* (DD-373), which flew on the stern, was rescued by Lt. Berton A Robbins, Jr., the ship's executive officer, about 9:30 a.m., after the *Shaw* was bombed in drydock at Pearl Harbor, December 7, 1941.

Left: press credentials issued to Pat by the Army and the Associated Press. The Navy also issued credentials. Many of Pat's Pearl Harbor aftermath images are credited instead to the military as official photos or to the AP.

Immediately after the attack, Hawaiian police faced a new, "strange aspect of law enforcement": the orders of the Military Governor. "Honolulu experienced a phenomenal growth in population during the latter part of 1941 and during 1942 due to the increases in the strength of the armed forces. Despite an almost doubled population there was a decrease in criminal offenses," attributed to operations of the Provost Court presided over by military judges which conducted all criminal trials. Other factors included "blackout regulations, early curfew, and other restrictions of movements and activities of the general public. Nearly every employable person was working, and many worked a considerable amount of overtime."[3]

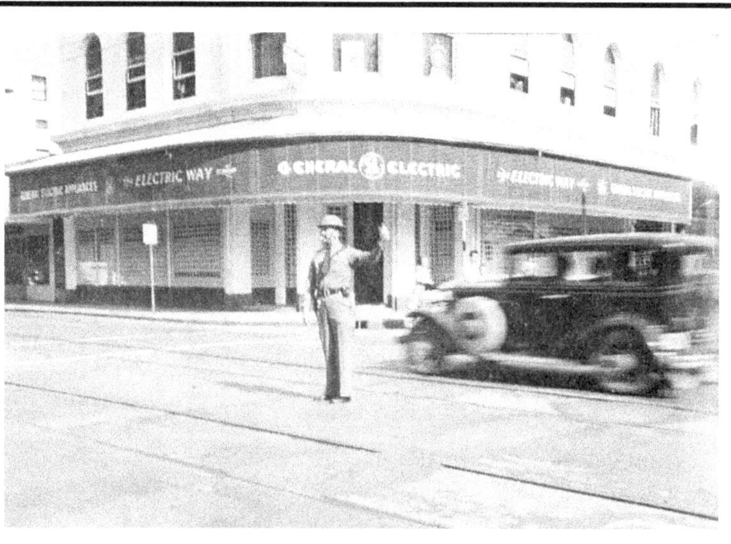

Honolulu policeman Ah Num Ho, complete with helmet, downtown, December 1941. No traffic = no gasoline.

"There was no fear until later that night of the seventh when we started thinking about our rumbling stomachs and wondering where our father was," Carroll recalled, "and when our Mother cried for the first time."

The Mutual Telephone Company evolved from the 1883 establishment of the Hawaiian Telcom, founded as a charter company granted by King Kalakua, with deep ties to Hawaiian culture and people, the *Star-Bulletin* reported. Honolulu store owners taped windows to prevent glass shattering in an attack.

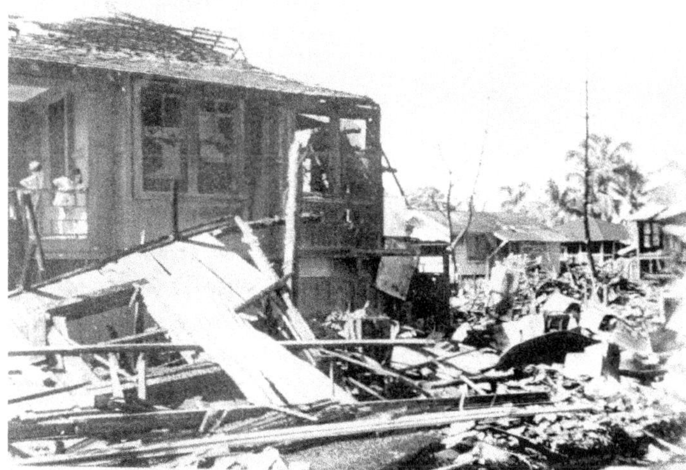

From a porch, Berton and Carroll survey wrecked houses near Pearl City, Oahu, caused by either Japanese bombs or falling ammunition from U.S. anti-aircraft fire, December 1941.

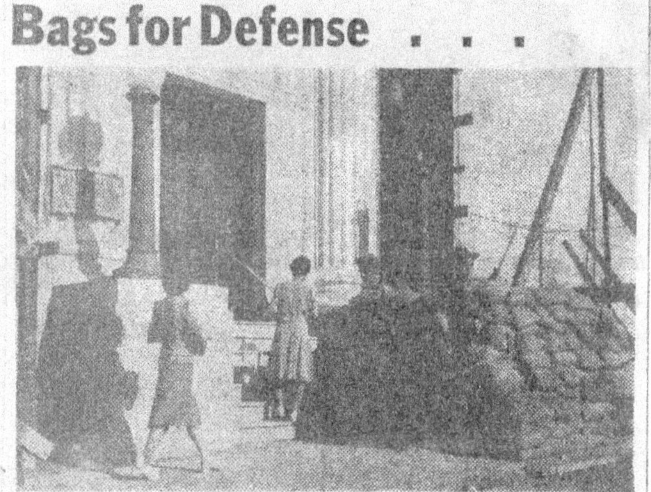

Bags for Defense . . .

BAGS AND BAYONETS—Alert guards stand watch with rifles and fixed bayonets behind a barricade of sandbags in front of the main building of the Mutual Telephone Co. on Alakea St. This defense scene is typical of scores to be found throughout the city.

'Bags for Defense,' Pat's Associated Press photo published in the *Honolulu Star-Bulletin*, January 2, 1942. The sandbags barricaded the strategic and essential Mutual Telephone Company building on Alakea Street downtown. 'The defense scene is typical of scores to be found throughout the city,' the photo caption says.[2]

Pearl City, located then eleven miles west of downtown Honolulu on Pearl Harbor, was in the attackers' approach routes and subject to intended or accidental damage. Pat took her children on all photo-shoot assignments. What else was she to do with them? Sometimes she rented an ancient, rickety vehicle for the trips. Carroll recalled, "Not only were the houses bombed out, but you could see Christmas toys and gifts. I burst into tears and Mother had to control me."

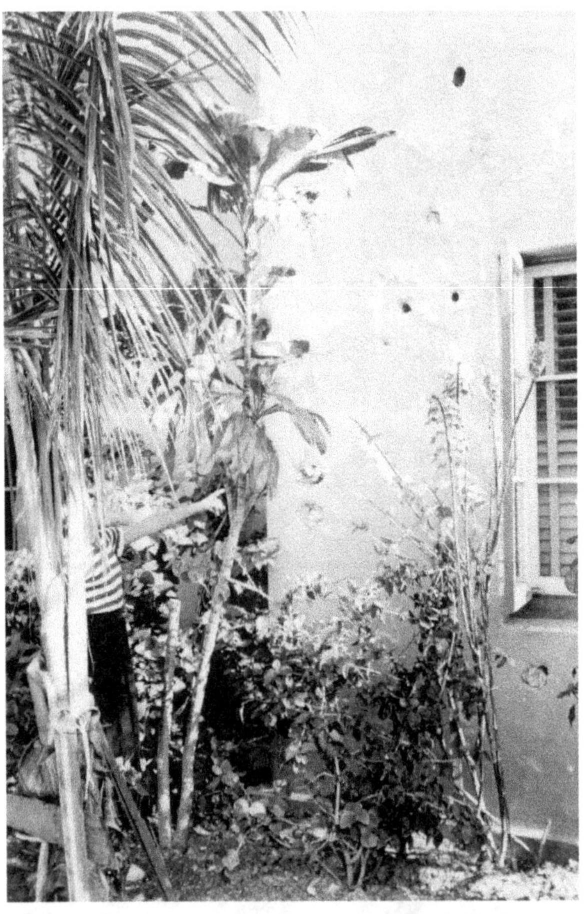

Berton points to pockmarks caused by shrapnel or bullets on a house one block from the Robbins' hotel, December 1941.

The Japanese targeted military facilities around Honolulu as well as ships in Pearl Harbor, the air fields, and Army posts, and primarily avoided commercial or residential areas. Much of the damage around Honolulu resulted from unexploded U.S. anti-aircraft shells falling in civilian areas.

Hundreds of defensive concrete pillboxes and heavy gun emplacements ringed Oahu beginning in 1942, along with numerous anti-aircraft batteries around the island. The enemy never returned.

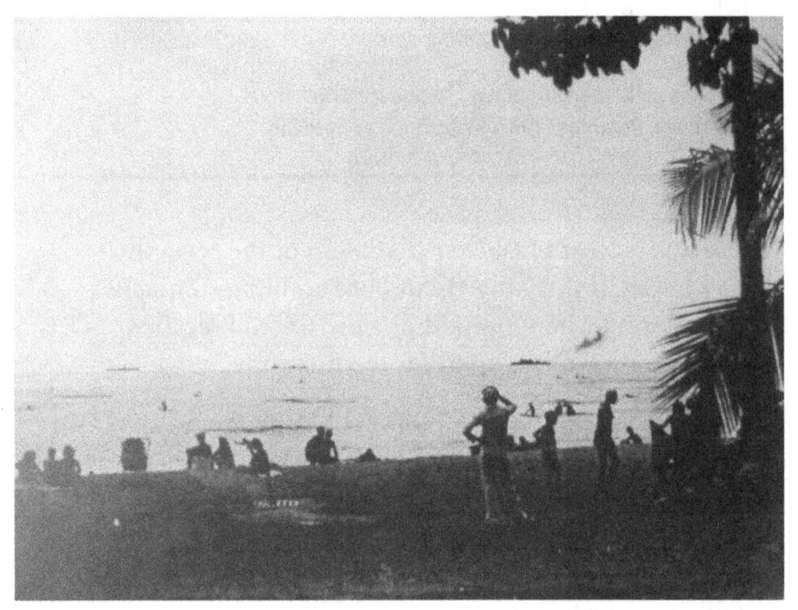

Above: watching the ships enter and leave the Honolulu area, 1942. This quickly became a pastime of Navy families.

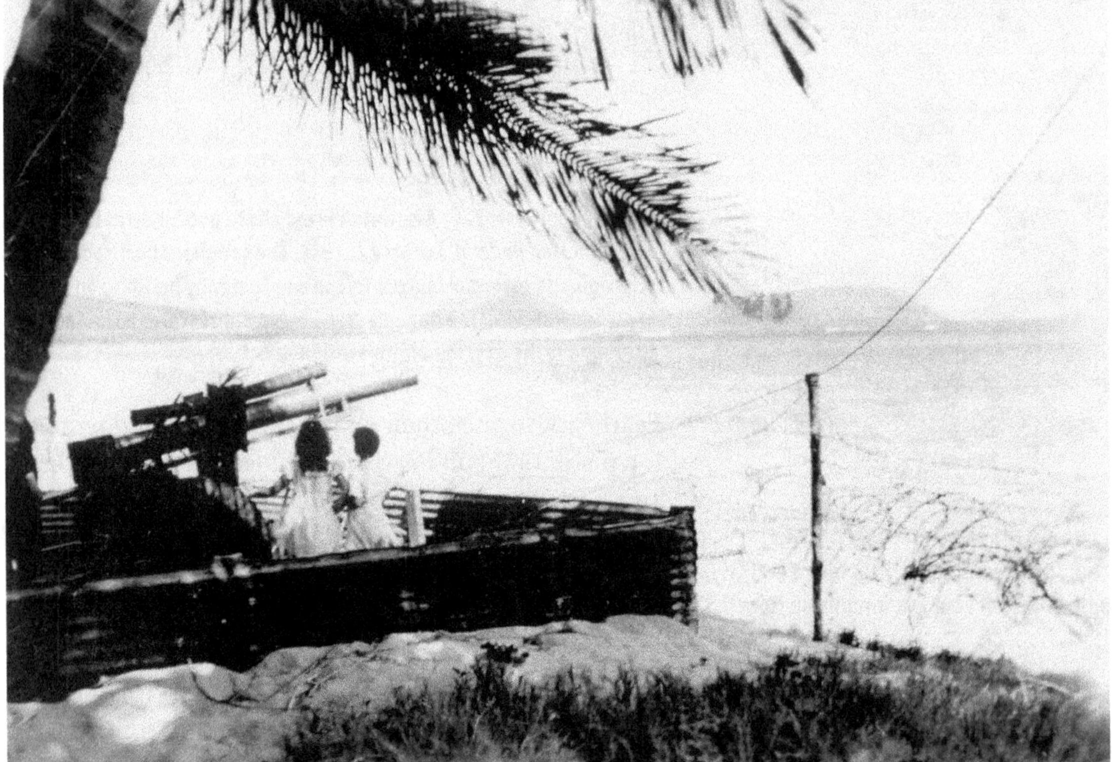

Left: Carroll and Berton play in an unmanned defensive gun emplacement and barbed wire along the Oahu coastline, early 1942.

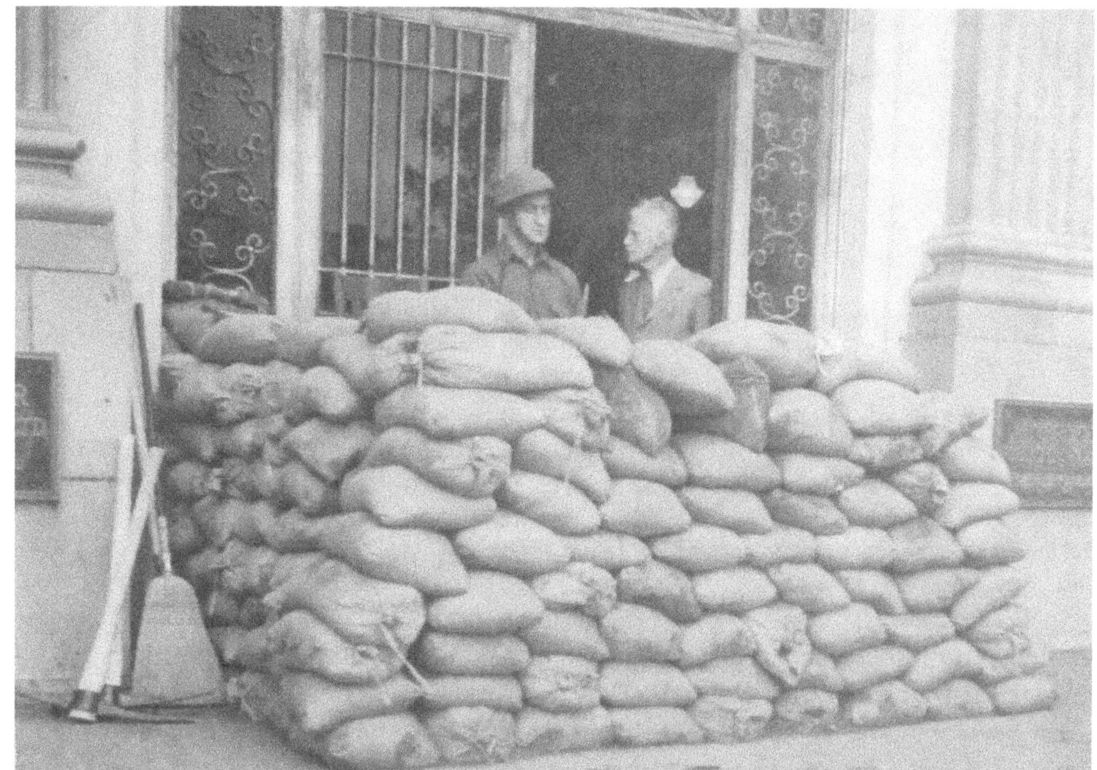

Sandbags and a soldier protect the *Honolulu Advertiser* newspaper offices, 1942.

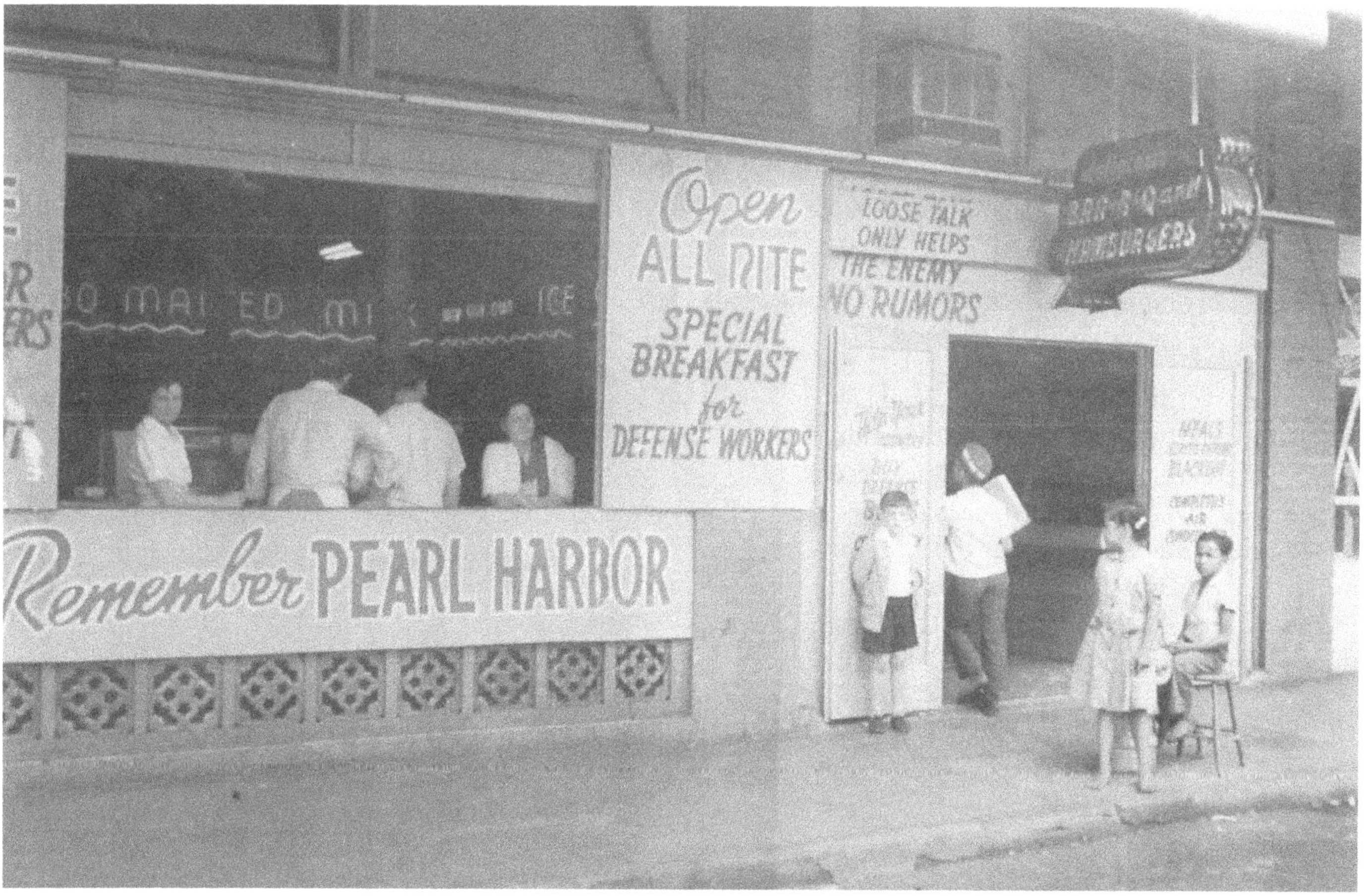

24-hour fast-food joint on infamous Hotel Street in downtown Honolulu. 'Mother wouldn't allow Berton to go inside; so he stood at the door.' 1942.

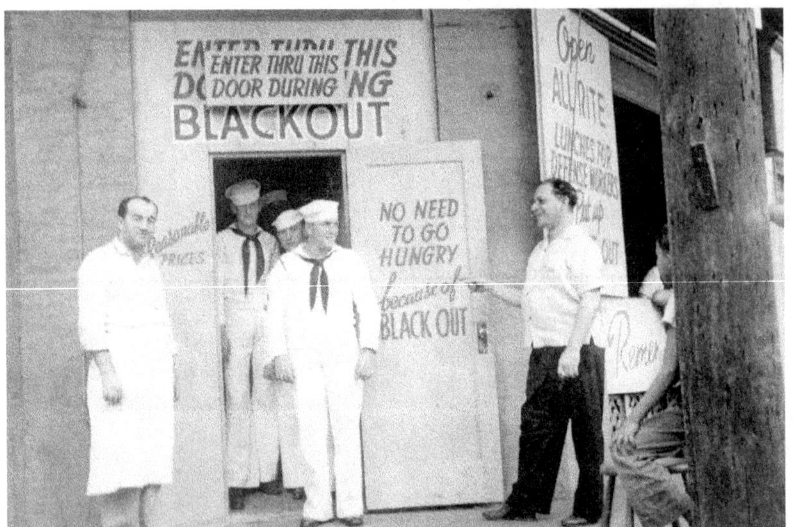

Sailors and management gather at the Times Square Grill on the infamous Hotel Street in downtown Honolulu, 1942.

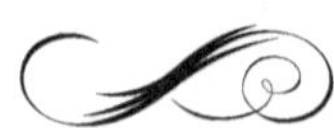

To Pacific sailors without a Paris, London, or Rome, notorious Hotel Street emerged as the fleet's only compromise "recreation zone." The street and vice rang synonymously: slop chutes (bars), juke (box) joints, dingy restaurants, tattoo parlors, games of chance, drunkenness, and brothels - prostitutes and fistfights everywhere. Both before and during the war, as part of their passage and indoctrination, sailors and soldiers with idle time prowled its establishments looking for entertainment or physical satisfaction, either resisting or falling victim to its temptations.

More specifically, here's one scene:[4] "The reality was that after the beginning of hostilities, the presence of over 30,000 soldiers, sailors and war workers on any given day in Honolulu's vice district had attracted hundreds of sex workers from the mainland. Bowing to that reality and believing that the women were important to the morale of servicemen, the military authorities elected to tolerate and regulate the situation. More precisely, they over-regulated": price, duration of an encounter, hours of service, and the women's physical condition, and "they also severely circumscribed their private lives."

Nevertheless, the women "thrived financially," making between $30,000 and $40,000 a year "when the average working woman was considered fortunate to make $2,000." In 1942 the women challenged authority, raising prices to $5.00 for three minutes, a move summarily dismissed by the police chief. Hotel Street experienced a twenty-two-day prostitutes' strike, causing "an enormous uproar" among the servicemen. The authorities relented.

During the seventieth anniversary week, I strolled Hotel Street and found many wartime-era structures still in use. I could easily visualize 1942.

Once the government instituted martial law on Oahu after the attack, about three hundred American ROTC students of Japanese descent joined the Hawaii Territorial Guard, were issued rifles, and began security details. One month later the government discharged the members without explanation and classified them as "enemy aliens."

During the war the military used the 'Iolani Palace, formerly the home of Queen Liliuokalani and Hawaii's governors, as its Hawaii headquarters.

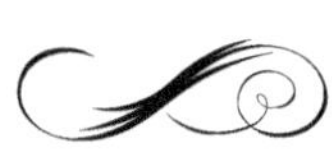

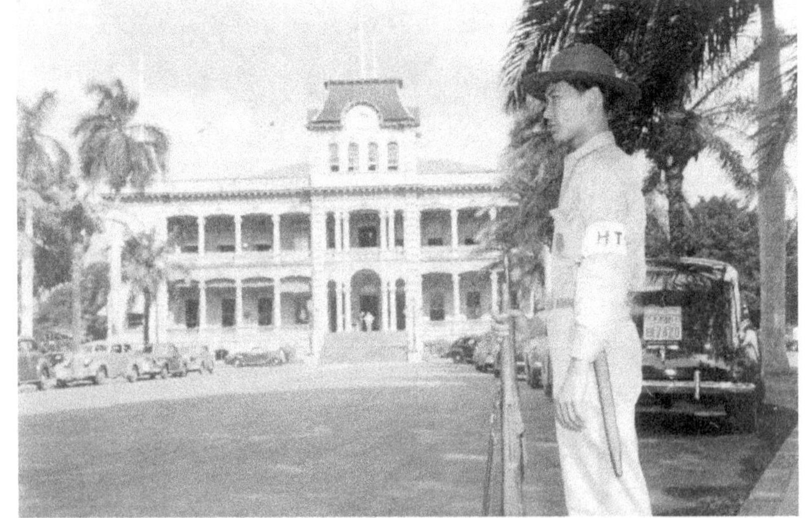
A soldier from the Hawaii Territorial Guard stands guard at the entrance to the 'Iolani Palace, South King Street in Honolulu, armed with Springfield rifle Model 1903, December 1941

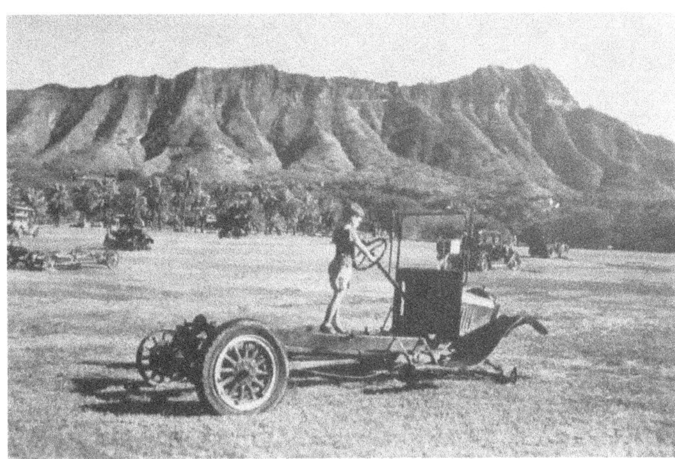

Near Waikiki Beach, with the famous Diamond Head looming, Berton plays on vehicles and other obstacles placed in fields to thwart potential Japanese landing attack sites, Honolulu, 1942.

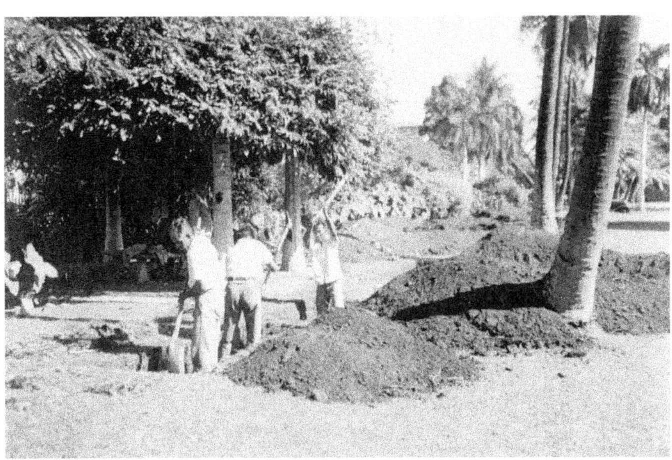

Inmates from the Oahu prison dig air raid trench shelters on parkland in downtown Honolulu, December 1941. Pat's kids played in air raid trenches prepared in open spaces.

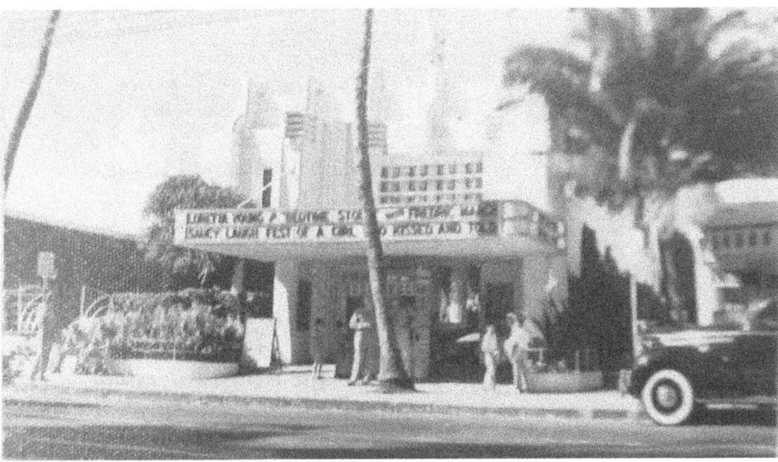

A Waikiki movie theater showing Pat's friend Loretta Young in *Bedtime Story*, billed as a 'Saucy Laugh Fest of a Girl Who Kissed and Told,' Honolulu, 1942.

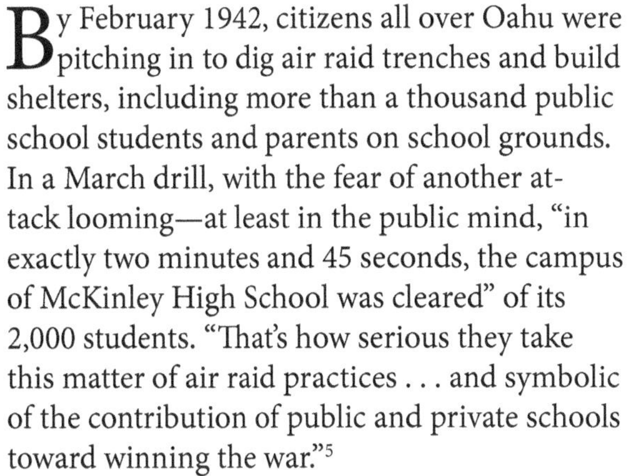

By February 1942, citizens all over Oahu were pitching in to dig air raid trenches and build shelters, including more than a thousand public school students and parents on school grounds. In a March drill, with the fear of another attack looming—at least in the public mind, "in exactly two minutes and 45 seconds, the campus of McKinley High School was cleared" of its 2,000 students. "That's how serious they take this matter of air raid practices . . . and symbolic of the contribution of public and private schools toward winning the war."[5]

Here we see the trench-shelters in use.

Mademoiselle magazine paid Pat $75 for the photos showing "War and Defense Problems of Women Students at the University of Hawaii" in its July 1942 issue. By May 1942, the Associated Students of the University of Hawaii had contributed $15,000 toward a national war bond drive among American universities.

"Mother could not find any place to leave us and took Berton and me on her shoots," Carroll said. "We were her bag carriers. The students thought we were oh-so cute."

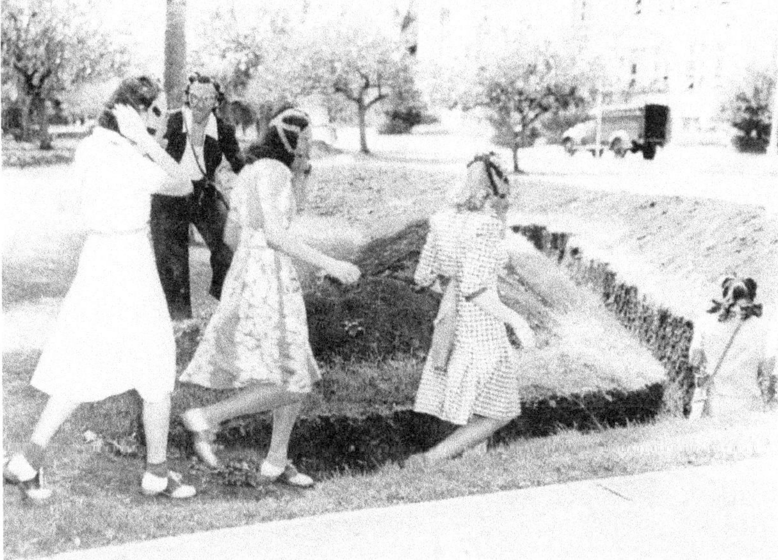

University of Hawaii coeds wearing gas masks heading into the trench-shelters during a drill, 1942.

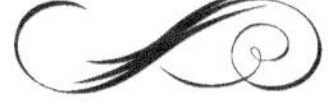

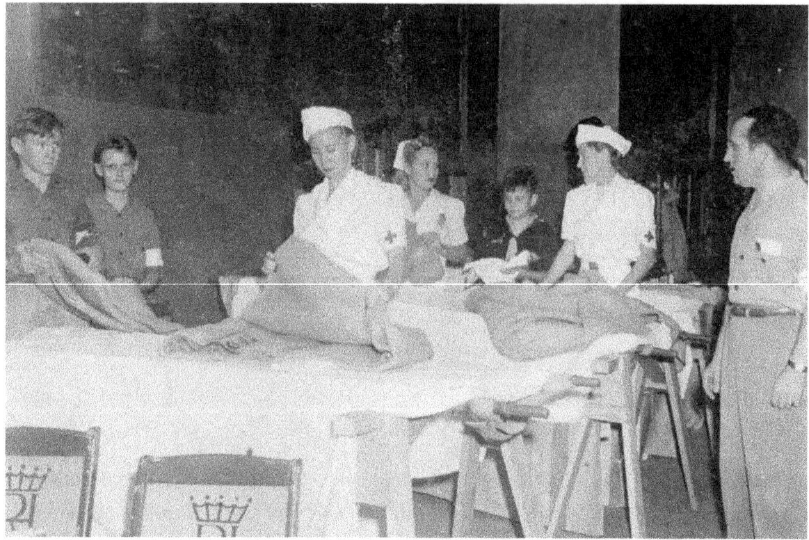

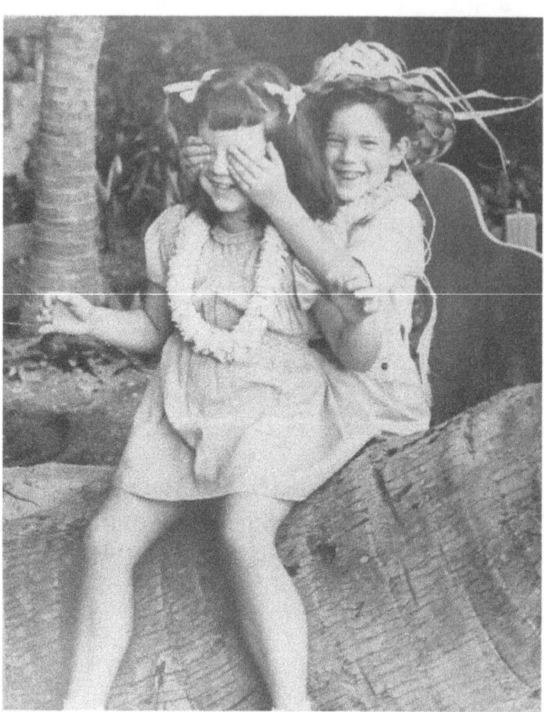

Above: Boy Scouts join Red Cross volunteers preparing blankets for first-aid care at the famous landmark Royal Hawaiian Hotel on Waikiki, Honolulu, December 1941.

Right: Carroll and Berton play among the air raid trenches and palm trees in Honolulu, Hawaii, December 1941.

"Each child had to be fitted with a gas mask and carry them with us at all times," Carroll said. On December 7, 1975 when I advanced President Gerald Ford's trip to Pearl Harbor, coincidentally I visited the old Comstock Apartments Hotel just a week before it was to be demolished for a shopping plaza. On my latest visit to the area in 2011, only the seemingly isolated but majestic Royal Hawaiian, surrounded by new development, remains recognizable in that area.

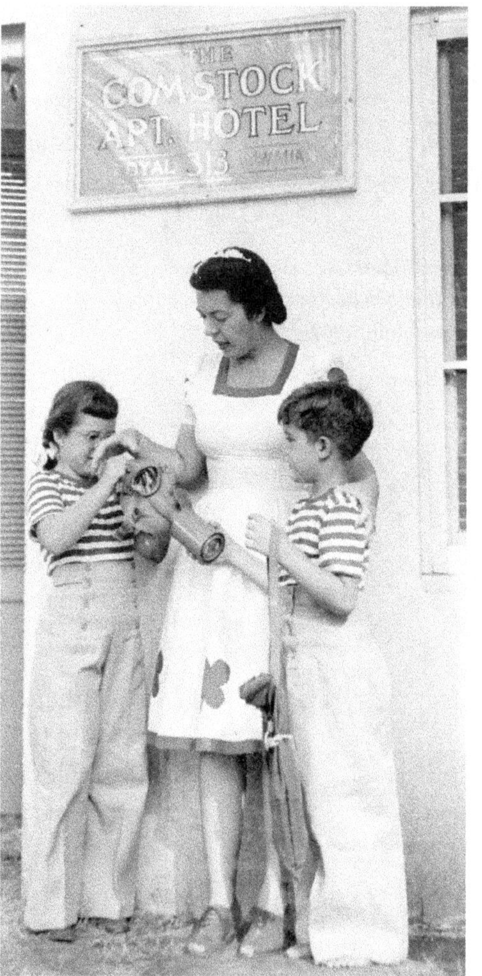

Pat Robbins with Carroll and Berton trying on gas masks at their Waikiki residence until August 1942, the Comstock Apartments Hotel across from the Royal Hawaiian Hotel, December 1941.

"Mother was asked to take photos showing how Hawaii was transitioning to war. We were told to expect another attack," Carroll said.

When the Royal Hawaiian opened in 1927, it "ushered in a new era of luxurious resort travel to Hawaii." Until World War II, it hosted numerous celebrities, financiers, and heads of state. In January 1942, the Navy obtained an exclusive lease as a rest and recreation center for Pacific Fleet Navy personnel. It re-opened to the public in 1947 after a nearly $2 million renovation.[6] My 6-day stay there in December 2011 found the restored "Pink Lady" still appearing as she gloriously did during the war.

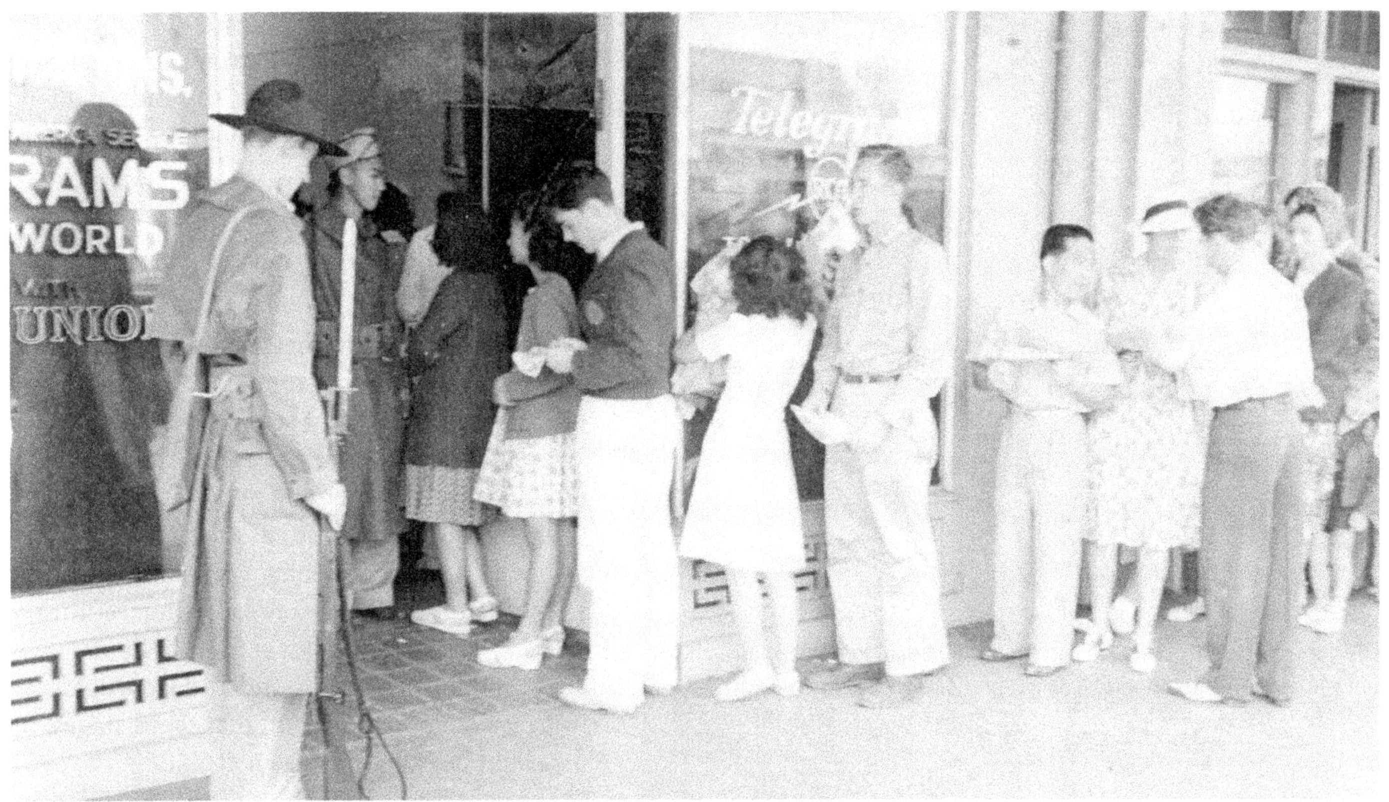

Under armed military guard, long lines form outside the Honolulu telegraph office; people wanted to let the folks back home know, 'I'm okay.'

The children "were supposed to have been trained so when she asked for a certain type of bulb or film or accessory or tripod stand we would be able to produce," said Carroll. "Her entire mind would be on what she was shooting, totally absorbed by what she was doing. She would frame a picture with her hands, then pose us and told us to hold things." One of them would carry a litter bag to pick up her trash. "Pretty soon a little kid's arm would fall off from holding it. Little kids can't keep still for hours. We would stand on one foot and then the other, and she would get mad: 'Stand up.'"

This went on often when Pat was on her missions. Looking back, Carroll saw early-on how natural it would be to misunderstand her, if not to dislike her.

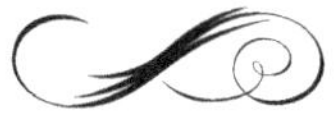

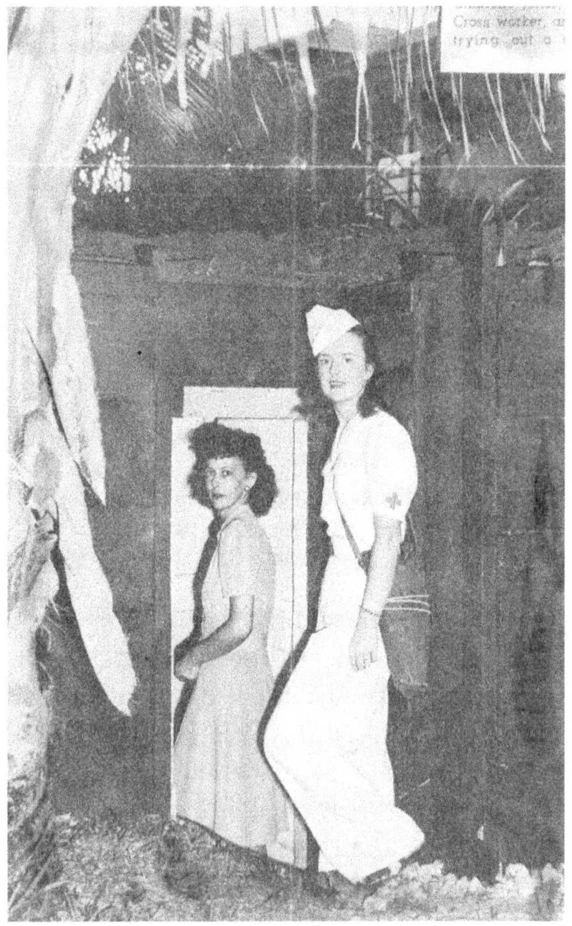

Pat shot a piece for *Mademoiselle* magazine on prominent young California women visiting Honolulu, which along with an assignment from *Look* magazine gave her 'legal' passage to Hawaii in November 1941. Here she catches them entering a downtown bomb shelter for her 'War Curbs Social Life of Southern Californians in Honolulu,' appearing in the Photogravure section of the *Los Angeles Times*, March 29, 1942.

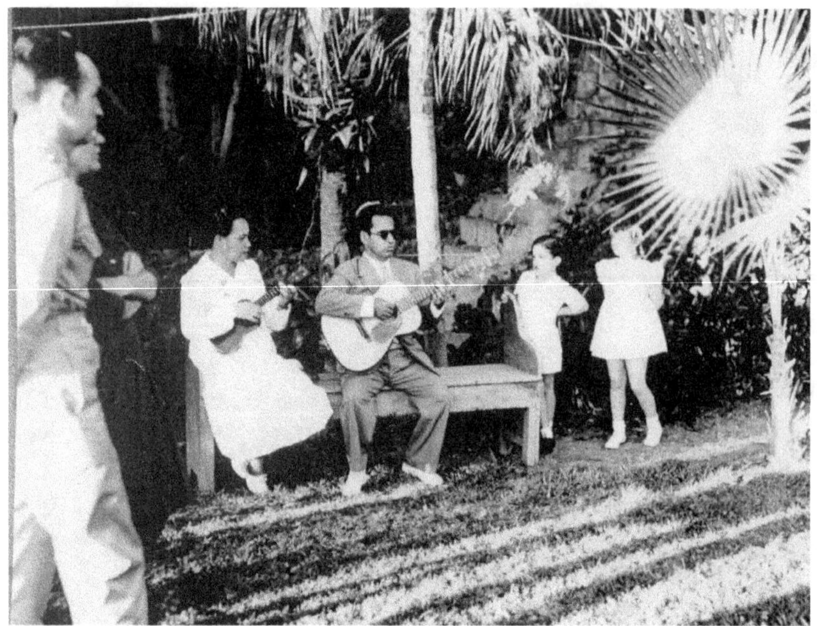

Life goes on at a Waikiki garden party despite the war; Hawaiian musicians with Berton and Carroll as spectators and, sometimes, fellow performers. Early 1942.

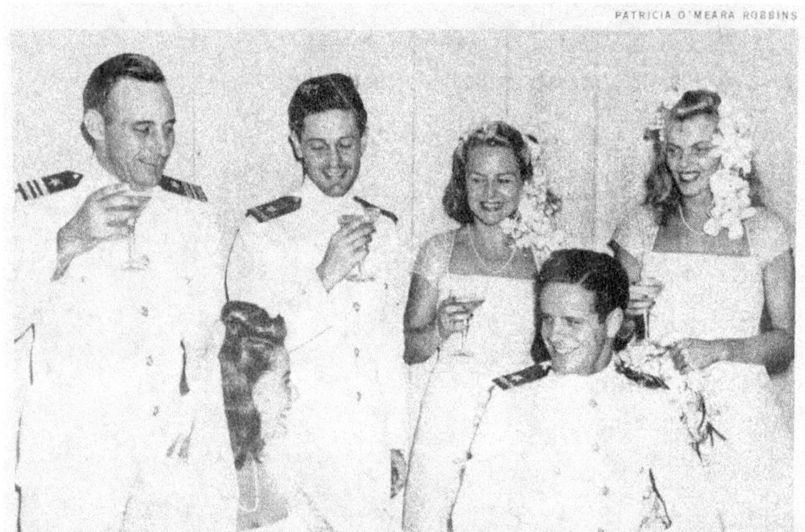

Navy wedding in Honolulu. Yes, Pat also shot a number of weddings. This one ran in *Town and Country* magazine, November 1942.

Social events attracted Pat and camera for both work and play. She knew one of the islands' most powerful couple, the industrialist Walter and Louise Dillingham. About him, *Time* Magazine stated: "Yet, for all his fondness for the old ways, Dillingham probably did more to mold a modern Hawaii than any other man . . . . During World War II, when Franklin Roosevelt wanted to know about the situation in Hawaii, he phoned Walter Dillingham." He was called "Hawaii's greatest builder."[7]

Military weddings and social life boomed. Carroll recalled, 'Berton and I [watching the musicians] were not shy and would often dance and sing Hawaiian songs for the crowd.'

"Adults would egg us on. At first we didn't know the Hawaiian songs so we just made it up. The entertainers got a kick out of us and taught us the movements, and we'd be called on to 'entertain the troops' so to speak." With her husband at sea, Pat often attended, dressing the children in their finest. Carroll and Berton learned the music and movements of Hawaiian songs and started doing the hula. Once at a luau, "Sailors and soldiers were watching and laughing. Mother almost lost it and told us to stop. Pretty soon the word got around and we would be asked to 'perform' on makeshift stages, would be called up because onlookers thought it was funny to see little kids dancing. We were compensated in food."

Carroll and Berton finagled invitations to weddings. She remembered: "'Pat, they're a riot,' people said about us. There weren't many white kids on the island. We loved weddings because we could eat lots of food."

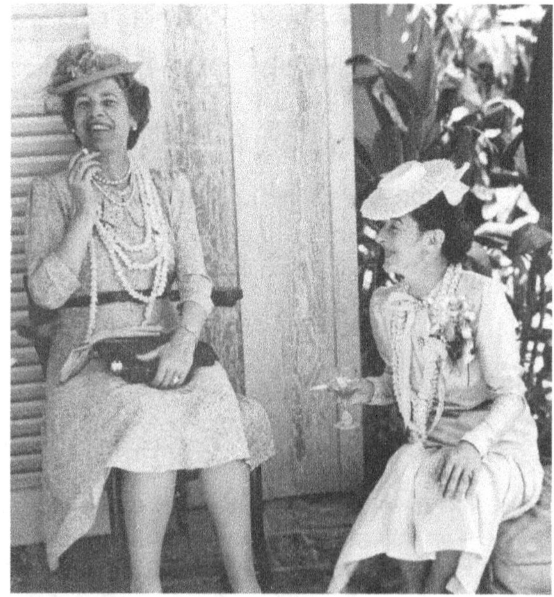

Mrs. Walter F. (Louise) Dillingham (left) at a Navy wedding, Honolulu, 1942.

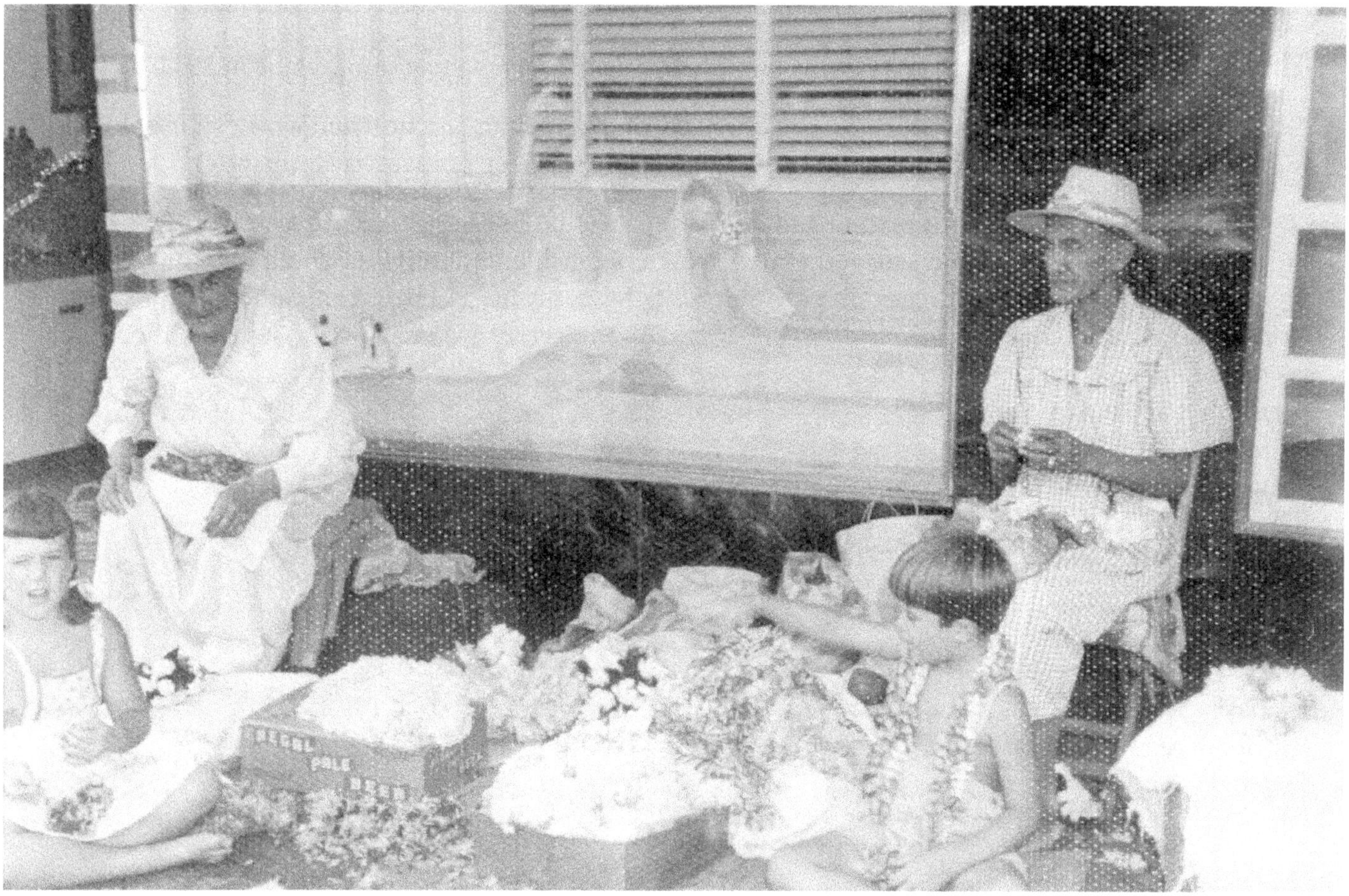

Caroll and Berton with the lei makers of Waikiki Beach, a Hawaiian institution, Honolulu, 1942.

Carroll recalled, "Sometimes Mother would leave us with the lei-makers on Waikiki. They made a lot of money off of us because it was very unusual to see white kids working with the leimakers on the sidewalks. We made leis right along with them. We loved them, they loved us. They would sit there and hum Hawaiian songs, and taught us the hand movements. It was good for their business to have two haole (how-o-lee) kids talking pidgin English with them. People would toss money down there even if they didn't buy a lei.

"We were also friends with the Waikiki beach boys who showed us how to walk on coral and not get bitten by an eel. We learned how to body surf, pull outriggers, and were very good swimmers. We got into the movies for free by going around to the side door exit. Of course, we were not attending school either."

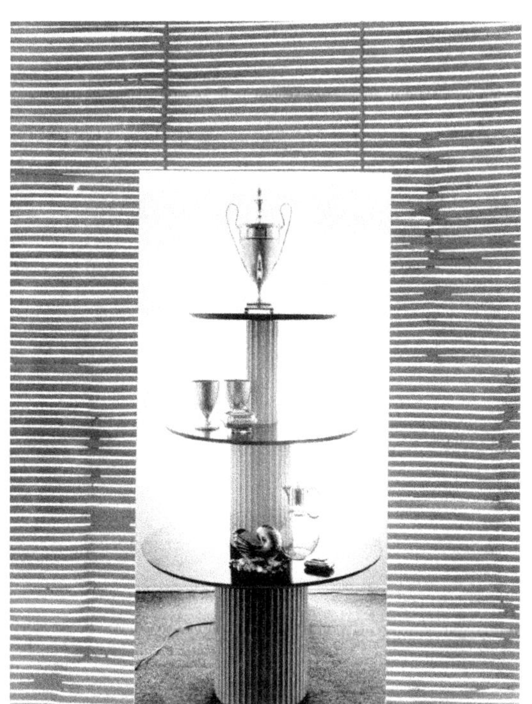

Advertisement: Cups on a tri-level stand, for the George Mellon Agency and Gumps department store, Honolulu, 1942.

The advertising agency placed a backdrop of venetian blinds behind the cup and stemware and dishes to help the merchandise stand out. This effect became the signature for the upscale Gumps department store, located next to the landmark Royal Hawaiian Hotel on Waikiki and across the street from the Robbinses' hotel. Pat shot numerous photo ads for Gumps and other businesses, which ran in Honolulu and California magazines and newspapers.

This is Pat's story in her words, as published in *Popular Photography* magazine in 1944:[8]

"War wives at home have an ideal opportunity to make photography a practical and worthwhile hobby. It is a mystery to me why more of us haven't taken it up in order to keep our faraway husbands posted . . . .

"I was in Hawaii when the war broke out and was fortunate to be able to help record a bit of history in the making there. I made pictures for Associated Press as a pinch hitter until they could get a staff photographer . . . . For a couple of weeks after the outbreak of war, my life as a newspaper photographer in Honolulu was rather a ticklish business. No one was allowed to carry a camera on the streets without the army's OK. I had to get permission and a photographer's card from army intelligence. More than once when I was out taking pictures, a 'doing his duty' soldier came running at me with his rifle aimed squarely at my stomach . . . . They were just about ready to shoot first and ask questions afterward . . . .

"My habit of doing my own developing and printing—even in far-off lands—has found me mixing my solutions in some of the oddest places, and projecting by means of such queer contraptions that only facetiously could be referred to as enlargers. I had my two-by-four bathroom blacked out in Hawaii and borrowed an enlarger

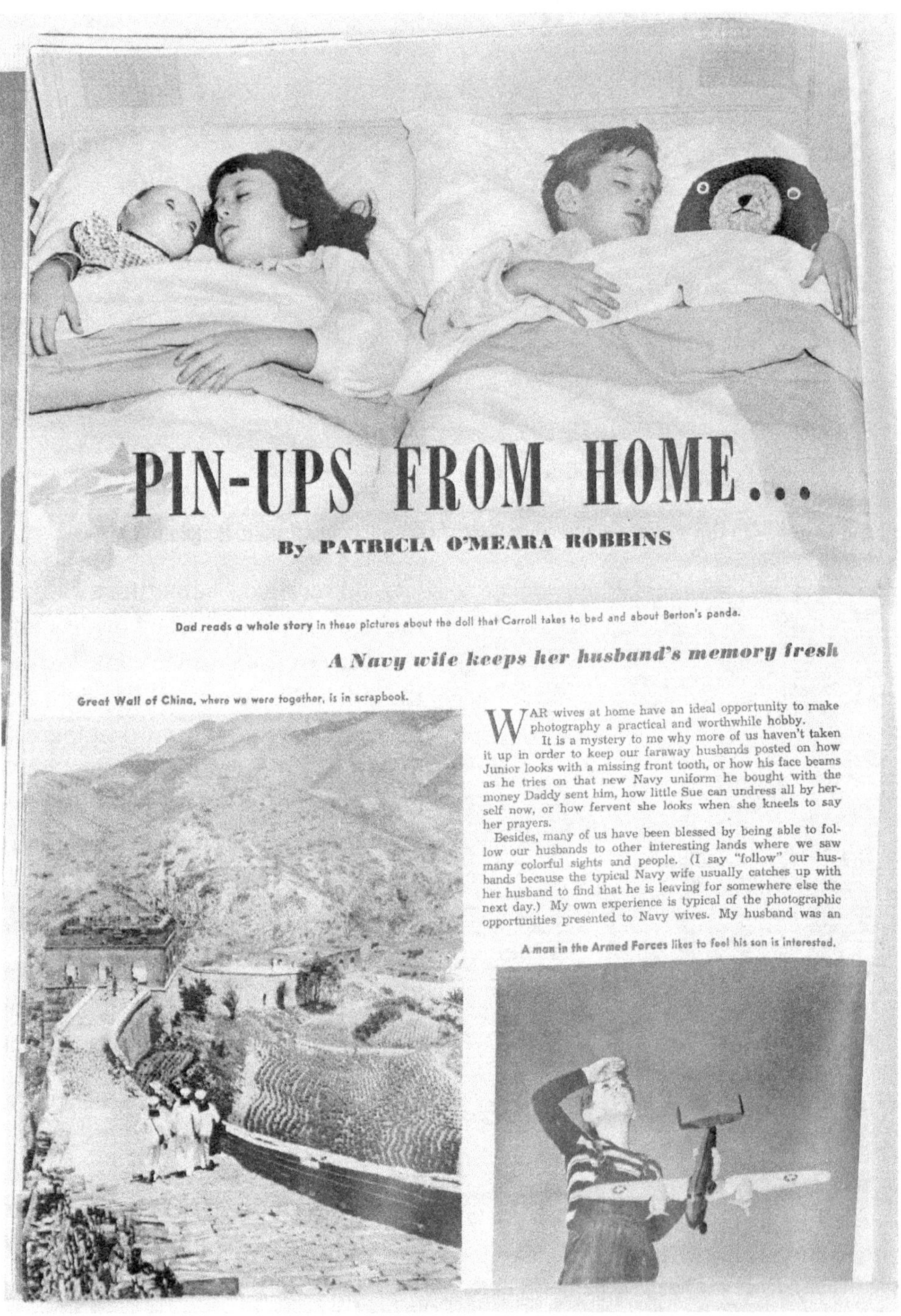

PIN-UPS FROM HOME...

By PATRICIA O'MEARA ROBBINS

Dad reads a whole story in these pictures about the doll that Carroll takes to bed and about Berton's panda.

A Navy wife keeps her husband's memory fresh

Great Wall of China, where we were together, is in scrapbook.

WAR wives at home have an ideal opportunity to make photography a practical and worthwhile hobby.

It is a mystery to me why more of us haven't taken it up in order to keep our faraway husbands posted on how Junior looks with a missing front tooth, or how his face beams as he tries on that new Navy uniform he bought with the money Daddy sent him, how little Sue can undress all by herself now, or how fervent she looks when she kneels to say her prayers.

Besides, many of us have been blessed by being able to follow our husbands to other interesting lands where we saw many colorful sights and people. (I say "follow" our husbands because the typical Navy wife usually catches up with her husband to find that he is leaving for somewhere else the next day.) My own experience is typical of the photographic opportunities presented to Navy wives. My husband was an

A man in the Armed Forces likes to feel his son is interested.

'Pin-Ups from Home . . . ,' Pat's photojournalism piece in *Popular Photography* magazine, February 1944, an illustrated essay about the importance of photography to help keep servicemen in touch with the families during wartime.

that looked like a shoe box with a strange bulge at one end and some sort of lens at the other. A good hot day spent in such a cubbyhole, coupled with the anticipation of seeing whether the next negative would bring a salon print or just an everyday shot, plus the excitement when I would on occasion find a print that had possibilities . . . .

"The only way my husband, who has been in virtually every major naval engagement in the present war, has been able to keep well-acquainted with his children is through photography. He takes great delight in receiving pictures . . . . In the past three years he has been able to be with us only two months. I try to mirror my husband's America—his family—for him . . . [such as] every new expression on our children's faces, every new trait . . . .

"I have done many morale shots and publicity photographs as one of my contributions to the war effort, but how better could I add to Navy morale than by making pin-ups of my family . . . . Pictures of his children mean more to him than all of Hollywood's glamour girls or Varga filmily clad curvaceous creatures. How better could my husband get his mind off the rigors of a heavy siege of duty as an admiral's aide in action at Midway . . . or after strenuous days in the South Pacific and more recently in the Aleutians . . . ?

"I have trained the children to pose ever since they were babies, and consequently they now fall automatically into a pose . . . . [They] have their own cameras and have made wonderful headway learning to develop and print."

The children at play or their daily routine pictured in a snapshot brings faraway fathers closer to home.

with pictures of their children and travels

ensign fresh out of Annapolis when we were married ten years ago, and he was immediately assigned to China. I tagged along.

I had been taking pictures ever since I was seven years old and had studied art. I loved the drama and color of old China, and spent much time capturing, both with still and movie cameras, the quaintness, the Oriental color, and the slow-moving pageant I found there.

However, it was difficult to obtain pictures of the Chinese themselves. They have a superstition that your little black box will capture their souls along with their images. Most of them would hide their faces or turn their backs when I approached with one of my Graflexes ready for action. It didn't take long, though, to find some who would gladly let me "capture their souls" for a small coin.

I followed my husband over most of the Orient—usually finding that Uncle Sam wanted him somewhere else just as I caught up with him. From Shanghai I played follow-the-leader with him to Hong Kong, then to Peking, Nankow, Tsingtao, Chingwangtao and Shankaikuan, where the Great Wall reaches the sea . . . clicking my camera shutters merrily all the way.

My daughter, Carrol Eloise, was born in Shanghai a year after we were married, and almost immediately I began keeping a camera record of her week-to-week changes.

My husband and I did manage to make the trip together over the Great Wall of China by sedan chairs, and I made a film record of this colorful trek.

Then on to Manila where I was on hand to take movie shots of the historical first landing of the China Clipper in Manila Bay. Then more playing hop-scotch from place to place—Olongapo, Cavite, and Raugio in the (*Continued on page 86*)

Rare moments Dad shared with his children are precious shots.

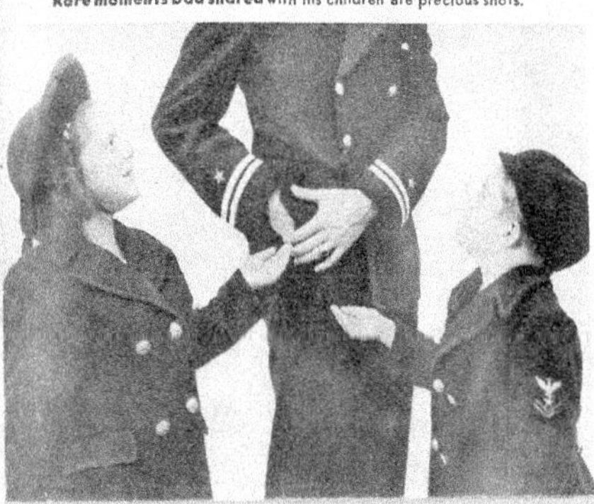

Sea voyages are part of a Navy family's routine.

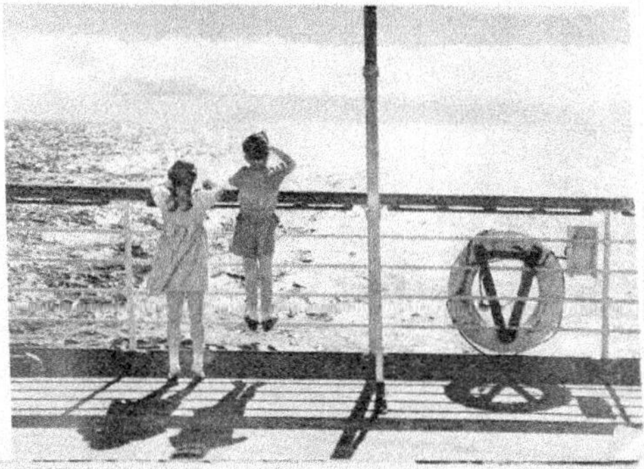

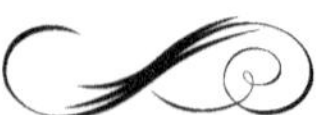

Pat and the children returned by ship to California in August 1942, ironically escorted by the destroyer USS *Shaw* with its temporary bow replacement. Pat immersed herself in her career and social life while Bob was away. O'Meara relatives in California faithfully supported her and the children; Bob's relatives all lived in New England.

Like so many thousands of American spouses and parents during wartime, on March 3, 1945, two weeks after he was hit, Pat received a Western Union telegram notifying her of Bob's combat wounds.

"THE NAVY DEPARTMENT REGRETS TO INFORM YOU THAT YOUR HUSBAND COMMANDER BERTON ALDRICH ROBBINS JR USN HAS BEEN WOUNDED IN ACTION WHILE IN THE SERVICE OF HIS COUNTRY. THE DEPARTMENT APPRECIATES YOUR GREAT ANXIETY BUT EXTENT OF WOUNDS NOT NOW AVAILABLE AND DELAY IN RECEIPT OF DETAILS MUST NECESSARILY BE EXPECTED BUT WILL BE FURNISHED YOU PROMPTLY IF RECEIVED. TO PREVENT POSSIBLE AID TO OUR ENEMIES PLEASE DO NOT DIVULGE THE NAME OF HIS SHIP OR STATION."[9]

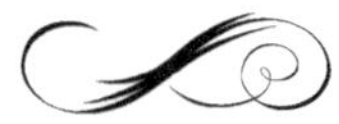

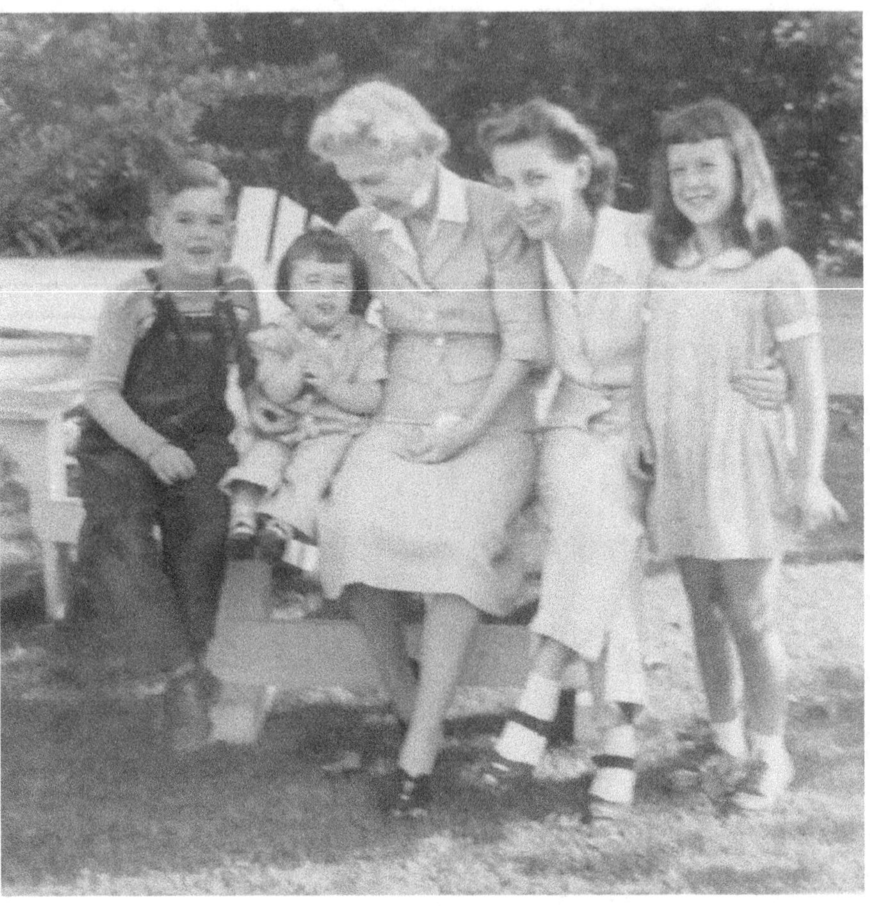

Robbins-O'Meara people, Los Angeles, 1942. Berton III, Kathleen O'Meara (Jean and Carroll O'Meara's daughter), grandmother Kitty O'Meara, radio actress Jean van der Pyle (O'Meara), and Carroll.

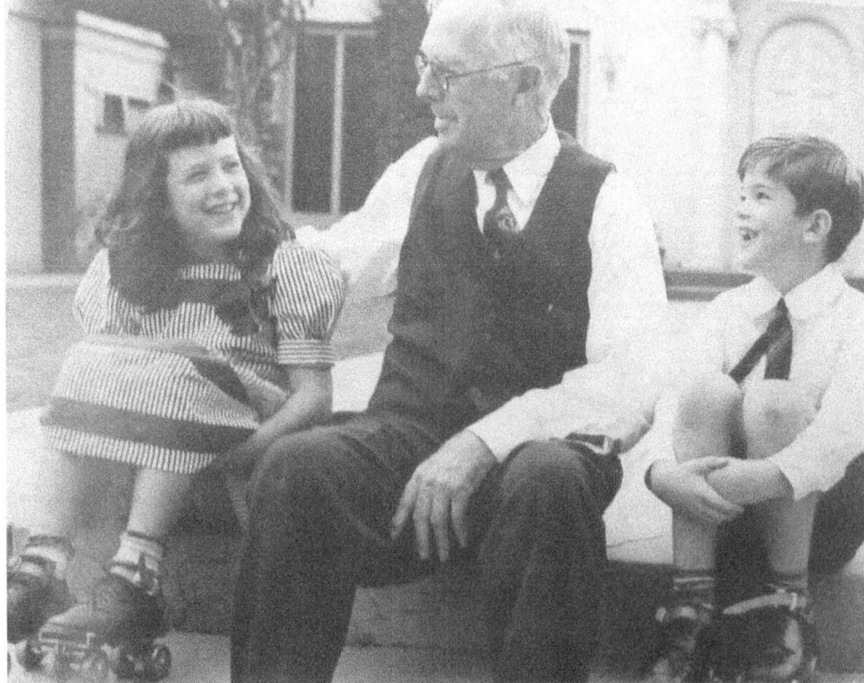

Carroll and Berton with grandfather William Patrick O'Meara, Los Angeles, mid-1940's. The kids played this very structured 'old family/old school' gentleman, and he let them.

A Bureau of Naval Personnel letter to Pat of May 19 provided more details than the telegram contained. "Your husband received sustained multiple shrapnel wounds on 17 February 1945 while serving in the Asiatic area . . . . He is receiving treatment at the United States Receiving Hospital, San Francisco, California. More detailed information is not available . . . but it is hoped that you have heard . . . directly from your husband. You may be assured that everything possible is being done to hasten his recovery."

Meanwhile, she received a March 1 letter from Bob in the U.S. Naval Hospital in Hawaii.

"My Darling, This is a brief, and as you can see, dictated note . . . . The ship got slightly damaged and we had a few wounded, the one point out of the ordinary being that this time I was one of the wounded. As a result I am enjoying a long-needed rest . . . .The wound in itself is not serious, but it is temporarily disabling, and it will take a little time for full recovery.

"The damage was done by a fragment of a Japanese mortar shell [sic; actually was from pillbox gun] which struck the ship. The fragment hit me in the neck at the right shoulder, and passed through coming to rest under the left shoulder. This fragment passed so close to the spinal column that it apparently induced a nerve shock, causing a temporary paralysis which is gradually wearing off. I addition I collected two or three small flesh wounds which don't amount to anything. I'm getting very fine attention and care, and expect to be up and around very shortly . . . . /s/ Your sweetheart, Bob."

A shell from a Japanese beach gun hit the destroyer he commanded, the USS *Leutze* (DD-481), while close-in, supporting underwater demolition teams, on February 17. That was two days before the Marines invaded Iwo Jima. Although it caused severe and partially paralyzing wounds to Bob's left arm and leg, he remained on active duty and retired as a rear admiral in 1959.

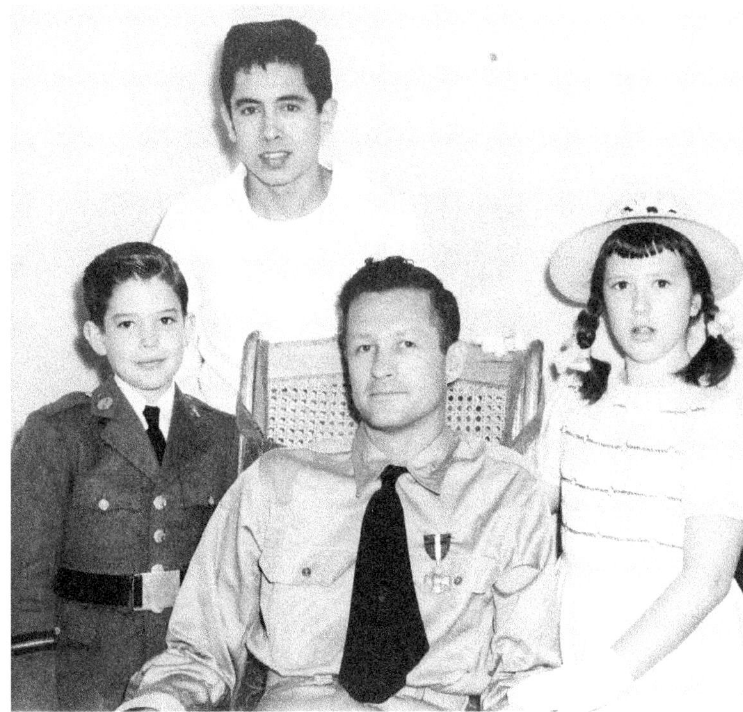

Cdr. Berton A. Robbins, Jr., and children Berton III and Carroll, while he was recovering from Iwo Jima wounds at the Long Beach Naval Hospital, Long Beach, Calif., May 18, 1945. He just received the Navy Cross for valor as commanding officer of the destroyer USS *Leutze* (DD-481) at Surigao Strait, The Philippines, as part of the victorious Battle of Leyte Gulf in October 1944. His torpedo attack helped sink the Japanese battleship *Fuso*.

"Dad was in a wheelchair and could not walk," Carroll said. "Mother took me down separately to see him—so this was the second time. They had a ceremony and lot of people with lots of stripes. They pinned the medal on him, and some of his friends in the Long Beach area attended. Seeing him so restricted during his long recovery frightened and saddened me."

"My grandparents would have wounded soldiers and Marines over to their house for dinner. My grandfather loved to talk to them. They had a standing open house to send over a few; they did that almost every Sunday including when we had family birthdays and events."

"It is a very sad thing that we must fight wars in these days," Bob wrote nine-year old Carroll on June 15, 1943, while at sea on the cruiser USS *Richmond* (CL-9), two months after the ship helped defeat the Japanese in the Aleutians Battle of the Komandorski Islands.[10]

"As long as there are so many stupid and bad people able to cause trouble there will be times when the rest of us will have to fight them in order to protect our homes and our freedom. Wars are like a bad sickness and the bad people that start them are the bad germs that cause sickness. When a person becomes sick we help the organisms of our body fight the bad germs with medicine. In this war our soldiers, sailors and aviators are like the organisms of the body. The ships, guns and planes they fight with are like the medicines we take . . . to destroy the bad germs.

"We have been fighting harder than usual lately and there are quite a few men that will never be able to go home again . . . . I want you to pray for them and the loved ones they have left behind. Do not feel badly about those who have gone because they have gone to their reward in heaven."

Heaven spared him, and in a few weeks he would see his family.

CHAPTER 5

Joan Crawford, Jack Benny, Maureen O'Sullivan, et al.: Flying Among the Stars in the 'Golden Age of Hollywood'

Pat Robbins mastered a strong suit of warmth, enthusiasm, and confidence, essential qualities for breaking ice and establishing rapport with a person she'd just met, particularly if in her own self-interest. Add a knack for unthreatening small talk; a polite aggressiveness (a little "muscle" occasionally if discreetly applied); a flair for selective gossip (know what the person you're sharing it with might already know . . .); and the right social, family, and business connections; and you have access into the "Golden Age of Hollywood." She believed in herself.

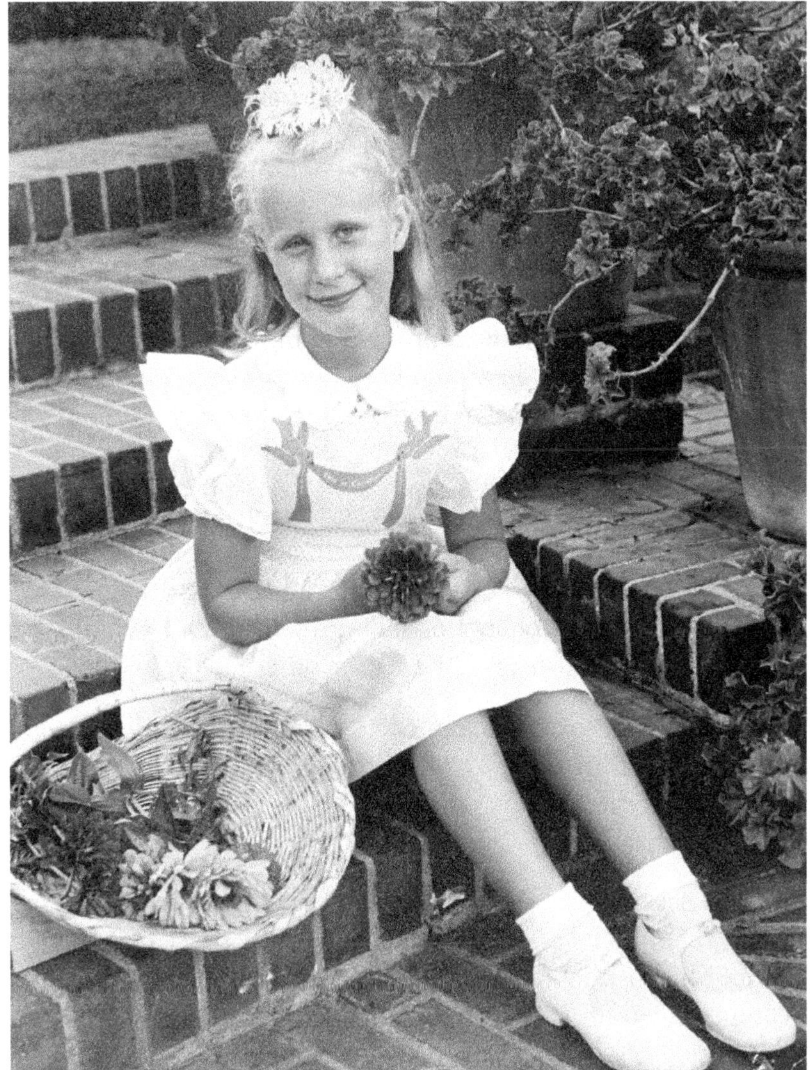

Christina "Tina" Crawford, daughter of actress Joan Crawford, age approximately nine, at her home in Los Angeles, late 1940s.

The ability to circulate and cultivate relationships personified Pat. The movie stars and wannabees, the celebrities, society's hangers-on, captains of industry, the right people to party with. Both she and they approached each other seeking mutual satisfaction. She sought clients and friends, and, during World War II with her husband at sea, companionship. They sought public attention to enhance their careers, and likely also relationships outside the grind of work. Quite suddenly, word-of-mouth spread and Pat was in demand, a "must-have" photographer of the stars and prominent families.

For example, take the unorthodox way Pat and Joan Crawford met.

Late one night Joan called Pat. "A throaty-voiced woman asked to speak to Pat Robbins," Carroll recalled. "Mother didn't recognize the voice and said, who's this? She said this is Joan Crawford. And Mother said yeah, and I'm the queen of England. They got into a conversation. Mother got her number to call her back." Joan had seen Pat's work and wanted her to do a photo book on her children Christina and Christopher. "She invited all of us to her house for lunch the following Sunday and said the children should bring their swimming suits. Joan had learned about our family." This was in the late 1940s. "Dad was still walking with a cane" from war wounds. "Mother didn't know this was for real and called her friend George Wasson [general counsel for 20th Century Fox Studios] who told her, 'that sounds right to me.'"

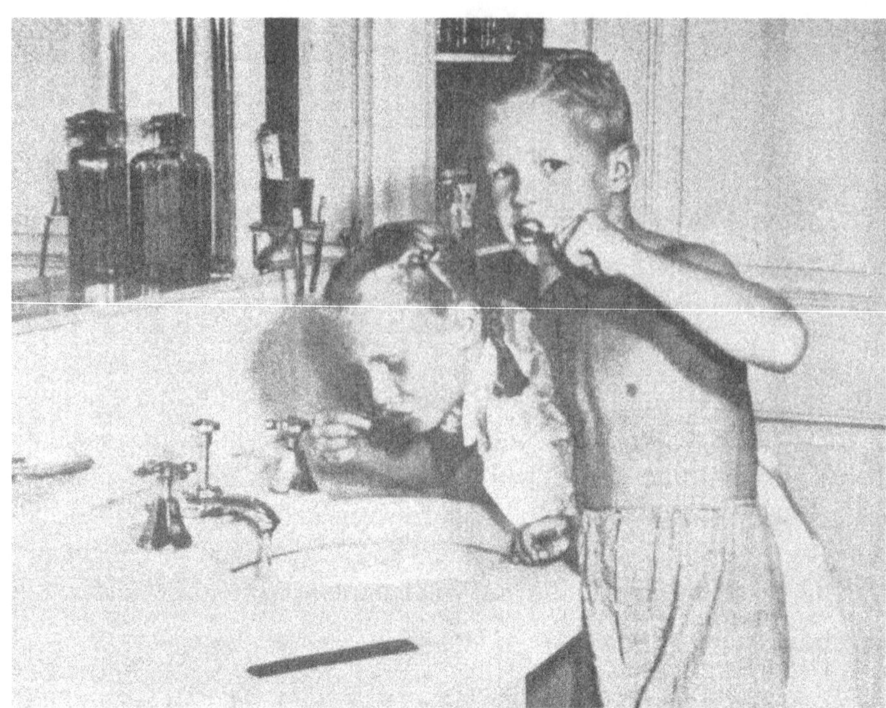

Christina Crawford and her brother Christopher share a family bathroom. Los Angeles, 1940s.

So, it was on.

Joan, a single woman, adopted Christina in 1940 at one year. Some witnesses saw the girl as "demanding, bratty, rotten . . . . She was a spoiled brat who demanded more and more of Joan Crawford and when Christina didn't get her way she acted out against Joan." Sent to a boarding school, not uncommon among the stars' children with their parents' hectic careers, she saw her mother on school breaks and special occasions. By the late 1960s, they appeared to reconcile their differences, but that was later.[1]

To Carroll, the Crawfords' 1940s relationship differed. "She was scared to death of her mother. I saw Joan in action a number of times." Once Christina was in her bedroom and Joan wanted Pat to take a picture of her asleep in her canopy bed, and told Christina to pretend she was asleep, "just like Mommie is doing it. If Christina smiled or blinked Joan would scream at her. She used to go on rages. She would keep her from going to birthday parties at the last minute, send her in a dirty dress, make her come home and wash all her clothes. Joan would get her up at midnight.

"I got yelled at by her," Carroll continued. "Christina wasn't demanding or bratty at all. She ran away from home one time and Joan decided to get even with her, and sent her away to the Chadwick School. Joan told the school she wasn't allowed to leave and make her work in the kitchen. She was there to help work her way through school, including scrubbing floors. Chadwick was an accredited school but horribly expensive. A lot of radio and movie kids went there. They never had a chance to take part in social activities the other kids enjoyed."

Servants called Joan "Mama Mean." "She had a reputation, liked sex and had men into her room right near where Christina's room was. One servant took Christina under her wing but was fired." Joan lived in Brentwood on Bristol, and actress Barbara Stanwyck lived across the street.

"I really didn't like being around Joan at all," Carroll said. "She scared me. I wasn't awed by these people. I had been around so many of them. Most were very nice." Christina wasn't allowed to have random kids over to play in her house. "Mother would take me when she went to shoot photos, and I would help her by carrying bags and things. I didn't like going over to that house. Once I lost my balance going through a hall and had to lean against a wall. Joan snapped: 'Don't do that—don't touch the wall!'"

Christina got even by penning her account of family relations in her blockbuster book, *Mommie Dearest,* in 1978, converted into a 1981 movie. In the book's Third Edition (Seven Springs Press, Ida., 2008), she and her

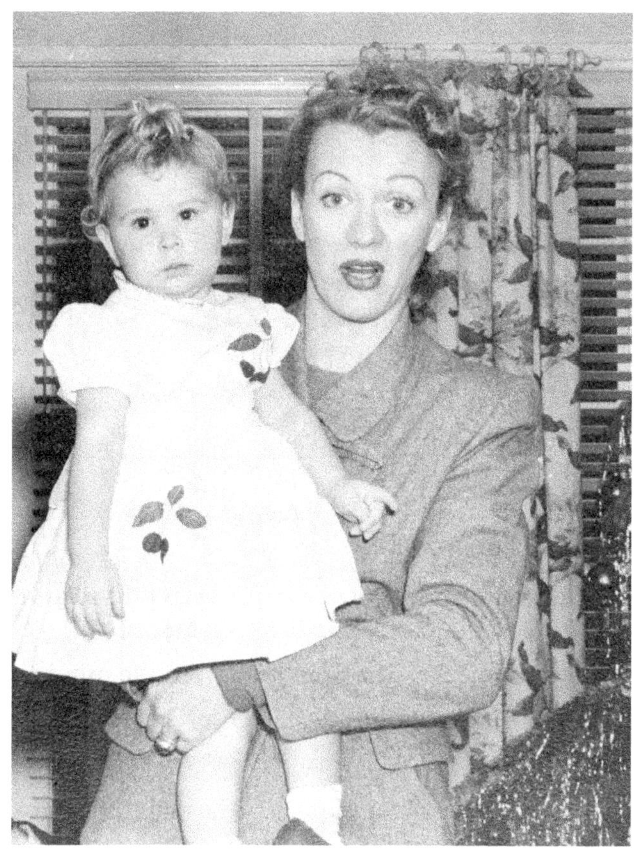

Actress Eve Arden and daughter Liza. Los Angeles, Christmas 1946.

brother Christopher are shown in at least two more of Pat's photographs.

Pat embraced clients and friends as soul mates. Having grown up in LA, she "knew a lot of the movie people. They passed her name around," Carroll said. "She did a lot of work for the *Los Angeles Times* and other media. She was very social and kept very busy. Some people she didn't like she'd just tell them. She didn't need an introduction to anybody."

Some of these business and personal relationships began before World War II, expanding after she returned to California from Hawaii in August 1942. Once her husband received orders in 1951 to command the Rhine River Patrol in Germany, her contacts with the Hollywood and society crowds dwindled and generally didn't rekindle even when he got reassigned to San Diego, California, in 1953. The whole thing could have been one of convenience for all parties, but while it lasted, Pat flourished professionally and socially. Carroll believes it was the "time of her life."

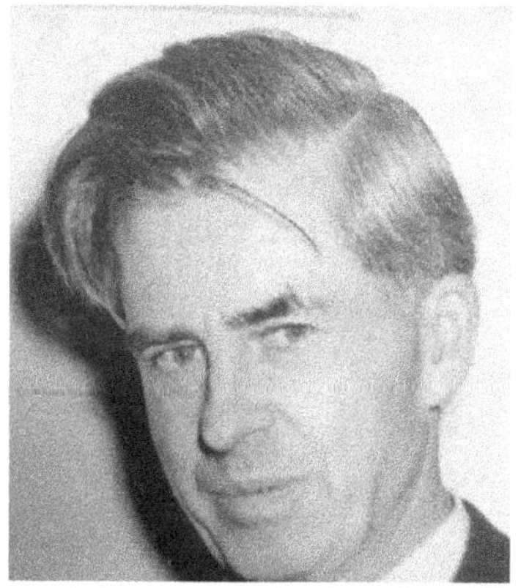

U.S. Vice President Henry A. Wallace at a party in wartime Los Angeles.

She enjoyed close friendships with several stars, notably Eve Arden, Maureen O'Sullivan, Loretta Young, and Jean Vander Pyl, regardless of how many others were clients or social acquaintances. With Joan Crawford, however, it was strictly business. In common with Pat, these four women were married to very successful men and raising children. Their mutual interests and concerns blended. The fact that Pat's husband Bob was a highly decorated naval war hero usually appearing in uniform, handsome, informed, and a captivating conversationalist, increased her demand and embellished her repertoire.

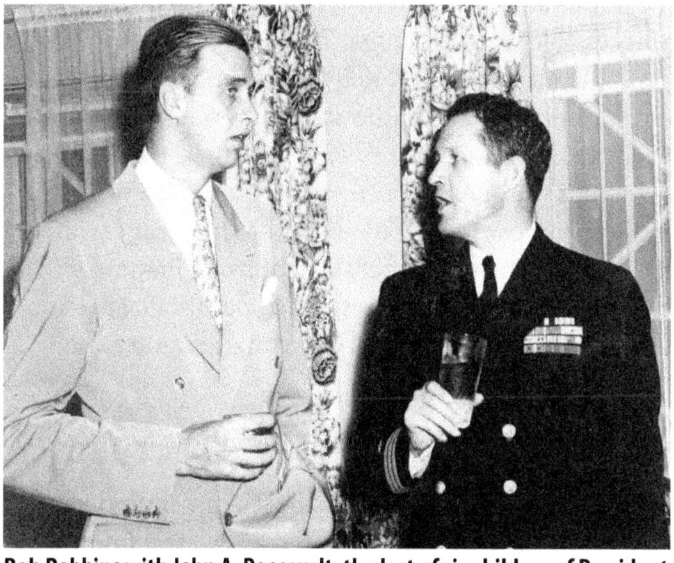

Bob Robbins with John A. Roosevelt, the last of six children of President Franklin D. and Eleanor Roosevelt, Los Angeles, late 1940s.

Although not political, she saw social openings with political figures, including Vice President Henry Wallace and John Roosevelt, the president's son. And, too, featuring at parties her friend the Princess der Ling, the last lady-in-waiting to the Empress Dowager Ci Xi, didn't hurt at all.

The Robbinses' robust social circle included pianist and wit Oscar Levant, and song writers George and Ira Gershwin. Carroll recalled listening to their music in their home, once hearing Levant play the classic *Rhapsody in Blue*. In July 1945, Ira autographed for Carroll a

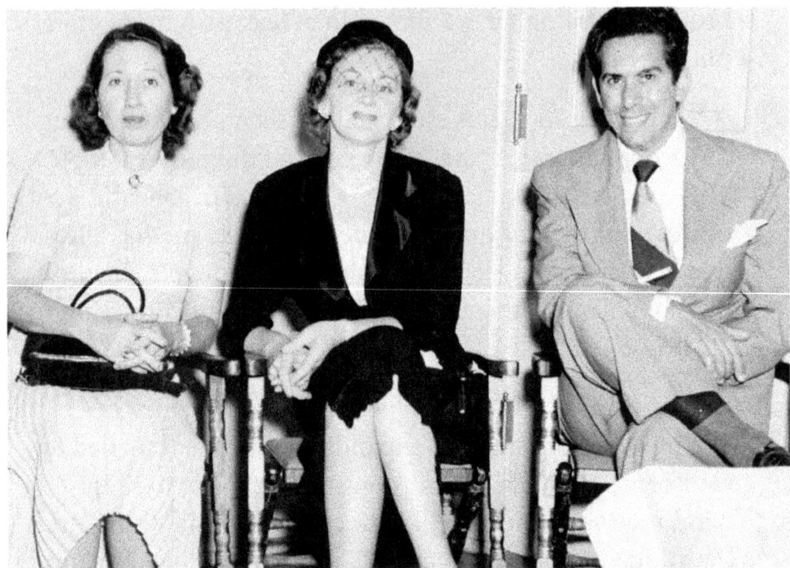

Bandleader and pianist Carmen Cavallero and his wife with Mary Jergens (left), wife of Jergens Lotion magnate Andrew Jergens. Los Angeles, 1950.

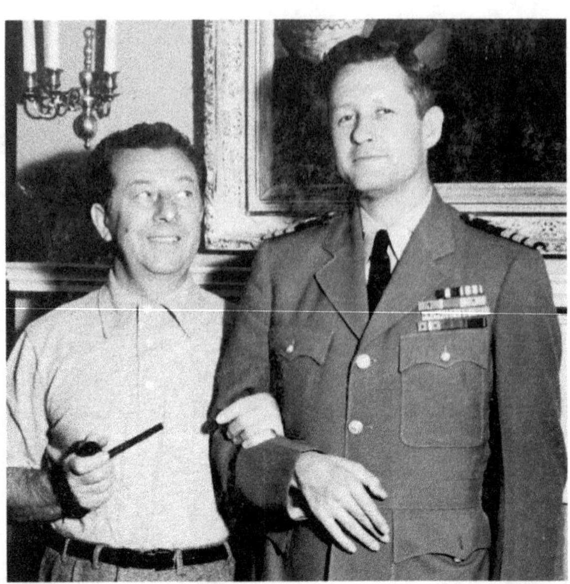

Restaurateur Dave Chasen, owner of Chasen's, the exclusive Place To See and Be Seen, with Bob. Los Angeles, 1947.

Decca 78-rpm album of Gershwin selections from the movie *Girl Crazy*, starring Mickey Rooney and Judy Garland. We still have it.

Other regulars were bandleader and pianist Carmen Cavallaro and restaurateur Dave Chasen, whose exclusive Chasen's on Beverly and Doheny drives was The Place To See and Be Seen. Naturally, that meant the Robbinses, too. "But, if you messed up, you were asked to leave," Carroll reminded me when we dined there in the 1960s. "He ran the greatest restaurant in Los Angeles."

She found star spouses, film studio executives, industrialists, and society mavens whose careers and lives were established outside the glitter and bright lights generally easier to shoot and more accessible to friendships. They included Ann (Mrs. Lou) Costello, Walter Chrysler, Kelly and Sonia Anthony (automobile dealerships and radio station KECA), George and Eleanor Wasson (general counsel, 20th Century Fox), Andrew and Mary Jergens (Jergens Lotion), Horace and Helen McCoy (screenwriter, novelist), William and Moya Lear (aviation, Learjet), and Princess Conchita Sepulveda Pignatelli (*Los Angeles Examiner* columnist and establishment social grande dame). The latter four couples and Conchita became close friends.

What was the Golden Age of Hollywood?

Inclusive dates vary, but generally it's considered to be from 1930 into the 1950s, highlighted by the war and the 1940s cinema boom. One prominent history source states:

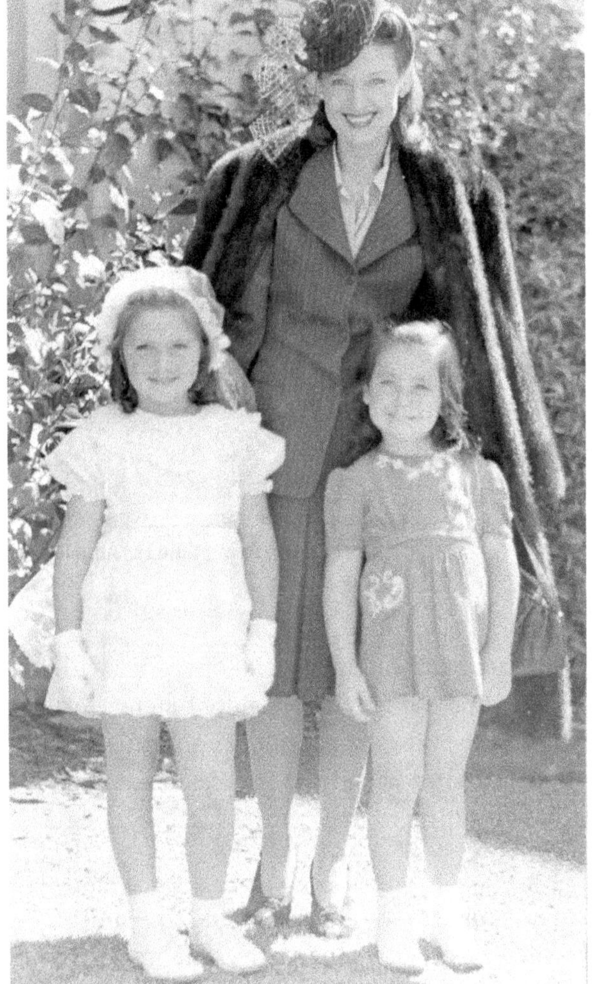

Ann Costello, wife of actor Lou Costello, with daughters Paddy Ann (left) and Carol Lou, at Marymount School for Girls for Paddy Ann's first communion. Los Angeles, late 1940s.

"New stars were born, and the studio system rose to mammoth status . . . . The eight major studios, each known for its distinctive style and stars, collectively produced 95 percent of all American films. More than 7,500 features were released by the studios between 1930 and 1945. More than 80 million people took in a least one film per week at the height of the cinema's popularity.

"This period also saw the introduction of the Production Code, B-Films, and the first animated feature of *Snow White*. Hollywood's Golden Age began to decline in the late 1940s due to the introduction of television, Hollywood blacklisting, and the ability of actors to become 'free agents.' A final blow to the industry occurred in 1948, when antitrust suits were filed against the major studios."[2]

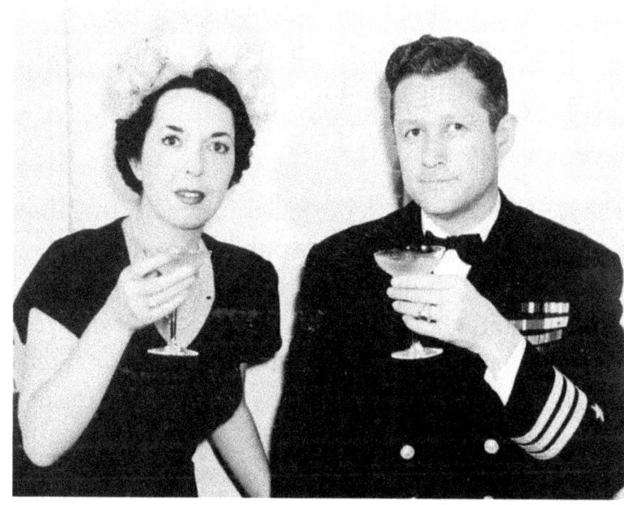

Pat and Cdr. Bob Robbins celebrating their 15th wedding anniversary at a party with friends, Los Angeles, 1948. In those days Bob usually wore his uniform socially even though not on duty.

Loretta Young and her husband Tom Lewis clicked with the Robbins duo. Pat, Bob, and other friends knew Young by her real name, Gretchen. Married three times, she "consistently made headlines for her personal life," particularly her love life. She won an Oscar for the romantic comedy *The Farmer's Daughter* in 1947, and a second Best Actress nomination for *Come to the Stable* in 1949. She was one of the first female stars to earn a six-figure salary.[3]

World War II buffs can check her 1944 fictionalized film *Ladies Courageous*, reissued as *Fury in the Sky*, about pilots of the Women's Auxiliary Ferrying Service.

For many years, Carroll maintained contact with Judy Lewis, the daughter of Loretta and Tom Lewis, a good friend during youth and later an actress, who died in 2011. Judy's sensational story shook Los Angeles in the mid-1930s. "It was one of Hollywood's best-kept secrets for decades until the truth came out after 60 years," a news source reported on her death. "Now Judy Lewis—the secret love child of film stars Clark Gable and Loretta Young, who conceived her on the set of *The Call of the Wild* in the 1930s—has died of cancer aged 76.

"Lewis sensationally revealed in her 1994 memoir *Uncommon Knowledge* that she was conceived in 1935 when Young, 22, and the married Gable, 34, were shooting the classic movie. Young, a single Catholic woman, concealed her pregnancy and placed her daughter in an orphanage at eight months. She brought her into public view at 19 months, saying she was her adopted child. Terrified her secret would come out, Young did all she could to

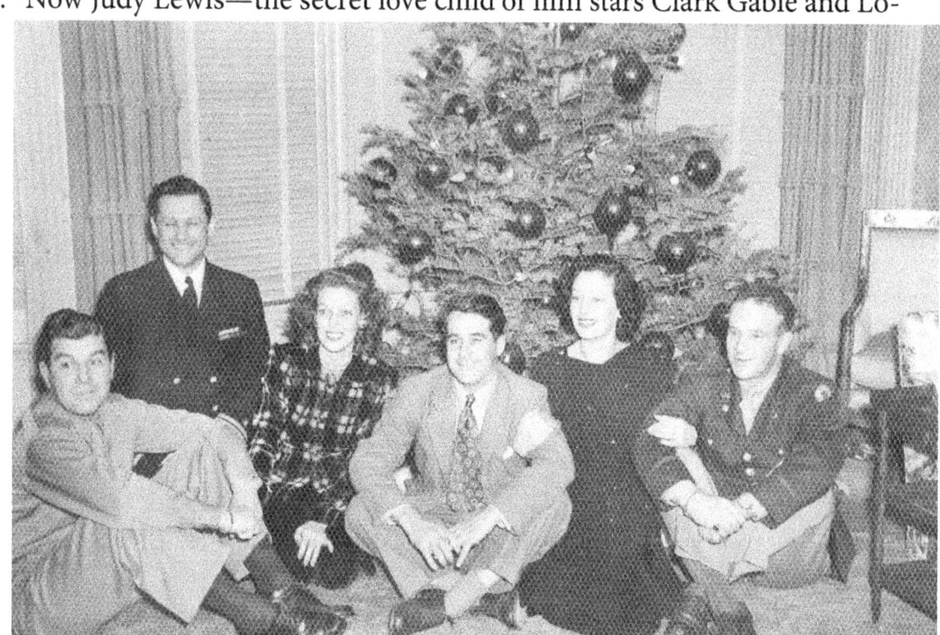

Actress Loretta Young (third from left), husband Tom Lewis (left), Cdr. Bob Robbins (next to Tom) and friends at Christmas party, Los Angeles, 1943.

cover up clues about her daughter's origins. There are no photographs of Lewis up to two. Up to seven they show her wearing a bonnet."[4]

Well, see below.

The New York Times reported at Judy's death, "In interviews after her book was published, Ms. Lewis was philosophical about the secrecy in which she grew up. If Young and Gable had acknowledged her in 1935, she said, 'both of them would have lost their careers.' Much of Ms. Lewis's account was painful to recall, she said. She quoted Young as saying, 'And why shouldn't I be unhappy?,' explaining her decision to give birth. 'Wouldn't you be if you were a movie star and the father of your child was a movie star and you couldn't have an abortion because it was a mortal sin?'"[5]

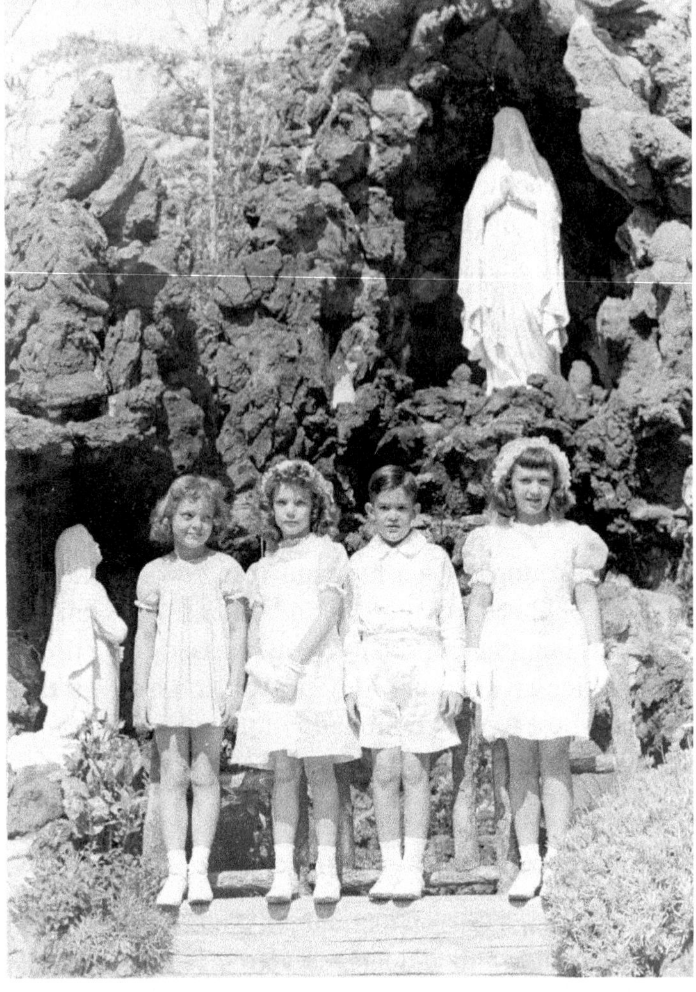

The Grotto at Marymount School for Girls, West Los Angeles, mid-1940s. Left to right, Judy Lewis, her first cousin Gretchen Foster, Berton III, Carroll, all making their first communion.

Marymount School, across Sunset Boulevard from UCLA, is now Marymount High School. In the 1940s its female and male students included children of Hollywood stars and celebrities, and the city's important and influential business leaders and society stalwarts. The mother of Gretchen, Sally Blane, Young's sister, appeared in more than 100 films over four decades. Her husband was film director, screenwriter, and former actor Norman Foster. Gretchen became a film actress.

A 1944 color photograph of Loretta and Judy credited to the Everett Collection/Rex Features appears to be Pat's work, her signature, her style. Her clients were free to use their images however they desired, and we believe a number have ended in private collections without original source attribution.

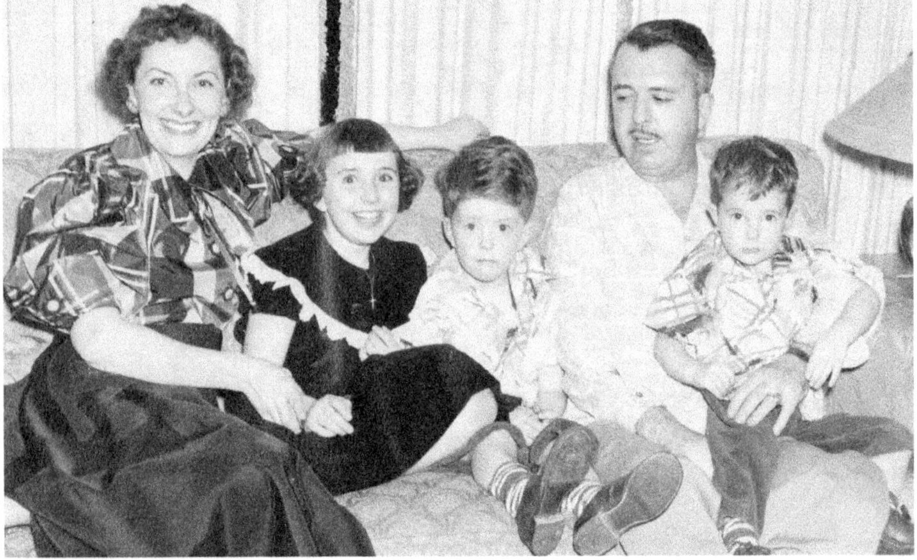

Actress Jean Vander Pyl and husband, television producer and Pat's brother Carroll O'Meara, with children Kathleen, Tim, and Michael. Los Angeles, 1948.

Yes, the voice—and radio, the electronic medium of the time. "By voice alone, without benefit of movement, gestures or facial expression, its performers love, suffer, thrill with terror or radiate with joy," wrote Pat.[6]

That described Jean Vander Pyl. Primarily a Hollywood radio star at the time, playing various characters, she married Pat's brother, Carroll O'Meara, a Young & Rubicam advertising executive and later television producer. They had children Kathleen, Tim, and Michael. O'Meara, then a writer and producer for station KHJ, hired her in 1941 for the show *The Phantom Pilot*.

Before the advent of television, she played on *The Silver Theater*, *Woodbury Playhouse*, *Big Town*, and *Lux Radio Theater*. Her career expanded into TV where she will always be best-known as the voice of Wilma (and her daughter Pebbles) on the 1960s series, *The Flintstones*"—her trademark yell "Fre-e-e-ed!"—and later on *The Jetsons* series.

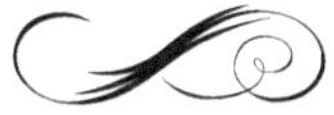

Through their mother's business and their parents' social life, Carroll and brother Berton developed relationships with adults and their children through their elite schools, dances, and other events. Thrust into the social mix, they often hung around adult parties in their home and accompanied their parents. Although not granted general freedom through the neighborhoods like "ordinary children," Carroll recalled ("We were rather regulated and scheduled"), they became playmates of sort with the stars' kids, such as Jack Benny's daughter, Joan.

"Mother had a hard time getting all three of them together for a family picture because of wife Mary Livingstone's schedule," Carroll recalled. "He was wonderful, very natural." Mary blossomed as his top radio sidekick.

An American entertainment icon, the versatile Jack Benny was a violinist, comedian, Vaudevillian, and radio, television, and film actor. He "portrayed his character as a miser, playing his violin badly. In character, he would be 39 years of age, regardless of his actual age." Known for "comic timing, and the ability to create laughter with a pregnant pause or a single expression, such as his signature exasperated 'Well!' His radio and television programs, popular from the 1930s to the 1960s, were a major influence on the sitcom genre."[7] "Many of Benny's best films were made during his last four years in Hollywood," including *Charlie's Aunt* (1941), *The Meanest Man in the World* (1943), *To Be and Not to Be* (1942) and *The Horn Blows at Midnight* (1945).[8]

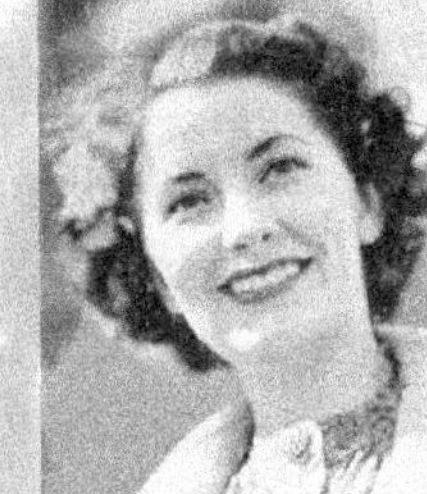

Radio actress Jean Van der Pyl, young but still experienced commercial and dramatic "voice"

ACTING ON AIR

Radio actors, the modern Mr. Anon.'s, who within a half-hour, play to vaster audiences than immortals of the stage reached in a lifetime

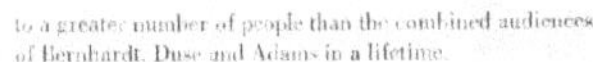

by Patricia O'Meara Robbins

HOUR AFTER HOUR, seven days and nights a week, the great radio chains pump their endless flow of entertainment into the ether. They blanket the great metropolis which has all the other forms of entertainment at its command, and penetrate the wilderness to distant mountain regions whose inhabitants have never seen even a motion picture.

Much of this entertainment is drama, some good and some bad, old stories from books and the stage, and a preponderance of "originals" written especially for the medium. By voice alone—without benefit of movement, gesture or facial expression—its performers love, suffer, thrill with terror or radiate joy.

Who are these people who enact the lives of dowagers and gangsters, salesmen, beggars and kings? In a few cases they are celebrities—like Loretta Young or William Powell in Hollywood, or Helen Hayes of the Broadway stage. But more likely they are just radio actors, generally unknown performers who in a single broadcast will play to a greater number of people than the combined audiences of Bernhardt, Duse and Adams in a lifetime.

A few radio actors—such as William Farnum, Jane Morgan, Gayne Whitman and Lionel Belmore—are veterans of the boards who came to prefer the microphone to the stage or screen. Others came when more and more stages were darkened or when they had lost their drawing power in films. But most of them, like Jean Van der Pyl, are young actors who have entered radio directly after small triumphs in school theatricals and perhaps a brief career in little theatres or on the professional stage.

Jean lives and works in Hollywood. She is typical of the 500 or more successful actors in radio throughout the country. Only twenty-one years old, she is younger than most radio actresses, but her career is representative in her field. She has been heard in all kinds of rôles—teen-age girls, sweet ingénues, tough old hags and dialect characters (often a combination of two in one broadcast). She has played important rôles with Edward G. Robinson, William Powell, Irene Dunne, Tyrone Power and other Hollywood headliners—on *The Silver Theatre*, *Woodbury Playhouse*, *Big Town*, *Lux Radio Theatre*.

As a little girl Jean began acting in neighborhood and grammar-school plays. At Beverly Hills High School, under the direction of Gene Nielson, she acted in the leading rôles of *The Royal Family* and *The Warrior's Husband*. Before she entered the University (*Continued on page 177*)

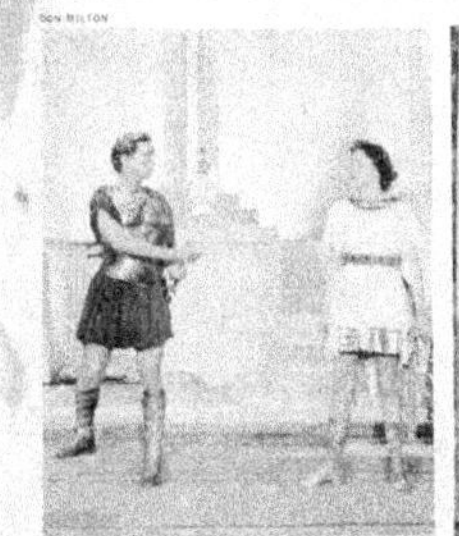

Jean's talent blossoms early. Above, she is a glittery Antiope in a Beverly Hills High School production of *The Warrior's Husband*

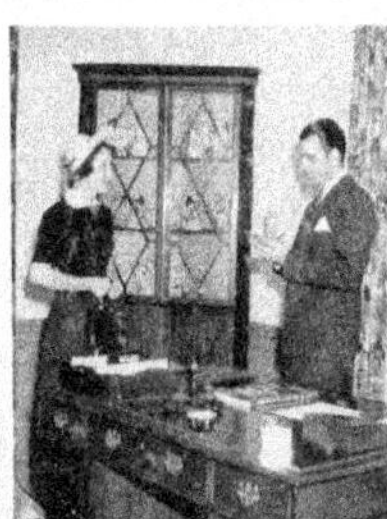

As a result of her first interview, Walter Johnson, Hollywood talent agent, arranges for her first audition before a microphone

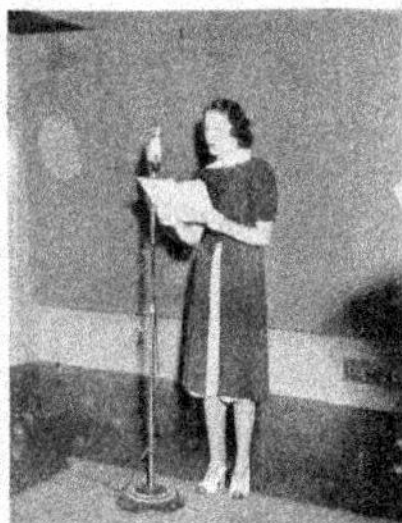

Within a year, Jean's radio assignments begin to interfere with her freshman studies at the U. of California. So, she deletes her degree

***Acting on Air*, a photo-piece in *Mademoiselle Magazine*, October 1941, about the budding career of actress Jean Vander Pyl, whose voice Pat considered 'young but still experienced, commercial and dramatic.'**

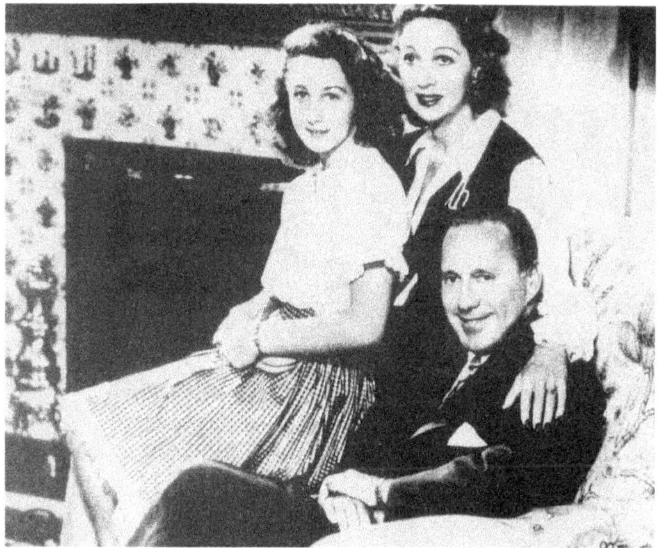

The Jack Benny family: wife Mary Livingstone and daughter Joan in their library, Beverly Hills, ca. 1947. Pat's photo in the Joan Benny family collection appears in *Sunday Nights at Seven: The Jack Benny Story*, by Jack Benny and Joan Benny (New York: Warner Books, 1991).

"The Bennys and the George Burnses—Gracie Allen—were very close friends," Carroll recalled. "They built identical homes on separate streets in Beverly Hills. They both had swimming pools, mosaic designs on the bottom. In the Bennys' was an octopus design, which scared Joan and me because the ripple of the water made it look like tentacles were moving. At the end of the pool were a pool house, one side for women and opposite for males. In between was a long bar with a refrigerator—they could have adult parties and ice cream socials for kids. They kept a boat for those afraid to get into the water because of the octopus." In the late 1940s, "I was friends with both girls [Joan and the adopted Sandra Burns] but at first would not get into their pools. The Andrew Jergens had something similar in their pool but they had to remove it because it scared [their children] Mary Ann and Andy."

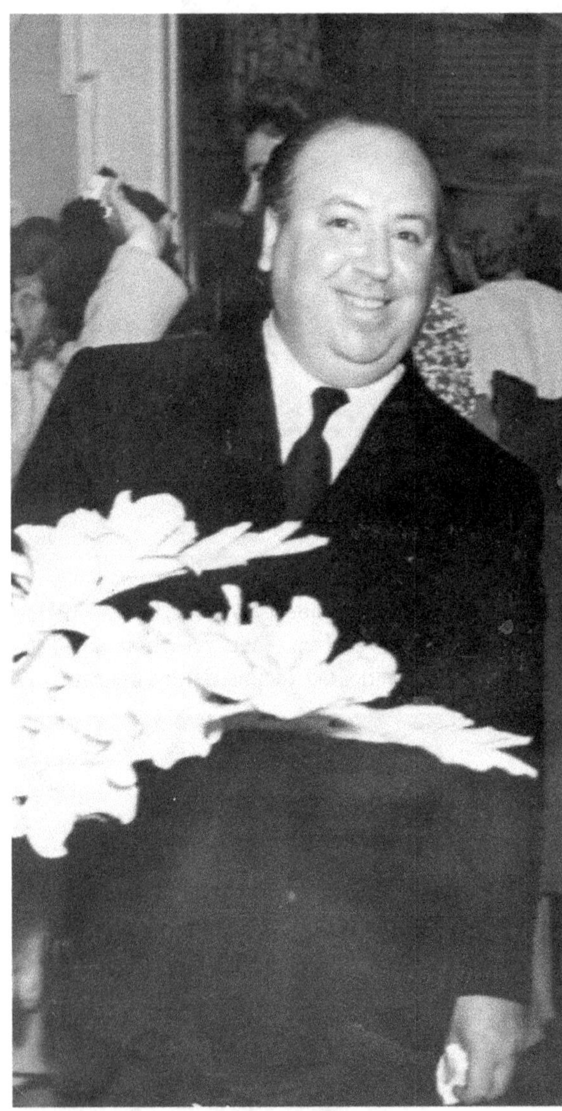

Film director Alfred Hitchcock at one of Pat and Bob's parties. Los Angeles, late 1940s.

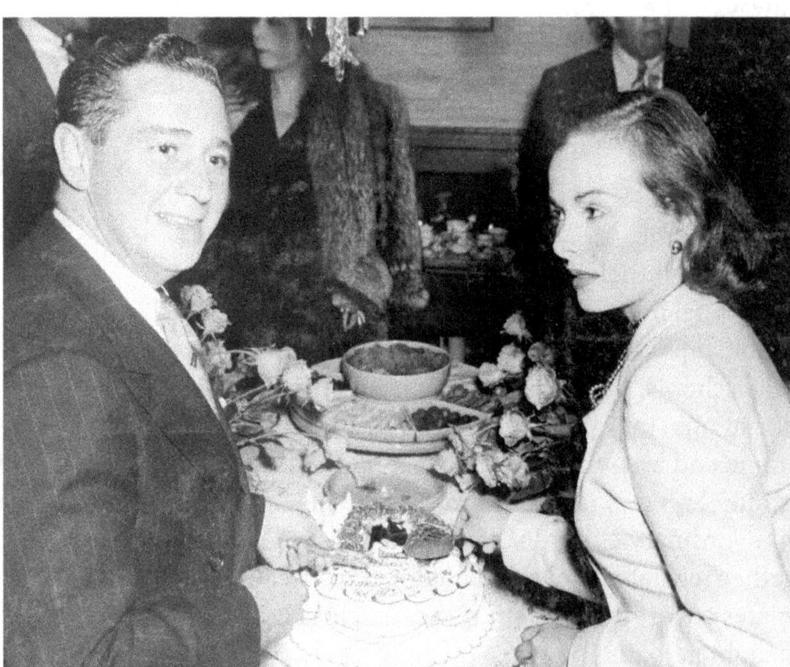

Industrialist Walter Chrysler, Jr. with actress Jeanne Crain. Los Angeles, 1949.

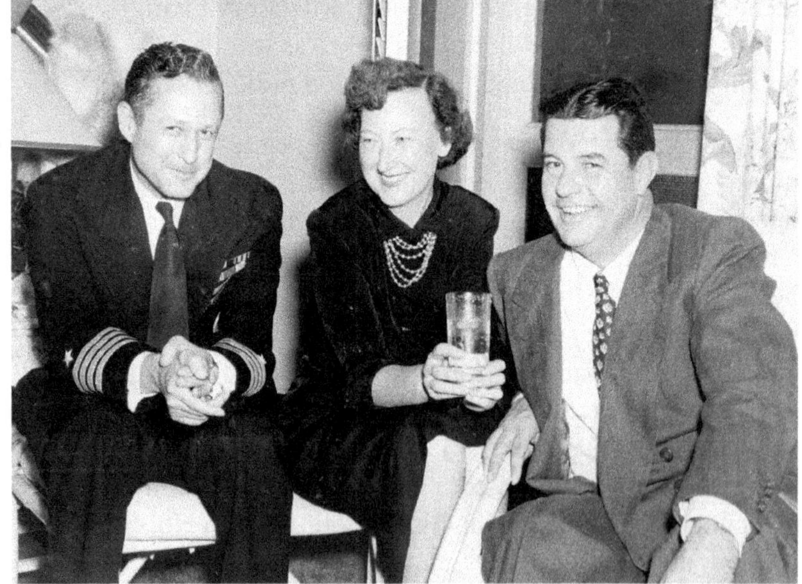

George Wasson, general counsel at 20th Century Fox, and wife Eleanor with Bob. Los Angeles, 1950.

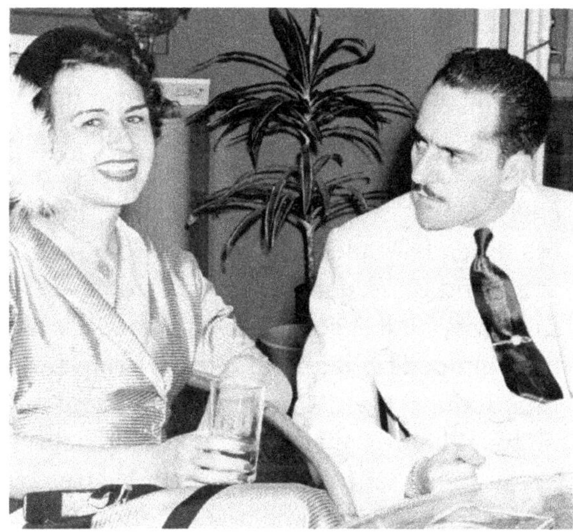

Sonia and Kelly Anthony, Los Angeles, August 1949. He was the son of Earle C. Anthony, a Los Angeles business pioneer icon who owned the Los Angeles Packard and Chrysler dealerships and radio station KECA (KFI).

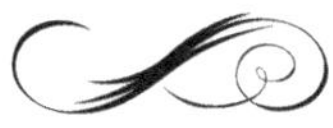

Earle C. Anthony's only son Kelly was disabled in a tragic World War II accident. "Kelly always wanted to be a prince in an operetta, always carried a cape and a walking stick," said Carroll. "They lived in a humongous house which looked like a medieval castle. He was a little cuckoo, and she was wonderful. Her mother-in-law told her she would give her a million dollars to stay married to Kelly, but they finally divorced."

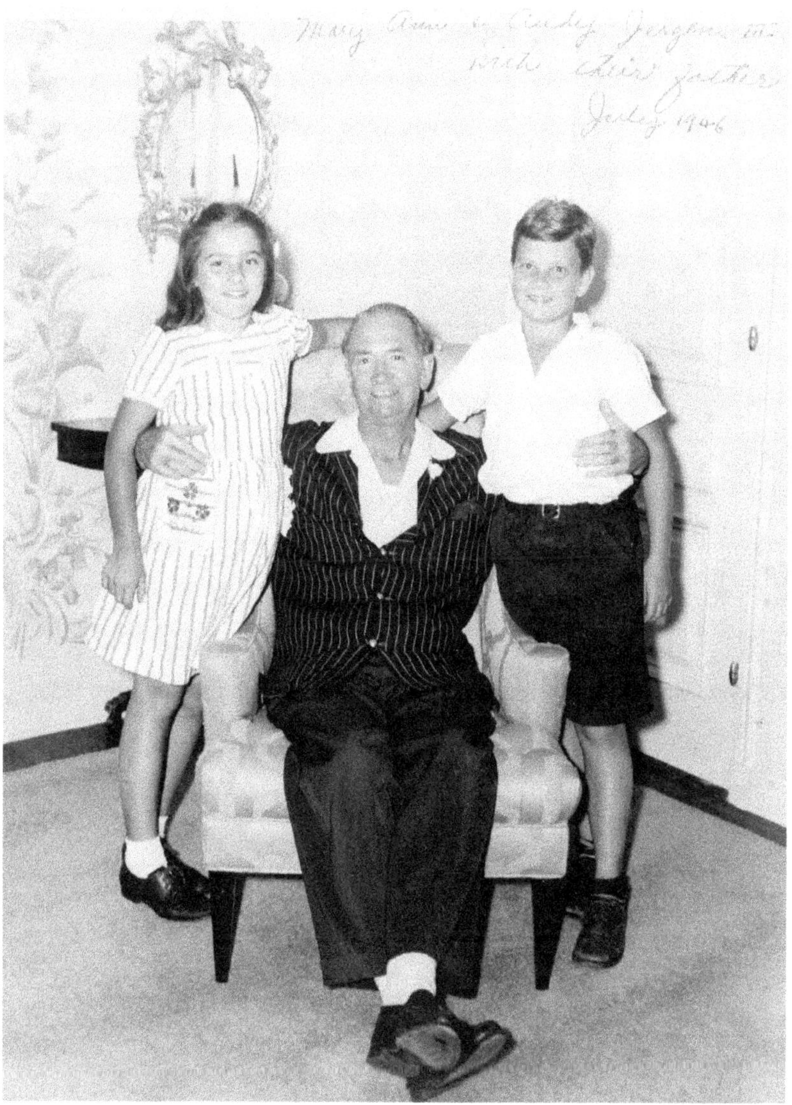

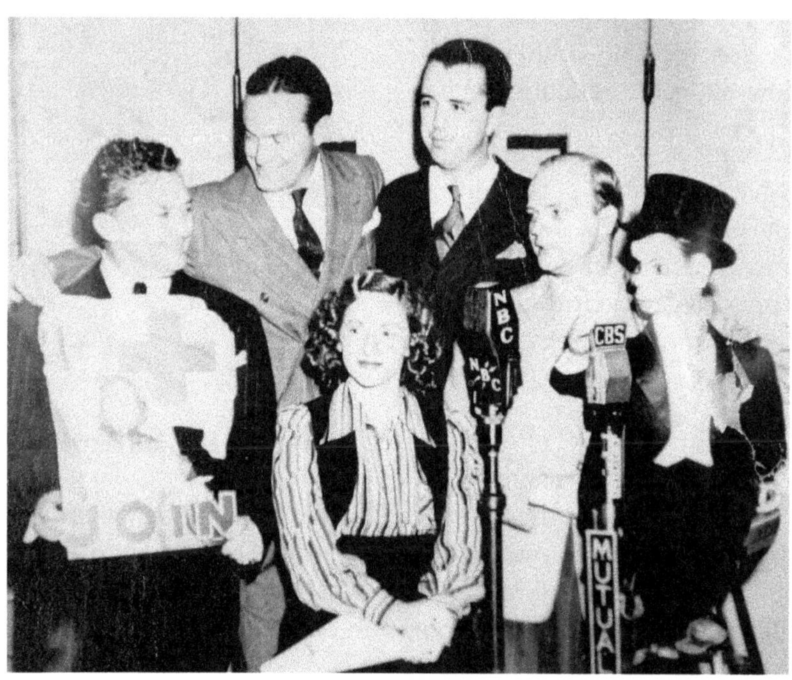

Top right: Andrew Jergens, Jr., owner of the Jergens Lotion company, with children Mary Ann and Andy. Los Angeles, 1946.

Bottom right: Show business ensemble endorses the American Red Cross, Los Angeles, wartime 1940s. Bob Hope is second from the left; radio producer Carroll O'Meara, Pat's brother, is on the right. Seated are singer/actress Ginny Simms, and Edgar Bergen and pal Charlie McCarthy. We believe that's Donald O'Connor on the left.

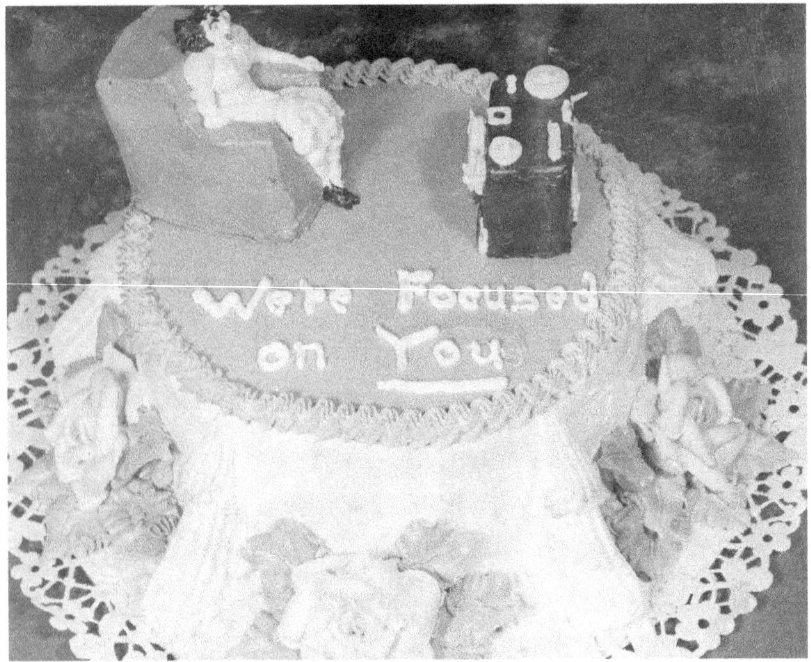

Pat's 39th birthday cake, appropriately, 'We're Focused on You,' Los Angeles, 1950.

Note the camera pointed at the seated female figure on the cake. That would be Pat, one of the very few times her own image appeared in one of her pictures during those years. Carroll remembered, "My parents had non-stop dinner parties and drop-bys. Friends would call and say, 'We're over at Pat and Bob's; come on over.' Dad never shot any photos because he had trouble with his wounded right arm and hand [from Iwo Jima action]. He had no interest in photography. Whatever made her happy and kept her from her tantrums he was for. He tread lightly with Mother; she was a shotgun. If she found someone she could push around, she would. But it was a real love affair—they loved each other."

Her friends and the public knew one side of Pat, her family another.

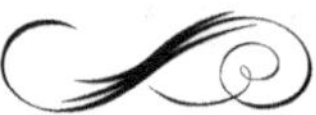

Edmund Lowe prospered in silent movies. In the 1930s he played leading man to Mae West, Claudette Colbert, and Jean Harlow, but settled as a valuable supporting actor at the major studios in a career of more than 100 films, "where his skills could bolster low-budget productions."[12]

"Although known for his somewhat flamboyant personality and purple ties (1920s code for homosexual), he was married three times," a gay website added.[13] He certainly had the 1930s-40s look, and was an occasional Robbins social accessory.

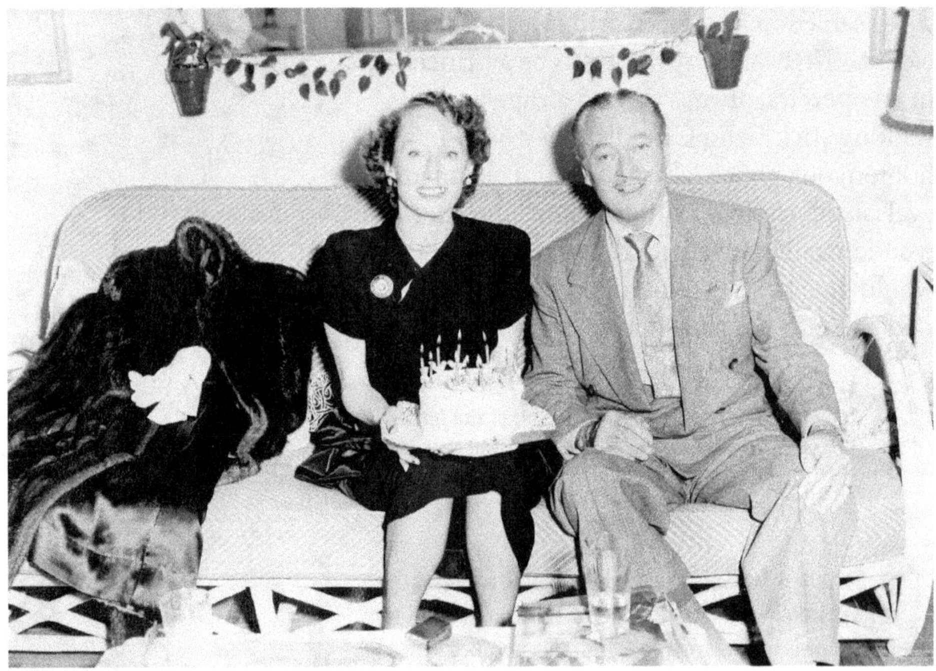

Actor Edmund Lowe and Betty Hirsch, at Lowe's home in Los Angeles, September 26, 1948.

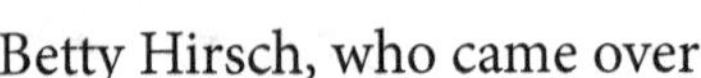

Betty Hirsch, who came over from London after the wartime Blitz, had boys at Marymount with Carroll, including in dancing classes. "Those were a hoot. When I was growing up, when Dad got out of the hospital it seemed like every weekend they were going to parties. Dad was not only good looking and a nice person, but he would beat others at various games. Berton and I stayed in our rooms unless someone needed another drink and then we would get it for them."

"Nancy Davis was under contract and had to do what the studio told her," said Carroll. In 1949 MGM gave Nancy a seven-year contract. "But success didn't come quickly. MGM found it difficult to cast her in the films they were making. Initially, she was typecast in minor roles such as the 'loyal housewife' or the 'steady woman.' She always said her favorite screen role was playing Mrs. Katherine Mead in *Night into Morning* with Ray Milland. After her 1952 marriage to actor Ronald Reagan, she became a housewife and mother and still managed to make three pictures before retiring.[9]

She "was in and out of her movie career in less than ten years . . . . Somehow the camera captured in the young Nancy Davis the poise and resolve that would become commonplace for the older Nancy Reagan. But those qualities weren't star-making ones in the 1950s."[10]

Pat completed several assignments for *Photoplay*, a popular American film fan magazine, like this Nancy Davis pose. The magazine was "considered quite influential within the motion picture industry . . . renowned for its artwork portraits of the film stars . . . ."[10]

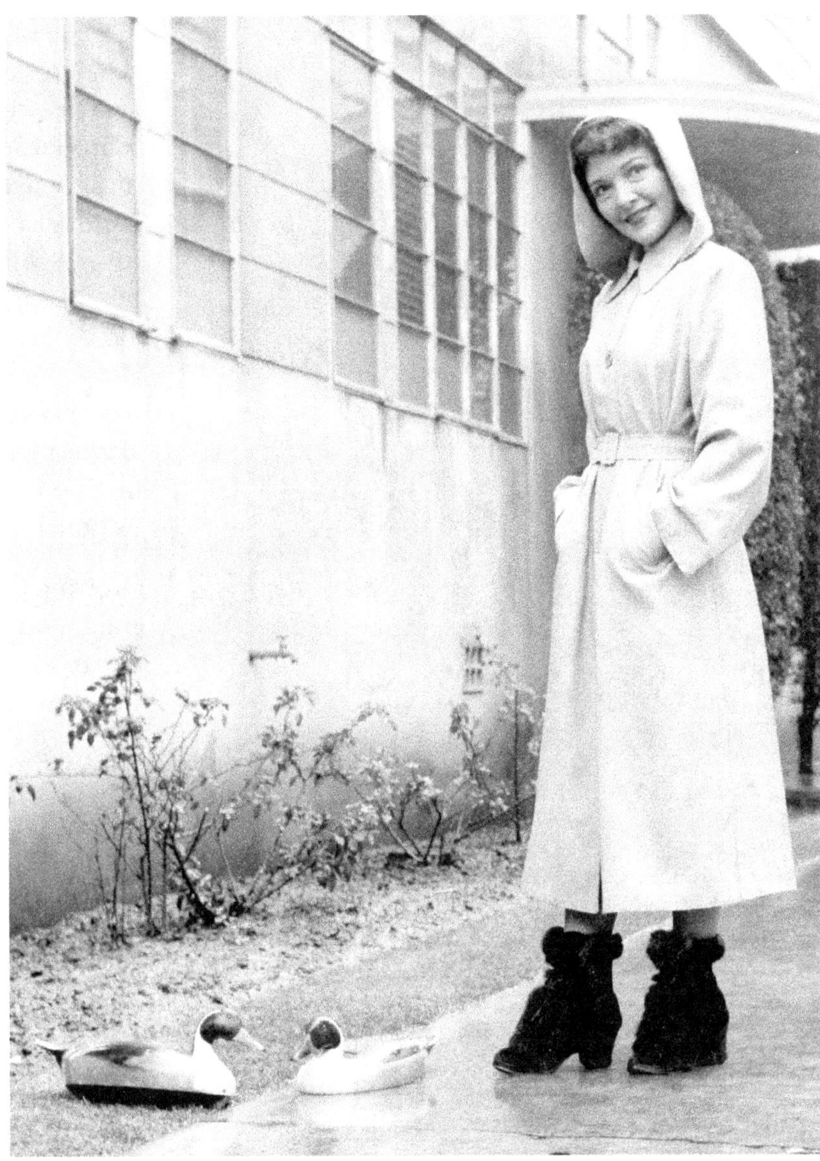

Actress Nancy Davis, future First Lady to President Ronald Reagan, for *Photoplay* magazine, outside the MGM Studio, Los Angeles, 1950.

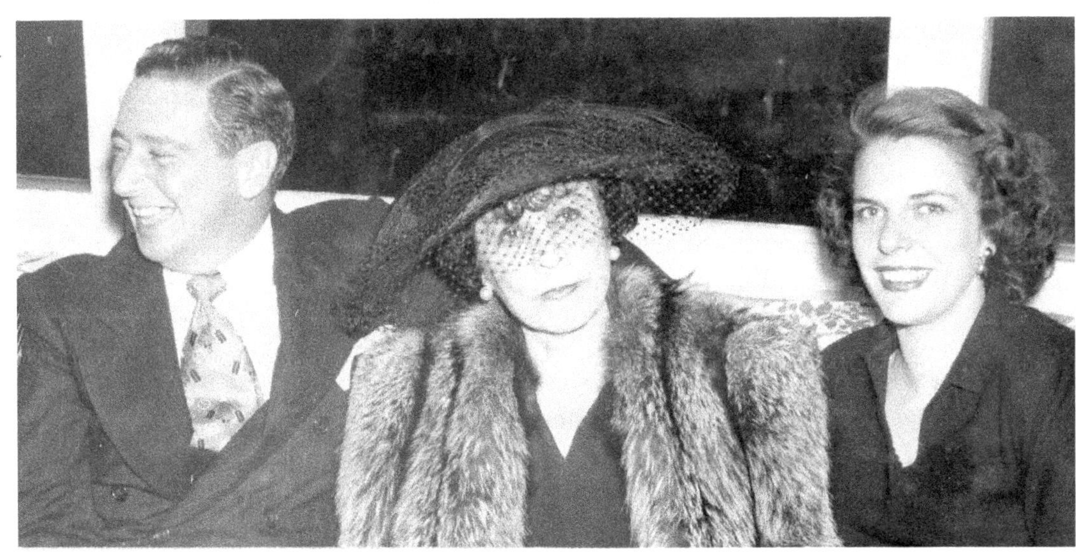

The industrialist Walter Chrysler, Jr., Princess Conchita Sepulveda Pignatelli, and her daughter Carlotta Munroe. Los Angeles, 1949. Conchita, from a prominent Southern California Spanish family who was born and educated in Mexico City, was the *Los Angeles Examiner*'s highly visible society columnist for thirty years. Pat and she were close friends.

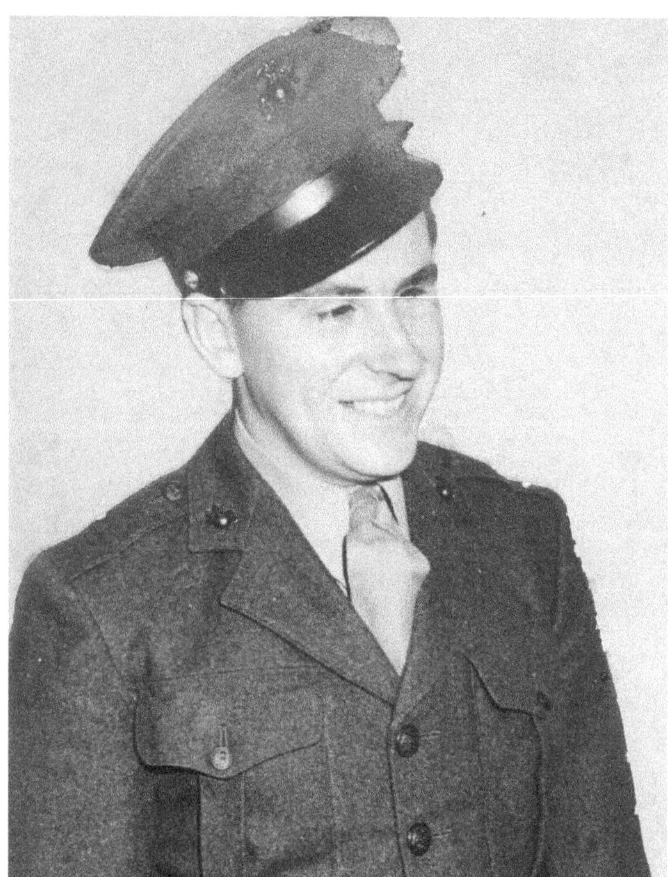

Sgt. Albert A. Schmid, USMC, aka 'Machine Gun Smitty,' Navy Cross recipient for heroism in combat at Guadalcanal, Solomon Islands, August 18, 1942. Photo in Los Angeles, 1943.

Requested by the studio, Pat took multiple images of Sergeant Albert A. Schmid. In 1945 Warner Brothers released the movie *Pride of the Marines*, starring John Garfield. His character was based on Schmid, nicknamed "Machine Gun Smitty," one of the war's earliest Marine Corps heroes. At the Battle of the Tenaru River, Schmid, blinded by enemy fire, and a mate (Corporal Leroy Diamond), wounded in the arm, manned a machine gun and held off sustained Japanese infantry attacks. Schmid loaded and fired the weapon as Diamond gave visual firing directions. He became a national sensation as a returning hero, regained partial sight in his only eye, died in 1982, and is buried in Arlington National Cemetery.

Growing up in Wilmington, N.C., during the war, my childhood buddies and I took special turns playing the role of Machine Gun Smitty during our neighborhood war games.

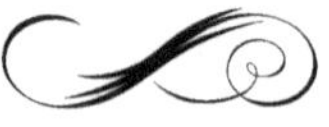

This photo from the Marymount School is another example of the crowd into which the Robbinses easily fit. Jean's father was the associate publisher of the *San Francisco Chronicle*; Joan's father was head of photography for MGM Studio. Cammie's stepfather Herbert Kalmus and two others invented Technicolor, which revolutionized the motion picture industry and produced the likes of *Fantasia, Gone With the Wind,* and *The Wizard of Oz.*

Carroll's Marymount boarding school experience was extremely important to her development and life. She communicated with some classmates and received mail from the school until she became too sick to engage.

Marymount was a French order of nuns started in Europe who were called madames, not sisters. Highly educated, they taught students classics, behavior, religion, manners, and to do good works. "Mother was not quite the mother," said Carroll, "and so she picked

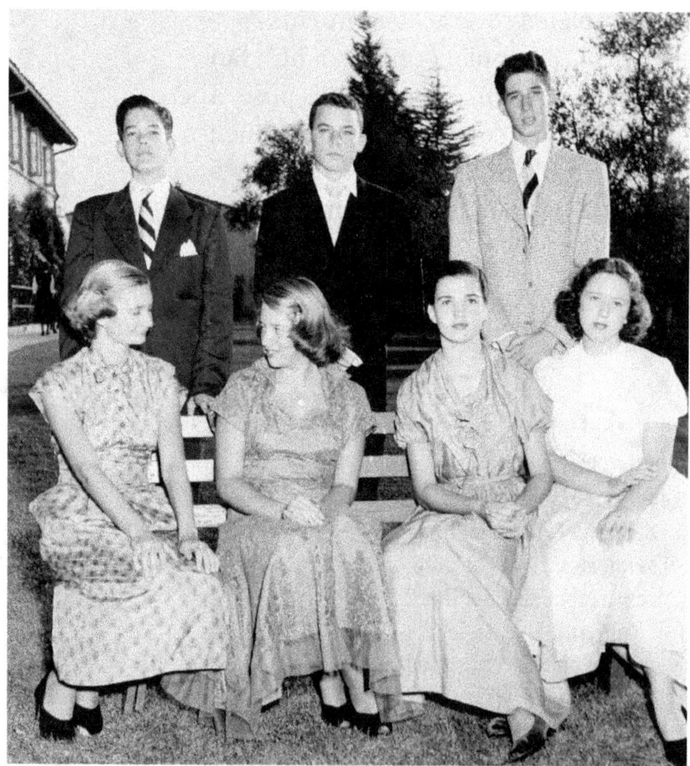

The Catholic Marymount School for Girls afternoon tea dance, West Los Angeles—across from UCLA, late 1940s. The classmates of Carroll (on the right), left to right, are: Jean Cannon, Joan Arnold, and Cammie King. Brother Berton is on the left.

this boarding school. My grandmother was glad we went there—she was every bit the lady." Carroll went there for several years, attended public school for the sixth and seventh grades, "then returned to Marymount because we weren't learning anything. I absolutely loved it."

"Eve Arden was a wonderful person, very warm, natural, down to earth, very polite, almost shy in a way, a comedian." said Carroll. "She wanted children but thought she couldn't have any," and knew about a pregnant girl. Meanwhile Eve had a nursery decorated for her in stuffed animals, red and white checks, ruffles around crib, red and white curtains, and did some of it herself. "She was all ready for this baby; she was a wonderful mother." Eve adopted Liza while married to Ned Bergen, a naval officer, and took her everywhere. When the war was over, "it just didn't work out—so they divorced. She was working heavily in movies and radio. She was a very nice lady. Mother said to Eve, 'I have to take care of you so you can start looking for someone who deserves you.'" Later, after she adopted another child, she became the single parent of two little girls.

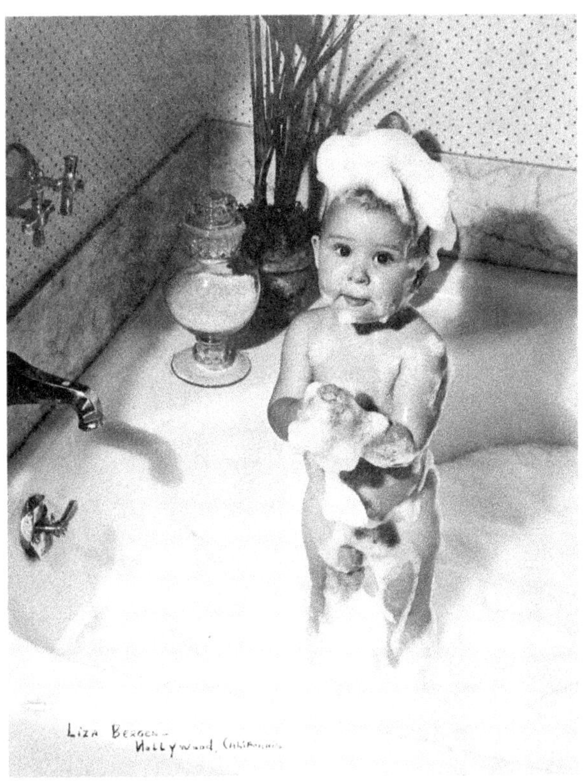

Liza Bergen, adopted daughter of actress Eve Arden and husband Edward G. Bergen, age two, Hollywood, late 1940s.

"She and Mother became very good friends and went around together. Eve came to our house occasionally. Mother introduced Eve to the [socialite] Alfredo de la Vega's party circle (Al's pals—he knew everybody in town, never married, was rich, always used his mother Tia Maria's house for parties). He would throw a party at the drop of a hat. Everybody would go to his parties. He collected people." Pat grew up with him. His mother, Tia Maria, was Carroll's sponsor at her Catholic confirmation, with Alfredo as godfather.

For an actress, Eve was "not a glamour girl," Carroll continued, "and played parts like the secretary working for a male boss. She did get pregnant later and named her son Brooks. Basically she was a homemaker and a very thoughtful woman." Eve hit the high note in Hollywood in the 1940s. Her role in *Mildred Pierce* earned a 1945 Oscar nomination. Expanding radio contracts culminated in the prime role in the popular *Our Miss Brooks* series on CBS in 1948, which fit her personality and character. In 1952 CBS moved the show to television, and in 1957 a movie of that name opened. She is perhaps best remembered for this role among her broadcasts and films.

"Tall, striking character comedienne, best known for her masterful delivery of snappy, sarcastic dialogue . . . Arden honed her sardonic powers on the stage and became typecast as the heroine's manless career-woman friend . . . . Arden's withering gaze, splendid lip-curling delivery and relaxed warmth stoke scenes in films including *Cover Girl* (1944), *Paid in Full* (1949) [and] *Anatomy of a Murder* (1959)."[15]

No wonder Pat found her friendship comfortable.

There was little distinction between Pat's paid work and her informal photography of friends and family. "Mother did across-the-board photography, advertising, portraits, magazine articles, casual scenes, and society," Carroll said. "She took her camera to every party. She was always late. She would come downstairs holding shoes he hadn't put on."

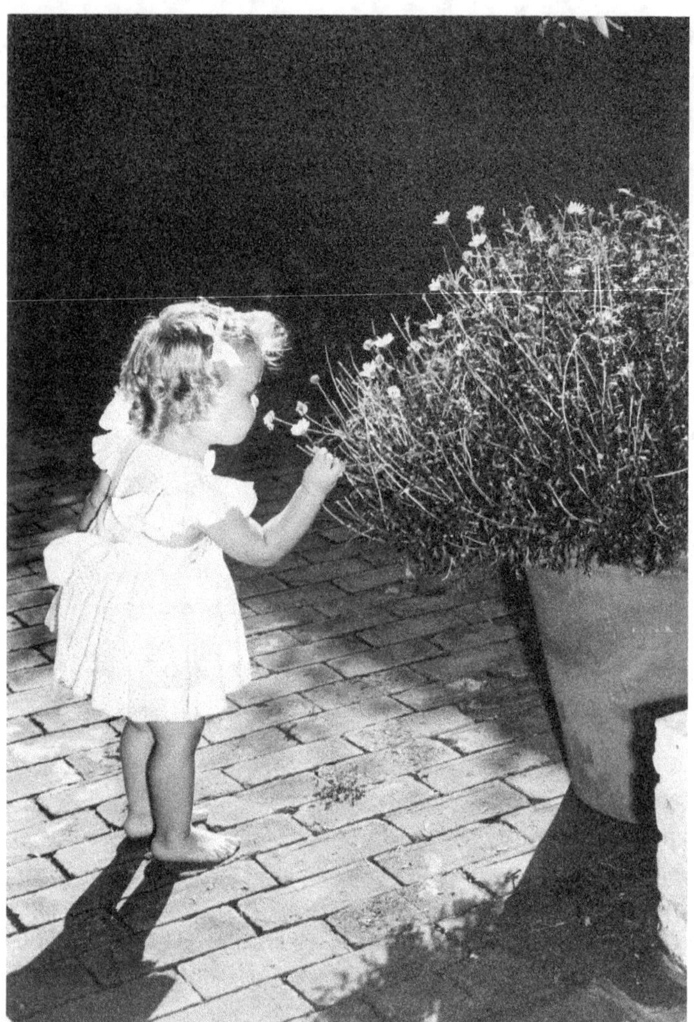

Barefoot Maria (Mia) Farrow, daughter of John Farrow and actress Maureen O'Sullivan. Beverly Hills, ca. 1947. For *Town and Country* Magazine.

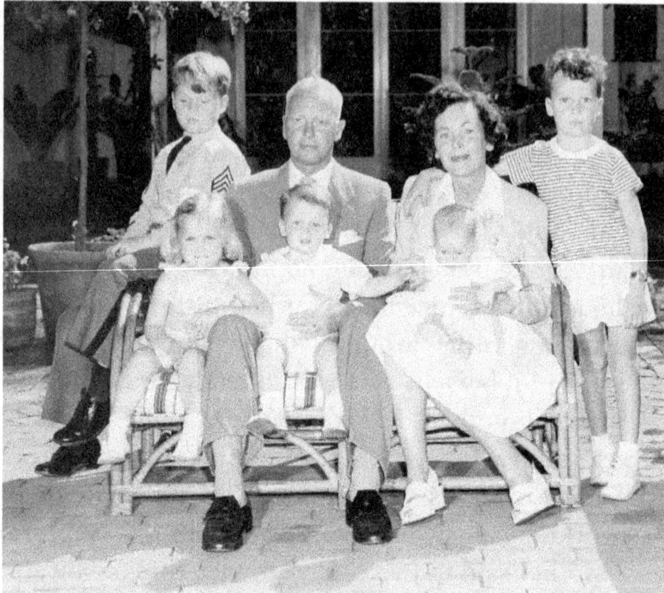

The John Farrow family of Beverly Hills, late 1940s. His wife is Maureen O'Sullivan. Their eventual seven children included daughter Mia Farrow, the future actress, seated on the left. Below, an ad for Acrobat Shoes featuring O'Sullivan and their children.

Maureen O'Sullivan played Jane with Johnny Weissmuller in many Tarzan movies, "which she hated, felt it was beneath her," Carroll recalled. She "despised working with the chimpanzee 'Cheetah' . . . at MGM," according to Mia Farrow, and "privately referred to the primate as 'that ape son of a bitch.'" Often called "Ireland's first film star," Maureen took time out from a 60-year career (until 1994) to raise a family.

The accomplished writer and director John Farrow received the 1956 Academy Award for the screen play of *Around the World in 80 Days*, and an Academy nomination for *Wake Island*. During the war he served in the U.S. Merchant Marine and Marine Corps, British Royal Navy, and the Royal Canadian Navy.[14]

"Mother and Maureen got along well," Carroll fondly remembered.

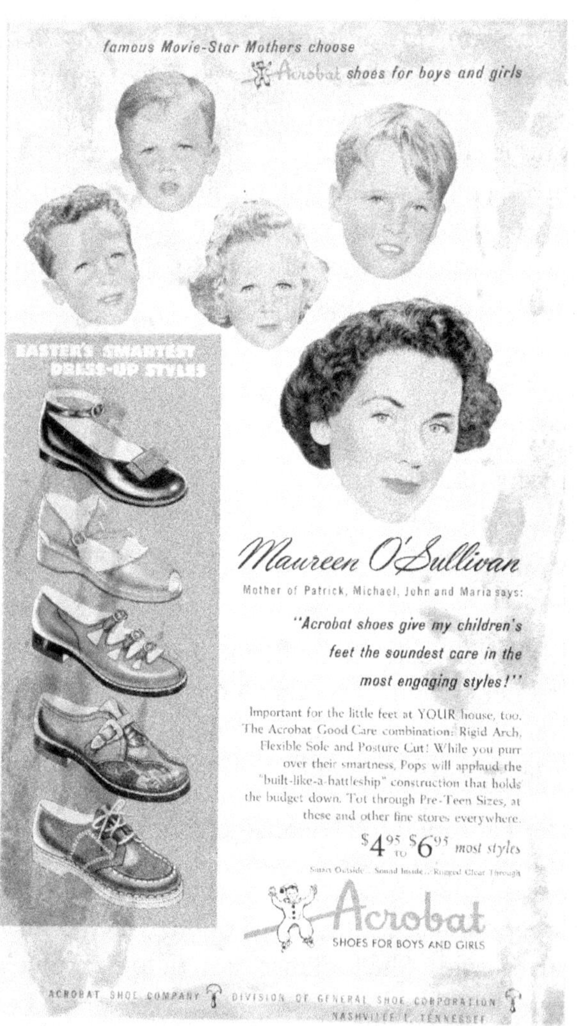

Horace McCoy was an established writer of books, screenplays, pulp fiction, and short stories. His most famous book, the 1935 novel *They Shoot Horses, Don't They?*, became a 1969 movie. He also wrote *I Should Have Stayed Home*, and *Kiss Tomorrow Goodbye. Time Magazine* called *Kiss Tomorrow Goodbye* "one of the nastiest novels ever published in this country. Literary caveman Horace McCoy has driven to an absurd extreme the hardboiled, feel-my-muscles style of James Cain and Dashiell Hammett . . . .The result is a gutter-minded, gutter-tongued shocker of alley-cat sex, sadism and unmourned murders. . . ."[16] Oh my gosh, but what would one expect in 1948?

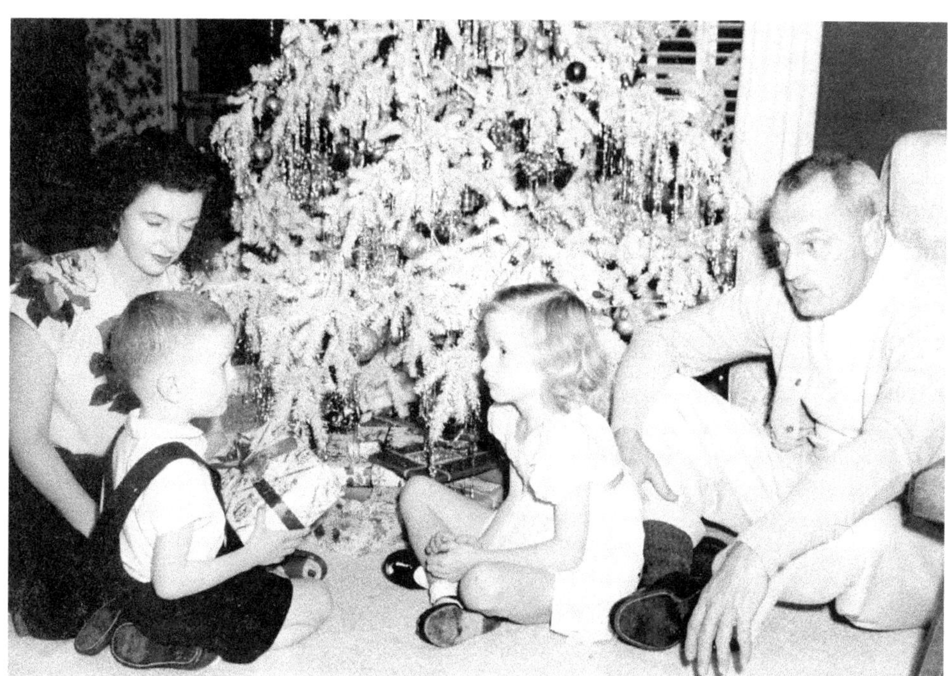

Horace McCoy and wife Helen with children Peter and Amanda, Beverly Hills, California, 1945.

The McCoys enjoyed throwing open houses and welcoming friends over for Christmas, remembered Carroll, whose family joined them on Christmas Eves. "Mother and Helen knew each other from childhood. If you went there you would see every celebrity in town. It was a tradition. You never knew who you would run into. Horace was a great raconteur and collected interesting people, and would keep you in stitches. Helen loved to cook. She would be in the kitchen wearing a $500 dress. Children were put in the back play room with food and toys, and after a few hours you can imagine what the place looked like. The circle of friends would give their nannies and cooks off for Christmas. We spent more time in Beverly Hills than anywhere else.

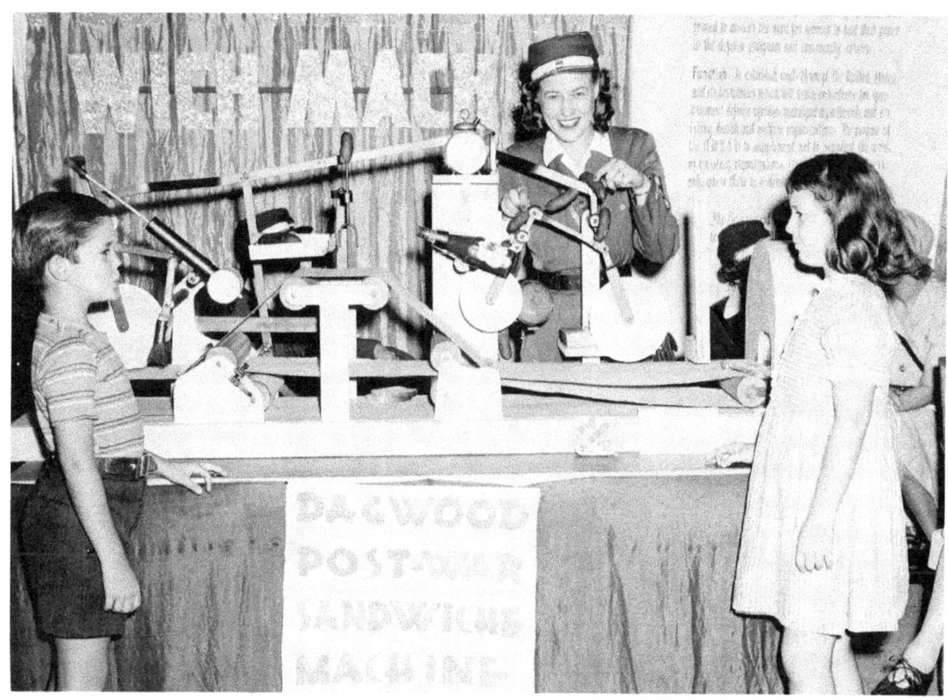

Helen Guggenheim, wife of M. Robert Guggenheim, Jr., of the wealthy and benevolent Guggenheim family, with Berton and Carroll at the ad-hoc 'Dagwood Post-War Sandwich Machine,' an effort to recruit and train war workers. Los Angeles, 1943.

"Horace was a great admirer of my father and the one person Dad could speak with. They were very good friends. This was the time that Communists were being rooted out in the film industry. Horace flew with the U.S. Army Air Service in combat in World War I, was wounded four times, and volunteered in the Spanish Civil War. He always wanted to write a book like *The Sun Also Rises* and he did, wrote three in a row. Peter, who had a deep voice as a child and always called his father Horace, served in the Reagan White House."

Horace died in 1955 while the Robbinses were living in Northern Virginia. He was writing a book and "needed to put a face on a female character: young-rich-bitch daughter." He saw the Zugspitze winter photo Pat took of Carroll in 1952 and used the image as the character. "The photo just fit," said Carroll.

The Robbins family lived in the central Los Angeles Parklabrea community in the 1940s and early 1950s. Its January 25, 1951, newsletter, with Pat's photos, reported: "Since a photographer is never happy except when exposing film, from her very first days at Parklabrea Pat Robbins was dashing around photographing this and that—and she's still doing it. Not much that's happened of significance in the area since March 1944 has escaped her camera."[17]

Still doing it. Not much has escaped her. Such was Pat, fatefully placed to record the "Golden Age of Hollywood."

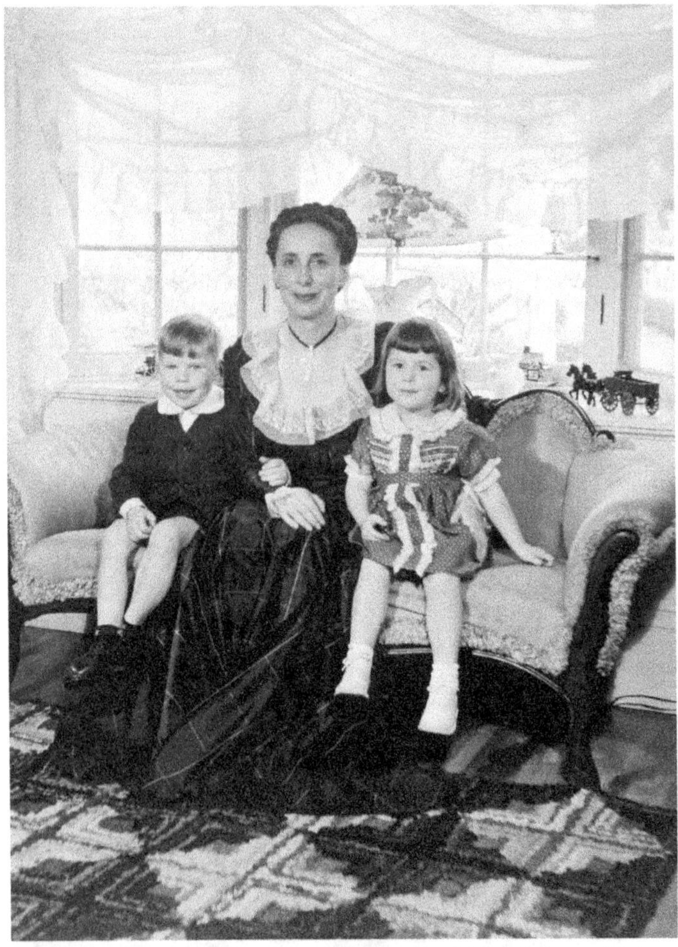

Mrs. William P. (Moya) Lear, wife of the aviation industrialist and jet pioneer, with children Shanda and Little John. Her father was 'Ole' Olsen of the popular comedy team Olsen and Johnson. Santa Monica, 1940s.

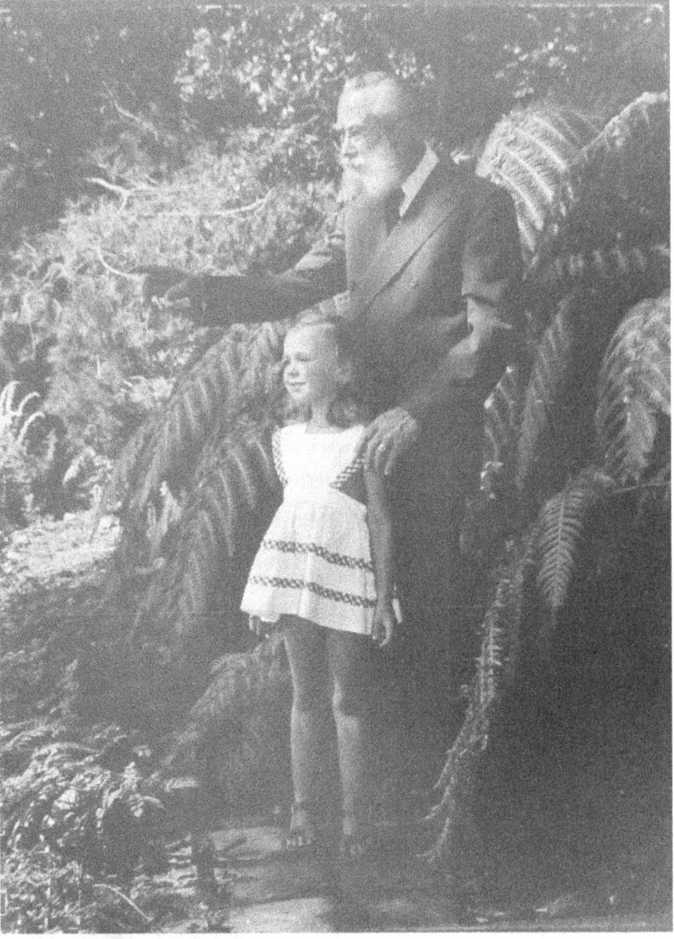

Dr. Bailey 'Earthquake' Willis, 'fearless' professor emeritus of geology at Stanford, who hunted earthquakes worldwide, with granddaughter Carol Smith at her parents' home in Hollywood Hills, California, 1940s.

CHAPTER 6

'Sticking Stalin,' the Rhine River Patrol, and Hitler's Bunker: Life in Post-War Germany and Europe

When Captain Bob Robbins arrived by ship with his family in Bremerhaven, West Germany, in early 1951 for duty, World War II's destructive evidence still covered much of Europe. Economies, transportation infrastructure, and communications of both victors and vanquished struggled slowly toward recoveries. For six years since, the war's Western Allies—France, Britain, and the United States—had occupied a defeated German nation split into their zones and those of their former ally, the Soviet Union, in the Eastern third.

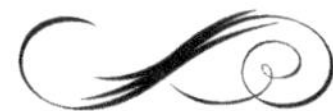

The Twentieth Century's Cold War, which began in 1945, matched two new enemies: the free West and the Communist East. It dominated the continent until the Soviet bloc began dismantling itself in 1989. New, divided, German states were called the Federal Republic of Germany—West Germany—and the German Democratic Republic—East Germany—respectively. The four Allies also controlled separate zones in Berlin, the pre-war capital and a constant flashpoint between the occupiers. West Germany established its capital in Bonn on the Rhine's west bank, south of Cologne.

U.S. financial aid to western European nations started in 1945, gradually guaranteeing their security, helping rebuild their armed forces, and promoting political stability. In 1947 President Harry Truman's new secretary of state, wartime Army chief of staff General George C. Marshall, crafted a huge European economic recovery package called the Marshall Plan. Through 1952, the Plan revitalized sixteen nations and consisted of food, staples, fuel, machinery, cash, and industrial investments. The Plan particularly resuscitated Germany, now a new ally, which served as a buffer to Communist forces of the Soviet Eastern Bloc, or Warsaw Pact.

The Allied occupation of Germany ended on May 5, 1955. In 1954 West Germany joined the Allies' North Atlantic Treaty Organization, which had been founded in 1949. By then, however, on July 1, 1953 the Robbinses had departed for the U.S. There, he assumed command of the attack transport USS *Pickaway* (APA-222) out of San Diego, for service during the Korean War.

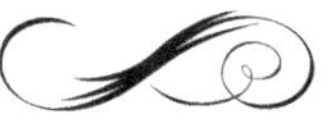

Following his three-year recovery from war wounds and limited duty in the Los Angeles-Long Beach area, the Navy sent Bob to command the Rhine River Patrol, a U.S. operation headquartered in Schierstein, West Germany. The family moved into a spacious rented villa on the east bank of the Rhine at nearby Eltville. Bob began traveling immediately on business, often taking Pat and sometimes Carroll and Berton, who were students at the American H.H. Arnold High School in Wiesbaden.

The family of four proceeded to the Schierstein area on arrival in Germany. Carroll remembered that "maids whom we called 'the girls' lived on top floor. We didn't move in there on arrival but were quartered temporarily in Villa Eltville. The Navy took over Villa Maria and paid the widow a stipend—she had lost everything during the war. The house had four floors counting a basement. We sat outside every day and watched the boats go by, and people on the boats waved back."

Besides his Rhine River Patrol duties, Bob's operational and diplomatic roles took him all over Occupied Germany and much of Europe, including behind the "Iron Curtain" separating West from East. Carroll believed he collected intelligence information. Pat's companionship, charm, wit, and confidence proved an exceptional asset and entre for the couple in both business and social situations.

Bob's wounds forever occasionally restricted his walking and left arm. "Dad used a cane during those days but only when his hand or leg bothered him. It was noticeable but hardly unusual. Yet, Mother for years bragged to others about the wounds and his Navy Cross, while failing to acknowledge that at least he came home alive. I felt she was out of place because so many men didn't."

Pat worked for both *Collier's* Magazine and the *Saturday Evening Post* while in Germany. Perhaps her most exciting and challenging assignment was taking the photos for the piece on the anti-Soviet White Russian Underground, which showcased her capabilities.

"She was not allowed to talk to us about it," said Carroll. "She said I had a big mouth. I had just graduated from high school. At this point I had become used to her going to odd places, as long as she let the American consul general know, because of Dad's job."

Pat teamed with writer Robert Shaplen. The piece featured Dr. Viktor M. Baydalakov, who fled Russia in 1920 and later founded the National Alliance of Russian Solidarists as an anti-Soviet organization, particularly opposed to the rule of Premier Joseph Stalin. Based in Limburg, West Germany, the young White emigre movement expressed dissatisfaction with older Russians' complacency for having lost the civil war, and championed a "second revolution" for reform without the past mistakes. (See more details about this piece in Chapter 1.) Their emblem, a gold trident, dated to Kievan Rus, the historical origin of the modern Russian state. Today, the same trident

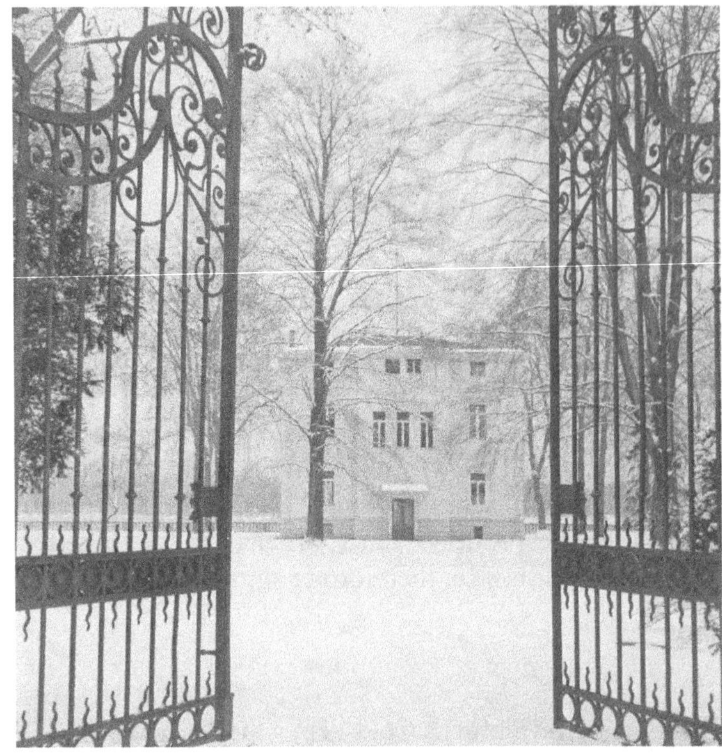

The Robbins family residence at Villa Maria in the village of Eltville on the Rhine's east bank north of Wiesbaden, West Germany, while he commanded the Rhine River Patrol, February 1952.

Rhine River boats passing the backyard of Villa Maria, Eltville, West Germany, the Robbinses' residence in the early 1950's.

symbol is used by post-Soviet Ukraine.[1]

Security concerns required that their interview be conducted clandestinely. Afterwards, Baydalakov wrote Pat on December 12, 1951: "Have many thanks for your kind letter and for sending the coloured pictures. I am quite touched by your attention." The innocuous envelope return address is an information agency in Limburg.[2]

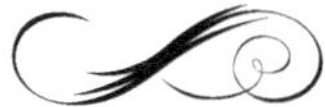

Activated in 1949, the Rhine River Patrol took over a wartime German naval base on the east bank. Capt. Robbins commanded the patrol from 1951 to 53. He reported to Rear Adm. Howard E. Orem, commander of the U.S. Naval Forces Germany, in his Heidelberg headquarters. A September 1952 *Collier's* piece (not Pat's) about the RRP reported that the American sector dominated about one hundred miles of river while the British, French, and Dutch monitored their northerly portions. "The 384 American sailors and the 125 carefully screened Germans who work with them would sweep their sector of all shipping, then go about the grim task of systematically demolishing anything that blocked the efforts of our forces or aided the enemy," defined as the Soviets and any of their Communist allies. "Our worry," said Capt. Robbins, "is defense, not occupation." The RRP employed 75-foot former German torpedo recovery boats. He designed an updated replacement boat.

They're Sticking Stalin with a Pitchfork

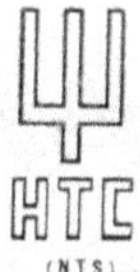

COLOR PHOTOGRAPHS FOR COLLIER'S BY PAT ROBBINS

Behind this trade-mark, a determined band of Soviet exiles has dented the Iron Curtain with eight million propaganda missives since 1949. The goal: a new Russian revolution

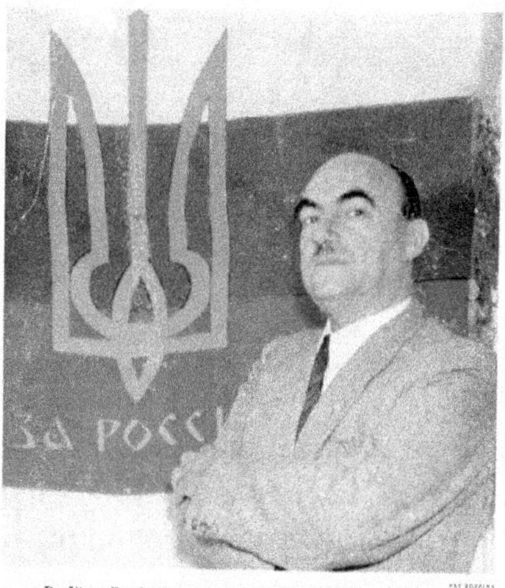

PAT ROBBINS

Dr. Victor Baydalakov, who fled Russia in 1920, heads Limburg staff of the NTS. Pennant is flag of the underground movement

'They're Sticking Stalin with a Pitchfork,' a photojournalism piece on the anti-Soviet White Russian underground, photos by Pat Robbins on assignment for *Collier's* magazine, February 22, 1952. The emblem on the flag is an ancient Russian-Ukrainian trident symbol, which has been revived by the post-Soviet Ukrainian state.

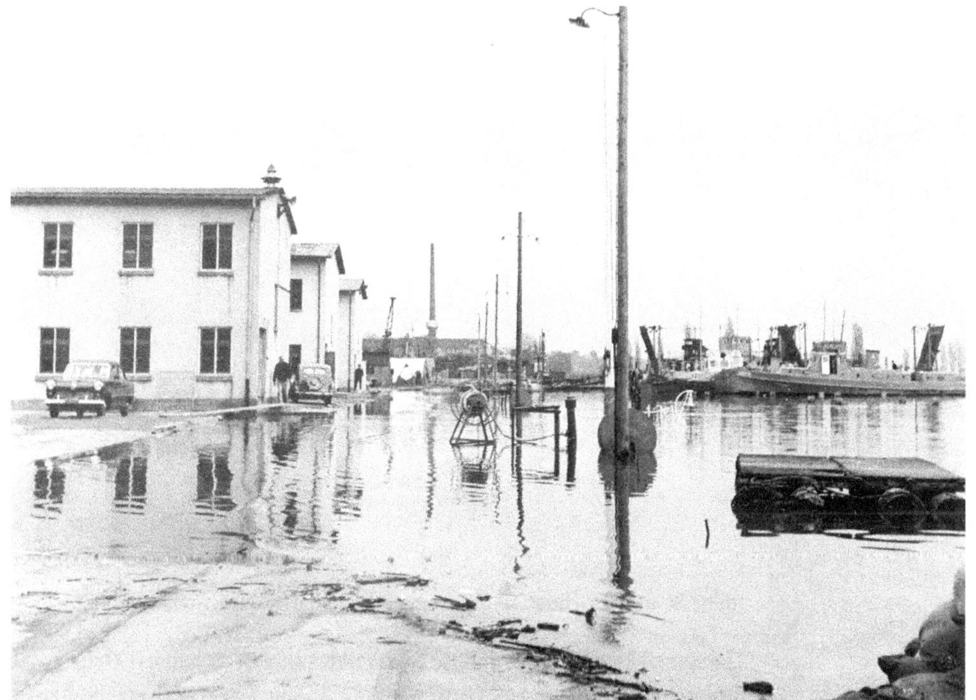

The Rhine floods the Rhine River Patrol base on the east bank at Schierstein, West Germany, 1952.

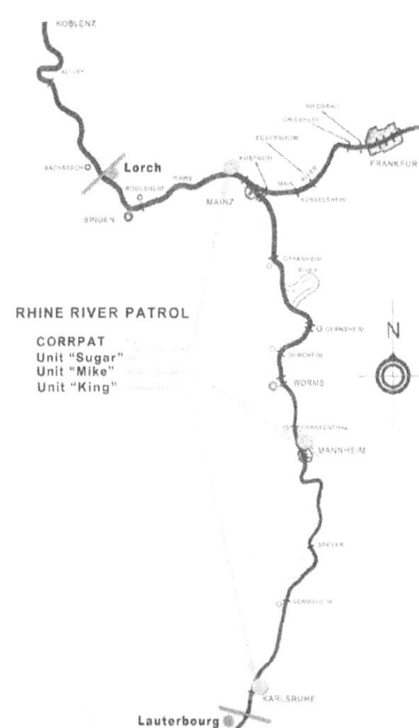

The U.S. Navy Rhine River Patrol's operational area, early 1950's.

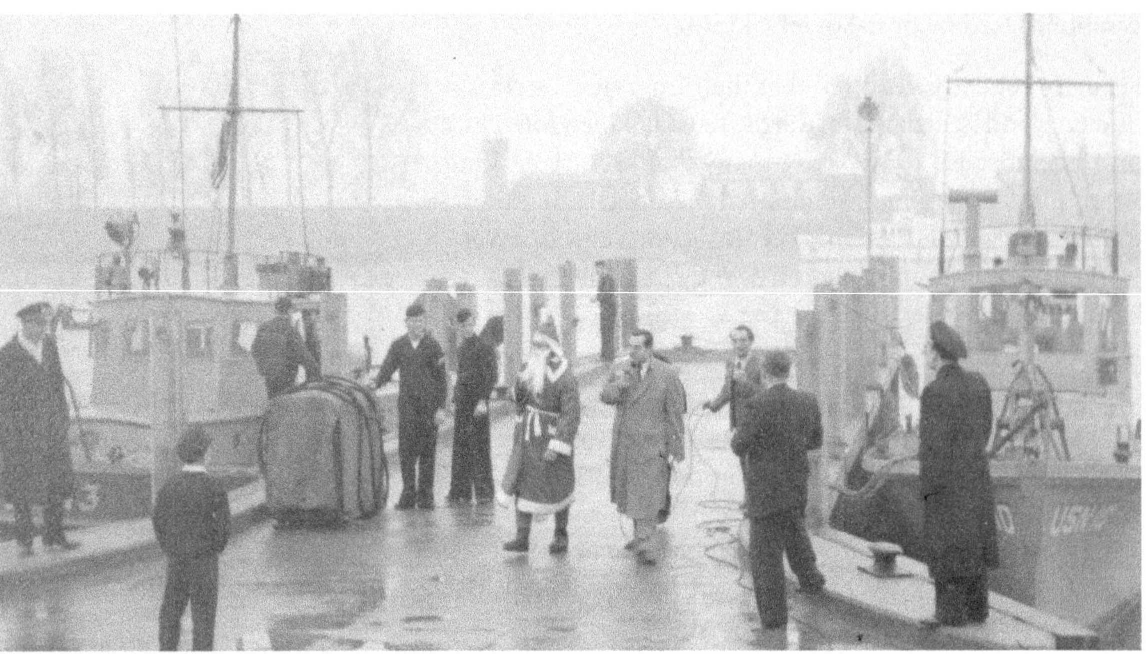

'Vater Weihnachten' (Father Christmas or Santa Claus) arrives for a Christmas party at the Rhine River Patrol Base, Schierstein, West Germany, 1951. Typical winter weather along the Rhine: overcast and dreary.

In 1975 after advancing President Gerald Ford's trip to Bonn, West Germany, I visited the Schierstein base and Eltville residence. I encountered a German civilian, a former naval chief petty officer, who had served under Capt. Robbins. He showed me around the office Robbins had used, and showed me photographs, documents, and boats. Fortunately I got there just before the man retired the following week. When I returned there in 2010, I recognized the cove area but no trace remained of the base, now a commercial marina. The villa remained but the neighborhood had grown.

From time to time, VIPs dropped in on the patrol. "President Truman's daughter Margaret Truman visited, wanted to take trip down the Rhine on one of Dad's patrol boats," Carroll recalled. "He said no, but it happened anyway." This was on August 11, 1952. "They wouldn't let Mother go because she wasn't credentialed by the White House. It required special treatment by the Navy. President Truman 'acted like a jerk' over the treatment his daughter was given there."

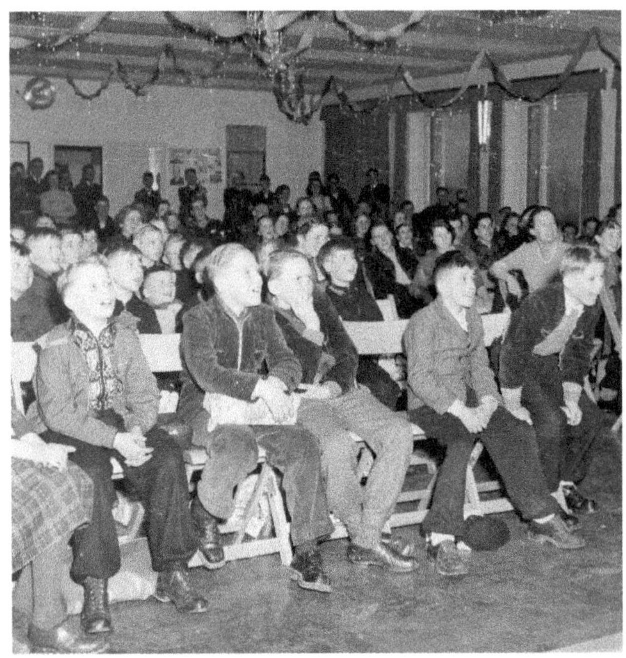

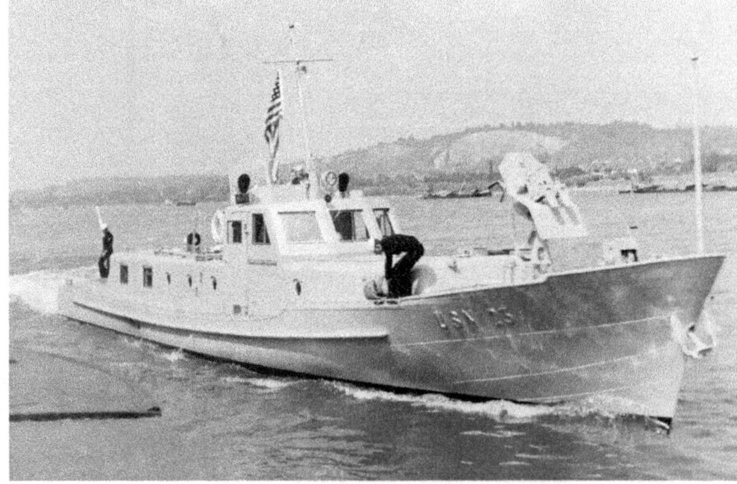

Rhine River Patrol boat, likely the type designed by Capt. Robbins, 1952.

Children of German Labor Service Unit workers enjoy a traveling USO show at Schierstein, West Germany, Christmas 1952. The base treated these children to a USO show with 'personalities you probably never heard of,' Carroll said.

A visit the following year was more in the chain of command. The industrialist Charles Wilson, former head of General Electric and known as "Electric Charlie," served in President Harry Truman's Office of Defense Mobilization before becoming secretary of defense. Wilson was escorted on his visit by Rear Adm. Orem, Capt. Robbins' immediate superior.

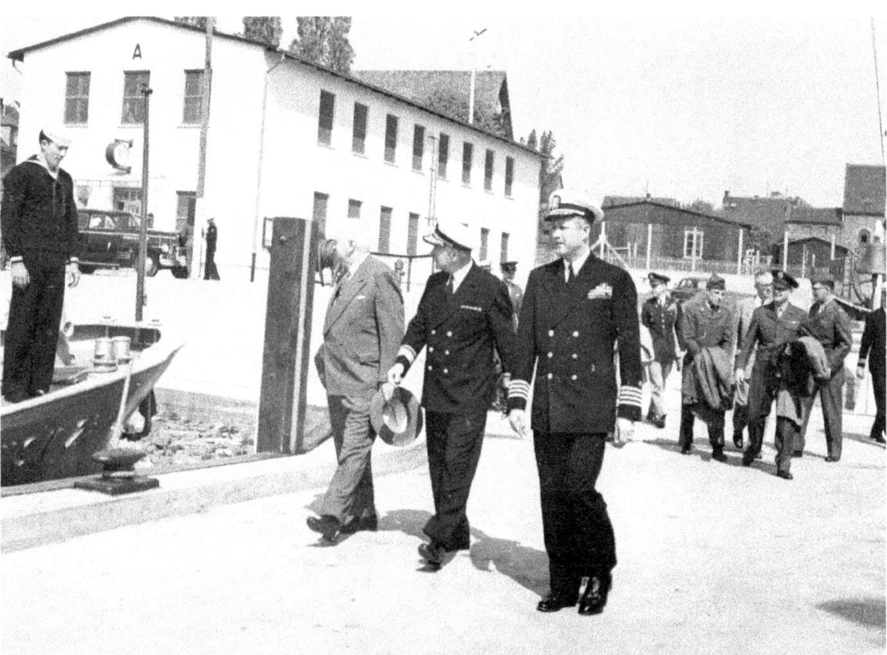

U.S. Secretary of Defense Charles E. Wilson, left with hat in hand, Rear Adm. Howard E. Orem, USN, Commander U.S. Naval Forces Germany, and Capt. Robbins, Commander, Rhine River Patrol, inspect the RRP base in Schierstein, West Germany, spring 1953.

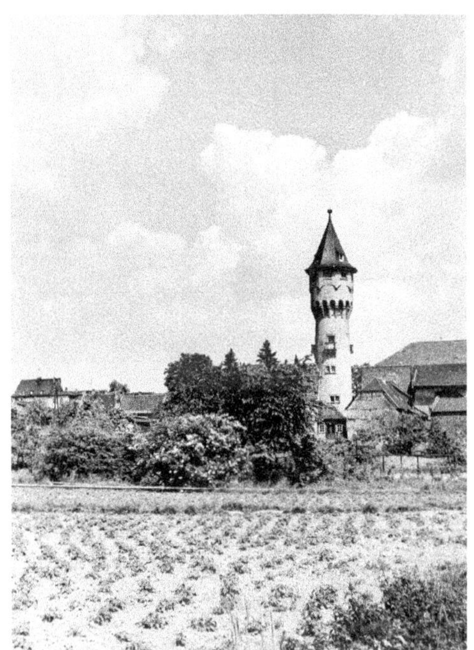

Farm and its tower on the Rhine next to Eltville where the Robbinses lived, West Germany, 1952.

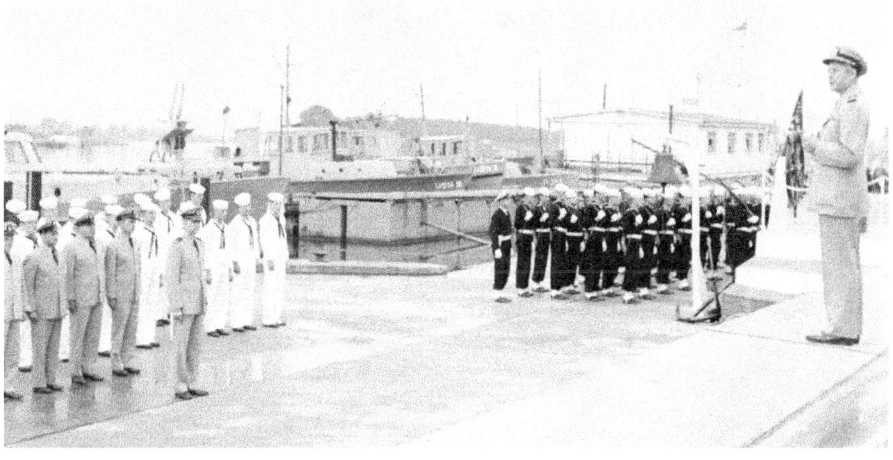

Capt. Robbins relinquishes command of the Rhine River Patrol at a ceremony at Schierstein, West Germany, June 1953.

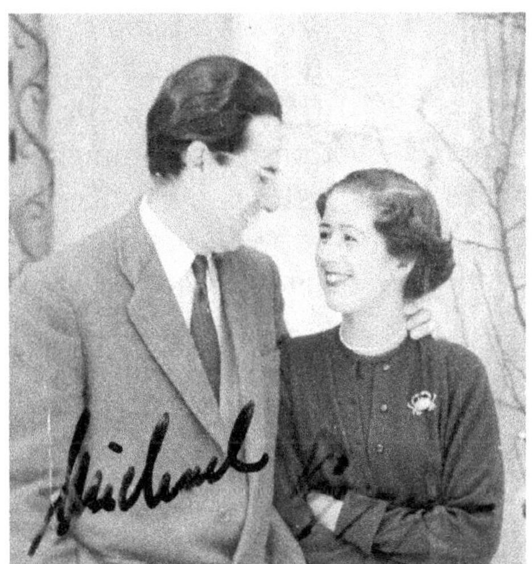

Count Michael Metternich and Baroness Inga Maria ('Poppy') von Ritter, husband and wife, West Germany, spring 1953.

Because of Bob's combined naval and diplomatic position and Pat's endless "connections," the Robbinses fit perfectly into what remained of Europe's society and old nobility. She thoroughly enjoyed seeking these new professional and social avenues, combining an appetite for attention with hostess skills, grace, and elegance, while adding their names to her resume. Carroll remembered the count and baroness as "delightful people and would come to dinner at our villa occasionally. They spoke French and English."

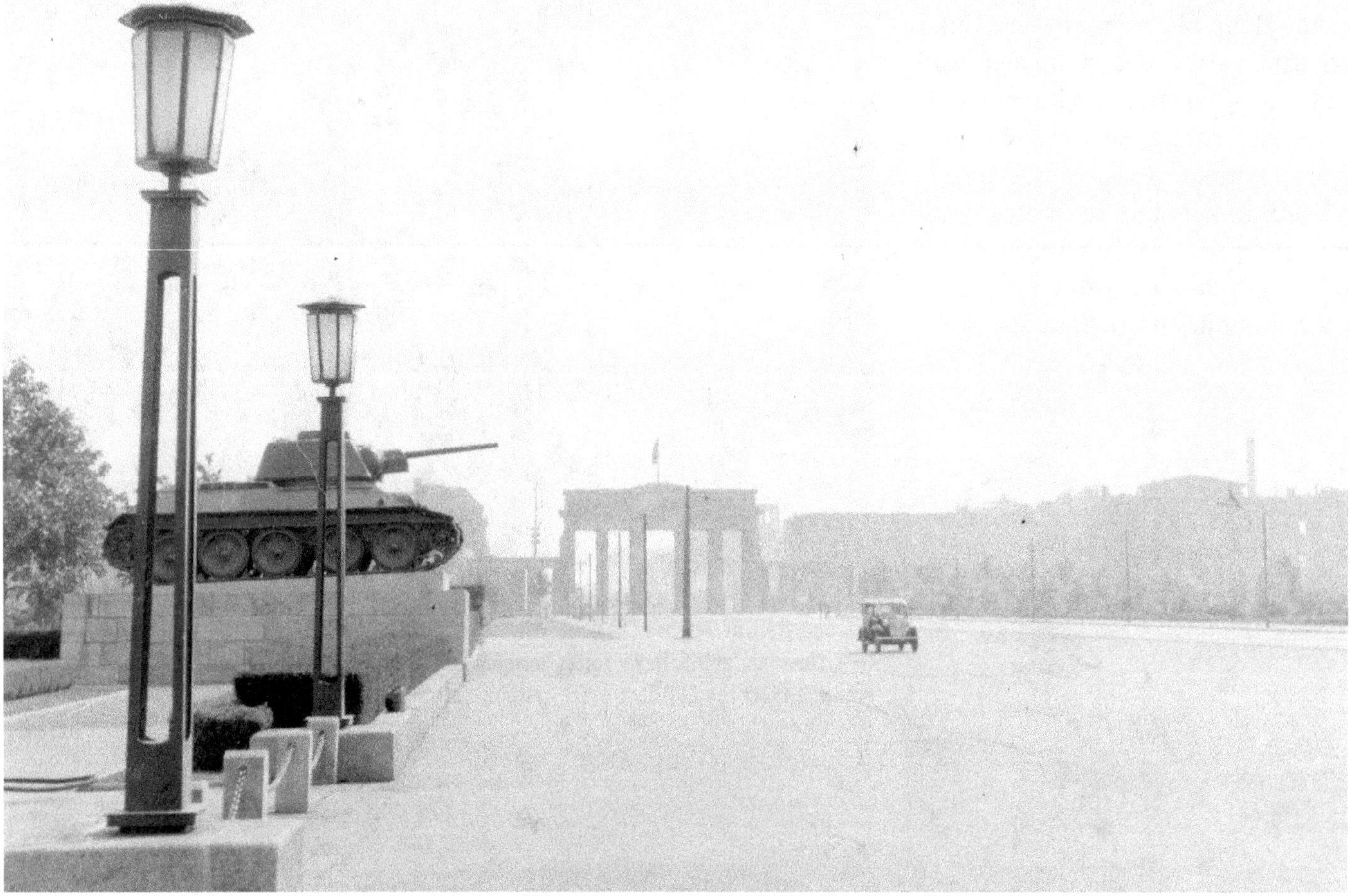

A characteristic scene of postwar Berlin: the starkness of a lone vehicle driving down the deserted Strasse des Siebzehnten Juni, past World War II T-34 tanks on display as part of Soviet war memorial, West Berlin. Beyond the Brandenburg Gate is Berlin's Russian Sector. May 1953.

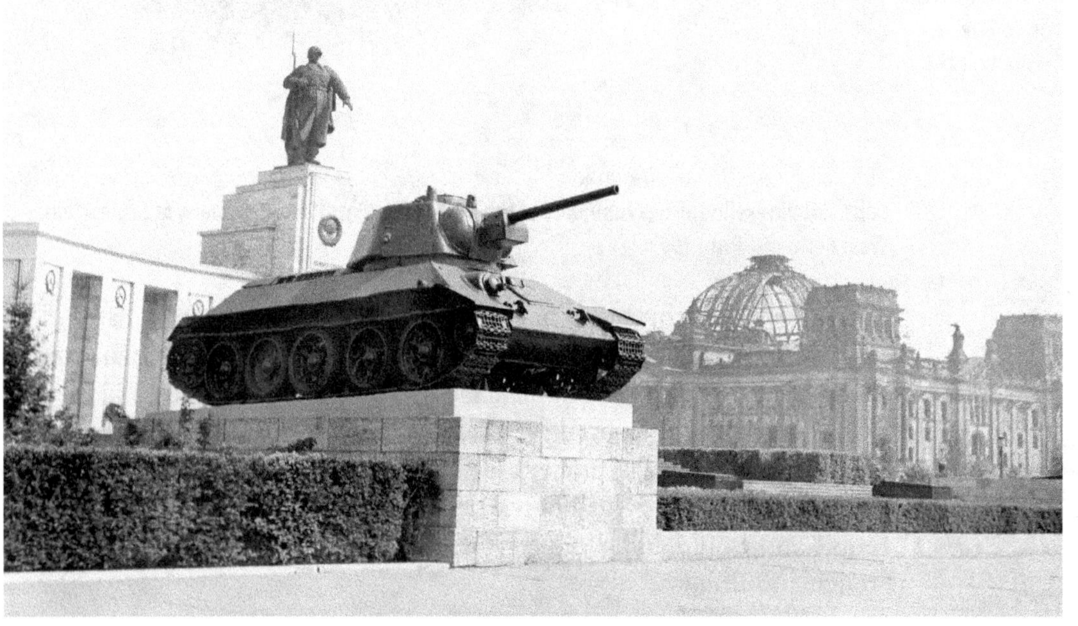

Soviet Victory Memorial in the Tiergarten Park, West Berlin, Germany, May 1953. In the background are the ruins of the pre-war German parliament building, the Reichstag. Now restored, it again houses Germany's parliament.

Amidst the Berlin ruins in late 1945, the Soviet Union constructed this monument to its victory over Nazi Germany. Constructed from war artifacts and flanked by two T-34 tanks reputed to have been the first to reach Berlin, the curved structure is made of Hitler's chancellery marble. Although in the British sector of Berlin before German unification, Soviet soldiers stood watch over it. The T-34

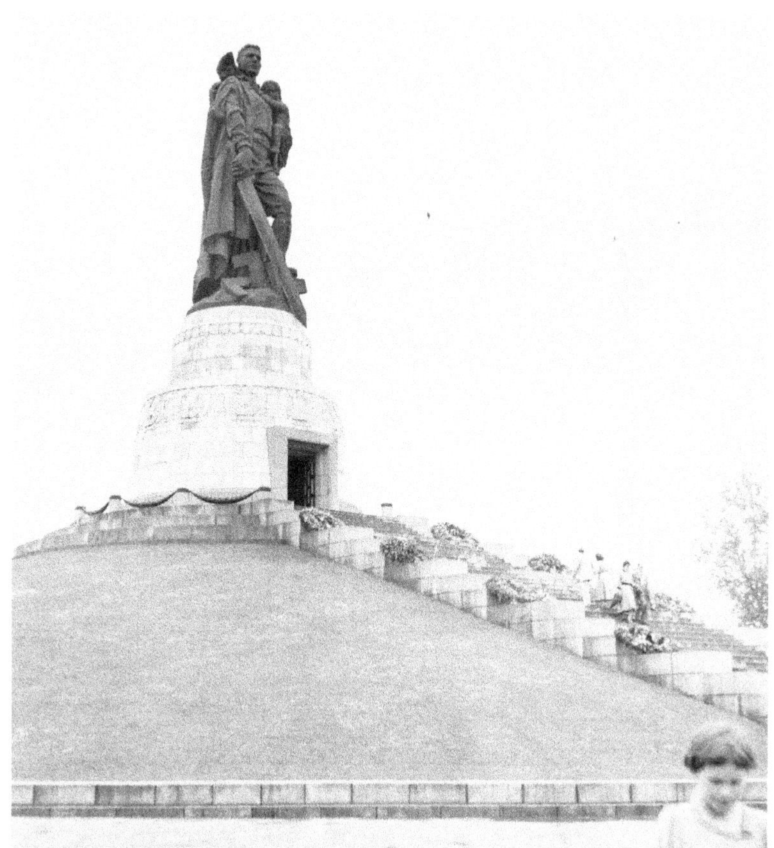

The Soviet War Memorial, dedicated to the USSR's victory in World War II and its dead, in Treptower Park, East Berlin, East Germany, May 1953.

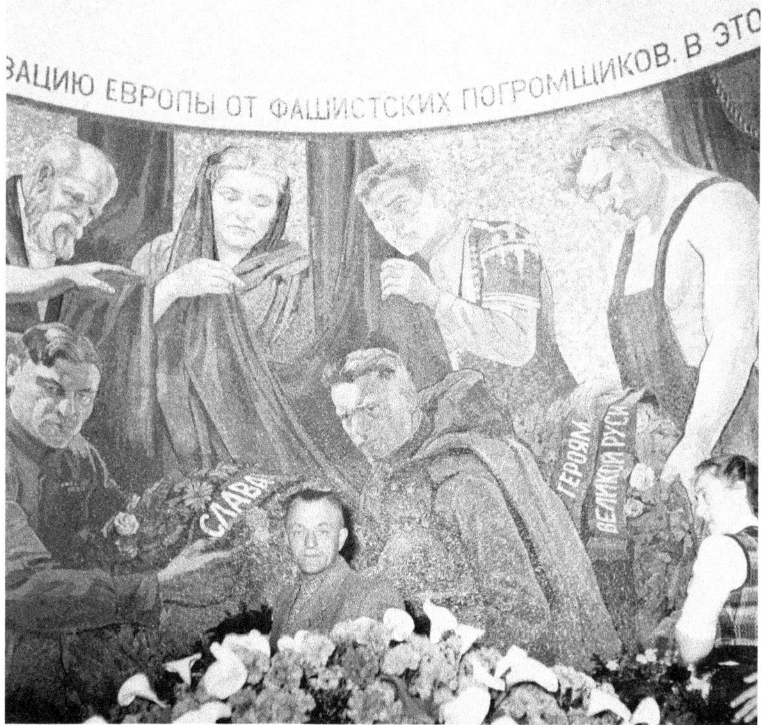

Inside Soviet War Memorial in Treptower Park, East Berlin, East Germany, May 1953. Note the muted look on the visitor's face as he blends into the montage.

was the Soviets' most famous and potent tank in World War II. On this business trip behind the Iron Curtain, Pat accompanied Bob but Carroll remained in Eltville. "They did get into the Soviet zone for a while. Her favorite thing was to play stupid and bluff to get some place," Carroll remarked.

Opened in 1949, this one is larger than the Tiergarten memorial near the Brandenburg Gate and includes a giant statue, museum, and a cemetery for some 5,000 Soviet soldiers who died in the Battle of Berlin in April-May 1945. The soldier on top brandishes a sword smiting a Nazi swastika while holding a child. Red Army troops guarded the memorial at the time of the Robbins visit. A large plaza surrounds the memorial displaying Joseph Stalin's words and combat scenes. The Soviets built a third memorial in Berlin's Pankow District.

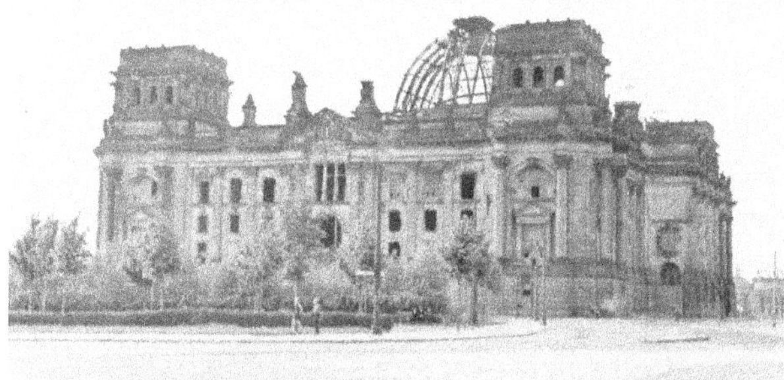

The ruined Reichstag, pre-war German parliament building taken by the Soviets in April 1945, was left standing as a war remnant, West Berlin, Germany, 1953.

The Reichstag served as the heart of the short-lived German democracy between World Wars I and II; the German Republic was proclaimed there in 1918. In 1933 Hitler ordered the building burned, blaming the Communists, as a means of grabbing national power. Until 1999 it remained an unused symbol.

Carroll didn't accompany her parents on the East Germany trip. "I had trouble traveling anywhere in Occupied Germany until I turned 18 and could get an American passport, which I got at the consul general's office in Frankfurt. Before that I had an ID as a military dependent born in Shanghai who could travel in Allied countries."

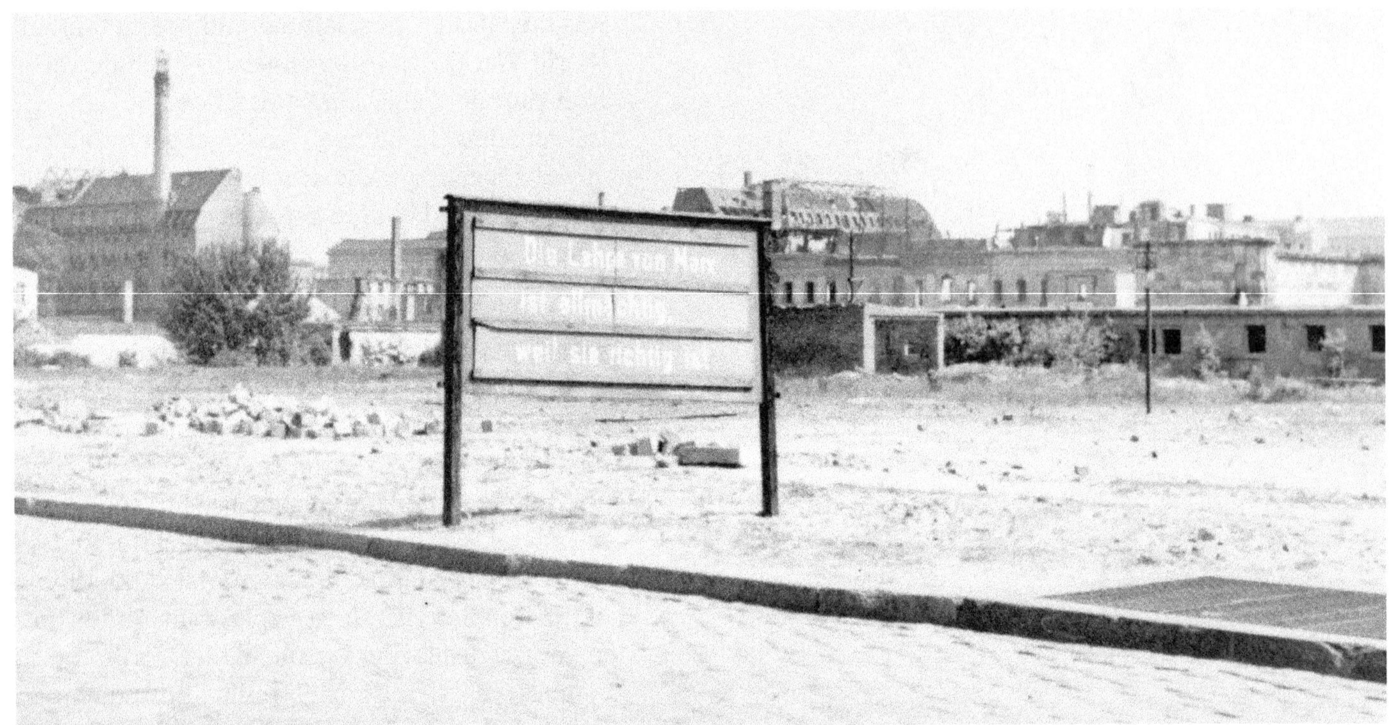

Site of Hitler's Berlin bunker amidst ruins, East Berlin, East Germany, May 1953.

Within his underground multi-level concrete bunker, Hitler and his die-hard cohorts, including his mistress Eva Braun, lived out their final days as the "Thousand-Year Reich" crumbled above them. Hitler and Braun committed suicide on April 30, 1945. Soviet troops captured this area in early May, and found Hitler's charred remains above ground within sight of this photo. The Soviets cleared the bunker wreckage, leveled the area, and discouraged visitors. The sign, referring to Karl Marx, on whose philosophy Communism was based, reads: "The doctrine of Marx is almighty because he is right."

Allied bombers destroyed up to 80 percent of German cities' historic buildings. Although much rubble still stood in 1953, reconstruction progressed. "Never before had so much been lost—and yet, never before were there so many new buildings. Never before had an entire country been rebuilt . .

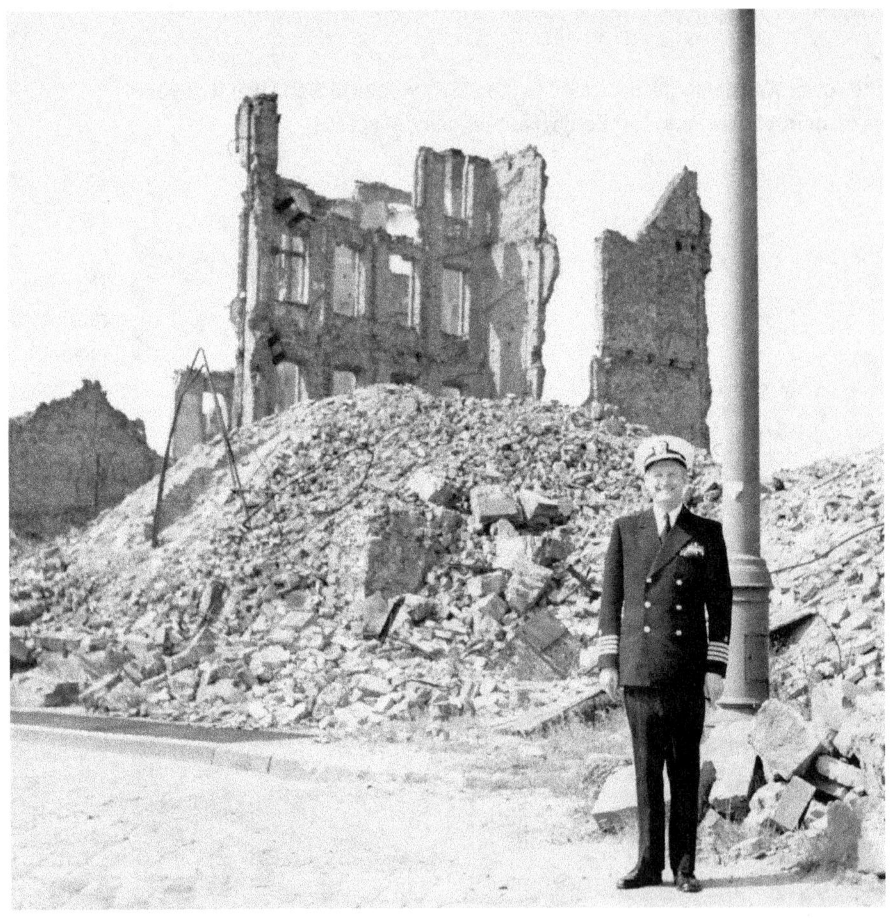

Bob Robbins and ruins, West Berlin, May 1953.

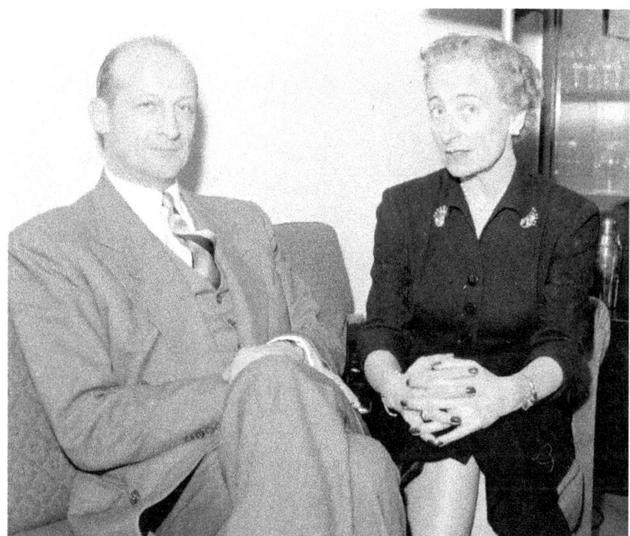

Princess Gabrielle of Liechtenstein and husband Harrison Day Blair, a New York banker, 1953.

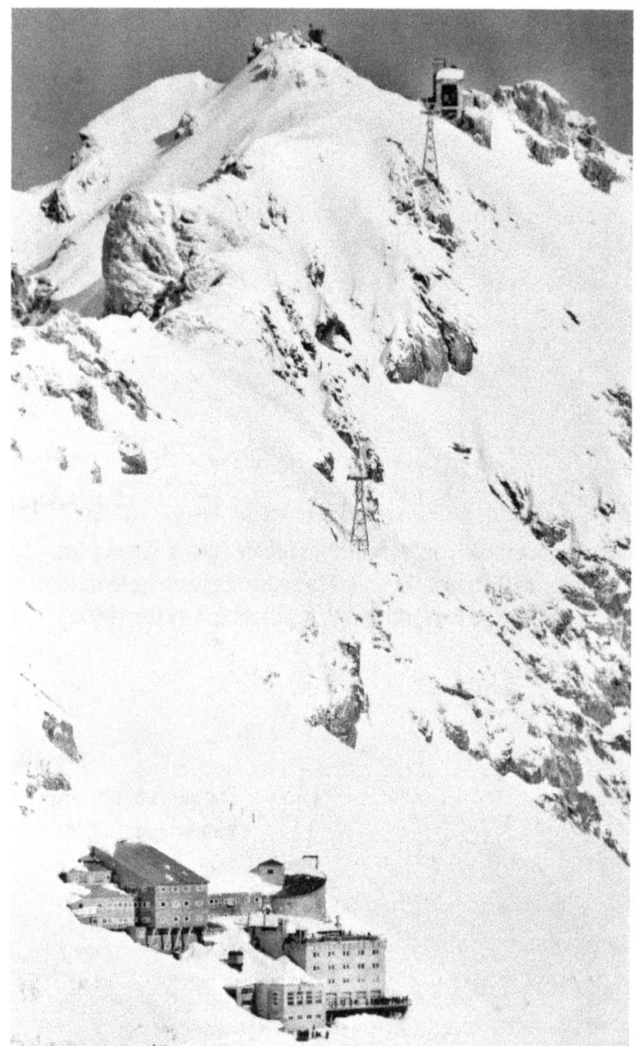

The Schneefernerhaus on the Zugspitze mountain, the Alps, West Germany, from its cable car, December 1952.

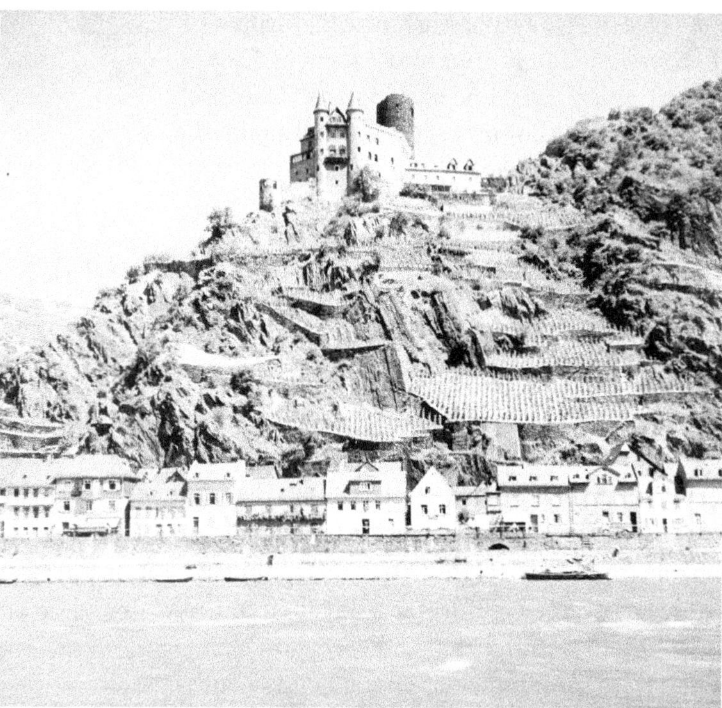

The famed Katz Castle on the east bank of the Rhine, early 1950's.

. . In West Germany alone, some 400 million cubic meters (14 billion cubic feet) of rubble was piled up . . . . Germany's phoenix-like resurrection from the inferno resembled a continuation of the wartime construction" as remaining buildings were leveled "to make way for the new."[4]

"Wiesbaden, near where we lived, had several bombed-out buildings as a reminder to the people of what had happened," Carroll recalled.

In its long history as a prominent Rhine landmark, Katz Castle was besieged, demolished (including by Napoleon in 1806), rebuilt, and extended several times. From 1946 to 1951 the castle served as the local high school "Institut Hoffmann." Private property since 1989, it is now the Hotel Katz Castle.

"Princess Gabrielle owned a castle in Trier which my parents went to several times," said Carroll. "The only times I saw her was when she visited us in Eltville. Sometime German nobility held balls and parties and would invite those Americans they deemed worthy of invitation. I was the 'eligible daughter' and attended some. Blair moved back to New York after the divorce and invited me to play tennis. He was on the make and obviously flirting. I said I had to meet some friends for lunch. I think he took that as a cue, the old goat. Mother kept admonishing me to go out with him."

A favorite getaway resort for Americans stationed in Europe and known as "Germany's grand old dame of ski towns," Garmisch is also near the country's highest mountain, the Zugspitze (9,714 feet).

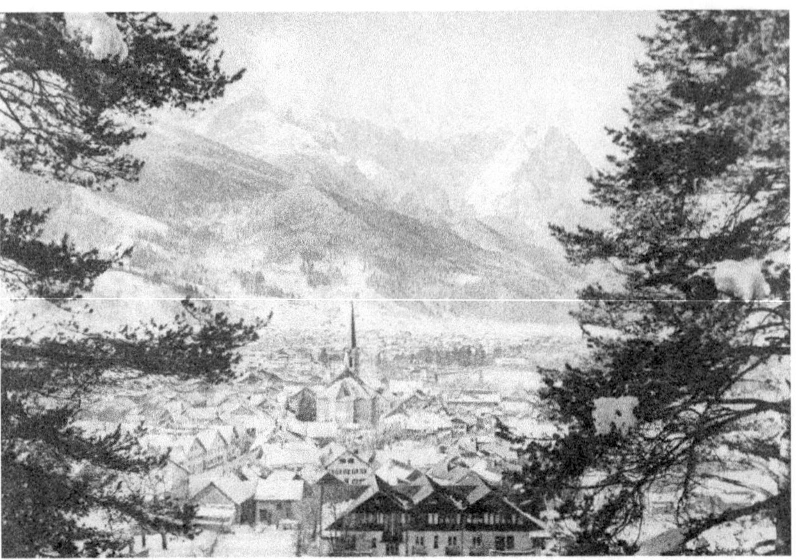

Garmisch-Partenkirchen in the Bavarian Alps, West Germany, winter 1952. The classic Bavarian winter scene.

On a trip to the Zugspitze (photo on previous page) Carroll remember being "scared shitless. The damned cable car had to wait to be repaired. I didn't have enough clothes on and was freezing to death. I didn't want to up there. It was snowing heavily; the wind was blowing; during winter Olympic tryouts. Oh, no, Mother was determined to go up there! Not many people get to the top of Zugspitze. I broke my left leg skiing on that trip. I just forgot to do the right thing, was taken to the hospital on a stretcher with bearers on skis. They were looking for my parents. My brother verified who I was and then returned to skiing. He did the Olympic ski run, but didn't qualify for the junior tryouts. I haven't been on skis since."

"Mother and I joined other mothers and daughters from Wiesbaden on a tour of Italy, eventually the two of us branching out on our own. She wanted to visit people she knew."

Other travels took Pat and her camera to the Netherlands and along the Danube River.

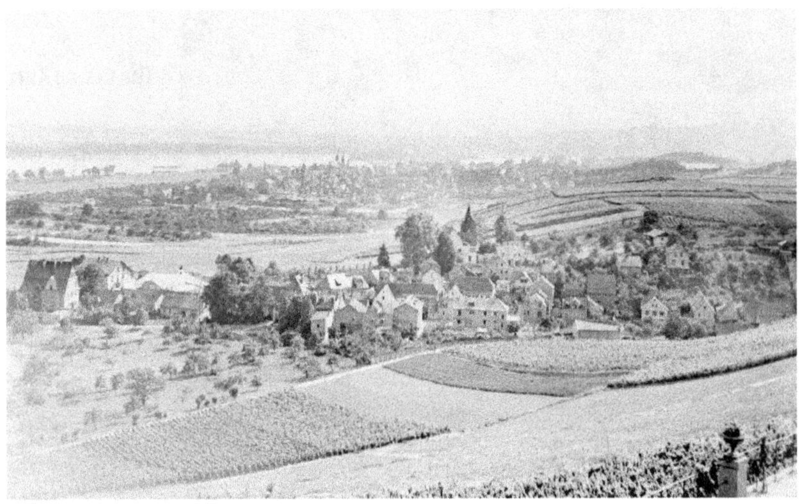

Looking southwestward across the Rhine from Schloss Johannisberg, famous for Riesling wines in the Rheingau District with claims to being the world's oldest Riesling vineyards, July 1952. Destroyed in World War II, it was rebuilt by the 1960's.

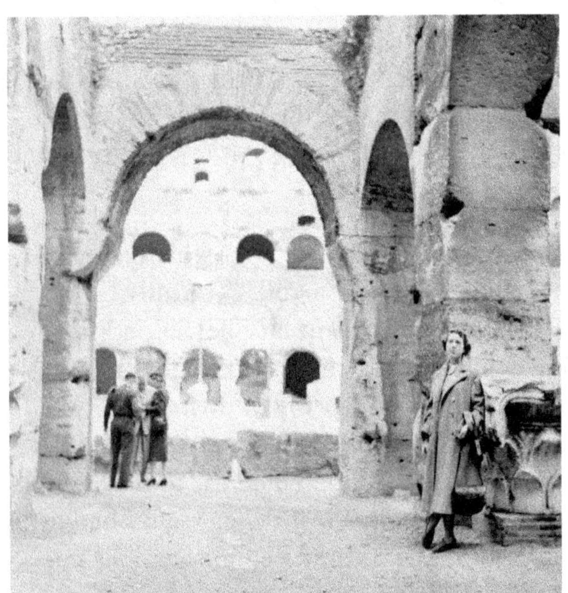

Carroll at the Coliseum in Rome, Italy, October 1952.

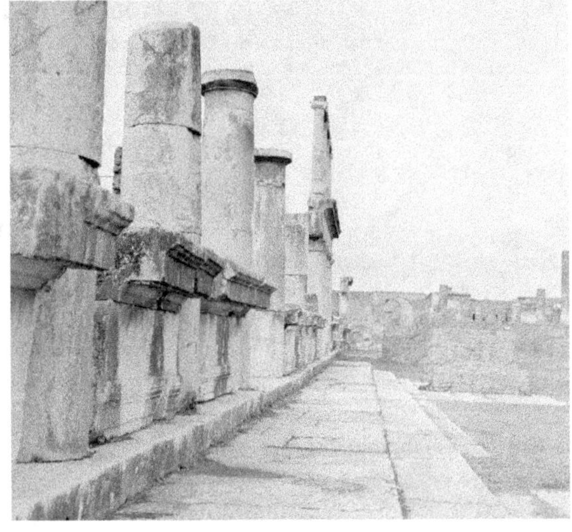

The ruins of ancient Roman Pompei, Italy, years before the onslaught of mass tourism, October 1952.

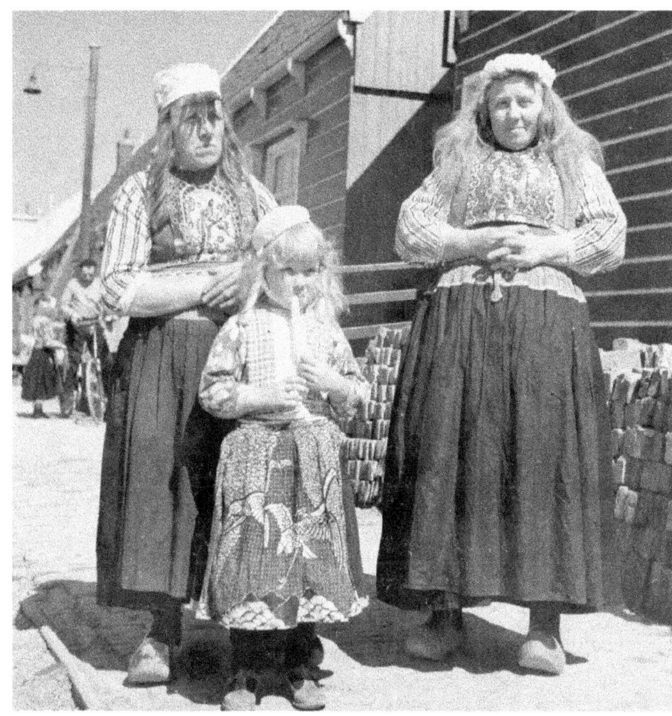

Native residents of Marken Island, The Netherlands, April 1953. 'They all looked alike because they intermarried,' Carroll said.

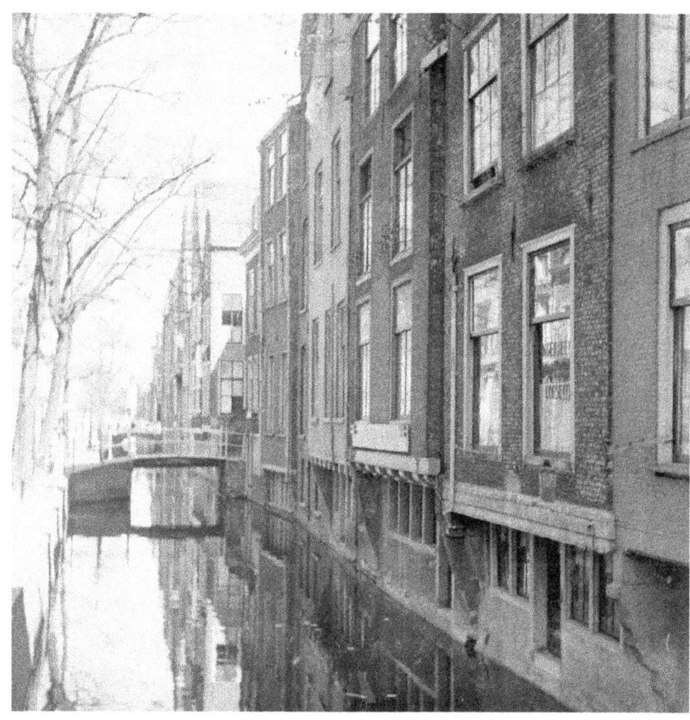

A canal in Delft, The Netherlands, home of the world-famous 'Delft Blue' porcelain industry, April 1953.

The mighty temple of Walhalla, a copy of Athens' Parthenon built in 1942, rises above the Danube. Its Hall of Fame contains 130 busts of German giants and legends. Recent additions include Albert Einstein and Sophie Scholl, student leader of the White Rose anti-Nazi movement executed in 1943.

"I remember the two bombed-out houses, which were left there deliberately," said Carroll. "Mother and Dad took a lot of trips together while I was left home in school. She went with him when allowed. I was picked up by school bus in front of our villa which wound through the Taunus Mountains, taking about 45 minutes via roundabout route. The Taunus were a great place to go boar hunting."

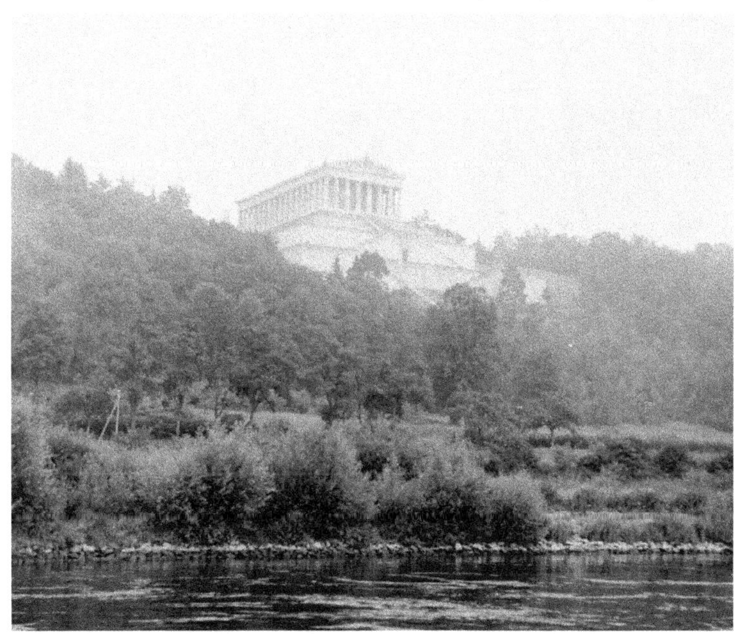

Walhalla (Valhalla) on the Danube River east of Regensberg, Bavaria, West Germany, August 1951.

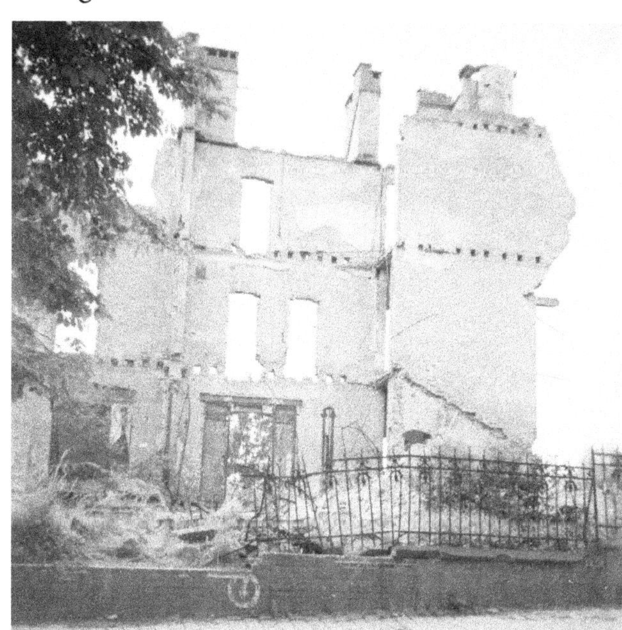

House in Neroberg, West Germany, destroyed during the war, 1951.

As she traveled in Europe, Pat employed framing and depth techniques developed in the 1930's China. "We drove a lot up and down the Rhine with whatever gas was available, especially to Koblenz," Carroll recalled. "We could get gas tickets only once a month. When Dad went on official business a driver took him in a military car."

Before school started in 1951, "Mother and I drove to Paris and met Dad and a couple who served on his staff. By that time I had eaten my way through three or four towns and had put on a lot of weight."

Indicative of her "ever-exploratory" mode, a determined Pat rode Vienna's "Riesenrad" Ferris wheel for some breathtaking shots. Bob accompanied her. Opened in 1897, the wheel served as a setting for the 1949 movie, *The Third Man*, starring Orson Welles, which undoubtedly attracted Pat and other sightseers.

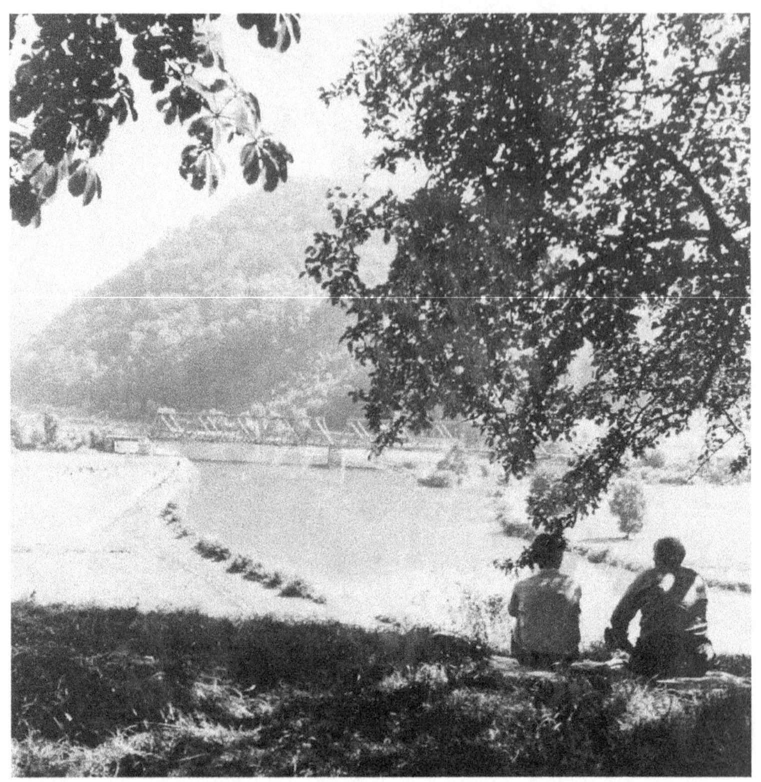

The Lahn River near Limburg an der Lahn, West Germany, August 1951.

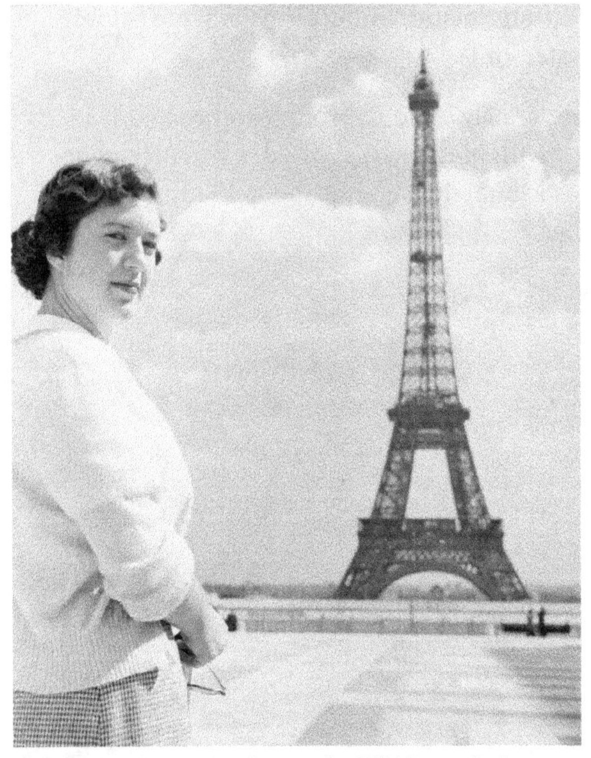

Carroll, age 17, appears alone at the Eiffel Tower, Paris, France, August 1951. As with the photo of a deserted Pompeii, where was the rest of Europe? August is their vacation month. Had the post-war recovery stalled?

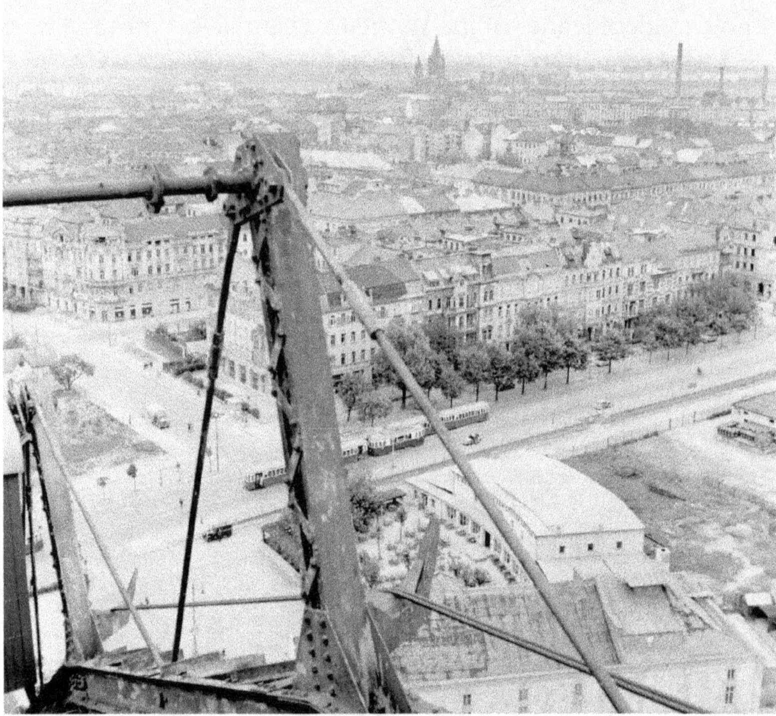

An overview of the City of Vienna, Austria, from the Riesenrad, the city's world-famous gigantic Ferris wheel located in the Prater park, May 1952. This wheel was the setting for a famous scene with Orson Welles and Joseph Cotten in the movie *The Third Man*.

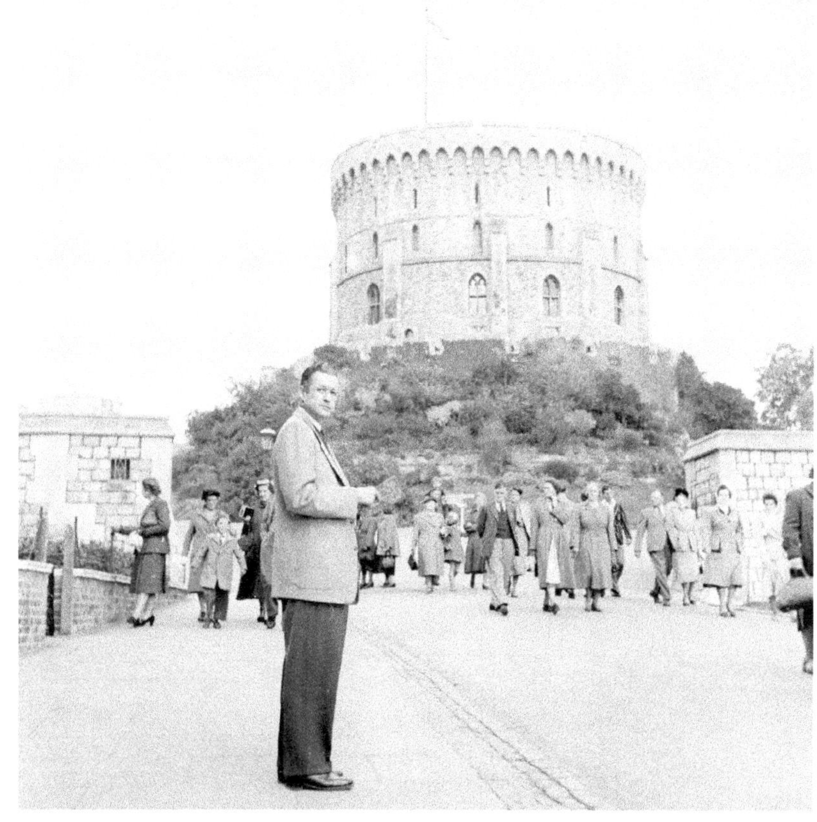

Bob at Windsor Castle, a residence of the queen of England, Elizabeth II, around the time she assumed the throne in 1952.

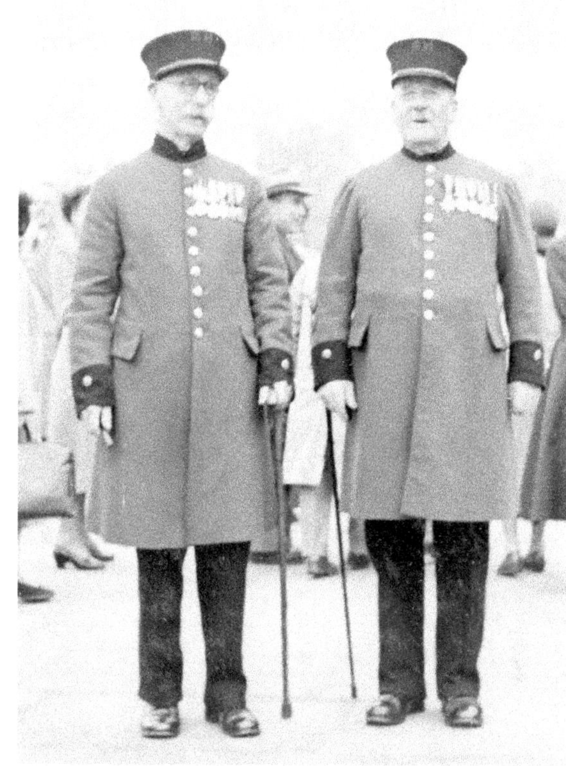

Old military pensioners, London, England, September 1952.

Germany loves festivals and carnivals, especially those celebrating wine along the Rhine. Fasching originated as a pagan festival but is observed primarily in Catholic parts of the country. "This is the week when people are allowed to 'flip out,' and behave recklessly before the beginning of Lent . . . ." Carroll enjoyed "their religious mardi gras. Everybody wore wild costumes, drank a lot of beer, partied from morning till night for three days. I thought it was pretty cool. They had balls all over town, and I did go to one."

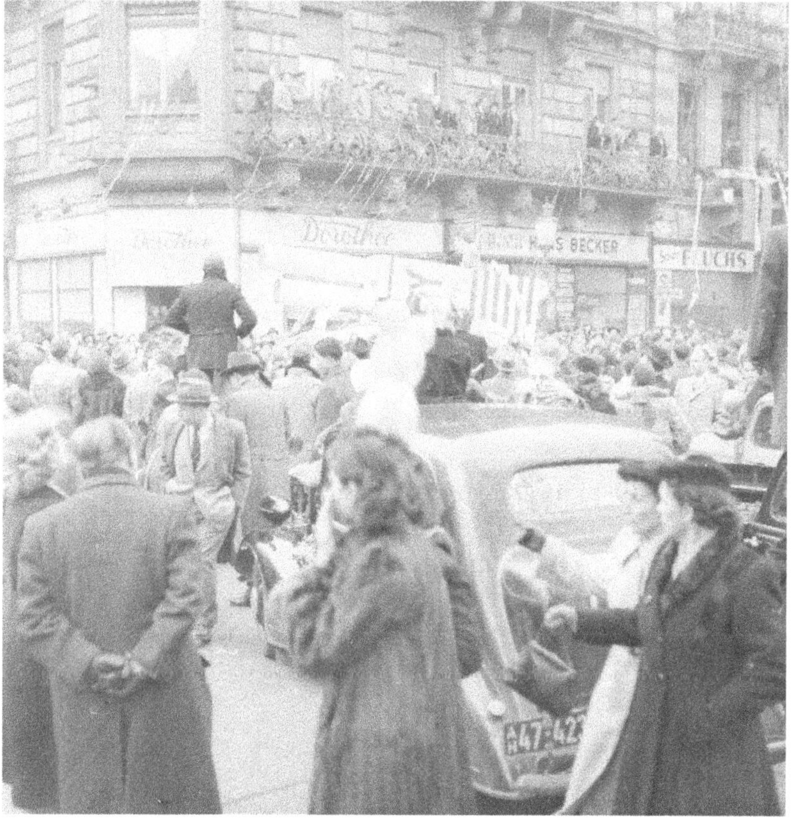

Celebrating Fasching in Munich, West Germany, 1951.

Carroll graduated from Wiesbaden's Arnold High School in 1952. The family relocated in 1952 to Coronado, California, where Bob embellished his reputation as commanding officer of the USS *Pickaway* (APA-222). Berton graduated from Coronado High School and earned his commission from the Naval Academy in 1958.

For whatever reasons, Pat apparently did not renew a relationship with the Hollywood community, whose Golden Age was sunsetting amid the Communist "black list" hysteria, or even her old Los Angeles friends—at least as her printed photographs show. She began shooting 2-2-inch color slides, rather than negatives, but never built a slide show or printed many. We have some. Is this my next project?

Pat regenerated her career during their move to the Washington, D.C., area in 1955.

CHAPTER 7

'With Full Honors': A Classic 'Saturday Evening Post' Image and the Washington Social Scene

"The military funeral marches at slow cadence," read the *Saturday Evening Post.* "The drum is muffled, swathed in black, as the caisson bears the flag-draped casket of one more warrior to his resting place in Arlington National Cemetery . . . . Here lie in glory men of every rank, from all the military services and from all the wars in our history. All together, nearly 100,000 rest in Arlington now. Photograph by Pat Robbins."[1]

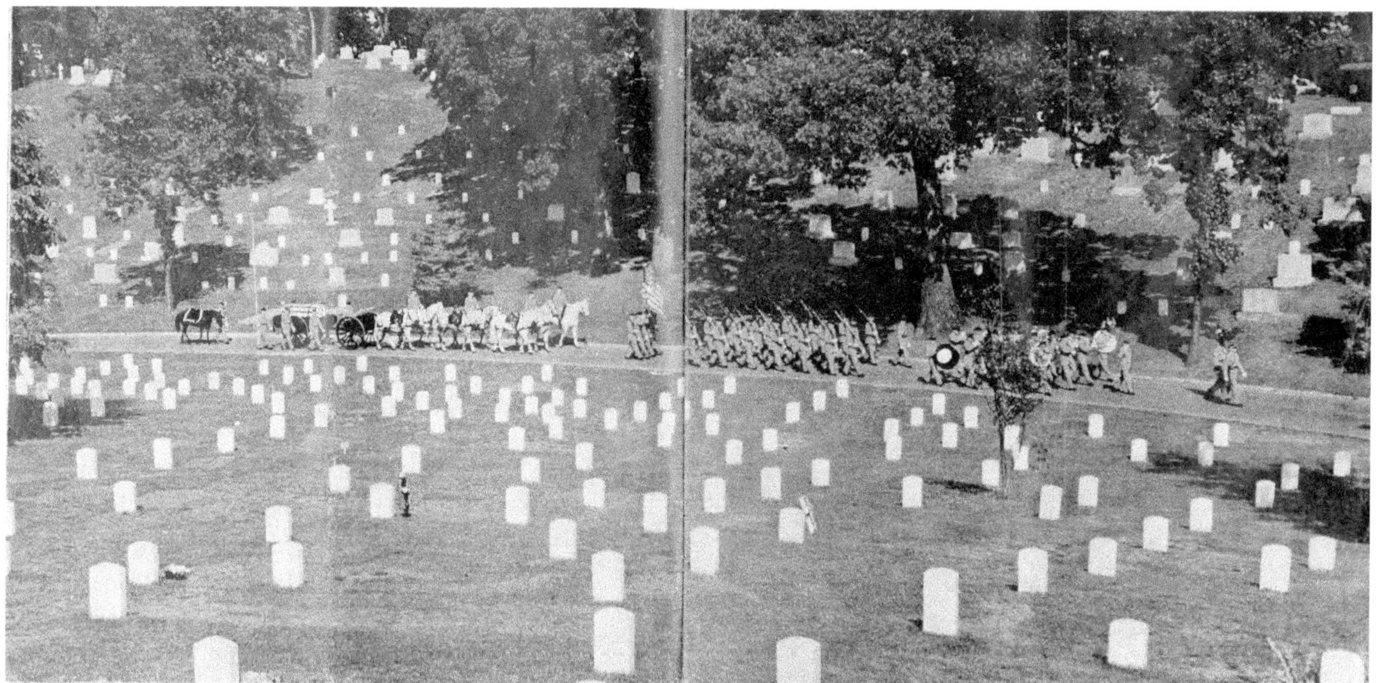

Military funeral procession at Arlington National Cemetery, Arlington, Va., a two-page spread in the *Saturday Evening Post*, May 31, 1958.

Pat planned this scene for days, scoping the territory, working with cemetery officials for the right time of day, devising her position and angles, for just the right aperture opening, lenses, and filter. "She was as proud of this one as any she took in her entire career," Carroll said.

This picture is nearly worth an entire chapter. Coincidentally, on my latest visit to Arlington National Cemetery to visit Pat and Bob in February 2014, a similar procession passed near their gravesite. Of course this picture came to mind.

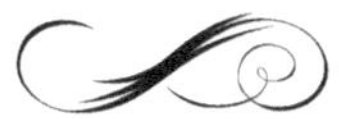

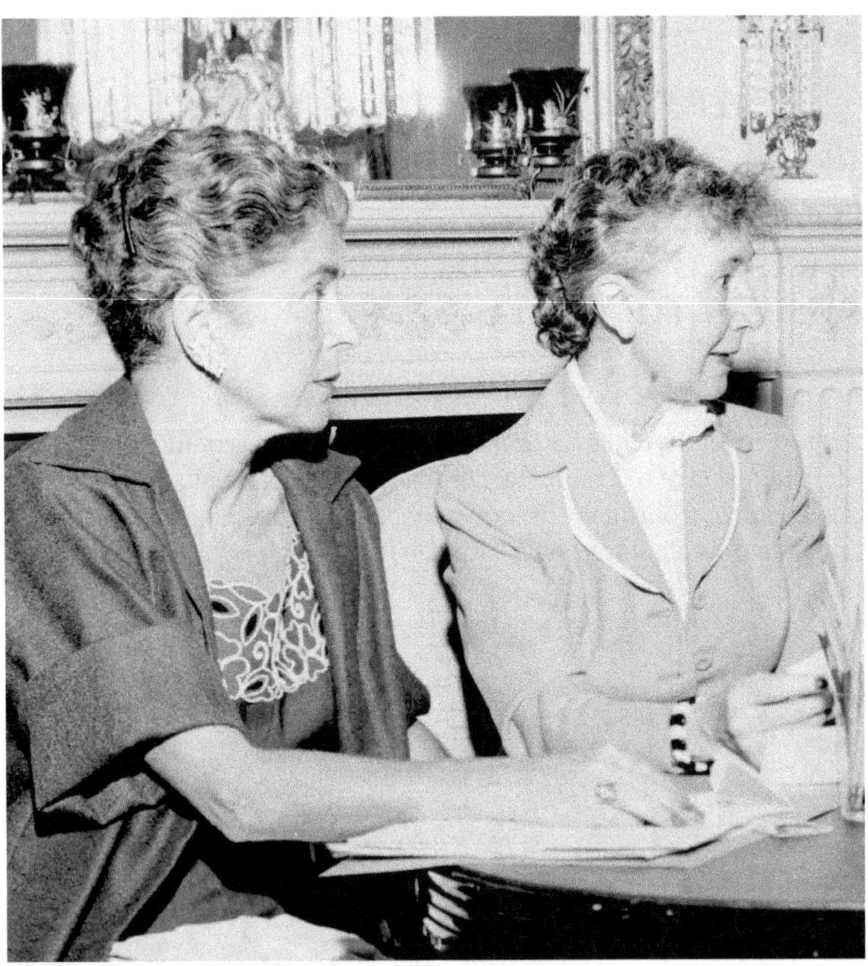

Mrs. Roland (Sally) Smoot (left) and Mrs. Arleigh (Roberta "Bobbie") Burke planning the annual Navy Ball, Washington, D. C., 1957.

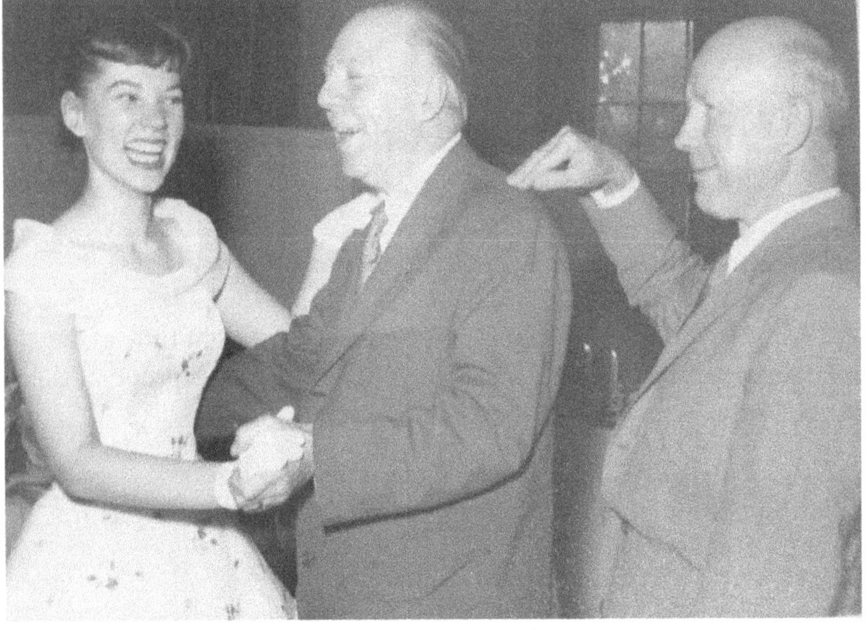

Miss Mary Elizabeth McLendon, daughter of *Washington Post and Times Herald* society columnist Winzola McLendon, with Secretary of the Army Wilber M. Brucker and Secretary of the Navy Charles S. Thomas at her debut, Washington, mid-1950s.

Although the wife of "only" a Navy captain, Pat, never reticent to advance her career or her husband's, put years of experience to work in their only duty assignment in Washington, DC. Whether through social graces and again, connections, or her professional reputation, she immediately gathered friends and even more acquaintances, particularly among senior military officers and government officials. It helped that Bob, a highly decorated World War II veteran, occupied a key Pentagon billet.

Sally Smoot was a long-time friend whose husband, Admiral Roland Smoot, was one of the Navy's most popular and heralded leaders and also a wartime hero. Their ties began early in Bob's career and lasted after both retired. Pat hadn't known Bobbie Burke as well. Her admiral husband served as chief of naval operations, the Navy's senior officer position, from 1955 to 1961, and historically was one of its most accomplished and respected commanders.

These ladies, along with First Lady Mamie Eisenhower, served as board members of the JANGOS (Junior Army-Navy Guild Organization), a capital-area group serving military enlisted personnel. Carroll, employed as an assistant buyer at Washington's prestigious Garfinkel's Department Store, served in the JANGOS kitchen on weekends.

"My Mother was the party-ingest person I ever knew. She was always going to parties," Carroll remembered. "The cream of the crop from Dad's Naval Academy class [1931] were gathering for duty in Washington at that time. Their admiral stars were beginning to emerge." Well suited and

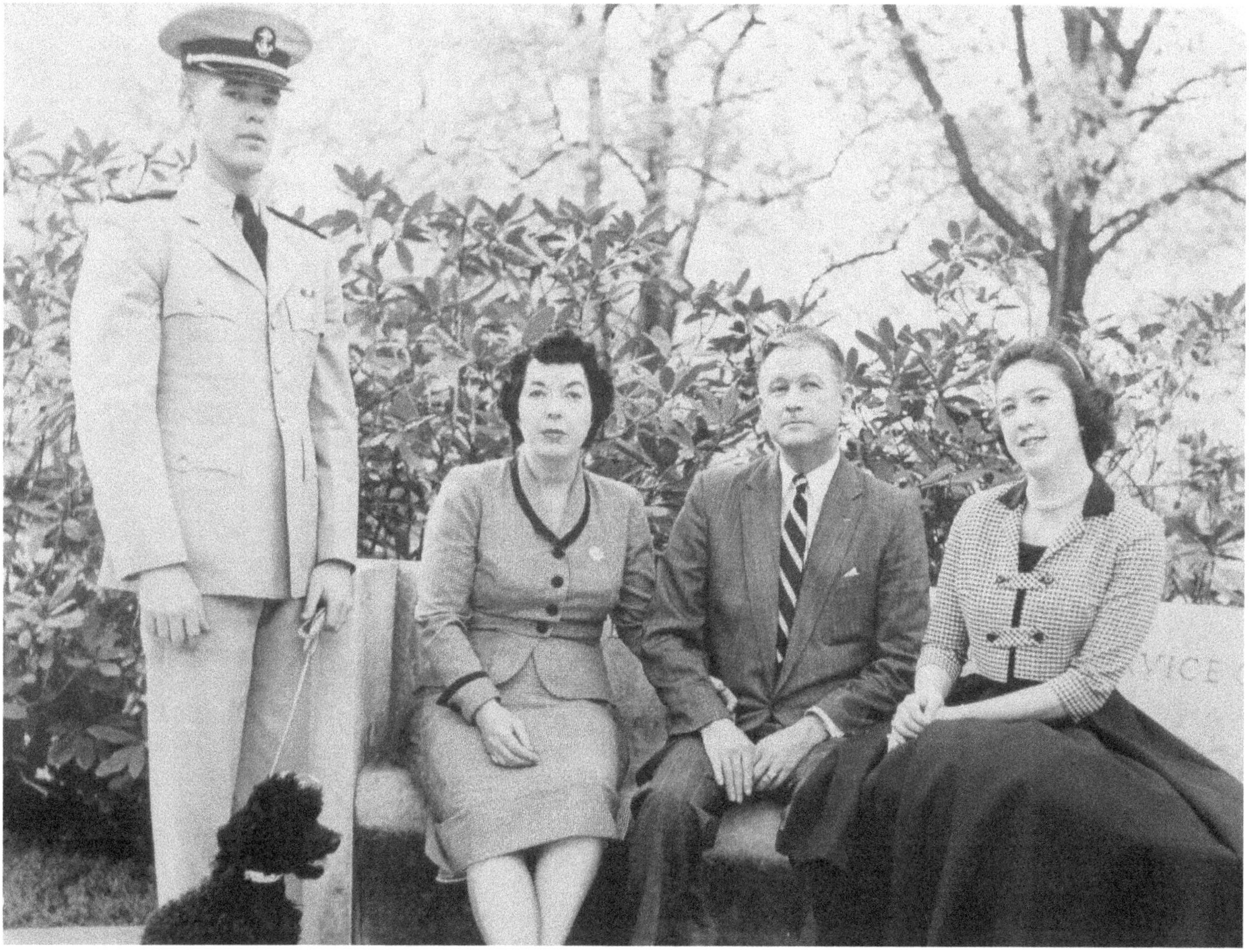

The Robbins family, ca. 1956. Naval Academy midshipman Berton III with poodle 'Baby,' Pat, Bob, and Carroll. This Alexandria, Virginia, house was the only one they ever built. Bob retired in 1959 as a rear admiral after twenty-eight years. Berton graduated from Annapolis in 1958; he retired as a commander with twenty-six years service.

primed for this lifestyle, Carroll often accompanied her parents to military and diplomatic functions, and herself partied in many embassies.

The Robbinses occasionally returned to Annapolis, Maryland, their late 1930s duty station, for football games and social activities. Here they encountered Old World royalty, including Queen Elizabeth II of Great Britain, who visited Annapolis in 1954.

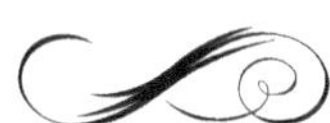

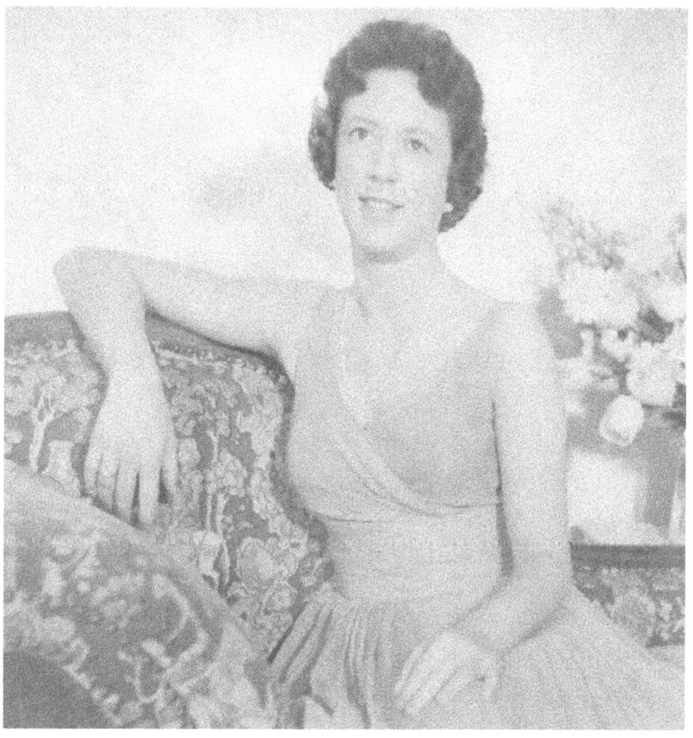

Carroll's 1959 engagement photograph, which ran in newspapers in Los Angeles, Wilmington, NC and elsewhere.

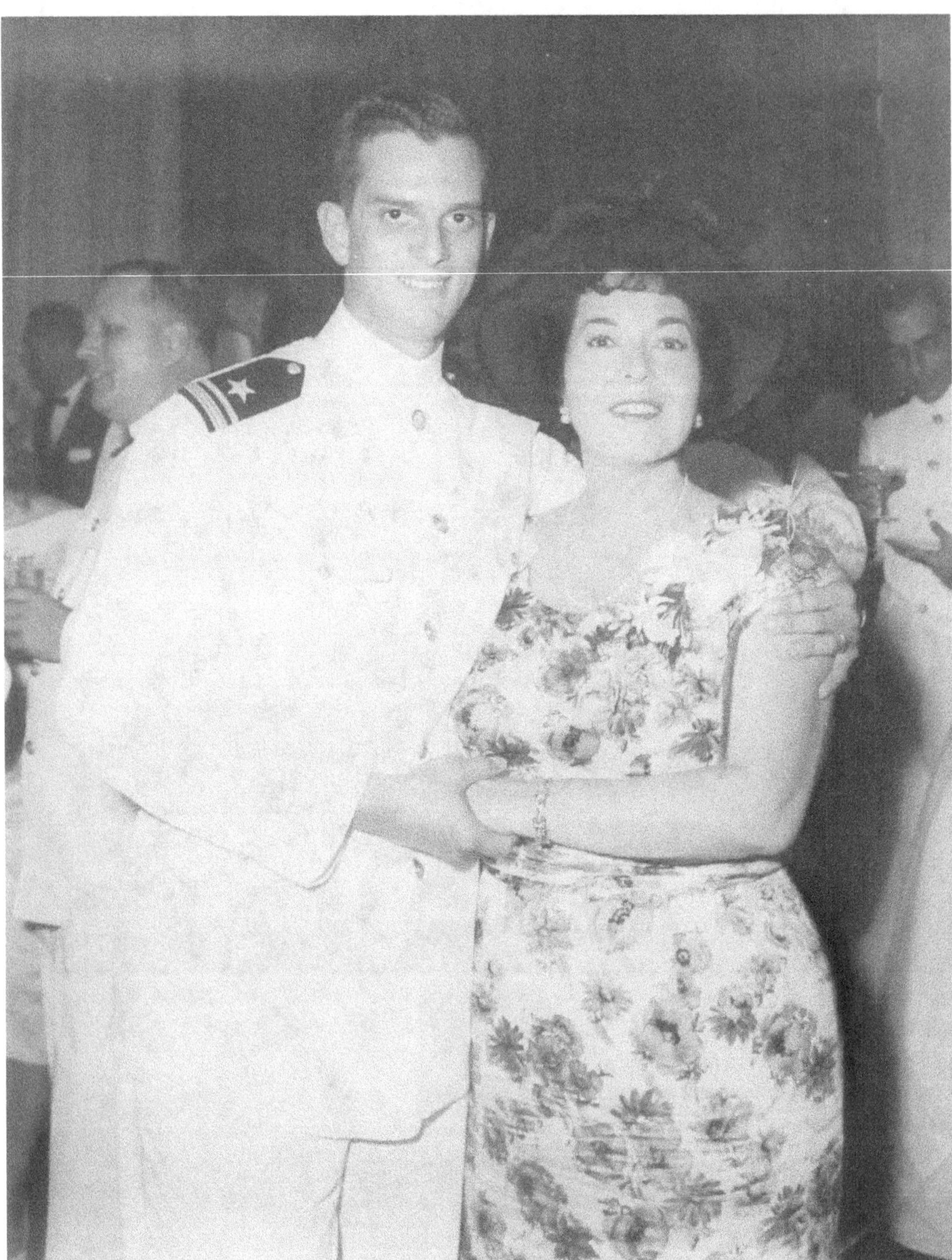

On the author's wedding day, Lt.(j.g.) Jones danced with his mother-in-law, still as lovely as in 1933. NATO AFSouth officers club, Naples, Italy, August 11, 1959.

PAT, BOB, AND CARROLL; FROM THE AUTHOR'S MEMORY BOOK:

A major change to the Robbins family occurred in 1959 when Capt. Robbins was stationed in Naples, Italy, as Commander Service Force Sixth Fleet/Commander Service Squadron Six, on board the flagship USS *Mississinewa* (AO-144). I was his flag lieutenant and staff communications officer, and accompanied him throughout the Mediterranean Sea on military protocol visits and at social events.

At Pat's request, Carroll left her assistant buyer position at Washington's Garfinkels to accompany her and Bob to Italy for their September 1958 change of duty assignment. Pat's health had declined, and she believed she needed Carroll's help in adjusting. As our ship sailed the Med, Pat and Carroll often joined us in port—Athens,

Barcelona, Cannes, and more. Those were the 1950s, the Cold War under control, Americans welcomed, and no terrorist threats.

Carroll intended to remain only a couple of months, then return to Washington, but two life-changing factors kept extending her stay. Pat made her feel guilty for "abandoning" her mother, and we began dating. The latter resulted after outright dares from my fellow wardroom junior officers. What, date the boss's daughter? The commodore's daughter? I guess I was nuts, but I liked her, and she reciprocated. (Also, Naples was devoid of other eligibles for each of us.)

Our first date was to Pompei. I had bought a German Opel Rekord sedan locally. We enjoyed Sunday or weekend drives to Rome, Cassino, Amalfi, Salerno, all over the region. We loved Italy and made ourselves at home there and comfortable with each other. We became friends, then good friends, then sweethearts. On April 27, 1959, the day before her twenty-fifth birthday, and after a day trip to Capri where I proposed, we announced our engagement to her parents over dinner at their apartment. I remembered the last words my mother (a Southern gentlelady of the Old School) said to me as I boarded an Air Force flight from Charleston, S.C., to Port Lyautey, Morocco, in early 1958: "Don't you bring back one of those girls from over there, you hear?!"

"Wilbur got all pink in the face when he started talking about it," Carroll wrote in her diary, "and the way he was leading up to it I felt sure they knew what was to come. Daddy got up from the table and was about to leave the dining room when Wilbur said, 'Come back and sit down, Commodore!!!' He did. Mother turned to me and said, 'You're kidding, really?' They both seemed more surprised than we expected, but at the same time pleased . . . . Later, after the dishes were done, we went out for ice cream and a drive."

In the end, for some time both parents couldn't help but realize where we were headed.

As I wrote in the Preface, ours was a classic storybook romance. On August 11 we said our vows in the Anglican Christ Church on a day she would recall as the hottest in Naples' history. Our honeymoon to Switzerland, Germany, Austria, and northern Italy, and later calls at other Med cities, an apartment at 94 Via Orazio overlooking Naples Bay, then home in 1960 on the SS *Independence* to New York, and a visit with my parents in Wilmington before driving to San Diego, my next duty station, with Carroll—now pregnant—dealing with scorching heat in a small, un-air conditioned car.

As a historian and nonfiction writer, I deal both in facts and in nostalgia. In 2007, after forty-seven years, one of us, me, finally returned to Naples. Once the Italian Campaign tour I'd led ended outside of Rome, I revisited Naples, retracing steps, searching for old familiar places we had known, yearning for a sense and feel of "yesterday, so long ago." I found Christ Church, still familiar, the Robbins and Jones apartments fronts, the NATO AFSouth officers building, a restaurant we frequented, the Santa Lucia waterfront Hotel Vesuvio where I picked her up for our first date.

I am planning a final visit to Italy in May 2017.

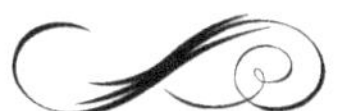

Health problems, namely COPD, which partially killed her in 1988—and eventually Carroll in 2013—by the 1960's curtailed Pat's ability to function professionally. She continued taking random 35mm shots of family, home, and trips, having most processed as slides, but by 1980 for all intents and purposes her cameras sat unused.

Unfortunately for the Robbins and Jones families and the history she recorded, she grew old an unhappy and accusatory woman. She found more negatives in life than positives despite her now distant professional reputation, successful children, and eight grandchildren who perpetuated both her clans' names.

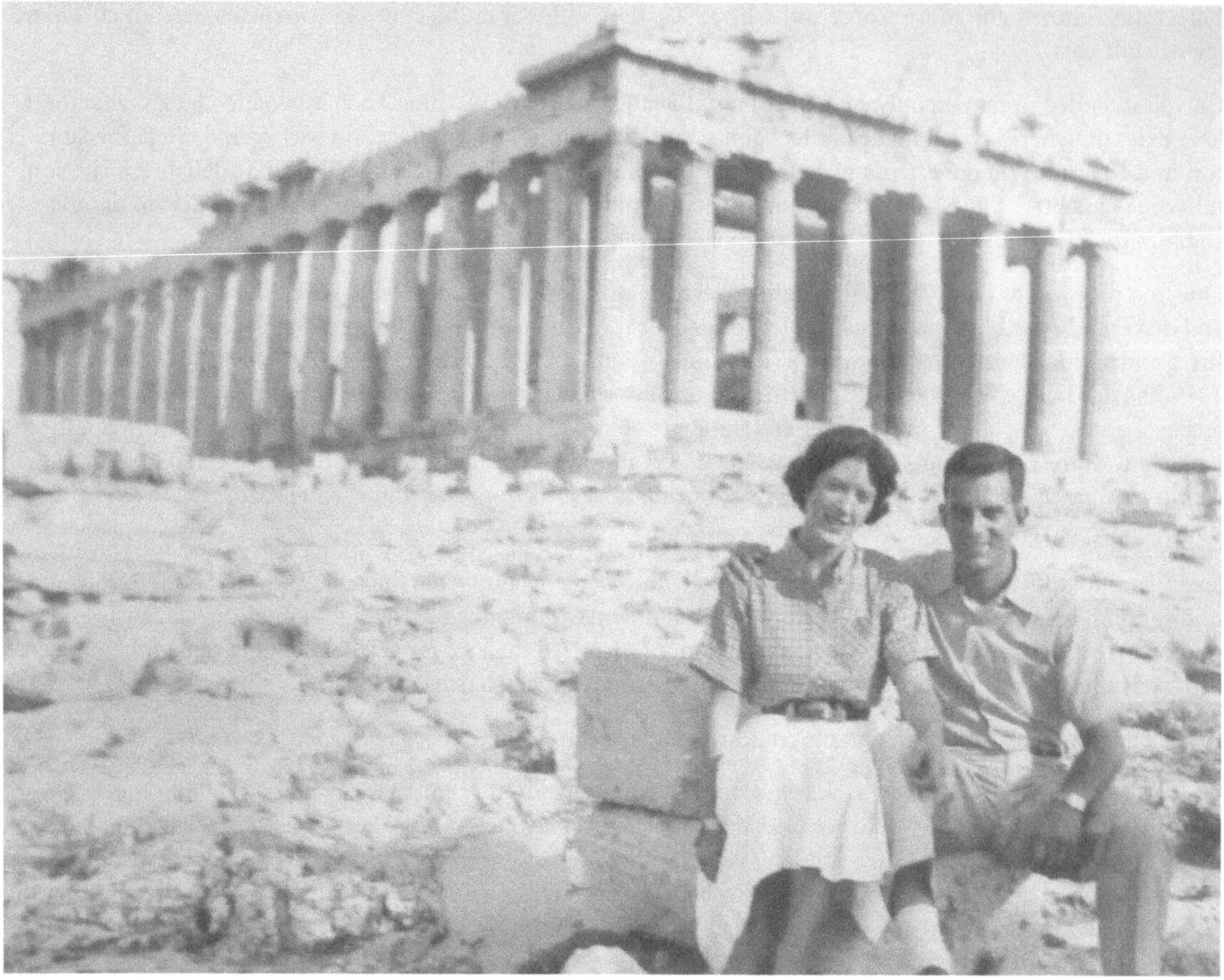

One of Carroll and Wilbur's favorites: Pat shoots the two at the Parthenon on the Acropolis in Athens, Greece, in 1959. The pair often socialized with her parents around the Mediterranean where the two men served.

She left several cameras and lens sets among the effects in her last California residence, but others subsequently just disappeared. With my sixty-year interest in photography, I used a couple of her Canons before giving them to my grandson-in-law, Matt Vaughan. She left a few letters but no diaries.

Carroll last visited her parents' grave in Arlington National Cemetery in 2009. Grave 6670, Section 13, lists Pat on the opposite side of Bob's marker.

With mutual respect and understanding, I always got along with Pat Robbins, and deeply respected her husband as my mentor. Because their son Berton, whom she idolized, was not around (he graduated in 1958 from the Naval Academy) perhaps she was just glad to see a young naval officer in their midst. From the beginning to the end, she was like a surrogate mother to me, and I a surrogate son.

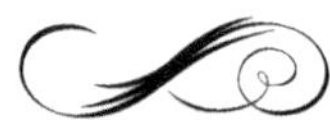

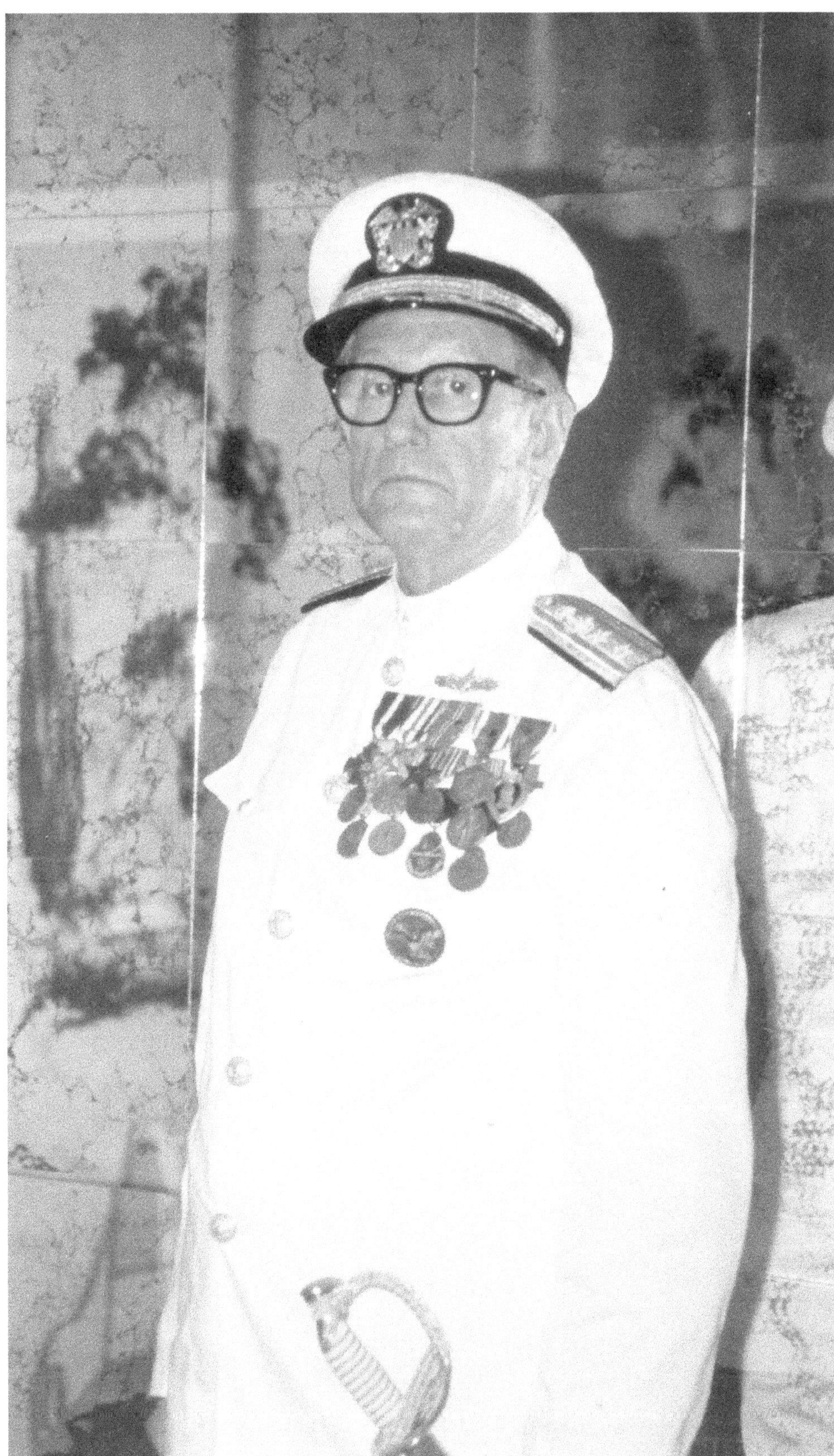

Ending her formal work, this was Pat's final 'portrait': Rear Adm. Berton A. Robbins, Jr., USN (Ret.), in 1980, in California. He died in the naval hospital in Camp Pendleton, California, in 1983.

NOTES

Preface

1 ocw.mit.edu/ans7870/21f/21f.027/empress_dowager/cx_essay01.html
2 en.wikipedia.org/wiki/Qing_Dynasty
3 www.smithsonianmag.com/arts-culture/Presenting-Chinas-Last-Empress-Dowager.html (October 2011); "Ready for Her Close-Up," by Owen Edwards, *Smithsonian* magazine, October 2011.

Chapter 1

1 Winzola McLendon in *Washington Post and Times Herald*, February 26, 1956. Includes the article headline: "She 'Shot' Her Way to Success."
2 "Society" column by Juana Neal Levy, *Los Angeles Times*, July 12, 1933.
3 *USS Chaumont* (AP-5) shipboard newsletter *Morning Breeze*, August 5, 1933.
4 "Miss Robbins Arrival Told," *Los Angeles Examiner*, May 1934.

Chapter 2

1 "Pin-Ups from Home," in *Popular Photography* magazine, February 1944.
2 www.navy.mil/navydata/cno/n87/usw/issue_17/chinapatrol.html
3 www.history.navy.mil/library/online/yangtze.htm
4 chinamarine.org/Diversions.aspx
5 en.wikipedia.org/wiki/Chefoo_School
jamesmcmullan.com/frameset_blog.htm
6 *Los Angeles Times*, February 6, 1938
7 www.earnshaw.com/shanghai-ed-india/tales/t-intro.htm
navalhistory.flixco.info/H/304842/8330/a0.htm
navalhistory.flixco.info/H/305978x110794/8330/a0.htm
wikitravel.org/en/Shanghai
8 forum.meremmelek.net/showthread.php?11639-***-China-***/page3
9 en.wikipedia.org/wiki/Manchu_people
10 en.wikipedia.org/wiki/Qing_Dynasty
11 www.history.com/topics/chinese-new-year
12 www.greatwall-of-china.com/
13 geography.about.com./od/specificplacesofinterest/a/greatwall.htm
14 en.wikipedia.org/wiki/Ruan_Lingyu
15 history.cultural-china.com/en/183H5986H11829.html
16 www.sacred-destinations.com/china/beijing-temple-of-heaven
17 visitourchina.com/guide/summer_palace.htm
18 www.chinahighlights.com/beijing/attraction/summer-palace/htm
19 chisineu.files.wordpress.com/2012/08/biblioteca_richardson.pdf
20 *Los Angeles* (Calif.) *Examiner*, May 1934.
21 www.submarineresearch.com/Bulletin97.html
22 en.wikipedia.org/wiki/United_States_Asiatic_Fleet#Chinese_Detachment
23 "Ramblings About Mayfair," *Los Angeles Examiner*, 1934.
24 journeytoforever.org/edu_silk_amah.html

www2.ucsc.edu/cwh/SocialBio.Chan.pdf
25 www.flickr.com/photos/ralphrepo_photolog/4079128019/
en.wikipedia.org/wiki/Jade_Belt_Bridge
26 en.wikipedia.org/wiki/Street_Angel_(1937_film)
27 en.wikipedia.org/wiki/Concessions_in_Tianjin
28 www.willysthomas.net/TientsinBuildings.htm
29 en.wikipedia.org/wiki/Yangtze_Patrol
30 www.chinatouristmaps.com/top-10s/cultural-symbols.html
www.greatwalltravel.net/China-Guide/China-Info/China-Info-Art-Chair.html

Chapter 3

1 muse.jhu.edu/journals/french_colonial_history/v010/10.lessard.html
2 en.wikipedia.org/wiki/French_Indochina
3 wikitravel.org/en/Vietnam
4 en.wikipedia.org/wiki/The_Peninsula_Hong_Kong
5 www.philippines-travel-guide.com/intramuros.html
6 www.manila-hotel.com.ph/history
7 manilacarnivals.blogspot.com/2009_05_01_archive.html
8 en.wikipilipinas.org/index.php?title=Manila_Carnival
9 www.hazegray.org/danfs/
10 www.emayzine.com/lectures/JAP1930.html
11 www.japanvisitor.com/index.php?cID=1702#ixzz1agid4nGf
12 Newspaper item believed to be from the *Washington Post and Times Herald*, ca. 1938.
13 latimesblogs.latimes.com/thedailymirror/2008/week6/page/2/
14 *Picture: The Snapshot Magazine*, March 8, 1940.
15 J.E. MacIntyre, *Los Angeles Times*, to Pat Robbins, August 21, 1940.
16 Virginia Hanson, *Mademoiselle* magazine, to Pat Robbins, January 25, 1938.
17 Johann E. Hoffman, *Mademoiselle* magazine, to Pat Robbins, May 27, 1941.
18 Column by Princess Conchita Pignatelli, *Los Angeles Examiner*, August 1941.

Chapter 4

1 thehonoluluadvertiser.com/specials/pearlharbor60/chapter3/html
2 *Honolulu Star-Bulletin*, January 2, 1942.
3 www.honolulupd.org/HPDmuseum/history4.htm
4 hawaiiantimemachine.blogspot.com/2011/02/great-hotel-street-sex-strike-of-1942.html
5 libweb.hawaii.edu/digicoll/hwrd/HWRD_html/HWRD42a.html
6 www.royal-hawaiian.com/resort/history.
7 *Time*, November 1, 1963.
8 "Pin-Ups from Home," *Popular Phtography* magazine, February 1944.
9 Western Union telegram to Patricia O'Meara Robbins, Los Angeles, March 3, 1945.
10 Lt. Cdr. Berton A. Robbins, Jr., to Carroll Eloise Robbins, June 15, 1943.

Chapter 5

1 www.legendaryjoancrawford.com/crawfordchildren.html
2 "Motion Pictures." *The New Encyclopedia Britannica*. Chicago: Encyclopaedia Britannica, 2002, in http://ils.

unc.edu/dpr/path/goldenhollywood/
3 gossiprocks.com/forum/hot-women/23019-loretta-young-actress.html
4 www.dailymail.co.uk/news/article-2068727/Judy-Lewis-dies-Clark-Gable-Loretta-Youngs-love-child-dies-cancer-76.html
5 www.nytimes.com/2011/12/01/arts/television/judy-lewis-secret-daughter-of-hollywood-dies-at-76.html
6 "Acting on Air," by Pat Robbins in *Mademoiselle* magazine, October 1941.
7 en.wikipedia.org/wiki/Jack_Benny
8 movies.nytimes.com/person/5438/Jack-Benny
9 webmail.ec.rr.com/do/mail/folder/view?l=en-US&v=twc_theme
10 en.wikipedia.org/wiki/Nancy_Reagan#Acting_career
11 en.wikipedia.org/wiki/Photoplay#History
12 en.wikipedia.org/wiki/Edmund_Lowe
13 gayhistory.wikidot.com/edmund-lowe
14 www.farrow-osullivan.com/JohnVilliersFarrow.html
www.imdb.com/name/nm0001577/bio
15 search.aol.com/aol/search?queryt=eve+arden+actress&s_it=keyword_rollover
www.tcm.com/tcmbperson/5233%7C49968/Eve-Arden/
16 *Time* magazine, May 10, 1948.
17 *Parklabrea News*, Los Angeles, Calif., January 25, 1951.

Chapter 6

1 www.absoluteastronomy.com/topics/National_Alliance_of_Russian_Solidarists
2 Viktor Baydarcoff to Pat Robbins, December 12, 1951.

Chapter 7

1 "With Full Honors," by Pat Robbins, *Saturday Evening Post*, May 31, 1958.

BIBLIOGRAPHY

PRIMARY SOURCES

The Estate of Patricia O'Meara Robbins: images, documents, clippings, records, etc.; Wilbur D. Jones, Jr.'s interviews and conversations with Carroll Robbins Jones, and items from her collection; and Jones' recollections of the O'Mearas and Robbinses.

OTHER SOURCES

Magazines

Collier's, September 6, 1952
"Acting on Air," by Pat Robbins, *Mademoiselle*, October 1941
"Pin-Ups from Home," *Popular Photography*, February 1944
Time, May 10, 1948
Time, November 1, 1963
"With Full Honors," by Pat Robbins, *Saturday Evening Post*, May 31, 1958
"Ready for Her Close-Up," by Owen Edwards, *Smithsonian* magazine, October 2011
Picture: The Snapshot Magazine, March 8, 1940

Newspapers

The Honolulu Advertiser, December 28, 1941
Honolulu Star-Bulletin, January 2, 1942
"Ramblings About Mayfair," *Los Angeles Examiner*, 1934
"Miss Robbins Arrival Told," *Los Angeles Examiner*, May 1934
Los Angeles Examiner, May 1934
Column by Princess Conchita Pignatelli, *Los Angeles Examiner*, August 1941
"Society" column by Juana Neal Levy, *Los Angeles Times*, July 12, 1933
Los Angeles Times, February 6, 1938
USS *Chaumont* (AP-5) *Morning Breeze*, August 5, 1933
Parklabrea News, Los Angeles, Calif., January 25, 1951
Newspaper item believed to be from the *Washington Post and Times Herald*, ca. 1938
"She 'Shot' Her Way to Success," by Winzola McLendon, *Washington Post and Times Herald*, February 26, 1956

Miscellaneous

Viktor Baydarcoff to Pat Robbins, December 12, 1951
J.E. MacIntyre, *Los Angeles Times*, to Pat Robbins, August 21, 1940
Virginia Hanson, *Mademoiselle* magazine, to Pat Robbins, January 25, 1938
Johann E. Hoffman, *Mademoiselle* magazine, to Pat Robbins, May 27, 1941
"Motion Pictures." *The New Encyclopedia Britannica*. Chicago: Encyclopedia Britannica, 2002, in http://ils.unc.edu/dpr/path/goldenhollywood

Internet

navy.mil/navydata/cno/n87/usw/issue_17/chinapatrol.html
history.navy.mil/library/online/yangtze.htm
chinamarine.org/Diversions.aspx
en.wikipedia.org/wiki/Chefoo_School
jamesmcmullan.com/frameset_blog.htm
history.cultural-china.com/en/183H5986H11829.html
earnshaw.com/shanghai-ed-india/tales/t-intro.htm navalhistory.flixco.info/H/304842/8330/a0.htm
navalhistory.flixco.info/H/305978x110794/8330/a0.htm
wikitravel.org/en/Shanghai
forum.meremmelek.net/showthread.php?11639-***-China-***/page3
history.com/topics/chinese-new-year
en.wikipedia.org/wiki/Manchu_people
en.wikipedia.org/wiki/Qing_Dynasty
greatwall-of-china.com
geography.about.com./od/specificplacesofinterest/a/greatwall.htm
en.wikipedia.org/wiki/Ruan_Lingyu
sacred-destinations.com/china/beijing-temple-of-heaven
chinahighlights.com/beijing/attraction/summer-palace/htm
chisineu.files.wordpress.com/2012/08/biblioteca_richardson.pdf
journeytoforever.org/edu_silk_amah.html
www2.ucsc.edu/cwh/SocialBio.Chan.pdf
flickr.com/photos/ralphrepo_photolog/4079128019/
wikipedia.org/wiki/Jade_Belt_Bridge
en.wikipedia.org/wiki/Street_Angel_(1937_film)
en.wikipedia.org/wiki/Concessions_in_Tianjin
willysthomas.net/TientsinBuildings.htm
en.wikipedia.org/wiki/Concessions_in_Tianjin
en.wikipedia.org/wiki/Yangtze_Patrol
chinatouristmaps.com/top-10s/cultural-symbols.html
greatwalltravel.net/China-Guide/China-Info/China-Info-Art-Chair.html
ocw.mit.edu/ans7870/21f/21f.027/empress_dowager/cx_essay01.html
smithsonianmag.com/arts-culture/Presenting-Chinas-Last-Empress-Dowager.html (October 2011)
legendaryjoancrawford.com/crawfordchildren.html
gossiprocks.com/forum/hot-women/23019-loretta-young-actress.html
en.wikipedia.org/wiki/Nancy_Reagan#Acting_career
tcm.com/tcmbperson/5233%7C49968/Eve-Arden/
search.aol.com/aol/search?queryt=eve+arden+actress&s_it=keyword_rollover
tcm.com/tcmbperson/5233%7C49968/Eve-Arden/
ils.unc.edu/dpr/path/goldenhollywood/
en.wikipedia.org/wiki/Jack_Benny
farrowosullivan.com/JohnVilliersFarrow.html
imdb.com/name/nm0001577/bio
movies.nytimes.com/person/5438/Jack-Benny
nytimes.com/2011/12/01/arts/television/judy-lewis-secret-daughter-of-hollywood-dies-at-76.html
en.wikipedia.org/wiki/Photoplay#History

en.wikipedia.org/wiki/Edmund_Lowe
gayhistory.wikidot.com/edmund-lowe
muse.jhu.edu/journals/french_colonial_history/v010/10.lessard.html
en.wikipedia.org/wiki/French_Indochina
http://wikitravel.org/en/Vietnam
en.wikipedia.org/wiki/The_Peninsula_Hong_Kong
philippines-travel-guide.com/intramuros.html
manila-hotel.com.ph/history
manilacarnivals.blogspot.com/2009_05_01_archive.html
en.wikipilipinas.org/index.php?title=Manila_Carnival
hazegray.org/danfs/
emayzine.com/lectures/JAP1930.html
japanvisitor.com/index.php?cID=1702#ixzz1agid4nGf
latimesblogs.latimes.com/thedailymirror/2008/week6/page/2/
the.honoluluadvertiser.com/specials/pearlharbor60/chapter3/html
royal-hawaiian.com/resort/history
hawaiiantimemachine.blogspot.com/2011/02/great-hotel-street-sex-strike-of-1942.html
honolulupd.org/HPDmuseum/history4.htm
libweb.hawaii.edu/digicoll/hwrd/HWRD_html/HWRD42a.html
absoluteastronomy.com/topics/National_Alliance_of_Russian_Solidarists
spiegel.de//international/germany/0,1518.702856,00.html
skigermany.com/skiing/garmisch/garmisch-partenkirchen.php

INDEX

Note: *italicized* page numbers are images

ABOUT THE AUTHORS

Wilbur D. Jones, Jr.

Wilbur Jones is a nationally known, award-wining author and military historian in Wilmington, N.C. A Wilmington native, he holds a history degree from the University of North Carolina, is a retired Navy captain and a former assistant and advance representative to President Gerald Ford. He served the Department of Defense for forty-one years, the last twelve as a professor and associate dean at the Defense Acquisition University.

This is his eighteenth book, seven of which have been about World War II. Doing business as Wilbur Jones Compositions, LLC (www.WilburJones.com), he writes, lectures and consults, spearheads efforts to preserve WWII history in North Carolina, and leads WWII battlefield tours to Europe, the Mediterranean, and Southeastern N.C. He chairs the all-volunteer, 501(c)(3) WWII Wilmington Home Front Heritage Coalition and is a recent Chairman of the USS North Carolina Battleship Commission.

Carroll Robbins Jones

The late Carroll Jones, Wilbur's wife and co-author, was born in Shanghai, China, to the late Rear Admiral Berton A. Robbins, Jr., USN (Ret.) and Patricia O'Meara Robbins. Carroll accompanied her mother traveling in old imperial China and North China and the Orient in the mid-1930s while her father served on ships of the U.S. Asiatic Fleet. She assisted her mother in taking photographs of the aftermath of the attack on Pearl Harbor, Hawaii; during photo shoots of Hollywood stars and Los Angeles celebrities in the 1940s and early 1950s; and in capturing European life during the Occupation of Germany and the social life of 1950s Washington, D.C.

Carroll enjoyed a twenty-year career as a Northern Virginia residential realtor, served for eleven years as a part-time research archivist at UNC Wilmington's Randall Library, and directed the UNCW oral history program.

Other Books by Wilbur D. Jones Jr. (Since 1997)

"Football! Navy! War!": How Military "Lend-Lease" Players Saved the College Game and Helped Win World War II

A Brief History of St. Andrews-Covenant Presbyterian Church: Written to Celebrate the 150th Anniversary (a monograph)

Forget That You Have Been Hitler Soldiers: A Youth's Service to the Reich, with Hermann Pfrengle

Condemned to Live: A Panzer Artilleryman's Five-Front War, with Franz A. P. Frisch

The Journey Continues: The World War II Home Front

A Sentimental Journey: Memoirs of a Wartime Boomtown

Hawaii Goes to War: The Aftermath of Pearl Harbor, with Carroll Robbins Jones

Gyrene: The World War II United States Marine

Arming the Eagle: A History of U.S. Weapons Acquisition Since 1775

Giants in the Cornfield: The 27th Indiana Infantry

www.ingramcontent.com/pod-product-compliance
Lightning Source LLC
LaVergne TN
LVHW061203120826
845149LV00011B/1894
9780998073507